THE GLOSSARY OF PROPERTY TERMS

THE GLOSSARY OF PROPERTY TERMS

Compiled by

JONES LANG WOOTTON
in conjunction with
THE ESTATES GAZETTE LIMITED
and
SOUTH BANK POLYTECHNIC

1989

A member of Reed Business Publishing Group

THE ESTATES GAZETTE LIMITED
151 WARDOUR STREET · LONDON W1V 4BN

First published 1989
Second Impression 1990
Third Impression 1990
Fourth Impression 1993
Fifth Impression 1996

ISBN 0 7282 0143 7

Typesetting by Digital Graphics Ltd
Printed by Hobbs the Printers Ltd, Totton, Hampshire SO40 3WX

CONTENTS

FOREWORD

A surveyor's effectiveness is limited by his ability to communicate. He must think, speak and write clearly and logically. As the skills of the surveyor become more widespread and the matters on which he is called to advise more complex, the need for precision in understanding the meaning of technical language is vital.

I am, therefore, delighted to welcome this Glossary of words and phrases which are used, and occasionally misused, in the profession. I congratulate all those who have been engaged for several years in this very important undertaking and I believe that their work will benefit not only surveyors but many others who from time to time are concerned with the meaning of terms relating to land and buildings and their associated interests.

In terms of the understanding of words, I hope that the Glossary will become a "bench-mark", an expression of which it states ". . . Commonly, a mark placed upon a permanent object of sufficient substance as to be unlikely to move . . .".

I believe that the contents are indeed "of sufficient substance" and that the Glossary will be of great and continuing usefulness for many years to come.

DAVID H R YORKE
President, The Royal Institution of Chartered Surveyors

December 1988

PREFACE

About eight years ago we at Jones Lang Wootton realised that with the growth in the size of the firm and the widening range of its activities there was a distinct risk of our using specialist words not so much loosely as with variations in meaning. We therefore decided to define and issue internally a list of standard terms.

After a good deal of work had been done we discovered that the South Bank Polytechnic were embarking on a similar project (although concentrating on valuation terms) for the benefit of students. They generously agreed to merge their work with ours and we subsequently, in conjunction with them and "Estates Gazette", set up an editorial panel to prepare a comprehensive glossary of property terms which would be of value to a wider, external audience.

This panel brought to bear a range of experience covering surveying, finance, law, education, writing and publishing and therefore occasionally initially differing points of view on a definition. The five members of the panel have assiduously selected and defined over 2,500 words which are now published in this book and I congratulate them on the outcome.

KEITH DOUGLAS-MANN
International Chairman of Jones Lang Wootton

December 1988

INTRODUCTION

This book has been prepared by Jones Lang Wootton, chartered surveyors, in conjunction with "Estates Gazette" and the South Bank Polytechnic to provide a reference work for those practising in public or private offices as surveyors, developers, lawyers, public authority officers and others who find it necessary to refresh their memories or confirm their understanding of specific words and phrases concerning property matters.

The work is a thoroughly revised and much enlarged version of the JLW Glossary of Property Terms which was published in 38 instalments in "Estates Gazette" between 1983 and 1987.

It is hoped that it will be particularly helpful to those who are not property professionals but whose work and interests necessitate some understanding of property terms.

During the time it has taken to compile this work it has become clear that many words are loosely, even wrongly, used in everyday dealings. Clearly this is undesirable and can only lead to misunderstandings. Great care has therefore been taken to ensure that, as far as possible, accurate, authoritative definitions are given. In instances where it might be a matter of opinion as to whether one meaning or another is the correct one, both the derivation and the most generally accepted terminology have been considered in selecting a particular meaning.

Certain Scottish and American expressions have been included where it was thought they would be helpful, especially where the same word may have different meanings because of the difference in legal systems or because of variations in common usage. However, the list of such expressions is not exhaustive, since the prospective American range of words alone would fill a large separate volume.

Although every possible care and attention has been exercised to ensure that all the definitions provided in this Glossary are accurate, no responsibility can be accepted for inadvertent errors or omissions (neither should this book be used or relied upon as evidence in legal proceedings).

EDITORS' NOTE

This Glossary has been compiled by an editorial panel comprising:

From Jones Lang Wootton:

Sir Jack Hughes BSc FRICS FRSA
Peter J A Lubbock TD FRSA MInstM MIAMA
Michael P Michaels LLB FRICS

From South Bank Polytechnic:

Geoffrey B Parsons MSc BSc ARICS ARVA AILAM

From "Estates Gazette":

Ernest G Speller

ACKNOWLEDGMENTS

Much helpful information, advice and suggestions have been provided by:

The Royal Institution of Chartered Surveyors
The International Stock Exchange
The Unit of Retail Planning Information Ltd
The South Bank Polytechnic
Mr R J Hickson BA BSc FRICS, partner, and other partners and specialists from Jones Lang Wootton.
Many readers of "Estates Gazette", in particular Mr W A Leach FRICS

While it is not possible to list by name all those who have made contributions or assisted in compiling this work, special mention must be made of the considerable help given by Richard Asher FRICS, Miss Gillian Mason and Miss Elizabeth Armah of Jones Lang Wootton, and Miss Audrey Boyle of "Estates Gazette".

NOTES ON COMPILATION

1. Cross references are provided in two different forms at the end of many definitions. These are:

(i) "Cf", which invites the reader to compare terms which appear to be similar, but are not; where confusion sometimes occurs over their proper use; or where there is direct contrast between them.

(ii) "See", which refers the reader to other terms which are either synonyms or may extend or add to the definition.

NB: Where other terms are mentioned in a definition, they are usually defined but not cross-referenced. It is left to the reader's discretion whether to refer to them.

Occasionally references are made to information outside the scope of this volume, eg to an Act of Parliament, statutory regulations or a law case. These are given to help those requiring more detailed knowledge of the subject.

2. Where the masculine gender has been used, this should normally be taken to refer to both genders, except where the text makes this manifestly inappropriate.

3. Rating terms apply to both the 1967 and the 1988 legislation, ie the General Rate Act 1967 and the Local Government Finance Act 1988. However, at the time of going to press the subordinate legislation required for the detailed implementation of the latter Act is not generally available.

4. For the benefit of students in particular, terms which occur as part of a major subject (such as "Valuation and Appraisal", "Rating" or "Landlord and Tenant") have been grouped in Appendix I so that each subject may be viewed in the light of the defined terms relating to it.

5. *Abbreviations* — A wide range of useful abbreviations which may be relevant to the subjects covered by the Glossary has been included at Appendix II. The abbreviations listed have not necessarily been defined in the main text.

6. A short section on citations for law reports has been included at Appendix III. Further abbreviations for law reports are given in Appendix II.

7. *Yields, rates of interest and returns on capital* — Because some terms under this heading are controversial, a short explanation has been included at Appendix IV.

8. Definitions show the position existing at the end of December 1988.

A

AAA (USA) An indication that an organisation possesses the highest credibility and financial standing in the view of one of the well-known credit rating agencies such as (in the USA) Moody's or Standard & Poor's. Usually called "triple A rating".

AAD certificate *See* CERTIFICATE OF APPROPRIATE ALTERNATIVE DEVELOPMENT.

A & S fees In insurance these are architect's, surveyor's, consulting engineer's, legal and other fees necessarily incurred in the reinstatement of a damaged or destroyed property.

abandonment **1.** Surrender of a legal right, especially a right of ownership of property. **2.** Relinquishment of a claim or part of a claim in a civil action or appeal.

abatement **1.** Reduction or cancellation of a debt. For instance, a lease usually provides for abatement of rent if the building demised is damaged or destroyed by fire. **2.** Removal or termination of a nuisance, especially the right of an aggrieved person himself to terminate the cause of the nuisance. If necessary, he may enter the property from which the nuisance arises, subject to giving notice where possible and not causing unnecessary damage.

abatement notice **1.** A notice served on the owner or occupier of a property from which a private nuisance arises warning him of the intention to enter on the land in order to abate the nuisance. **2.** A formal notice, especially one served by the local authority under the Public Health Act 1936, requiring a person creating a nuisance to eliminate its cause.

ab initio From the beginning. For example, a contract is void *ab initio* if it is (or should be) known to both parties that it is illegal from the start.

abortive expenditure Money which does not achieve the purpose for which it was spent, ie it has been wasted. A typical example is expenditure on professional fees for work done on a development scheme which does not mature. The reasons may be: changes in circumstances; misjudgment of the market; losing a bid for the site; failure to obtain the necessary consents, such as planning permission; intervention by a public authority exercising statutory powers, thereby establishing a right to compensation, eg on compulsory purchase or on revocation or modification of planning permission.

absolute *See* FEE SIMPLE ABSOLUTE IN POSSESSION; TERM OF YEARS ABSOLUTE.

absolute covenant In a legal document a positive or restrictive undertaking which is neither conditional nor determinable during its lifetime. *Cf* QUALIFIED COVENANT.

absolute title The right of ownership of a legal estate in registered land, it thereby being guaranteed by the state that no one has a better title, subject to any minor interests or overriding interests. *Cf* GOOD LEASEHOLD TITLE.

abstract of title In establishing a person's ownership of an interest in land, a summary of the evidence which has been extracted from the title deeds and other relevant documents as required by a purchaser or mortgagee.

abstraction of water The taking of water from a natural source of supply, eg a river. A licence is usually required from the water authority but not:

a for moderate quantities;

b when required for domestic or agricultural use (other than for spray irrigation); or

c when removed in the course of land drainage or for firefighting.

abut To adjoin or border on, to the extent of touching physically.

abutment A point at which one building provides lateral support to another.

abuttals The boundaries of a plot bordering and physically touching an adjacent property. *See* BOUNDARY.

acceleration In relation to property, the coming into possession of a future interest in land earlier than specified in the document creating the interest, eg where a tenant surrenders a lease, thereby accelerating the reversion to the landlord.

acceleration clause **1.** A clause used in a mortgage deed which gives the right, in certain specified circumstances, to demand repayment in full of the outstanding debt earlier than the due date. *See* ALIENATION CLAUSE 2. **2.** A clause in a deed or contract which provides for the early termination of an existing interest in land, in certain specified circumstances, thereby advancing the future interest. *See* ACCELERATION.

acceptance The written or oral agreement to the terms of an offer which creates, or may lead to the creation of, a legally binding contract, usually subject to the satisfaction of other requirements. *See* TACIT ACCEPTANCE.

access agreement Under the National Parks and Access to the Countryside Act 1949 section 64 and the Countryside Act 1968 section 18, an agreement drawn up between a local planning authority and a person having an interest in land which provides the public with certain rights of access.

access order Under the National Parks and Access to the Countryside Act 1949 section 65, an order made by a local planning authority, subject to confirmation by the Secretary of State for the Environment, requiring a person having an interest in land to provide the public with certain rights of access. Such an order can be made only where a local planning authority is unable to secure an access agreement.

accident book A record which (under the Health and Safety at Work etc Act 1974) must be maintained by the occupier of a building and in which brief details of all accidents sustained by those employed within the building must be kept.

accommodation agency A business which provides details of housing accommodation to let, usually looking to the prospective tenant for a fee or commission. The activities of such firms are restricted by the Accommodation Agencies Act 1953, which makes it an offence to demand or accept any payment merely for registering or undertaking to register a person's residential tenancy requirements or for supplying or undertaking to supply addresses or other particulars of houses to let.

accommodation land **1.** Land which, while having potential for development with buildings, is meanwhile put to temporary use. **2.** Sometimes understood to mean land close to market towns and used by butchers and others for holding animals temporarily prior to their disposal.

accommodation works On the acquisition of a property, or part of a property, by an authority having powers of compulsory purchase, works carried out by the authority to other property belonging to the same owner, so as to mitigate loss or damage to the latter property resulting from the acquisition. Typical examples would be the erection or reinstatement of a fence or wall or the diversion of drains or other services. The term is also applied colloquially to works carried out by the owner whose costs are reimbursed by the acquiring authority.

accord and satisfaction
This is "the purchase of a release from an obligation, whether arising under contract or tort, by means of any valuable consideration, not being the actual performance of the obligation itself. The accord is the agreement by which the obligation is discharged. The satisfaction is the consideration which makes the agreement operative". (*British Russian Gazette and Trade Outlook* v *Associated Newspapers Ltd* (1933).)

account (Stock Exchange) A term used by the Stock Exchange to name the principal division of its calendar. Accounts run usually for ten working days, each account being identified by a letter and a number, eg 6F. All bargains carried out during a particular account period are settled on one day — usually the second Monday following the end of the account (account day).

accounts method *See* PROFITS BASIS.

accretion A natural increase in an area of land caused either by the gradual accumulation of silt or other deposits from a river or the sea or by dereliction, ie the retreat of the sea exposing new land. *Cf* ALLUVION.

accrued depreciation At a given time, the accumulated amount of depreciation which has been entered in the accounts for a particular asset.

accrued interest The unpaid interest accumulated from an investment or a loan.

accumulative rate The rate of interest at which it is known or assumed that an annual sinking fund will grow. It may be expressed as gross or net of income taxation but, except in the case of a gross fund, can accumulate only at the net rate.

acknowledgement and undertaking Confirmation (in a title deed) that a named party may see and have copies of relevant deeds not in his possession, with an undertaking by the holder of the deeds to keep them safely, eg on a part disposal of land the vendor gives such an acknowledgement and undertaking to the purchaser in relation to the deeds of the whole.

a coelo usque ad centrum By custom, a phrase indicating that a right of ownership in land will theoretically extend both up to heaven and down to the centre of the earth.

acquiring authority A local authority, government department or other body exercising a statutory power of compulsory purchase or of acquiring a property by agreement in advance of (or under threat of) compulsory purchase.

action A proceeding in a civil court.

action area An area selected by a local planning authority for comprehensive treatment by development, redevelopment or improvement of the whole or part of the area, or by a combination of such measures, the proposals being set out in an action area plan.

action for implement (Scotland) The equivalent to specific performance in England and Wales.

active management An arrangement, additional to the routine duty of looking after the buildings as they are, whereby property managers undertake to keep a watching brief on properties under their management with a view to advising their principals when action should be taken in relation to the property concerned. It includes recommending the rearrangement of terms with the tenants to release marriage value, the disposal of properties with disappointing growth prospects, the purchase of adjoining properties and carrying out physical improvements or redevelopment. *See* PROPERTY PORTFOLIO MANAGEMENT.

active trust (special trust) A trust in which the trustees have duties beyond merely handing over the trust properties to the beneficiaries, eg obligations to safeguard or dispose of the trust property. *Cf* BARE TRUST.

act of God An event due to some natural cause, eg flood or earthquake, so severe as to be incapable of reasonable anticipation or safeguard.

Act of Parliament A formal document setting out a law which has been passed by Parliament and received the Royal Assent. *Cf* BILL (PARLIAMENTARY BILL). *See* SPECIAL ACT; PRIVATE ACT; PUBLIC ACT.

actual notice In law this means having knowledge of a fact by direct communication. *Cf* CONSTRUCTIVE NOTICE; IMPUTED NOTICE.

additional rent Part of a rent which is payable under a lease or tenancy as an extra amount in excess of a basic or initial rent. *Cf* SERVICE CHARGE.

add-on interest (USA) A method of charging interest, usually used in the financing of automobiles but sometimes used in real estate financing. Interest is computed on the total amount borrowed and added to the principal. Each payment is then deducted from this total amount. Interest on real estate loans is usually calculated on the balance owing after each payment is made (declining balance). *See* ROLLED-UP INTEREST.

ad hoc For the particular purpose. For example, an *ad hoc* committee is one set up to deal with a particular matter, as opposed to a standing committee.

***ad hoc* trust for sale** A trust for sale where the trustees are approved by the court or by their successors in office or by a trust corporation. A sale of land subject to such a trust overreaches equitable interests that would otherwise not be overreached, ie if the trustees were not so qualified.

ad idem Towards the same thing. The term indicates that parties are agreed.

adjacent Near or close to another property, especially (but not necessarily) having a common boundary. *Cf* ADJOINING; CONTIGUOUS; ABUT.

adjoining Near or close to another property to the extent that they share the whole or part of a boundary. *Cf* ABUT; ADJACENT; CONTIGUOUS.

adjoining owner Under the London Building Acts 1930 to 1939, the owner of a property contiguous with that of a person (the building owner) who wishes to carry out work to or in respect of an actual or proposed party wall or structure.

adjudication **1.** A judicial decision or formal judgment by a court or tribunal. **2.** The determination by the Commissioners of Inland Revenue of the amount of any stamp duty payable on a document.

adjusted net trading profit Depending on the type of valuation, the net trading profit (NTP) after particular deductions or adjustments have been made for items not actually payable in the circumstances, eg in compulsory purchase NTP is adjusted for any profit rent (for a lessee) or rental value (for a freeholder), for interest on capital and for an estimate of what the proprietor's remuneration, if appropriate, should be.

Adler clause A clause obliging a tenant, if he wishes to dispose of his lease, first to offer to surrender it to the landlord. Approved in *Adler* v *Upper Grosvenor Street Investment Ltd* (1957).

ad medium filium (viae or aquae) Literally up to a middle line. Used to define a boundary between adjoining lands in different ownership, eg where a road or a river divides the two properties, rather than by the legal or physical criteria which would be used in other cases. The middle line of a stream or way is adopted as the boundary in the absence of evidence to the contrary.

administration **1.** Where a person dies intestate or there is no surviving executor under the will (or the executor is not willing to act), the grant of letters of administration to an administrator of the deceased person's estate. *See* RULES OF INTESTACY; PERSONAL REPRESENTATIVE 1 **2.** The collection of assets, settlement of debts and distribution of the residue of a deceased person's estate to the beneficiaries. **3.** The carrying out of duties imposed by a trust concerning the property of a bankrupt or of a person of unsound mind.

administrative law That part of constitutional law concerned with the organisation, powers and obligations of administrative authorities, ie ministers of the Crown, local authorities and the officers employed on their behalf to carry out the relevant duties and enforce the powers.

admissible evidence Relevant evidence before a court which is not prohibited by one of the exclusionary rules, eg (i) the rule against hearsay, (ii) privilege, or (iii) unfair prejudice to an accused person. All irrelevant evidence is inadmissible.

adopted as holograph (Scotland) Manuscript words to be inscribed above signatures at the foot of every typewritten page of missives to form a legally binding contract under Scottish law.

adoption In a property context, usually either: **1.** the acceptance by a local authority of responsibility for the maintenance and upkeep of a road or of a sewer as a public highway or public sewer respectively; or **2.** the decision of a public body such as a local authority to enforce the optional ("adoptive") provisions of some statute, eg the rating of unoccupied premises under the General Rate Act 1967.

ad valorem Literally, according to the value. Applied, for instance, to a scale of stamp duty, inheritance tax or fees.

advance compensation Under section 52 of the Land Compensation Act 1973, the right of an owner of an interest in land to be paid up to 90% of the amount of any compensation agreed with the acquiring authority (plus interest), where possession of the property has already been taken, the balance being paid on completion of the purchase after the total compensation has been agreed or determined. In the absence of agreement, the sum is 90% of the compensation as estimated by the acquiring authority.

advance corporation tax (ACT) An early payment of tax on corporate profits, ie as corporation tax, the amount being calculated by reference to the income tax deducted at the standard rate from dividends distributed to shareholders.

advance factory A factory built before there is any specific tenant requirement, usually with a view to encouraging an occupier to lease or buy it, thereby increasing employment in the locality.

advance payments code For development projects, arrangements under section 219 of the Highways Act 1986 whereby the developer or builder makes early payment to the highway authority or enters into some kind of indemnity bond to meet the cost of roads which will eventually be adopted.

adverse differential In a valuation under the Leasehold Reform Act 1967, the difference in yield where the capitalisation rate applied to the modern ground rent is different from the decapitalisation rate applied to the site value when that rent was ascertained.

adverse gearing Where the total annual cost of borrowed money on a property or project exceeds the net rental income. *Cf* GEARING.

adverse occupation Occupation of property by a trespasser who is denying the lawful occupier or owner his rights.

adverse possession Under the Limitation Act 1980, occupation of land inconsistent with the rights of the true owner and without his permission. After such an unlawful — but undisturbed — occupation for over 12 years, the legal owner loses his right to recover possession. Likewise, if a rent of £10 per annum or more payable under a lease (£1 pa or more if the lease was granted before August 1 1980) is paid for 12 years to a stranger wrongfully claiming the reversion on the term, that is adverse possession and the true owner of the reversion will be barred.

advertisement For the purposes of control of advertisements under the Town and Country Planning Act 1971, defined in Regulation 2(1) of the Town and Country Planning (Control of Advertisements) Regulations 1984, as amended, as: "any word, letter, model, sign, placard, board, notice, device or representation, whether illuminated or not, in the nature of, and employed wholly or partly for the purposes of advertisement, announcement or direction . . ." with certain exclusions ". . . and (without prejudice to the preceding provisions of this definition) includes any hoarding or similar structure or any balloon used, or adapted for use." *See* AGENCY BOARD.

advertisement control Powers exercised by local planning authorities under section 63 of the Town and Country Planning Act 1971 and the Town and Country Planning (Control of Advertisements) Regulations 1984, as amended, to control the display of advertising material in the interest of amenity or public safety. A wide range of advertisements is exempt from the need for formal consent, but permission is required for material such as agents' boards above a certain size and most illuminated signs. *See* AGENCY BOARD.

advowson The perpetual right to install (or "present") a clergyman to a church living. It is real property and vests in the owner of the right, the patron, as an incorporeal hereditament. Until 1924 advowsons were capable of being sold, but by the Benefices Act 1898 (Amendment) Measure of 1923, they were in most cases made unsaleable after two vacancies had occurred. (It is of interest to note that when *Estates Gazette* was founded in 1858 its subtitle was "A Paper devoted to the Sale of Land, House Property, and Advowsons".)

aeolian soil Soil composed of materials deposited by the wind.

aerial survey A survey of an area made by taking sequential photographs from an aircraft; plans are then drawn from the photographs.

affidavit A statement in writing which is made under oath.

a fortiori With stronger reason.

aftercare Arrangements required of a mineral operator to put land from which minerals have been extracted into good condition for a specified use.

aftercare condition A condition in a planning permission for mineral extraction which provides that steps should be taken to bring the land up to a required standard for a specified use, such as agriculture, forestry or amenity, as the work of extraction proceeds or after it has been completed.

agency board An advertising board which is displayed outside premises by an estate agent who is acting on behalf of the owner or landlord in the disposal of the premises by sale or letting or in their development. It is a relatively inexpensive but effective method of giving brief details of a property in the market. Such a board bears the name, telephone number and often the address of the agent and also sometimes a brief synopsis of the accommodation available. Under the Town and Country Planning (Control of Advertisements) Regulations 1984 (as amended in 1987), there are restrictions on the number and size of the boards which may be displayed without express consent. Currently (1988), (i) the maximum permitted area for a board displayed on a residential property is $0.5m^2$ for a single board and $0.6m^2$ for two boards joined at an angle. For agricultural, industrial or commercial properties the limit is $2m^2$ for a single board and $2.3m^2$ for a joined board; (ii) only one sale or letting board may be displayed at a time on the property to which it relates.

agency by estoppel An agency created by operation of law when an agent oversteps his authority but action (or failure to act) by the principal leads the person dealing with the agent to believe the authority exists. *See* APPARENT AUTHORITY.

agent One who acts on behalf of a principal. *See* ESTATE/EXCLUSIVE/GENERAL/JOINT/JOINT SOLE/RETAINED/SOLE AGENT.

agent of necessity One who justifiably acts to protect the property or other interests of another which are threatened by an emergency. The essential requirements giving rise to the agency are that there must be urgent circumstances and that it must be virtually impossible for the "agent" to communicate with the person whose interests are under threat.

agreement *See* CONTRACT.

agreement for lease (or sale) A contract to enter into a lease (or sale). Under section 40 of the Law of Property Act 1925, to be enforceable either this must be evidenced in writing and signed by the person against whom action is taken for breach of the alleged contract or there must be a sufficient act of part performance.

agrément certificate A certificate issued by the British Board of Agrément giving an independent opinion on the performance of a product, component, material or system used in the construction industry. The French word *agrément* means "approval".

agricultural building allowance Under sections 68 and 69 of the Capital Allowances Act 1968 as amended, an allowance against income taxation in respect of capital expenditure on the construction of farmhouses, farm or forestry buildings, cottages, fences or other works. *See* CAPITAL ALLOWANCES.

agricultural fixtures *See* TENANT'S FIXTURES.

agricultural holding Defined by section 1 of the Agricultural Holdings Act 1986 as "... the aggregate of the land (whether agricultural land or not) comprised in a contract of tenancy which is a contract for an agricultural tenancy, not being a contract under which the land is let to the tenant during his continuance in any office, appointment or employment held under the landlord."

agricultural land **1.** Defined under the Agricultural Holdings Act 1986 as "(i) land used for agriculture which is so used for the purposes of a trade or business, and (ii) any other land which, by virtue of a designation under section 109 (1) of the Agriculture Act 1947, is agricultural land within the meaning of that Act". **2.** Defined under the Capital Allowances Act 1968 section 69, as amended, as "... land, houses, or other buildings in the United Kingdom occupied wholly or mainly for the purposes of husbandry", the latter including "any method of intensive rearing of livestock or fish on a commercial basis for the production of food for human consumption".

agricultural land tribunal Under the Agriculture Act 1947 as amended, a body set up by the Lord Chancellor in each of eight areas of England and Wales to determine, mainly, disputes between landlords and tenants of agricultural holdings. For each hearing a tribunal consists of a chairman who is a lawyer, a person representing landowners and a person representing farmers.

agricultural licence A licence to occupy agricultural land. Most purported agricultural licences are automatically converted into tenancies from year to year by section 2 of the Agricultural Holdings Act 1986, the exceptions being:

a one with prior ministerial approval;
b one made in contemplation of the use of the land for grazing and/or mowing during some specified period of the year;
c where the licence was granted by a person whose interest in the land is less than a tenancy from year to year and has not taken effect as such a tenancy by virtue of section 2.

Agricultural Mortgage Corporation (AMC) A body offering loans on agricultural property in England and Wales secured as first mortgages on freehold land. First incorporated in 1928 and operating under the provisions of the Agricultural Credits Acts 1928 and 1932, it normally grants loans for periods of between 5 and 40 years at fixed or variable rates of interest. In recent years it has also granted mortgages on forestry investments.

agricultural tenancy The tenancy of an agricultural holding, the tenant having statutory protection under the Agricultural Holdings Act 1986 as to security of tenure, determination of rent and compensation on termination of the tenancy.

air conditioning Apparatus for cleaning the air supplied to a room or building and bringing it to the required humidity or temperature or both.

airspace The air above a parcel of land, ownership of which is included with the land concerned, subject to the rights of others and any restriction on its use imposed by or under statutes. *Cf* FLYING FREEHOLD. *See* CUJUS EST SOLUM EJUS EST USQUE AD COELUM ET AD INFEROS.

alienation The transfer of an interest in property to another, eg sale of a freehold or grant or assignment of a lease.

alienation clause **1. (UK)** A clause controlling a lessee's right to assign and/or sublet. **2. (USA)** A type of acceleration clause calling for a debt under a mortgage or deed of trust to be due in its entirety upon transfer of ownership of the secured property.

alpha, beta, gamma, delta Descriptions used to grade domestic equities according to the view taken by the stock market of their marketability and the degree to which they can be traded without affecting the price. Shares are grouped as: alpha — the most active shares; beta — the next most active; gamma — the remainder, provided they have at least two market makers; delta — unpopular shares which are difficult to sell/buy and for which bargain match-making is necessary. *Cf* BLUE CHIP.

alimentary liferent (Scotland) A liferent which cannot be sold or assigned by the liferenter and cannot be attached by his creditors.

alimentary trust (protective trust) A trust which lasts for a period no longer than the beneficiary's life but ends on the occurrence of certain events, eg bankruptcy. At the end of the period the income from the trust property is used at the absolute discretion of the trustees for the beneficiary or his family.

allotment Any small parcel of tenanted land used for cultivation. It can constitute an agricultural holding and for compensation purposes is defined as being greater than 2 acres (Allotments Acts 1922 and 1950).

allotment garden A parcel of land not exceeding 0.1 of a hectare (originally 40 poles) occupied for the production of vegetables and fruit for the consumption of the occupier and his family. A tenant has security of tenure and is entitled to compensation if his lease is terminated. Because it does not satisfy the use for trade or business under the Agricultural Holdings Act 1986, it cannot be defined as an agricultural holding, but its use is regarded as being agricultural for planning purposes (Allotments Acts 1922 and 1950).

all risks yield (ARY) (market yield) The remunerative rate of interest used in the valuation of freehold and leasehold interests, reflecting all the prospects and risks attached to the particular investment. Current, reversion and term yields are examples of all risks yields.

alluvion The gradual building up or accretion of soil caused by the flow of a river or the sea. The owner of the land which is thereby increased becomes the owner of the new land. *Cf* AVULSION; DERELICTION.

alterations In property terms this normally means physical changes to a building or structure which may or may not amount to improvements.

alternative use value The value of land and buildings which reflects a prospective use which is different from that of the current use. In exceptional circumstances, which are more likely to arise on leasehold land, an alternative use value may be negative.

ameliorating waste (meliorating waste) Such "voluntary" waste as improves the demised premises, ie an unlawful improvement to a property.

amendment of documents Changes in draft legal documents, eg a lease or a building agreement. Such amendments are traditionally marked in colour as follows: a first amendment in red, a second in green, a third in violet, followed by brown, orange, light blue, magenta and yellow. In modern practice it has become common, with the widespread availability of photocopying, for amendments to appear in black.

amenity In property terms something tangible which makes the human environment more pleasant, eg a landscaped open space within an urban area or a swimming pool in a private garden.

amenity land A term often used in town planning to describe an area of land which is dedicated to, or available for, public enjoyment, eg public open space or children's play areas.

amortisation **1. (UK)** The concept of writing off the capital cost of a wasting physical asset by means of a sinking fund. **2. (USA)** Payment of a debt in equal instalments of principal and interest, as opposed to interest-only payments.

amortisation rate The rate of interest used for purposes of amortisation.

amortisation term The period, usually expressed as a number of years coinciding with the useful life of an asset, over which the value of the asset is written off. *See* SCRAP VALUE; WASTING ASSET; WRITTEN-DOWN VALUE.

amount of £1 The amount to which £1 invested now will accumulate in a given number of years at a selected rate or rates of interest, compounded over the period at the appropriate intervals. This is the reciprocal of the present value of £1.

amount of £1 per annum The amount to which £1 invested at the end of each year for a given period of years will accumulate at a selected rate or rates of interest, compounded over the period at yearly or other intervals. This is the reciprocal of the annual sinking fund.

anchor tenant(s) One or more department or variety chainstores, or supermarkets, introduced into a shopping centre in key positions to attract the shopping public into the centre for the purpose of encouraging other retailers to lease shops en route. The larger the development the more anchors required. (Although semantically wrong, this term is used interchangeably with magnet stores; strictly speaking, it should be remembered that a magnet store can both attract and hold shoppers, whereas an anchor tenant can only hold them, once they have been attracted.)

ancient demesne An obsolete form of land tenure comprising land held by freehold tenants in any manor belonging to the Crown in the time of Edward the Confessor or William the Conqueror, such tenants enjoying certain immunities but being subject to certain restraints. It was abolished in 1926 by the Law of Property Act 1922.

ancient lights Windows and other apertures for the admission of light to a permanent building for which the owner of the building has an established right of light. The right, which is an easement, may be acquired at common law but is usually claimed under section 3 of the Prescription Act 1832, which declares the right to be absolute if it has been enjoyed without interruption for not less than 20 years. *See* PRESCRIPTION.

ancient monument A "scheduled monument" and any other monument which, in the opinion of the appropriate Secretary of State for environmental matters, is of public interest by reason of the historic, architectural, traditional, artistic or archaeological interest attaching to it (section 61(12) of the Ancient Monuments and Archaeological Areas Act 1979). In the National Heritage Act 1983, section 33(8), the term is defined as: "any structure, work site, garden or area which in the [Historic Buildings and Monuments] Commission's opinion is of historic, architectural, traditional, artistic or archaeological interest". *Cf* PROTECTED MONUMENT.

Ancient Monuments Boards Bodies, one each for England, Scotland and Wales, which were established under the Ancient Monuments Consolidation and Amendment Act 1913 to advise the appropriate Secretary of State on the preservation, maintenance and management of ancient monuments. The English board was replaced in 1983 by the Historic Buildings and Monuments Commission for England, but the boards for Scotland and Wales continue in being under the Ancient Monuments and Archaeological Areas Act 1979. *See* ANCIENT MONUMENT; HISTORIC BUILDINGS AND MONUMENTS COMMISSION; MONUMENT; PROTECTED MONUMENT; SCHEDULED MONUMENT.

ancillary accommodation The parts of a property which are put to ancillary use, eg offices forming part of a principally industrial property.

ancillary building A building which is used for purposes ancillary to the principal buildings within a site, eg a self-contained office building or a boiler house within a predominantly industrial complex.

ancillary use A planning term describing the use of a property in a manner different from, but functionally related to, its main use. *Cf* PRIMARY USE.

animus possidendi The intention to have possession. Defined in *Powell* v *McFarlane* (1977) as "the intention, in one's own name and on one's own behalf, to exclude the world at large, including the owner with the paper title if he be not himself the possessor".

animus revertendi The intention of returning. The expression is sometimes used in deciding whether an absent tenant has security of tenure under the Rent Acts.

annual equivalent Having regard to the tenure involved, the annual income calculated to correspond to a capital sum, such as a premium, paid for an interest in land.

annual percentage rate (APR) For a loan at a stated rate of interest, the annual rate of interest which takes account of the amounts and dates of repayment of capital and other expenses associated with the loan. Under the Consumer Credit Act 1974 the APR must be publicised to prospective or actual borrowers.

annual sinking fund (ASF) A sinking fund where payments and interest accumulated are calculated yearly.

annual sinking fund rate *See* ACCUMULATIVE RATE.

annual value 1. In general parlance, the rental value of an interest in property for 12 months subject to the benefits and/or disadvantages either attaching to the property generally (eg a planning restriction or estate covenant affecting use) or imposed on a tenant or prospective tenant by the terms of letting (eg an absolute covenant against assignment or subletting). **2.** Under section 837(1) of the Taxes Act 1988 this "shall be taken to be the rent which might reasonably be expected to be obtained on a letting from year to year if the tenant undertook to pay all usual tenant's rates and taxes, and if the landlord undertook to bear the costs of the repairs and insurance, and the other expenses, if any, necessary for maintaining the subject of the valuation in a state to command that rent". For the purposes of Schedule B, under section 16(13) of the Act, the annual value of woodlands is determined "as if the land, instead of being woodlands, was let in its natural and unimproved state". *See* PRAIRIE VALUE.

annuity A sum of money paid each year during the life of the recipient. An annuity is usually paid as a legal obligation under a contract or undertaking, as through a pension scheme, and may be paid in instalments more frequently than once every twelve months.

annuity £1 will purchase Having regard to the rate of interest applicable, this determines the amount which would be payable annually for the period of the income for each £1 invested at the outset. The resultant figure is the reciprocal of the years' purchase.

anti-avoidance Descriptive of taxation provisions which are designed to counter arrangements which taxpayers have made or may otherwise make to reduce their liability to one or more taxes. Section 776 of the Income and Corporation Taxes Act 1988 is an example. *Cf* EVASION. *See* AVOIDANCE.

apartment hotel (USA) A building combining features of an apartment building and an hotel. The units are furnished and may offer hotel facilities such as maid service or a restaurant, but residents may stay for months or years paying on a weekly or monthly basis.

apparent authority Action (or failure to act) by a principal which leads one to believe that his agent has authority which in fact the agent does not have.

apparent easement An easement which, by external signs of its existence, is evident to a person of ordinary intelligence from inspection of the servient tenement, eg a right of way.

appeal An application to a superior court or authority for the administrative or judicial examination of a decision or an issue determined by a lower court or inferior body or authority. In most cases the superior court, administrative tribunal, Minister of the Crown or other appellate body conducts the appeal in the form of a hearing of the entire case or dispute, but appellate courts usually use transcripts or notes of the evidence before the lower courts rather than hear oral evidence and seldom overrule the decisions of lower courts on questions of fact as distinct from points of law.

appellate committee The judicial committee of the House of Lords which hears appeals.

appendant Descriptive of a subordinate right or interest attached to a larger interest in land by operation of law and automatically passing with the conveyance of the greater interest. *Cf* APPURTENANT.

appointed day The day when a statute or part of a statute comes into effect. It is usually specified in the Act itself or by an order, ie an appointed day order.

apportionment The division of a benefit or liability proportionate to the interests of the various parties concerned, and where the necessity arises owing to an event occurring during a period defined for payment. The process is used, for example, to determine how the amount of rent, rates, service charges and other costs are to be borne between landlords and tenants or among owners on sale, or occupiers on assignment of tenancies. The basis for the calculation is set out in the Apportionment Acts 1834 and 1870.

appraisal (appraisement) 1. Another term for valuation; more commonly used in the USA. **2.** An evaluation which extends to matters beyond a "valuation" as such; for instance consideration of taxation, funding and other subjective factors of particular market segments.

appraiser One who carries out appraisals (valuations). The term is used in the USA for a valuer.

approvement The common law right of a lord of the manor to enclose waste land in his manor for his own benefit, so extinguishing the rights of others, eg to graze sheep or cattle on the land enclosed. Approvement cannot now be exercised without the consent of the Secretary of State for the Environment (following a public inquiry).

approved inspector A person who, in accordance with building regulations, is approved by the appropriate Secretary of State or by a designated body (The Royal Institution of Chartered Surveyors being one such) for the supervision of building work under powers conferred by Part II of the Housing and Building Control Act 1984. An approved inspector may be appointed and paid by a developer as an alternative to the older system of supervision by a local authority building inspector.

appurtenance Something belonging or attached to a property and passing with it on sale or other transfer, even if not expressly mentioned. The term is applied particularly to incorporated rights, but can include other land or buildings.

appurtenant Descriptive of a subordinate right annexed or attached to and benefiting a larger interest in land by act of parties, eg an easement must be appurtenant to the dominant tenement. *Cf* APPENDANT.

aquaculture The farming of either fresh water or sea fish using intensive methods. *Cf* MARICULTURE.

arbiter The term used in Scotland for an arbitrator.

arbitrage The system by which dealing in securities is carried out in order to profit from a variation in the price quoted in different markets. Often effected by buying and selling in two different markets at the same time in order to profit from the margin.

arbitrary zoning *See* GEOMETRICAL ZONING.

arbitration A method of resolving a disagreement between two parties by presenting their different views to an independent arbitrator (in Scotland called an arbiter). The award is binding on the parties but an arbitrator's decision can be challenged in a court of law in certain circumstances. *Cf* INDEPENDENT EXPERT.

arbitration agreement A contractual agreement to refer an existing or possible future dispute to arbitration. Such an agreement need not be in any special form but should appoint the arbitrator(s) or set out the manner in which they are to be appointed if not agreed between the parties, eg by the President of the Law Society or the President of the RICS.

arbitration clause A clause in a contract providing for disputes arising from the contract to be referred for the decision of a third party (arbitrator). Common examples are disputes over rent review clauses in leases or the terms of building contracts.

arbitrator An impartial person who is

appointed to settle a difference between two parties. *Cf* INDEPENDENT EXPERT.

arcade A covered way or gallery for pedestrians, usually only 4m to 6m wide, flanked by shops on one or both sides. Historically the roof was arched.

archaeological area *See* AREA OF ARCHAEOLOGICAL IMPORTANCE.

architect One who designs buildings and is qualified to do so in accordance with the Architects Registration Acts of 1934 and 1938. *See* ROYAL INSTITUTE OF BRITISH ARCHITECTS.

architect's certificate A term used colloquially to describe a certificate for payment which is issued by a supervising officer, usually an architect advising a client, to release funds to the contractor in payment for work completed under the terms of a building contract.

area of archaeological importance An area designated as of archaeological importance by an order made under Part II of the Ancient Monuments and Archaeological Areas Act 1979 by either the appropriate Secretary of State for environmental matters or the local authority or, in London, the Historic Buildings and Ancient Monuments Commission for England and Wales. In such an area it is an offence to carry out, or cause or allow to be carried out, operations which disturb the ground or involve flooding or tipping without serving an "operations notice" on the local authority or unless specific exemption has been granted.

area of outstanding natural beauty (AONB) An area designated under the Countryside Act 1968 as being of that quality.

area of special control An area defined by an order made under the Town and Country Planning (Control of Advertisements) Regulations 1984 as an area of special control in respect of the display of advertisements. Within such an area no advertisements may be displayed except those of certain specified classes and descriptions, eg traffic signs, and the seven classes of advertisement which have deemed consent under the regulations, and also advertisements of certain types for which express consent is required.

arithmetical zoning *See* GEOMETRICAL ZONING.

arm's length Description of a transaction between individuals or bodies who are not associated in any material way.

arrears **1.** Money unpaid after the due date. Thus a debt is in "arrears" if unpaid after the due date. **2.** Rent is said to be paid in arrears where the lease provides for the rent for a particular period to be paid at the end of that period. (In modern leases rent is usually payable in advance, ie it is due at the beginning of the period.)

article 4 direction The colloquial name for a direction under article 4 of the Town and Country Planning General Development Order requiring planning application to be made for a class of development which would otherwise be permitted under the GDO. Such a direction is usually restricted to properties of a limited class or within a defined area — or even to a specific property — and if made by the local planning authority requires confirmation by the Secretary of State.

articles of association A document setting out the rights and duties of the directors and members of a company in relation to its internal organisation. *Cf* MEMORANDUM OF ASSOCIATION.

articles of roup (Scotland) The document containing the conditions of sale for heritable property when it is sold by public roup, ie by auction. The properties for sale are described, together with the date and location of sale, the upset price, if any, as well as details of any deposit and the date when the properties will be handed over.

asking price The price at which a vendor offers a property for sale. The eventual selling price may be different after negotiation with the purchaser.

assart The clearing of wooded areas by grubbing up trees and bushes by the roots, usually to convert the land to agricultural use.

assembly of land *See* LAND ASSEMBLY.

assent A document transferring property from personal representatives to a beneficiary under a will or on intestacy.

assessment **1.** A measure of a person's liability to tax, made by an inspector of taxes unless otherwise provided by the relevant statute. **2.** The process of obtaining the gross value or net annual value, as appropriate, of a rating hereditament.

assessor **1.** In rating in Scotland, the official who makes rating assessments on behalf of the government. **2.** In a public inquiry, a person with expert knowledge who sits with the presiding official and proffers advice based on that expertise.

asset For capital gains tax purposes, any form of property, whether situated in the United Kingdom or not, including:

a options, debts and incorporeal property generally,
b any currency other than sterling, and
c any form of property created by the person disposing of it, or otherwise coming to be owned without being acquired.

asset valuation In the property market this expression is applied to the valuation of land and buildings or plant and machinery. The term is often used to describe an expert opinion of the worth of a property which may be incorporated into company accounts, where the ownership of the asset is not necessarily to be transferred but the valuation is of interest to, for example, shareholders or is required for company takeovers, share flotations or mortgages. The RICS publication *Guidance Notes on the Valuation of Assets*, 2nd edition, is the valuer's standard work of reference.

assign To transfer an interest in a property, especially a lease.

assignation (of lease) (Scotland) The disposal or transfer of a lease. Scottish law is fundamentally different from that in England and Wales, since on assignation the tenant who assigns steps out and is free of all obligations under the lease as from the date of the assignation, except as to arrears of rent, and the assignee takes his place and is responsible for all obligations of the lease. *See* PRIVITY OF ESTATE.

assignee One who receives an assignment, eg the assignee of a lease for so long as he retains that interest and stands in the position of tenant under the lease.

assignment The transfer of a property interest, especially a lease, from one party to another. (In Scotland "assignation".)

assignor One who makes an assignment.

assisted area A part of the country where government funds and other aids and incentives are available to encourage the creation of infrastructure and business and hence economic and social recovery from local depression or decline.

assurance A formal guarantee of a calculable sum being paid on the happening of an inevitable event, eg a payment on death. *Cf* INSURANCE.

assured shorthold tenancy Under section 20 of the Housing Act 1988, this is an assured tenancy which is also a fixed term tenancy of at least six months, not determinable by the landlord within the first six months, where before the assured tenancy is entered into notice has been served in the prescribed form by the proposed landlord on the proposed tenant stating it is to be a shorthold tenancy. From January 15 1989 such tenancies supersede protected shorthold tenancies under section 52 of the Housing Act 1980.

assured tenancy Under section 1 of the Housing Act 1988, as from January 15 1989, a tenancy of a dwelling-house let as a separate dwelling and (i) which is not in one of the categories listed in Part I of Schedule 1 to the 1988 Act or (ii) which is already an assured tenancy under sections 56 to 58 of the Housing Act 1980 (tenancies granted by "approved bodies"), the latter provisions being replaced by those under the 1988 Act. Among the classes of tenancies excluded under Schedule 1 are existing tenancies entered into (or already under contract) before the commencement of the Act, those of dwelling-houses with a rateable value exceeding £1,500 in Greater London or £750 elsewhere, tenancies where the landlords are local authorities, various other public bodies or housing associations, secure tenancies and various other tenancies already excluded from Rent Act protection.

at best A Stock Exchange expression for an instruction to a dealer to buy or to sell shares at the best price in the market at the time, ie the lowest purchase price or the highest selling price.

atrium An entrance hall of a building, often rising through a number of storeys and containing lifts, reception areas and plants. Originally the hall or chief apartment of a Roman house.

attest To testify or bear witness to; to affirm by signature or on oath. The signature is known as an attestation.

attorney A person appointed or empowered to act on behalf of another. Usually one qualified and legally authorised to present a case in a court of law; a solicitor. More commonly used in the USA.

attornment The transfer of property upon sale.

attour (Scotland) Besides, over and above.

auction A sale (usually in public) in which property is sold to the highest bidder, provided the amount offered exceeds any reserve, ie the lowest acceptable price, fixed by the vendor. Occasionally, but not often, properties may be offered without a reserve price, in which event the highest bid will be accepted however low it may be.

auction by candle *See* CANDLE AUCTION.

auction, Dutch *See* DUTCH AUCTION.

auctioneer At an auction an agent who conducts the sale of property or offers it for sale. Anyone may act as an auctioneer provided his full name and address are displayed at the place of auction in accordance with section 7 of the Auctioneers Act 1845.

audi alteram partem Literally hear the other side. The principle that both parties to a dispute should be heard prior to a decision.

authorised Descriptive of a use of land which is, or would be, permitted or allowed: (i) by a valid planning permission, (ii) by having become an "established" use or (iii) by being within the same "use class" as the "permitted" or "established" use.

authorised development Development which has been allowed by a planning permission. *Cf* PERMITTED DEVELOPMENT.

authorised use A use of land which is, or would be, permitted or allowed by a valid planning permission. *Cf* LAWFUL USE. *See* PERMITTED USE.

autre vie The life of another. An estate *pur autre vie* is an estate to be held during the life of another person.

autumn tenancy A yearly agricultural tenancy which commences in the period from 1st September to 31st December.

average A principle of insurance (particularly insurance of property) where the insurer will pay for only the same proportion of a loss as the sum insured bears to the cost of reinstatement or to the actual value of the property at the time of the loss, eg if an item is insured for only half its value at the time it is damaged, the insurer will pay only half of any claim for repair or reinstatement.

avoidance The arrangement of one's affairs within the law so as to make full use of exemptions, reliefs and other advantages to mitigate taxation. *Cf* EVASION. *See* ANTI-AVOIDANCE; SECTION 776.

avulsion The severance of land by a change in the course of a river but where it remains the property of the original owner.

award A decision made by an unbiased third party, especially an arbitrator, after consideration of two opposing views, eg on rent reviews. *See* PARTY WALL AWARD.

away-going crop (way-going or off-going crop) A crop, generally of winter wheat, which an outgoing farm tenant holding under a spring (Candlemas or Lady Day) tenancy has the right, based on custom or written agreement, to retain on quitting the land, since it is not ready for gathering until after the termination of his tenancy. At one time the outgoer was allowed either to hold over or to re-enter in order to harvest the crop, but under modern practice the right is usually commuted to monetary compensation.

B

backhanded rent (Scotland) Rent reserved in a lease to be paid on a specified future date which falls after the end of the period to which the rent relates, eg rent for a period from 15th May 1988 to 14th May 1989 but payable on 11th November 1989 would be referred to as an annual rent "six months backhanded". *Cf* ARREARS 2.

back land Land having no frontage to a highway and, frequently, inadequate access for the purpose of development.

back-letter/back-bond A document which qualifies the legal effect of some other document which otherwise would purport to give an absolute right of ownership in property.

back-to-back loan A loan made by one party secured on a property, or other acceptable security, at the same time as a loan of an equal amount is borrowed by that party, on the security of another property, from the borrower of the first loan. It is generally adopted to raise money in one country where one of the parties has no adequate cash resources and, in effect, the debt is supported by a security in another country. Each loan is in the local currency, possibly subject to fluctuation in exchange rates. In the event of one of the debts becoming repayable at a time when the security cannot be realised at a high enough figure to redeem the loan, the lender may have recourse to recovering the deficit by a reduction of his debt in the other property. Such adjustment in the lender's mortgage would probably reflect any change in the values of the respective currencies.

badges of trade A cluster of principles, derived from case law, by which the distinction is made for taxation purposes between a dealer in land and an investor in land. The principles cover such matters as: intention and circumstances at date of acquisition (or disposal); use; nature, purpose and extent of any work carried out on the property; form of documentation; method of financing; repetition of activity (reiteration); and professional or trade knowledge.

bailee One to whom goods are entrusted by another (the bailor) for a specific purpose, the transfer of the goods being known as bailment, eg a contract for hire or safe custody.

bailiff An officer of the court concerned with executing writs and processes and enforcing its orders, including levying distress. Commonly applied to a sheriff's officer.

balance sheet A statement of financial accounts which for a particular date, eg at the end of a financial year, lists the assets and liabilities of a business including such reconciling items as are needed to equate the two totals.

balancing allowance *See* CAPITAL ALLOWANCES.

balancing charge **1.** An amount payable by or to a person after a charge for goods, work or services has been made based upon an estimate which proves to be inadequate or excessive when the full facts are known and the figures reconciled. **2.** For taxation purposes *see* CAPITAL ALLOWANCES.

balloon frame A type of timber-framed construction in which the vertical timbers (studs) extend from ground level to the roof. Support for the upper floors is provided by a horizontal beam, or beams, and joists which are fixed to the studs.

balloon payment A repayment of a loan or bond, usually but not necessarily the final repayment, which is larger in amount than other instalments. In America this kind of arrangement is referred to as "ballooning" a loan.

bank holiday A day on which banks are legally closed and which is generally accepted as a national holiday. Established in 1871 by banker and Member of Parliament Sir John Lubbock, it was originally called "Lubbock's Day".

bank rate Formerly a rate of interest which was set by the Bank of England but has been superseded by minimum lending rate. *See* BASE RATE.

bankrupt An individual debtor whose property is vested in a trustee for translation into money or calculable money's worth and then divided among his creditors in pursuance of an order of court adjudicating him a bankrupt.

bar chart A form of statistical tabulation shown diagrammatically by comparable vertical or horizontal columns.

bare licensee A person whose entry or presence on a property has the permission of the occupier, so that he is not a trespasser. Such permission, or licence, can be revoked at any time and is non-assignable.

bare trust (naked or simple trust) A trust in which the trustees hold the property for the absolute benefit of beneficiaries who are of full age (and under no disability) and the trustees have no obligations other than to transfer the trust property to the beneficiaries at their request.

bargain **1.** In the Stock Exchange, a transaction involving the sale and purchase of securities. In this sense it does not imply a specially low price. **2.** The purchase or leasing of a property or other asset where the price or rent is on terms which are ostensibly below the market value.

barren rent *See* RENT SECK.

barring the entail *See* DISENTAILMENT.

base fee A fee simple which will cease on the death of the descendant(s) of a tenant in tail in remainder, because the entailed interest has been barred without all the due formalities. *See* ENTAIL; FEE SIMPLE 1; FEE TAIL.

basement Rooms and other areas in a building which are below ground level and are at the lowest level except for any sub-basement, which is lower still.

base rate The underlying rate of interest first fixed by the Bank of England and charged to other borrowing banks of the highest repute. The base rates form the foundation for other rates (and hence returns and yields) and the rate charged to a particular borrower will be fixed according to his financial status. Historically, various terms have been used to indicate such rates of interest. *See* BANK RATE; MINIMUM LENDING RATE.

base rent Where there is provision in a lease for the total rent to be reviewed periodically (by some method of indexation or other formula), the minimum rent (if any) quantified in and payable under the lease, even if the review formula produces a lesser sum. *See* DEAD RENT; HARDCORE RENT; PERCENTAGE OR TURNOVER RENT.

base value Under the now repealed Development Land Tax Act 1976 there were three bases (A, B and C), the highest of which, known as the "relevant base value", was offset against the net proceeds of the disposal to determine the realised development value.

bear A Stock Exchange term for a person who undertakes to sell, at a specified future date and at an agreed price, securities he does not own. He does so in the hope/belief that the requisite securities can be bought cheaper during the intervening period and transferred at a profit. *Cf* BULL. *See* BEAR MARKET.

bearer bond A certificate of debt which entitles the holder to repayment with interest thereon in due course but does not require registration (or proof) of ownership.

bearer security A bond, stock or share, where no indication of the holder's name is given on the certificate and no record of ownership is maintained in the issuing company's records. Apart from its realisable cash value, it might give rights to dividends which would be payable on presentation of a coupon attached to the certificate. Physical possession is *prima facie* evidence of its ownership.

bear market The financial market at a time when prices generally are falling, and in which "bears" would prosper.

bed (of a stream) Land covered by water at the average or mean state of the stream/river throughout the year. Whether the bed of a tidal river includes the foreshore appears to be a matter of doubt, there being conflicting decisions.

before-and-after valuations Valuations which arise where some change is contemplated in the nature of an asset being valued. The asset is valued first in its existing state and secondly on the basis that the change will be made. The difference between the two values can provide a measure of the likely gain or loss due to the change. The method is also used in such cases as:

a injurious affection on compulsory purchase; and
b planning compensation, eg following a revocation order.

belvedere *See* GAZEBO.

bench-mark In land surveying, a physical reference point of known level above, or below, the selected base level, eg sea level. Commonly, a mark placed upon a permanent object of sufficient substance as to be unlikely to move, such as a rock, stone plinth or building. *See* ORDNANCE SURVEY.

beneficial interest An interest in property held by a beneficiary who is not necessarily the owner of the legal interest, eg where a legal estate is owned by a trustee (trustees) under a trust entitling the beneficiary to the financial rewards available after meeting all due obligations.

beneficial occupation The physical possession and control of land and/or buildings in a manner entitling the occupier to full use and enjoyment of the premises. *See* RATEABLE OCCUPATION.

beneficial occupier One enjoying beneficial occupation.

beneficial owner **1.** A person enjoying or entitled to property for his own benefit, not, for instance, as a trustee who holds the legal estate in land for the benefit of another. The owner of the legal estate is usually the beneficial owner, but if the legal estate is vested in trustees, the beneficial owner has only an equitable interest. He is then known as the beneficiary or *cestui que trust*. **2.** The person who is the real owner of a security, and thereby entitled to all consequential benefits, as distinct from a nominee who holds securities on behalf of another.

beneficiary A person entitled to benefit, eg under a trust or will. *See* BENEFICIAL INTEREST; CESTUI QUE TRUST.

benefit/cost ratio In assessing the financial potential of projects, the ratio of the total discounted value of the benefits to the sum of the discounted costs. This is a discounted cash flow technique.

best efforts The process of relying exclusively on the market for the purchase of all or part of shares being issued, ie without the benefit of indemnities from underwriters who guarantee to acquire any unsold shares at a pre-determined price.

best rent The highest rent which can reasonably be expected by a landlord in the circumstances of a particular case. *See* RACK-RENT.

beta value A coefficient measuring the comparative volatility of a specific investment through time, eg an ordinary share relative to the variability of the investment market as a whole.

betterment **1. (UK)** Any increase in the value of property which arises from action by government, either local or national. Such action may be positive, eg the building of a new road, or negative, eg when restrictions are imposed on other land to the advantage of the property concerned. **2.** The increment of value added to a property by virtue of any improvement. **3. (USA)** An improvement in the structure which increases the value of the property but is not a repair, redecoration or enlargement, eg the addition of aluminium sheeting over a frame wall; paving a street adjoining the structure; or adding a fireplace.

betterment levy Under the now repealed Land Commission Act 1967 a tax of 40% raised on the actual or deemed disposal of land reflecting development value, subject to exemptions, reliefs and concessions. It was abolished by the Land Commission (Dissolution) Act 1971.

betting office Shop, office or other premises open to the public and licensed for the placing and taking of bets under the Betting, Gaming and Lotteries Acts.

bid An offer to buy at a particular price, especially at an auction or by tender.

bidder One who makes an offer, or bids, to buy or lease chattels or property, especially at an auction or by tender.

bidding agreement (also known as knock-out agreement) *See* RING.

Big Bang A colloquial expression given to the great changes to the rules and practices of the Stock Exchange which came into force in 1986. These were designed to bring British practices into line with those of principal foreign exchanges. The changes permit banks, insurance companies and other financial institutions to own Stock Exchange subsidiaries. They also abolished the strict segregation which existed between jobbers and brokers and the arrangements for fixed commissions. *See* CHINESE WALL.

bilateral contract (synallagmatic contract) A contract in which each party undertakes to do or refrain from doing some act, thus creating mutual obligations. *Cf* UNILATERAL CONTRACT.

Bill (Parliamentary Bill) A proposal for legislation which is presented to Parliament for consideration by both Houses. After receiving the Royal Assent a Bill becomes an Act of Parliament.

bill of quantities A document, usually prepared by a quantity surveyor, describing in cost terms the detail of the quantities of labour, plant and materials required for building or engineering works, together with the contractual conditions under which the works will be carried out. It is usually used as a guide in deciding whether to proceed to tender and is therefore often the basis of documentation upon which tenders are prepared and submitted. The bill of quantities for the accepted tender then becomes a basis for estimating:

a costs before any variation in design,
b costs due to any variation in works during the construction programme and
c the final cost of works.

The document is usually based on the rules of measurement that are laid down in *Standard Method of Measurement of Building Works* issued by the Royal Institution of Chartered Surveyors and the National Federation of Building Trades Employers.

bill of sale A document for passing the title to chattels, either absolutely or by way of mortgage, possession remaining with the grantor. Bills of sale are subject to many statutory provisions.

blench (less commonly blanch) (Scotland) Descriptive of a feudal holding where rent to be paid (or service rendered) by a vassal is merely nominal, eg a rose. *See* PEPPERCORN RENT.

blight *See* PLANNING BLIGHT.

blight notice A notice that may be served under the Town and Country Planning Act 1971 sections 193-207 (as amended) on a statutory body by certain owner-occupiers of land when the value of that land is substantially decreased as a result of published proposals which indicate that the property may be acquired by the public body under compulsory purchase powers. *Cf* PURCHASE NOTICE.

block plan A plan, usually of small scale, showing in simple outline the buildings and other important physical features in an area and their relationship one with another. *Cf* LOCATION PLAN; SITE PLAN.

block width The wall-to-wall dimension across an office block or similar, adjusted to a consistent effective width in the case of premises of irregular shape, eg for the purpose of assessing rental value or judging the internal spread of natural light.

blue chip A colloquial term for a security of the highest repute. It is derived from the name of the highest value chip used in the game of poker.

boarding house A private dwelling where accommodation with services, such as meals and cleaning, is provided to paying guests who occupy as licensees rather than as tenants.

board, estate agents' *See* AGENCY BOARD.

body of deed The main and operative part of a deed, as opposed to the recitals.

bona fide Genuine; in good faith. *Cf* MALA FIDE.

***bona fide* purchaser** A person who, in good faith, is willing and able to purchase for valuable consideration.

bona vacantia Goods and land without any apparent owner. In the case of a person dying intestate and having no relatives qualified to succeed, under the Administration of Estates Act 1925 all his property passes to the Crown (or, as the case may be, to the Duchy of Lancaster or the Duke of Cornwall). Previously in such circumstances land passed to the Crown under the medieval custom known as escheat. The term also applies, under section 654 of the Companies Act 1985, to certain property of dissolved companies.

bond **1.** An investment by way of a loan at interest to a public body, a corporate body or a financial institution. The rate of interest may be nominal and the price on issue discounted to below the face value at which it will be repayable at the due date. **2.** A legally enforceable undertaking by one party to another to do or refrain from doing some act, eg a performance bond or, by analogy, a surety.

bonded warehouse (excise warehouse) A place of security approved by the Commissioners of Customs and Excise under section 92 of the Customs and Excise Management Act 1979 for the storage and/or processing of alcoholic beverages, tobacco and other goods subject to excise duties. *See* QUEEN'S WAREHOUSE; WAREHOUSE.

bonus issue An issue of new equity shares given free to the existing shareholders. Sometimes called "scrip" or "capitalisation" issue. It has the effect of reducing the price of individual shares and is of especial merit where prices have become "heavy" (relatively large in cost terms). *See* CAPITALISATION OF RESERVES.

book cost The cost to date of expenditure on an asset as carried in the accounts ledger. *See* BOOK VALUE.

book depreciation *See* DEPRECIATION.

book gain/loss A notional gain or loss represented by the difference between the acquisition cost of an asset, as shown in the accounts, and its market value at a particular time.

book value The value which is ascribed to a property shown in the accounts as a capital asset but is not necessarily current market value, since it may be based on actual cost (less depreciation, if any) or on an earlier valuation after acquisition.

Books of Council and Session (Scotland) A popular title for the Register of Deeds and Probative Writs in which, according to direction given, deeds may be registered for preservation, or preservation and execution.

boosey pasture A right of holdover whereby an outgoing farm tenant retains possession of pasture land to enable his cattle to feed on the preceding season's hay and straw.

bote *See* ESTOVERS.

boundary The line which separates property in one ownership from its neighbour(s); it is therefore the limit in all directions to which the ownership extends.

Bowcock's Tables A set of valuation tables, compiled by Philip Bowcock BSc ARICS, which are based on the assumption that income is to be received quarterly in advance and interest, where payable more frequently than once every twelve months, is converted into its effective annual equivalent.

breach of close Entering upon land belonging to another person, or upon common land, without a legal right to do so, ie a form of trespass.

breach of contract An act, or omission, contrary to one or more of the provisions in a contract and therefore giving the aggrieved party a right to enforce specific performance, to rescind the contract and/or to claim damages, the remedy available depending upon the nature of the breach.

breach of trust Failure of a trustee, or other person, to act properly in discharging his fiduciary duties, thus making him legally liable for any loss thereby sustained.

breach of warranty Failure to comply with a contractual undertaking, eg the failure of a vendor to pass title or give vacant possession when such has been warranted. Such a breach normally entitles the innocent party to damages, although the breach of a warranty in an insurance contract by the insured normally entitles the insurer to treat the contract as discharged.

break In Stock Exchange parlance, a drastic fall in prices. *Cf* BULGE.

break clause A clause in a lease which gives the landlord and/or the tenant a right, in specified circumstances, to terminate the lease before its normal expiry date. It usually defines the length of notice to be given and may be subject to contractual or statutory financial provisions.

break-even (point) In a cash flow appraisal of a project, eg house building for sale or a break-up operation, the time at which turnover is equal to the sum of fixed costs and variable costs. *See* BREAK-EVEN ANALYSIS.

break-even analysis A cash flow technique, which, on such assumptions as are made, shows the profit (or loss) of a project and its break-even point.

break point (break date) The date at which a lease terminates when a break clause has been invoked. Not to be confused with the date when notice of the intention to break requires to be served.

break-up operation In the property sense, when property has been acquired or held as a whole, the disposal of that property in parts to maximise the total sum realised.

break-up value The value of a specific property, eg an estate of land and buildings, based on the assumption that it is lotted and sold in parts, in such a manner as to achieve the best possible price.

bridging finance A short-term loan often made available as building finance, eg to a developer, for a period which may be from the beginning of a building programme until such time as the developer has secured funds of a more permanent nature, from which source the bridging finance is repaid. The repayment will include rolled-up interest (unless interest is payable during the period of the loan). It could extend to include an advance of part or the whole of the cost of site acquisition (site finance). In effect, where a developer has insufficient funds to meet his total commitment until permanent funds are available, the short-term loan "bridges" the time gap. *Cf* BRIDGING LOAN.

bridging loan Usually money made available, eg a bank loan, to a borrower enabling him to purchase a property. Repayment will normally be made from the proceeds of sale of the borrower's existing premises. *Cf* BRIDGING FINANCE.

bridlepath (bridleway) A public footpath along which there is also a right to ride or lead a horse. Sometimes there is an additional right to drive animals, in which case this was formerly known as a driftway or drove road. *See* HIGHWAY.

British Board of Agrément (BBA) A body which is principally concerned with the testing, assessment and certification of products for the construction industry, to secure the ready acceptance of the products concerned and to ensure their safe and effective use. The subjects for assessment are normally new or innovatory products, but existing products may be assessed should the need arise, eg as a result of changes in building regulation requirements. For certain products the board also approves and monitors installation contractors. The board was set up in 1966 by the Minister of Public Building and Works as The Agrément Board, adopting its present name in 1982. Its chairman and council members are appointed by the Secretary of State for the Environment.

British Council of Shopping Centres (BCSC) A body which represents the professional and commercial interests of shopping centre development in the United Kingdom. Membership is open to individuals or companies concerned with shopping centre property as owners, developers, managers, surveyors, retailers or consultants.

British Standards Institution (BSI) A non-profit-making organisation incorporated by Royal Charter in 1929. Its principal objects include the co-ordination of efforts by producers and users to improve and regularise standards of quality in materials, products and practices, and to eliminate waste through unnecessary variations in sizes and patterns of articles used for the same purpose. The BSI sets standards of quality and dimensions and promulgates their use.

British Venture Capital Association A body which represents financial organisations offering venture capital.

brochure A relatively expensive form of descriptive booklet or leaflet containing illustrations and full details of the main points necessary to inform and persuade a prospective purchaser or lessee of the desirability of a property or to describe to a client or prospective client the merits of a firm.

broker An agent or middleman who acts for a vendor or a purchaser in a transaction.

broker/dealer A broker who, as a member of a Stock Exchange, is permitted to deal in securities on behalf of a buyer, a seller or himself. Prior to the Big Bang, only brokers could deal with the public, and then as agents, they were not permitted to trade in securities as principals.

brokerage **1.** Commission paid to a broker. **2.** The activity of a broker in bringing together two parties in a transaction.

buffer zone A tract of land left undeveloped and often intensively planted with shrubs and/or trees in order to shield one land use from another, eg residential from industrial.

building A structure built to provide shelter for people, animals or goods. Usually an enclosed structure with walls and a roof, as in a house or factory. A building is intended to be permanent, or at least to stand for a reasonable period of time. Self-standing walls or fences do not constitute a building, but a wall adjacent to a building and supporting a roof could be construed as part of the building.

building agreement An agreement between the owner of a site and a developer, usually in the form of a licence, whereby the developer undertakes to construct the building(s) and on due performance becomes entitled to a lease of the land and building(s). This is a less attractive security to the developer and to a prospective lender than a direct building lease.

building byelaws Local authority control of building standards which was replaced in 1966 by national building regulations, except in inner London, where the London Building (Constructional) Byelaws (SI 1985 No 1936) set out the requirements. *See* BUILDING REGULATIONS.

building contract A contract between an owner or occupier of land and a building contractor, setting forth the terms under which construction is to be undertaken. A contract will normally include details of work to be carried out, basis of remuneration, time-scale, and penalties, if any, for failure to comply with terms of the contract. *See* JOINT CONTRACTS TRIBUNAL; COST-PLUS/DESIGN AND BUILD/FIXED PRICE/LUMP SUM/AND REMEASUREMENT CONTRACTS.

building contract certificates *See* INTERIM CERTIFICATE; CERTIFICATE OF PRACTICAL COMPLETION; CERTIFICATE OF MAKING GOOD DEFECTS; FINAL CERTIFICATE; PARTIAL COMPLETION CERTIFICATE.

building contractor A builder who enters into a contract with an employer under which he becomes obligated to carry out building or engineering works of a nature, extent and specification described in the contract and usually within a prescribed period.

building control The function of setting standards by building codes or regulations, approving an owner's proposals for building works and monitoring the builder's work as it progresses in order to ensure compliance with the standards or approved departures from them. Under Part II of the Housing and Building Control Act 1984 the supervision of plans and work in accordance with the regulations is carried out either by the local authority or, if the developer wishes, by an "approved inspector".

building cost indices A series of indices published by the Building Cost Information Service of the RICS relating to the cost of building work. They are based on cost models of "average building", which measure the changes in costs of labour, materials and plant which collectively cover the basic cost to a contractor. *See* TENDER PRICE INDICES.

Building Cost Information Service (BCIS) A subscriber service set up in 1962 under the aegis of the Royal Institution of Chartered Surveyors to facilitate the exchange of detailed building construction costs. Originally open only to chartered quantity surveyors, the service is now available to those of any discipline who are willing and able to contribute and receive data on a reciprocal basis. It is a sister service to the Building Maintenance Cost Information Service. *See* BUILDING COST INDICES; TENDER PRICE INDICES.

building finance *See* BRIDGING FINANCE.

building frontage *See* FRONTAGE (LINE).

building lease A long-term lease imposing an obligation on the lessee to erect one or more buildings which will pass to the landlord as part of the reversion, subject to any statutory rights of occupying lessees under, for example, the Landlord and Tenant Act 1954 or the Leasehold Reform Act 1967. Any rent payable by the lessee is a ground rent. *Cf* BUILDING AGREEMENT. *See* GROUND LEASE.

building licence **1.** An official licence issued by the Board of Trade between 1945 and 1951 and without which building was not permitted to take place during that period. **2.** A building agreement in the form of a licence.

building line (set-back line) A line, usually at a fixed distance from the centre of a highway, in front of which building is not permitted. It is intended to enhance the environment by setting buildings back from a road, thus improving the appearance of the locality and increasing road safety. In cases of loss of use of land due to the enforcement of a building line, compensation may be payable. (Highways Act 1980 sections 73 and 74.) *Cf* IMPROVEMENT LINE; SIGHT LINE.

Building Maintenance Cost Information Service (BMCIS) A subscriber service for the collection, analysis and dissemination of cost data and other information about building maintenance and property occupancy. Set up in 1971, the service is self-supporting and works closely with, but independently of, the Royal Institution of Chartered Surveyors. Like its sister service, the Building Cost Information Service, it operates on a reciprocal basis with subscribers providing data on their own buildings and receiving information made available by other members.

building of special architectural or historic interest. *See* LISTED BUILDING.

building owner Under the London Building Acts 1930 to 1939, the owner of a property who wishes to carry out work in respect of an existing or proposed party wall or structure. *See* ADJOINING OWNER.

building preservation notice (BPN) A notice served under section 58 of the Town and Country Planning Act 1971 by a local planning authority on the owner and occupier of a building which is unlisted but is considered by the authority to be of special architectural or historic interest and in danger of alteration or demolition. In effect the BPN protects the building for six months while the Secretary of State gives consideration to the possibility of its being listed.

building preservation order (BPO) An order, formerly made by a local planning authority subject to confirmation by the Minister, which prohibited the demolition or alteration of a building of special architectural or historic interest. Such orders were abolished by the Town and Country Planning Act 1968 (subsequently consolidated in the Town and Country Planning Act 1971), which introduced the present listed buildings procedures and building preservation notices.

Building Regulations A code of practice issued as a statutory instrument under the Housing and Building Control Act 1984 by the Secretary of State for the Environment, which lays down methods of construction for England and Wales (except inner London, where requirements for the London boroughs are set out in building byelaws). The regulations also specify the type and minimum quality of materials to be used in building. The Building Regulations are legally enforced by district councils.

Building Research Establishment (BRE) A group of government laboratories which carry out research and development in building and construction, housing and planning, prevention and control of fire, and general environmental factors. The work ranges from fundamental research to the study of practical problems arising from current change and innovation.

building scheme (scheme of development) In property law a development project in which land is laid out in plots and sold to different purchasers or leased to different lessees, all of whom enter into restrictive covenants with the common vendor or lessor. Provided it can be shown that there was an intention to impose a scheme of mutually enforceable restrictions in the interest of all purchasers or lessees and their successors, anyone in such a category can enforce and will be bound by the restrictions, even though they may not have been a party to them.

building society Under the Building Societies Act 1986, sections 5 and 119 and Schedule 2, this means a UK society "whose purpose or principal purpose is that of raising, primarily by the subscriptions of the members, a stock or fund for making to them advances secured on land for their residential use", thereby qualifying for establishment and, on complying with the "scheduled requirements", for incorporation under the Act. The latter involves registration with the central office of the registry of friendly societies, except in Scotland, where registration is with the assistant registrar of friendly societies for Scotland.

building survey An examination of a building by a surveyor (which may include specific tests by the surveyor or other experts) in order to produce a written or verbal report. Such a report would cover for instance the condition of the structure, fixtures and fittings, services and plant installations. Depending upon the instructions given to the surveyor these physical features would be described in relation to safety, stability, strength, efficiency and economy in use, ease of maintenance and other factors as required.

building surveyor An individual who is competent to undertake building surveys, prepare building specifications, place contracts with builders, supervise repair, restoration or new work and generally manage allied works on behalf of clients to whom he will owe the normal duty as an agent or employee, depending on the terms of his engagement.

built depth The maximum external measurement from front to rear walls of a building, especially a shop.

bulge In Stock Exchange terms a sharp rise in the prices of securities. *Cf* BREAK.

bull A Stock Exchange term for a person who buys a security (eg stock, share or bond) in the hope/belief that prices will rise, enabling him to sell later at a profit. *See* BULL MARKET. *Cf* BEAR.

bull market The financial market at a time when prices are rising and in which "bulls" would prosper.

bullet A borrowing in which the repayment of all the principal is made at maturity.

bundle of rights theory The hypothesis that ownership of real property is an agglomeration of a number of separate rights which together constitute absolute ownership. These rights include the right to occupy; the rights to use and to profit from; the rights to develop, to sell or bequeath.

bungalow A single-storey dwelling.

burden (of contract or covenant) The obligation(s) into which a party to a contract or a covenantor has entered in favour of the other party or covenantee.

burial ground In section 128 of the Town and Country Planning Act 1971 this is defined as including "any churchyard, cemetery or other ground, whether consecrated or not, which has at any time been set apart for the purpose of interment." Provisions governing the use and development of burial grounds are contained in the above section of the Act.

Bürolandschaft A German word for a landscaped office.

business **1.** Broadly described as an activity which is principally of a commercial or mercantile nature but which may also include industrial undertakings. It concerns work seriously carried out to provide a means of livelihood and with the intention of producing a profit. **2.** For the purposes of the Landlord and Tenant Act 1954 business "includes a trade, profession or employment and includes any activity carried on by a body of persons whether corporate or unincorporate". *See* BADGES OF TRADE; BUSINESS TENANCY; TRADE.

business expansion scheme A tax relief scheme which allows certain individuals to invest in a company involved in a particular kind of business. A specified maximum sum may be invested and set off against taxable income. The shares must be held for at least five years to qualify for exemption from capital gains tax and to avoid claw-back on the income tax relief.

business name A name under which a business activity is carried on; where appropriate it is registered for business purposes under the Business Names Act 1985.

business park A landscaped area containing high-tech, other specialist buildings and leisure facilities with other amenities for business purposes, as distinct from high-tech buildings in a science park. Building density is lower than would be usual in a traditional industrial estate. Business parks are preferentially located where motorway, rail and airport communications are within a short distance. *Cf* SCIENCE PARK.

business premises **1.** Generally used to describe premises occupied or capable of being occupied for commercial or retail purposes. **2.** Premises occupied under a lease to which Part II of the Landlord and Tenant Act 1954 applies. *See* BUSINESS 2.

business space A combination of "light industrial" and "office space."

business tenancy A tenancy of premises used for a "business" by an occupier who enjoys security of tenure under Part II of the Landlord and Tenant Act 1954.

butt *See* ABUT.

buyer's behaviour analysis In marketing, the function of examining the ways in which those in the market go about the acquisition of a property or service; such an analysis will usually be undertaken with a view to applying the knowledge gained to the marketing of a product.

buyer's market In the property market, a condition of supply and demand in which those seeking to purchase are in a relatively strong negotiating position because of a degree of oversupply. *Cf* SELLER'S MARKET.

buy in **1.** To acquire a subordinate interest in a property in which the purchaser already has an interest. **2.** A term indicating that the highest bid at an auction is being made by the vendor, or by someone acting on his behalf, which, in effect, means that the property remains unsold. **3.** When a security is purchased at market price to complete a deal when the seller has failed to deliver. The buyer then goes elsewhere in the market to "buy in" the agreed quantity of securities. Also, in futures markets, to close (cover) a short position.

buy on close To purchase at the end of the trading session at a price within the closing range. *Cf* BUY ON OPENING.

buy on opening A Stock Exchange term meaning to purchase at the beginning of a trading session within the opening range. Used mostly in commodity futures markets. *Cf* BUY ON CLOSE.

buy-out **1.** The purchase of a completed development by a body which has provided forward finance. **2.** Where the managers and employees of a company, having arranged the necessary finance, acquire a proportion or all of the equity shares and undertake the running of the business.

buy-out rate In a funding agreement between a developer and a prospective purchaser, the pre-determined investment yield which will be used to capitalise the annual income receivable at the time of sale to determine the buy-out price.

byelaw (by-law) A local law operating in the area of a particular authority, made by the authority under statutory powers, confirmed by the appropriate Minister, administered by the authority but enforceable in the courts of the realm.

C

cadastral Derived from the French *cadastre* and meaning related to a register of land ownership, usually for taxation assessment purposes.

cadastral map A map showing the boundaries of property ownership for the recording of title and for taxation purposes.

cadastral survey A survey carried out to record the boundaries of a property on a plan.

calendar month One of the twelve periods of 28 (or in leap years 29), 30 or 31 days into which a calendar year is divided. *Cf* LUNAR MONTH.

calendar year (civil year) A period of 365 consecutive days or, if the period includes February 29, 366 consecutive days (leap year). *Cf* FINANCIAL YEAR; FISCAL YEAR.

call The process of calling upon the holder of a security to pay an outstanding amount or balance, in the case of a security issued at a price of which only part is payable at the outset, the remainder being due at a later date only when required by the issuing company. The date and amount of any call will be governed by the terms stated at the date of issue. A call should be distinguished from an instalment, which is automatically due to be paid at a fixed date determined at the time the security was issued.

call-in Under the current town and country planning legislation, a requirement by the appropriate Secretary of State that a planning application be transferred to him for decision instead of by the relevant local planning authority.

call loan A loan which is repayable in full to the lender on demand.

call option **1.** A contract whereby one party has the option to purchase the other party's interest in a property, usually within a specified time, at a stated or calculable price and/or in defined circumstances. It is binding against a third party only if registered as an estate contract. **2.** The Stock Exchange term for a right to buy securities at a specific future time and at a defined price. *Cf* PUT OPTION. *See* PUT AND TAKE OPTION.

CALUS An abbreviation for Centre for Advanced Land Use Studies, a department of the College of Estate Management. The centre organises conferences and study tours for qualified surveyors and others and encourages research which will be of practical value to the profession.

candle auction An auction which is continued while a candle is burning. The last bid before the flame goes out, or reaches a pre-determined level, is the one which is accepted.

Candlemas February 2. The Feast of the Purification of the Virgin Mary. One of the half quarter days or, in Scotland, term days. *See* QUARTER DAYS.

capital Wealth, usually derived from direct or indirect savings, in the form of permanent or durable assets or employed in industrial, commercial or other productive enterprises as the financial base upon which they are established and operate. This is with a view to making a profit which may be either income or a capital gain, or both. Typically it is the money invested by the purchase of stocks and shares in a corporate body, the aggregate of which represents the capital of that company. In taxation, the distinction between capital and income has to be drawn, as different rates of tax often apply to each. Since it is not always obvious whether something is capital or income, rules have been made enabling the Inland Revenue to determine which is which. *Cf* INCOME.

capital allowances Under the Capital Allowances Act 1968 as amended, allowances available to owners against income tax or corporation tax for capital expenditure on certain buildings and structures (including site clearance). Generally the kinds of allowances available include one or more of the following:

a *initial allowance* — made to a person who incurred capital expenditure on the construction of a building or structure or on the purchase of a new unused one. In the case of plant and machinery the term "first-year allowance" is used instead of "initial allowance". Currently (December 1988), applies only in enterprise zones.

b *writing down allowance* — made annually to a lessor or trader currently owning and/or using the eligible building or structure.

c *balancing allowance/charge* — an adjustment which occurs if the building is sold, demolished or ceases to be used within the period when the writing down allowance is still available, so as to adjust the total allowance to the net cost.

Allowances are available for the following categories:

Industrial buildings — The rates of industrial building allowances (IBAs) have varied from time to time and are now restricted to writing down allowances, but a balancing allowance/charge may arise on disposal or in other circumstances.

Hotels — Allowances on capital expenditure apply to costs incurred after April 11 1978 in respect of the construction, extension or alteration of hotels which qualify under the 1968 Act as amended.

Certain residential buildings — Allowances for residential buildings constructed for letting under the assured tenancy scheme (originally introduced by the Housing Act 1980 and to be replaced on January 15 1989 by the scheme under the Housing Act 1988).

Enterprise zones — Allowances of 100% for the construction of buildings within enterprise zones apply to qualifying industrial buildings, hotels and commercial buildings and structures constructed within 10 years of the designation of the zone. Buildings in enterprise zones are treated more favourably than similar buildings elsewhere.

Plant, machinery and equipment —Allowances for expenditure on the installation of certain plant, machinery and equipment in qualifying industrial, commercial and residential property. In addition, expenditure on fire safety, thermal insulation and safety at sports grounds may be eligible.

Other categories — Allowances may also be available on expenditure related to agricultural or forestry buildings, scientific research and a variety of structures, eg sea walls and river embankments.

capital appreciation The increase in the capital value of an asset over a given period, usually expressed as a percentage of the initial value.

capital expenditure Money spent on acquiring or improving capital assets, such as land, buildings, plant and machinery, as distinct from expenditure of a revenue nature such as money spent on the maintenance of existing assets.

capital gain For capital gains tax purposes, an increase in the value of a capital asset, not being stock-in-trade, as computed in accordance with the Capital Gains Tax Act 1979.

capital gains tax (CGT) A tax on the gain accruing to a taxpayer through the disposal of a capital asset if sold on or since April 6 1965. Special rules applied where the asset was acquired before that date. There are various exemptions, reliefs and concessions. Companies pay a form of corporation tax on capital gains. Since April 1982 the taxpayer has been enabled to receive some allowance for inflation during the period of ownership, ie indexation. Under the Finance (No 2) Act 1988 for disposals on or after April 1 1988 CGT is generally only payable on gains arising since April 1 1982. *See* ROLL-OVER RELIEF; TIME APPORTIONMENT; WASTING ASSET.

capital gearing *See* GEARING.

capital improvement Work carried out on an asset with a view to enhancing its value, but not including repairs or maintenance. *See* ENHANCEMENT EXPENDITURE.

capitalisation **1.** At a given date the conversion into the equivalent capital worth of a series of net receipts, actual or estimated, over a period. *Cf* DECAPITALISATION. *See* DISCOUNTING; TIME VALUE OF MONEY. **2.** A method of calculating a final purchase price for a development using an agreed formula to convert actual, or assumed, income from initial lettings into a capital sum. Such capitalised sums may be offset against a purchasing fund's interim finance payments, any excess being paid to the developer.

3. In relation to a company's reserves, the conversion into capital of money, which is then distributed as a capitalisation issue. *Cf* DECAPITALISATION. *See* CAPITALISATION OF RESERVES.

capitalisation of reserves (bonus, free or scrip issue) A procedure whereby the issued capital of a company is increased by converting reserves into new shares, which are distributed to the shareholders, without payment, in proportion to their existing holdings. It has the effect of reducing the price of individual shares and is of especial merit where share prices have become "heavy", ie relatively large in cash terms.

capitalisation rate The yield at which the net income from an investment is discounted to ascertain its capital value at a given date. *Cf* DECAPITALISATION.

capital loss For capital gains tax purposes, a reduction in the value of an asset not being stock-in-trade, as computed in accordance with the Capital Gains Tax Act 1979. A capital loss is allowed for tax purposes when the capital asset has been the subject of a disposal at a loss.

capital market The market for securities of a medium- or long-term nature in contrast to the money markets for short-term debt.

capital money Money from certain transactions, eg sales, the granting of certain leases, mortgage loans or the proceeds of insurance claims, in respect of settled land or land held on trust for sale. Capital money must generally be received by the trustees, rather than the beneficiaries, of a settlement and unless raised for some special purpose such as authorised improvements must be invested and held by the trustees on the same trusts as the land. *See* SETTLED LAND; TRUST FOR SALE.

capital transfer tax (CTT) A former capital tax on gifts charged progressively on successive gratuitous transfers of value (those made in the previous ten years) by an individual during his or her lifetime and on death, subject to exemptions, reliefs and concessions. CTT replaced estate duty from 1975 and was itself superseded by inheritance tax in 1986.

capital value The value of an asset as distinct from its annual or periodic (rental) value. *Cf* RENTAL VALUE.

capital, working *See* WORKING CAPITAL.

carriageway A highway along which there is a right to drive vehicles, and also — except where prohibited by statute — to lead or ride animals and to pass on foot.

carrying charge Expenditure incurred, whether by a freeholder or the owner of a subordinate interest, in the course of holding a property vacant.

case **1.** A court action, something forming sufficient grounds for bringing an action, or the collective arguments put forward by one of the parties to such an action. **2.** One of a number of categories of assessment for income taxation under Schedule D or Schedule E. There are six under Schedule D and three under Schedule E. **3.** One of twenty sets of circumstances detailed in Schedule 15 to the Rent Act 1977, as amended by the Housing Act 1980, in which possession of a dwelling-house let on, or subject to, a Rent Act protected or statutory tenancy may (or in some instances must) be ordered by a court.

case law The body of law established by judicial decisions. *Cf* STATUTE LAW. *See* CITATION.

case stated A written statement of the material facts in a decision by a magistrates' court, by certain tribunals (such as the Lands Tribunal or an agricultural land tribunal) or by an agricultural arbitrator for the opinion or judgment of the High Court or Court of Appeal on one or more questions of law. The case is prepared by the court or tribunal at the behest of a party who wishes to appeal against its decision and it usually sets out specific questions on the various points at issue.

cash and carry (warehouse) An outlet where goods can be bought in bulk by traders or retail customers. Goods are exchanged for immediate payment by cash or such equivalent as is acceptable to the store. No delivery service is provided.

cash back A payment made by a property owner to a prospective tenant to secure a letting in times of oversupply on terms which would otherwise be unacceptable. In essence it can be regarded as the opposite of a premium and, as such, is a form of reverse or negative premium.

cash flow The actual or estimated movement of money by way of income and outgoings during the life of a project.

cash flow analysis/statement Cash flow portrayed as a table of successive periods, eg monthly, quarterly or yearly. It has many applications relating to financial viability, eg forecasting loss, breakeven or profit; discounted cash flow exercises; or as a basis for budget control.

cash on cash (USA) The mathematical relationship between the net income receivable, after servicing any mortgage debt including amortisation, together with other outgoings and the net purchase price paid for an investment with a continuing liability for the mortgage debt secured on the property.

catastrophic perils (dry perils) In property insurance those special or unusual risks which may be covered on payment of an additional premium and subject to special conditions. Such risks include destruction or damage (by fire or other hazard) of, or to, the property caused by aircraft or any other aerial devices, explosion, earthquake, riot and labour disturbances. *Cf* NON-CATASTROPHIC PERILS (WET PERILS).

catchment area **1.** The area of land from which water finds its way into a particular watercourse, lake or reservoir. **2.** By analogy, the area which contains those people who can be expected to obtain goods, services, employment or other benefits from a particular property. More especially related to retail premises, where the success of forecasting depends on the accuracy of estimating the number of purchasers (catchment population) likely to be attracted from the different parts of the area and the average expenditure which might be expected from them.

catchment population *See* CATCHMENT AREA 2.

cattle In cattle trespass "cattle" — in the sense of livestock — includes horses, oxen, sheep, swine, goats, asses, fowls, geese, ducks, and probably peacocks and turkeys, but not dogs, cats or bees. Tame deer may now be included.

cattlegate A right to graze animals for a limited period on someone else's land. The word also means an area of pasture sufficient to support five sheep or one cow.

cattle trespass Originally a tort in common law whereby the owner of trespassing cattle was strictly liable for any damage caused by the cattle, this is now in England and Wales an offence under the Animals Act 1971. Under that Act the owner of straying livestock that damages another's land or property is liable for the damage and for any expenses of keeping or ascertaining the ownership of the livestock. *See* TRESPASS.

caution In land registration, one of the methods of protecting minor interests; in particular it entitles the cautioner to record his interest to ensure that:

a any application for first registration of title is notified to him, whereupon he can take appropriate action to protect his interests;

b no dealing or notice of deposit can be effected without similar notice.

Cf INHIBITION; RESTRICTION.

caveat actor Let the doer beware.

caveat emptor Let the buyer beware. An old legal maxim stating that the buyer takes the risk regarding quality or condition of the item purchased, unless there is misrepresentation or he is protected by warranty or statute. Recent consumer protection laws have placed more responsibility for disclosure on the seller and broker.

caveat subscriptor Let the signer beware, eg of a contract.

caveat venditor Let the vendor beware.

ceiling value A term applied to the maximum compensation payable for compulsory acquisitions under Parts IX and XVII of the Housing Act 1985, ie of unfit properties acquired at "site value". Section 589 of the 1985 Act coupled with section 10 of and Schedule 2 to the Land Compensation Act 1961 provides that such site value compensation must not exceed the open market value of the property.

central activities zone (CAZ) Originally defined by the City of Westminster to describe that area of the city where central London activities predominate; subsequently adopted as a planning term by the former Greater London Council to describe a broader area of central London but now adopted as a planning term by some other central London boroughs.

central business district (CBD) The functional centre around which the rest of a city is structured. Characterised by the presence of comparison shopping, office accommodation, leisure facilities, buildings for recreational use, public museums, art galleries and governmental functions. Generally the area of highest land values within a city.

central non-domestic rating list Under section 52 of the Local Government Finance Act 1988, a list compiled and maintained by the central valuation officer containing data about non-domestic hereditaments prescribed in regulations yet to be issued (1988).

central valuation officer Under section 61 of the Local Government Finance Act 1988, a person appointed by the Commissioners of Inland Revenue to compile and then maintain the central non-domestic rating list in accordance with sections 52 and 53.

certificate of appropriate alternative development A certificate issued under section 17 of the Land Compensation Act 1961 by a local planning authority — or by the Secretary of State on appeal — stating what development, if any, would have been permitted if the land in question had not been proposed for acquisition by an authority with powers of compulsory purchase. Such a certificate is for the purpose of establishing the basis of compensation where the land is not zoned for commercial, industrial, residential or comprehensive development and is not in an action area.

certificate of discharge A certificate issued by the Capital Taxes Office of the Inland Revenue on application by a deceased person's personal representative(s) who, having supplied all the information required, has (have) agreed the figures with the Revenue office and paid the taxes due. The taxpayer is then absolved from further tax liability arising as a result of the death unless there has been fraud or non-disclosure of facts.

certificate of fair rent A certificate issued by a rent officer stating the fair rent of a dwelling-house within the Rent Acts, which has been determined by either the rent officer himself or a rent assessment committee.

certificate for payment *See* ARCHITECT'S CERTIFICATE.

certificate of immunity *See* CERTIFICATE OF NON-LISTING.

certificate of making good defects Under a building contract, a certificate issued by the architect, surveyor or supervising officer at the end of the defects liability period stating that the contractor has satisfactorily made good any defects. This certificate will have the effect of releasing the balance of the retention money for the payment of the contractor. *See* BUILDING CONTRACT CERTIFICATES.

certificate of non-listing (certificate of immunity) Under section 54A of the Town and Country Planning Act 1971, a certificate issued by the Secretary of State for the Environment stating that for a period of at least five years (following an application by any concerned person) a building will not be listed as one of special architectural or historic interest. Such application can be made only in cases where the building has been the subject of a planning application and/or a planning permission for development involving its alteration, extension or demolition.

certificate of partial completion *See* PARTIAL COMPLETION CERTIFICATE.

certificate of practical completion Under a building contract, a certificate issued by the architect, surveyor or supervising officer stating that the works have been substantially completed and the building is ready for occupation. This certificate will:

a release an agreed percentage of any retention money,
b begin the defects liability period, and
c transfer responsibility for insurance from the contractor to the employer.

See BUILDING CONTRACT CERTIFICATES.

certificate of value **1.** A form signed by the purchaser of a property attesting to the price paid, eg for stamp duty purposes. **2.** A document issued by the Lands Tribunal certifying the value of property being sold to an authority possessing compulsory powers (Land Compensation Act 1961, section 35). It is issued on the written application of the vendor and is of especial use to trustees in that the value certified is deemed to be the best price that can be obtained. *Cf* VALUATION CERTIFICATE.

certiorari Originally a prerogative writ. Subsequently an order of the Queen's Bench Divisional Court quashing decisions of inferior courts, administrative tribunals or administrative bodies because they are founded on errors of law. Since 1981 orders of certiorari have been obtained by an application for judicial review, which enables the Divisional Court as an alternative to issue a declaratory judgment or injunction. *Cf* MANDAMUS; PROHIBITION.

certum est quod certum reddit potest If something is capable of being made certain, it should be treated as certain, eg if the amount of rent in a lease can be ascertained, it is treated as certain and the lease is therefore valid and enforceable.

cesser The premature cessation of a right or interest, eg on destruction of premises where provision is made for the lease to be terminated in such an event.

cesser of rent Permanent or temporary release from the obligation to pay rent, usually arising only in certain circumstances specified in the lease, eg on the total loss of a building as a result of a fire.

cestui que trust A beneficiary or beneficial owner under a trust.

chain **1.** A traditional measure of length being 22 yards, ie the length of a surveyor's Gunter's chain, and also the distance between the wickets on a cricket pitch. **2.** A traditional rule of metal links with metal tags to denote rods, poles and perches. **3.** A series of property transactions, each of which is dependent upon at least one other, especially in residential sales, where purchaser B will only be able to buy a property from vendor A if purchaser C buys B's property and so on.

chain store One of a series of retail outlets under a single ownership, but now more commonly called a multiple retail outlet. Each store within such a group will probably sell the same range of goods and have the advantage of central buying.

champerty (champertous maintenance) Derived from the Latin *campi partito* (a division of the land). A term used since medieval times to describe the illegal act of a person, who otherwise had no interest in the outcome of a court action, in giving support to a litigant on the basis of receiving a share of any benefit arising from the court decision. Under section 14 of the Criminal Law Act 1967, champerty is no longer either a crime or a tort, but a contract involving champerty may be treated as void on grounds of public policy. *See* CONTINGENCY FEE.

Chancery Division That division of the High Court which replaced the former Court of Chancery and deals principally with questions concerning rent, property, trusts, the administration of estates, patents and company law. Its nominal president is the Lord Chancellor but it is really headed by the Vice-Chancellor.

change of use, material *See* MATERIAL CHANGE OF USE.

chapter The description given to an Act of Parliament as part of the volume of statutes for a year, each Act being given a separate number.

charge An interest in land which secures the payment of a present or future debt.

charge by way of legal mortgage A deed charging the mortgagor's land in favour of the mortgagee to secure the repayment of the mortgage debt. This is one of the only two forms of legal mortgage subsisting since the Law of Property Act 1925 (the other being a mortgage by demise, ie a lease subject to a cesser on redemption).

charge certificate A certificate issued to a mortgagee by the Land Registry, subject to deposit of the land certificate during the period of the mortgage, and giving evidence of his title.

charge, equitable *See* EQUITABLE CHARGE.

charge, legal *See* LEGAL CHARGE.

chargeable realised development value (CRDV) The realised development value on which development land tax was chargeable, ie after allowing for any exemptions, reliefs or concessions available to the taxpayer.

charges register One of the three parts into which the register of each individual title to land is divided under the Land Registration Rules 1925. It shows interests which are adverse to the registered proprietor, eg restrictive covenants or easements. *Cf* LAND CHARGES REGISTER. *See* LAND REGISTRY; PROPERTY REGISTER; PROPRIETORSHIP REGISTER.

charging authority Under section 144(1) of the Local Government Finance Act 1988 this is a district council, a London borough council, the Common Council of the City of London and the Council of the Isles of Scilly. Such authorities will be empowered to levy community charges and non-domestic rates.

charitable trust A trust set up exclusively for charitable purposes as recognised by law, ie for the furtherance of religion, the advancement of education, the relief of poverty, or other purposes beneficial to the community.

charity A body which, without profit to itself, administers funds for the direct or indirect benefit of deserving persons or causes. Normally charities have to be registered with the Charity Commissioners and this gives the charities certain benefits, eg exemption from taxation.

chartered surveyor A surveyor who is a qualified member of the Royal Institution of Chartered Surveyors, being a Fellow or Professional Associate in one of seven divisions, each covering a different field of activity.

chattel A property other than a freehold interest in land. *Cf* REAL PROPERTY. *See* CHATTEL REAL.

chattel personal A tangible item of personal property, eg an item of furniture. *Cf* CHOSE IN POSSESSION.

chattel real A leasehold interest in land.

checkout The part or parts of a supermarket or other self-selection store at which the actual sale of goods takes place by payment of cash or, where permitted, by credit card or cheque. There will usually be several tills, at points which are located for easy egress to a street or car park. These exits are usually designed to facilitate the conveyance of goods by trolley to a car park or other area close to transport facilities.

chief rent Not in general use, but in certain parts of the country, eg Lancashire, a synonym for "rentcharge".

Chinese wall A term used, particularly in relation to the world of business and finance, to describe an intangible barrier existing within an organisation to prevent the improper flow and subsequent use of information from someone who is on one side of the barrier to anyone, whether or not a member of that organisation, who is on the other side. The type of information not allowed to cross the barrier is that which, if disclosed, would be a breach of confidentiality and prejudicial to one or more clients of the organisation or to anyone else to whom they owe a duty. Such improper disclosure can only be prevented if the operational system adopted by an organisation is efficient, understood by all to whom it applies, and imposes adequate penalties if breached.

chose An article of personal property.

chose in action An intangible right which can be enforced by legal action, eg a right to a payment or the recovery of a debt.

chose in possession A tangible object which is capable of being possessed and enjoyed, eg an article of furniture. *See* CHATTEL PERSONAL.

Church Commissioners A body established in 1948 by the amalgamation of Queen Anne's Bounty and the Ecclesiastical Commissioners. Its main duty is to manage the financial affairs of the Church of England.

church rate *See* RECTOR'S RATE.

circulation ratio The ratio of the net internal area to the gross internal area of a building, usually expressed as a percentage. *See* FLOOR AREA.

circumstantial evidence (indirect evidence) Evidence tending to establish the existence of a fact in issue by inference from known facts. *Cf* ORIGINAL EVIDENCE.

citation The quoting of a decided case or authority as guidance to the court. *See* CASE LAW.

Civic Trust A voluntary body set up in 1957 to promote the protection and improvement of the built environment. It encourages the formation of local amenity societies and makes annual awards for schemes of development which enhance the environment.

civil year *See* CALENDAR YEAR.

claim holding Under the former Town and Country Planning Act 1947, the prospective right of a landowner to receive payment in respect of an established claim for the loss of development value. From January 1 1955, outstanding claim holdings in a parcel of land were aggregated, together with a capital supplement (interest), to become the original "unexpended balance of established development value".

clause A sub-division of a Bill before it is enacted, when it becomes a section of the Act.

claw-back A lawful recovery of part or the whole of a payment which was properly due at the time it was made. The term is specifically used in relation to tax — originally as "the clawing back" by a taxpayer of some element of tax paid by him which proved to be excessive or on other grounds recoverable; more recently it tends to be a "clawing back" by the Inland Revenue of some element of payment previously made to a taxpayer by way of tax relief.

clean air zone A colloquial term for a smoke control area under the Clean Air Act 1956.

clearance Indication by the relevant officer of the Inland Revenue that a particular tax provision does not apply to an actual or proposed transaction, eg under section 776(11) of the Income and Corporation Taxes Act 1988.

clearance area An area which is to be cleared of all buildings in pursuance of a declaration of the local housing authority, made under section 289 of the Housing Act 1985, where they are satisfied that the houses in the area are unfit for human habitation or, by reason of the narrowness or bad arrangement of the streets, are dangerous or injurious to the health of the inhabitants of the area, and that other buildings (if any) in the area are for the like reason dangerous or injurious to the health of the inhabitants of the area. Such a declaration is normally followed by the acquisition of the land and the clearance of the area, but under section 301 there is power for the authority to postpone clearance and render the houses capable of providing accommodation of a standard which is adequate for the time being. *Cf* CLOSING ORDER; DEMOLITION ORDER. *See* CEILING VALUE; SITE VALUE 3.

cleared site approach Under the Leasehold Reform Act 1967, the use of the direct comparison method to find the site value and hence the modern ground rent. The comparison is made with other residential sites which have been sold. *Cf* NEW-FOR-OLD APPROACH; STANDING HOUSE APPROACH.

clear height Defined by the *RICS/ISVA Code of Measuring Practice* as "The height between floor surface and lowest part of roof trusses, ceiling beams, roof beams or haunches at the eaves".

clearing house A place where, at agreed dates, transactions of a commercial nature are settled by financial payments which equal the net result of any transactions carried out by the parties concerned since the last date. In particular, that part of a financial market for commodities, securities or other assets which arranges for settlements of transactions at regular intervals.

clear lease A lease under which the landlord has no actual or contingent liability for outgoings (other than tax), eg one let on full repairing and insuring terms or one where the full cost of meeting the landlord's obligations is recoverable from the tenant by an adequate service charge additional to the rent.

clear title Unencumbered title to real property, against which there are no claims, mortgages, voluntary liens etc.

clog on equity of redemption A restriction contained in a mortgage deed on the mortgagor's right to redeem the mortgage on payment of the outstanding debt or performance of any other obligations for which the security was given. All such restrictions are null and void.

close company A company which is controlled by not more than five participators. There are special tax provisions which affect such companies.

closed tender *See* PRIVATE TENDER.

closing order An order made by a local authority under section 265 of the Housing Act 1985 in respect of an unfit dwelling-house which is beyond repair at reasonable cost but where the building is listed or a demolition order would be inexpedient because of its effect upon another building. Such an order prohibits the use of the premises for any purpose other than one approved by the local authority.

clustering The grouping of shops (usually for comparison goods) or of service outlets, eg estate agents, building societies, insurance offices and banks. Such grouping is the result of landlord control, operators' decision or planning process, so as to achieve maximum convenience for customers and the optimum return for tenants.

Code of Measuring Practice Guidelines for the measurement of buildings published jointly by the Royal Institution of Chartered Surveyors and the Incorporated Society of Valuers and Auctioneers.

Code on Takeovers and Mergers A non-statutory set of rules, produced by the Panel on Takeovers and Mergers, with which participants in takeovers or mergers and their advisers or agents are expected to comply. They are designed to ensure that all activities in connection with such matters are conducted in a manner which is fair to the shareholders involved. The rules, although not being legally enforceable, are an effective sanction against improper behaviour, since a company in breach of them incurs the displeasure of "the City" and would thereafter be refused the support, or advice, which it would usually require at some subsequent date for the successful operation of its business.

collateral (security) Traditionally used to mean some security in addition to the personal obligation of the borrower but commonly used to refer to a security provided in addition to the principal one. *Cf* NON-RECOURSE LOAN.

collateral agreement An agreement subsidiary to the main contract, such as one whereby professionals, eg architects or structural engineers, employed by a developer acknowledge direct responsibility and an additional duty of care to whomsoever purchases the development when it is completed.

collective insurance An arrangement whereby insurers, while remaining fully liable to the insured, pass on a proportion of the risk to other insurance companies. This situation arises where the company has a limit beyond which it cannot, or is unwilling to, accept liability unless re-insured by another insurer.

collector of taxes An officer of the Department of Inland Revenue responsible for collecting taxes under assessments made by an inspector of taxes.

College of Estate Management (CEM) An independent body, now based on the campus of Reading University, empowered under Royal Charter to offer educational courses and to encourage research, and publish the results, in all matters of interest to the landed professions. *See* CALUS.

combination mortgage A mortgage loan where repayment is agreed to be by a mixture of methods, eg part in cash and part from the proceeds of a matured endowment policy.

comfort letter *See* LETTER OF COMFORT.

command papers Documents presented to Parliament by the government, officially by royal command, eg White Papers and reports of Royal Commissions and committees of inquiry. They are numbered serially in sets of 1-9999, each set having a distinguishing prefix, ie Cd; Cmd; Cmnd; and, since 1987, Cm.

Commercial Court A court made up of judges from the Queen's Bench Division of the High Court (of which it forms part) and specialising in commercial cases, eg transport, insurance, banking and commodity transactions. Among its powers it also deals with applications relating to arbitration but where no significant point of arbitration law or practice is raised, the application(s) may be transferred to another court, eg in the case of rent review arbitrations to a judge of the Chancery Division.

commercial waterway Under section 104 of the Transport Act 1968, a broad canal or inland waterway designated as suitable for commercial carriage of freight.

commission The remuneration (usually on a percentage basis) of an agent or professional adviser for services provided, eg that of an estate agent who effects the sale or lease of a client's property. *Cf* FEE 3.

Commissioners, General *See* GENERAL COMMISSIONERS.

Commissioners, Special *See* SPECIAL COMMISSIONERS.

Commissioners of Customs and Excise Members of the body who, *inter alia*, are charged with the duty of administering value added tax in accordance with the statutes. (See Schedule 4 para 1 to the Customs and Excise Management Act 1979.)

Commissioners of Inland Revenue Members of the Board of Inland Revenue responsible for the administration of tax, including assessments, collection and enforcement, as well as the appointment of inspectors of taxes and collectors of taxes. *Cf* GENERAL COMMISSIONERS; SPECIAL COMMISSIONERS.

Commission for the New Towns A body corporate, first established under the New Towns Act 1959 and continued under the New Towns Act 1981 sections 35 and 36, for the purpose of taking over ". . . and, with a view to its eventual disposal, to hold, manage and turn to account the properties of development corporations transferred to the Commission . . ." having regard to the convenience and welfare of persons residing, working or carrying on business there. Pending disposal the Commission has a duty to maintain and enhance the value of the property and the return obtained therefrom.

common 1. *See* RIGHT OF COMMON. 2. *See* COMMON LAND.

common area The space within a shopping centre or other estate or campus-type development which is not intended to be let. It may include landscaped areas, pedestrian precincts and service facilities. *Cf* COMMON PARTS.

common area charges The amounts paid by tenants for operating and maintaining a common area. Such charges in shopping centres are usually calculated on a pro-rata basis related to retail floorspace or volume of sales.

common in estovers *See* ESTOVERS.

common interest (Scotland) An interest, as of adjoining users of a common wall, floor or garden, not amounting to common property but entitling the party interested to a say in the subject's use.

common land Land over which commoners, eg the inhabitants of a particular locality, enjoy rights in common with the owner of the land. In many instances members of the public have the right of access over common land. Several statutes cover commons, eg the Commons Registration Act 1965.

common law That part of the law of the realm built up over the centuries from the principles and rules laid down by the judges in cases decided in the courts of law and not by express legislative enactment by legislative authority. *Cf* ADMINISTRATIVE LAW; EQUITY; STATUTE LAW.

common ownership *See* CO-OWNERSHIP.

common parts The parts of a multi-occupied building which are not let to individual tenants but are either retained by the landlord, eg for the provision of services, or held in common by the tenants for the purpose of providing access for themselves and their visitors, eg halls, passages, lifts and stairways. *Cf* COMMON AREA.

common property (Scotland) Common ownership of property without demarcation of individual boundaries but characterised by each owner's having the right to insist on a division of the property. It is contrasted with property held jointly, where the rights of a joint owner pass on death to the others and cannot be disposed of separately. This may be compared with a tenancy in common in England and Wales. *Cf* COMMON INTEREST.

community charge A flat rate personal tax, colloquially known as a poll tax, which is to replace domestic rates in each rating authority area (to be called a charging authority) on April 1 1990 under Parts I and II of the Local Government Finance Act 1988. There are three kinds of community charge:

a *personal community charge*, payable to a charging authority by adults (broadly those aged 18 or over) whose sole or main residence is in that authority's area and who are not in an exempted category. Exempted persons include the severely mentally impaired, prisoners, students on a full-time course, members of religious communities and those without a fixed abode;

b *standard community charge*, payable by the owner of a freehold or a lessee for six months or more of a domestic property which is not the sole or main residence of any person;

c *collective community charge*, payable by the owner or manager of a multi-occupied building which is used by residents for short periods.

community land scheme The arrangements enacted in the Community Land Act 1975 and the Development Land Tax Act 1976 (both now repealed) to meet the twin objectives stated in the White Paper "Land" (Cmnd 5730), namely "to enable the community to control the development of land in accordance with its needs and priorities, and to restore to the community the increase in value of land arising from its efforts".

community shopping centre (USA) A neighbourhood shopping centre, where a small group of shops serves a community such as a village or a housing estate. *See* HIERARCHY OF SHOPPING CENTRES.

Companies Court A title attributed to the Chancery Division of the High Court or to a county court when hearing cases under the Companies Acts, particularly those concerning winding-up.

company A legal entity where a group of persons holding shares (shareholders) have a common purpose in carrying on through it some business activity and operating according to such rules and regulations as they see fit to introduce. (Most companies are subject to the Companies Acts.)

company limited by guarantee A company where the liability of members for its debts is limited to the amount which they each undertake at the outset to contribute if the company is wound up. *Cf* UNLIMITED COMPANY. *See* LIMITED COMPANY; PUBLIC LIMITED COMPANY.

company registration The obligation of most companies to be registered with the Registrar of Companies and receive by way of legal identification a certificate of incorporation and, if a public company, a trading certificate authorising the company to conduct its business.

comparable In determining the value of a particular property, a transaction, or other relevant evidence, involving another property (or possibly similar units within the same property) which is sufficiently similar in character and location to enable the details to be analysed to find a unit of comparison.

comparative method *See* DIRECT COMPARISON METHOD.

comparison goods Goods which, before making a purchase, the consumer is likely to wish to compare, as regards appearance, quality and price, with alternatives available in one or more shops. Principally applies to clothing and footwear; do-it-yourself goods; household goods, eg furniture, carpets, major appliances, furnishings and hardware; recreational goods, eg radio and television sets, sports goods, toys, games and camping equipment; toilet articles, perfumery, jewellery, silverware, watches and clocks. *Cf* CONVENIENCE GOODS. *See* CONSUMER GOODS.

comparison shop/store A retail outlet selling comparison goods, sometimes with a limited range of convenience goods.

compensation A payment to make amends for the removal or curtailment of rights in property or for an injury, including the payment to the owner for lawfully taking a property against his wishes, eg by compulsory purchase. In the latter instance the normal rules for compensation are set out in section 5 of the Land Compensation Act 1961. *See* DISTURBANCE; EQUIVALENT REINSTATEMENT; INJURIOUS AFFECTION; SPECIAL SUITABILITY OR ADAPTABILITY; SIX RULES.

competent Legally fit, having the necessary age, ability and authority to accomplish any given acts or duties.

competent landlord The landlord, not necessarily the immediate landlord, who is empowered to serve, and receive, notices under the Landlord and Tenant Act 1954 Part II in respect of business tenancies.

completion The final step in the legal process of transferring ownership of property, eg when the documents in connection with a sale of land are signed, sealed and delivered. *See* CONVEYANCE.

completion notice **1.** Notice served on the owner and occupier of land (and on any other person likely to be affected) by a local planning authority who are of the opinion that an uncompleted development will not be completed within a reasonable period. The notice provides that after a stated period — of not less than 12 months — the planning permission will cease to have effect, so that the development has to be completed within that period (unless a further planning permission is obtained). **2.** A notice served under section 17 of the General Rate Act 1967 on the owner of a new or substantially altered and unoccupied property to enable the rating authority to charge unoccupied rates (empty rates) from a specified date. *Cf* NOTICE TO COMPLETE; PRACTICAL COMPLETION CERTIFICATE.

completion statement A statement prepared by solicitors, usually those acting for a purchaser and a vendor respectively, following the conveyance of an interest in property, giving a schedule of sums paid and sums received leading to a balance being the final amount due to the vendor. In some cases the statement is prepared at a later date and may show a figure recoverable by the purchaser from the vendor.

composite hereditament For rating purposes under the Local Government Finance Act 1988, a hereditament which is part domestic and part non-domestic.

compounding The collection of rates from the owner of several small hereditaments rather than from the individual occupiers.

compound interest Interest paid at given intervals on accumulated interest as well as on the principal.

comprehensive development area (CDA) An area defined as such in an old-style development plan which, in the opinion of the local planning authority, should be developed, or redeveloped, as a whole to deal with extensive war damage, bad layout, or obsolete property. It should then provide for the relocation of population or industry, or the replacement of open space or any other purpose specified in the plan. The equivalent in the new-style development plans (which have largely superseded the old ones) are "action areas" in local plans.

compulsory liquidation (winding-up) The winding up of a company by court order at the request of the creditors or other qualified persons, eg the Secretary of State for Trade and Industry. *Cf* VOLUNTARY LIQUIDATION.

compulsory purchase The acquisition, in accordance with statutory procedures and practice, of interests in land by a public or private body empowered so to do by an Act and authorised so to do by the appropriate minister's confirming a compulsory purchase order with or without amendment. Such a purchase entitles the purchaser to deprive the, usually unwilling, owner of his property on payment of such compensation as is provided for by statute.

compulsory purchase order (CPO) An order made by a private or public body (usually a local authority or government department) with the relevant statutory powers which, after confirmation by the appropriate minister, gives the right to acquire specified land compulsorily.

concession *See* EXTRA-STATUTORY CONCESSION.

concessionaire Usually the holder of a licence to trade within part of an area open to the public, such as a department store, retail shop, theatre, trade fair or leisure park. The licensee maintains his own identity but benefits from the concentration of prospective customers in the area and generally pays an all-inclusive licence fee plus, possibly, a percentage related to turnover. *Cf* FRANCHISE.

concessionary rent A rent which is lower than otherwise obtainable, granted as a privilege, sometimes with gratuitous intent, to a particular tenant.

conclusive evidence Evidence which, by law, must be taken to prove a fact in issue and cannot be disputed, eg a land certificate is conclusive evidence of ownership by the registered proprietor. *Cf* PRIMA FACIE EVIDENCE.

concurrent interests Two or more interests involving joint ownership of land, eg a joint tenancy or tenancy in common.

concurrent lease A lease granted to run at the same time as and subject to an existing lease of the same premises so that the lessee of the concurrent lease becomes the immediate lessor in respect of the other lease. For this to apply, the so-called "concurrent" lease must have at least a nominal reversion so as to terminate after the existing lease. The grantor would not be able to distrain on the original lessee for any rental due. *See* OVERRIDING LEASE.

condemnation **1. (UK)** The act of deciding that a building is unfit for use or is dangerous. **2. (USA)** The acquisition of a private property by a public authority where the owner is entitled to compensation.

condition **1.** Provision in a contract that its commencement or continued operation depends upon an external event (condition precedent or condition subsequent respectively). **2.** A term in a contract so vital that on breach thereof the injured party may treat the contract as discharged. **3.** A provision in a planning permission restricting the manner or timing of its implementation, breach of which may lead to enforcement action by the planning authority. *Cf* SECTION 52 AGREEMENT.

conditional contract A contract which is subject to either a condition precedent or a condition subsequent (or both).

conditional interest An interest which, under the Law of Property (Amendment) Act 1926, qualifies as a fee simple absolute in possession despite the fact that it can be forfeited by the grantor in certain specified circumstances. *Cf* CONTINGENT INTEREST; DETERMINABLE INTEREST.

conditional planning permission Planning permission subject to one or more conditions. For these to be valid and enforceable, they have to comply with certain criteria, eg they must be imposed only for a planning purpose, they must be fairly and reasonably related to the development permitted and they must not be manifestly unreasonable. *Cf* CONDITION 3.

condition precedent A stipulation not forming part of a contract but specifying some prerequisite to the contract's coming into force, eg when a contract for the sale of a property is conditional upon the grant of planning permission or upon the vendor's first acquiring some other interest.

conditions of sale Conditions subject to which one or more properties are offered for sale. Two standard sets are available, the National Conditions of Sale and the Law Society's Conditions of Sale, and one or the other is usually incorporated in the conveyance of a property with any necessary adaptations for the particular circumstances of the sale. In an auction sale it is common practice to include in the printed particulars of sale or the catalogue a set of general conditions applying to the conduct of the auction and to all the lots on offer, followed by a set of special conditions relating to the particular circumstances of individual lots. In a private treaty sale of a substantial property the printed particulars or brochure may set out the relevant conditions.

condition subsequent A stipulation in a contract or in a collateral agreement that the contract will come to an end in certain eventualities, eg a provision in a contract for the sale of a property that the contract can be rescinded by one of the parties if planning permission for a specific development has not been granted by a given date.

condominium (USA) A building or structure of two or more units, the interior space of each unit being individually owned and the balance of the property (both land and building) being owned in common by the owners of the individual units.

consensus ad idem; consensus in idem **(Scotland)** Agreement on the same thing, ie there is no dispute as to the subject-matter involved or to what has been agreed with respect thereto. Such is fundamental to the formation of a contract.

consent Permission given by an empowered body, including that issued by a planning authority authorising the carrying out of some activity such as building work or changing the use of an existing property. It is frequently subject to compliance with conditions described in the form of consent.

consequential loss of rent Consequent upon an interruption in the occupation of premises of an insured following the occurrence of a loss, this is an item of insurance which will cover any loss of rent payable/receivable while the premises are unfit for occupation and until such time as they are reoccupied, but in any event not exceeding the indemnity period.

conservation area An "area of special architectural or historic interest the character or appearance of which it is desirable to preserve or enhance", which has been designated as such by the local planning authority under section 277 of the Town and Country Planning Act 1971 (originally under the Civic Amenities Act 1967). Any work contemplated by an owner within such an area is subject to strict constraint, eg with certain exceptions, no buildings within a conservation area can be demolished without conservation area consent.

consideration Strictly, the payment, promise, object, act or forbearance given by one party to a contract in return for a promise or pledge given by the other party. In property law the term is applied particularly to the price offered by the purchaser in a contract to acquire an interest in land. *See* GOOD CONSIDERATION; VALUABLE CONSIDERATION.

consolidation of mortgages Where a mortgagor has mortgaged two or more properties to the same mortgagee, the latter's right to insist that all the mortgages are redeemed at the same time, provided this is later than all their contractual dates of redemption. Under the Law of Property Act 1925 section 93, the intention to permit consolidation of the mortgages must be expressed in at least one of the mortgage deeds for this right to be exercised by the mortgagee.

constant rent An uplifted rent which has been calculated in accordance with constant rent tables. *See* EQUATED RENT.

constant rent tables Valuation tables of discount factors for the computation of uplift in rents, eg Rose's Tables, compiled by Jack Rose MPhil FSVA.

construction loan (USA) Short-term finance made available to meet the cost of undertaking a building or engineering project; it is usually repayable upon completion of the project or within a specified period thereafter. *See* BUILDING FINANCE.

construction period The length of time elapsing from the date a building or other similar project is started, or deemed to start, until the works involved are finished. The finishing date is frequently known as the date of practical completion, being the date when the architect certifies that all the relevant works have been carried out in a satisfactory manner.

constructive notice The legal presumption of knowledge by a person even if actually ignorant of the facts, eg the presumption that a purchaser of land is aware of all matters which would be disclosed on proper investigation of title. *Cf* ACTUAL NOTICE; IMPUTED NOTICE.

constructive trust A trust arising by operation of equity from a fiduciary relationship already in existence, eg where a trustee obtains a valuable interest in the trust property for himself, he is deemed to hold it on a constructive trust for the beneficiaries.

consumer goods Durable or perishable goods for personal or domestic consumption. *See* COMPARISON GOODS; CONVENIENCE GOODS.

contango A method used on the Stock Exchange in which, upon payment of an additional consideration, settlement for securities is deferred from one account to the next. The last dealing day of an account on which contangos are arranged is known as a contango day.

contiguous Touching by means of a common boundary. *Cf* ADJACENT; ADJOINING. *See* ABUT.

contingency fee (incentive fee) A fee related to the degree of success achieved in the task for which it is payable.

contingency insurance The protection offered by an insurance contract (policy) whereby on the occurrence of the risk or event insured against, eg death, the insurer will make a payment of an amount specified in the policy, irrespective of the actual loss suffered. *Cf* INDEMNITY INSURANCE.

contingent interest A future interest in land giving no right at all until the occurrence of some future event which either may never happen or will happen at an unpredictable date. *Cf* CONDITIONAL INTEREST; DETERMINABLE INTEREST; VESTED INTEREST.

contract A legally binding agreement. A contract for the disposal of an interest in land is unenforceable in the absence of a sufficient memorandum in writing (*see* section 40 of the Law of Property Act 1925) or a sufficient act of part performance by one or other of the parties.

contract deposit A sum paid, for instance, by a purchaser of property under a contract and usually held by a third party, eg an agent or a solicitor. It signifies that the payer will fulfil his obligations under the contract but in the event of his default he will forfeit the deposit. There is a statutory definition of "contract deposit" in section 12 (2) of the Estate Agents Act 1979. *Cf* PRE-CONTRACT DEPOSIT. *See* STAKEHOLDER.

contract for sale **1. of land:** An agreement whereby the seller (vendor) agrees to transfer an interest in land to a purchaser for a consideration. The agreement is effected by the exchange of copies of the agreement document between the parties. Rights to possession are not conferred upon the purchaser until the purchase is completed, but the purchaser has an insurable interest in the property from exchange of contracts. A non-returnable deposit is usually paid by the purchaser on exchange. **2. of goods:** The transfer of ownership of chattels from a seller to a buyer for a money price where ownership is transferred immediately.

contractor One who enters into a contract, especially a builder entering into a building contract.

contractor's basis/method A method of valuation used, particularly in rating, where there is an absence of market evidence of comparable lettings or sales and where the profits basis is inappropriate. At first the capital value of the property is found by adding:

a the current cost of construction of the building or structure or suitable substitute (deducting in each case an allowance for age, functional obsolescence and other factors) to
b the value of the land for its existing use.

The hypothetical rental value is then calculated by taking an appropriate percentage of the capital value. *Cf* PROFITS BASIS/METHOD. *See* DEPRECIATED REPLACEMENT COST BASIS.

contractual improvement An improvement to a property carried out under a legal obligation, eg an improvement by the tenant under the terms of a lease of business premises. *Cf* VOLUNTARY IMPROVEMENT.

contractual tenancy A tenancy created under contract as opposed to a statutory tenancy, the expression normally being applied to tenancies protected under the Rent Acts. *See* PROTECTED TENANCY.

contribution clause A clause in an insurance policy whereby if, when a claim arises, there are any other existing insurance policies in force covering the same risk, the respective insurers shall share the loss in proportion to the cover provided or premium paid. If the insured recovers the whole claim from one insurer, the latter is entitled to recover from the other insurer(s) their proportion of the total payment.

controlled rent Under the Rent Acts, a now obsolete rent for a dwelling-house let under a controlled tenancy.

controlled tenancy Now obsolete, a tenancy of residential accommodation which was protected under the Rent Acts 1957 to 1977 until abolished by virtue of section 64(1) of the Housing Act 1980. *See* CONVERTED TENANCY; SECURITY OF TENURE.

conurbation A coalescence of adjoining towns and villages to form a large and virtually continuous built-up area.

convenience goods Goods normally purchased without making any comparison with alternatives, other than by price, including food and drink, tobacco, matches, newspapers, cleaning materials. *Cf* COMPARISON GOODS. *See* CONSUMER GOODS.

convenience shop/store A retail outlet selling convenience goods. In the case of the larger outlets a limited range of comparison goods may also be included.

convenience shopping The process of buying one or more articles, not necessarily confined to convenience goods, either under one roof or from a number of units in close proximity to each other, providing for consumers' specific regular shopping needs.

converted tenancy Under the Rent Acts, a tenancy which has been converted from a controlled into a regulated tenancy. All former controlled tenancies have now been converted into regulated tenancies.

convertible bond A bond which can be converted into a different type of security in the issuing company or its parent company; the option can be exercised by the holder at specific dates and in specific circumstances, as explained at the original date of issue.

conveyance **1.** The transfer of a legal interest in land from one person to another. **2.** A document transferring a legal interest in land.

conveyancing The legal procedures employed in the creation, transfer and extinguishment of ownership in interests in land, including preparation of contracts, enquiries, searches, land registration (where appropriate) and completion of the transaction.

co-ownership An arrangement whereby two or more persons are entitled to the shared ownership of land, either by joint tenancy or by tenancy in common.

coppice Trees grown for cropping at regular intervals before maturity to provide a commercial crop, eg chestnut paling.

copyhold An obsolete form of land tenure enforceable only in the court of the lord of the manor, the title comprising a copy of the entry on the appropriate rolls of the court. Under Part V of the Law of Property Act 1922 all such tenures were converted into freeholds from January 1 1926.

corporate treasury function For companies and other bodies, the management function concerned with

a handling cash flows;
b seeing that cash requirements are met by raising funds;
c managing risk in interest and currency transactions; and
d investing surplus funds.

corporation tax Under the Income and Corporation Taxes Act 1988, a tax on the net income received by companies in their corporate capacity as distinct from the tax payable on dividends distributed to shareholders.

corporeal hereditament Tangible real property, eg lands, buildings, minerals, trees, fixtures and all other things which are part of, or fixed in a legal sense to, land. *Cf* INCORPOREAL HEREDITAMENT.

cost-benefit analysis A method or technique to assist in decision-making, involving the consideration and measurement in financial terms of all costs and benefits, including social aspects, when comparing alternative projects or courses of action.

cost-of-living clause A clause in a contract, eg a lease, providing for an adjustment in price, rent or other financial item based upon an index such as the Retail Price Index.

cost-plus contract A building contract where the price is based upon the estimated or actual cost of the works together with (ie "plus") a proportion or agreed amount to represent the contractor's profit.

cost rent (economic rent) A figure calculated to provide over a period of time a rent which is sufficient to meet the cost over the same period of time of actual or notional loan interest (on the owner's equity), sinking fund contributions and the cost of upkeep and management.

costs in use A discounted cash flow technique whereby the total cost of a building or project is expressed as the sum of the initial capital cost and the present value of recurring costs, such as repairs, maintenance, renewal of components, insurance, services and, perhaps, user activities. Alternatively, the initial capital costs and intermittently recurring costs can be expressed as annual equivalent sums and added to the regular annual costs, thereby giving the costs in use as an annual sum.

cottage holding Under the Smallholdings and Allotments Act 1908 and other statutes, a dwelling-house and not more than 1 acre of agricultural land which can be cultivated by the occupier and his family; but since 1970 no land can be let or sold by an authority as a cottage holding.

Council for Small Industries in Rural Areas (COSIRA) A government sponsored body for development and promotion of small industrial businesses in small towns, villages and the countryside. It offers a variety of services and provides grants for certain building works, eg conversion of buildings to workshops.

Council of the International Stock Exchange A body which governs the activities of the Stock Exchange and comprises 46 members elected by the members of the Exchange plus five lay members and the Government broker, who is *ex officio* and has no vote. All actions of the Stock Exchange are taken in the name of the council.

counterpart A duplicate legal document, especially the landlord's copy of a lease (the tenant's copy being termed the "lease").

Countryside Commission A statutory body, set up under the Countryside Act 1968, to advise the Government and other bodies on countryside policy to manage loans and grant aid for recreational amenity, conservation and similar purposes.

county Geographically a county or shire is an ancient division of the country. Some administrative counties correspond to the old geographical counties, but all are statutory creations.

county court One of the local civil courts of first instance which together cover the whole of England and Wales, with jurisdiction for actions in both contract and tort, where the amount claimed or the rateable value of the property the subject of the dispute does not exceed a prescribed amount or where, in excess of the prescribed limit, the parties nevertheless agree to the case being heard there rather than in the High Court. Every county court has a circuit judge and a registrar.

coupon **1.** A Stock Exchange term for the detachable part of bearer security certificates which may be exchanged for dividends. **2.** Commonly denotes the rate of interest on a fixed-interest security at its nominal price.

court **1.** A body set up to administer justice and/or to protect the interests of those unable to protect themselves. **2.** A forum for the hearings of such a body.

Court of Appeal The second highest court in the UK, which now comprises a Civil Division and a Criminal Division, presided over respectively by the Master of the Rolls and the Lord Chief Justice, the ordinary judges being Lord Justices of Appeal or, by invitation, puisne judges. The Civil Division hears appeals from the county courts and High Court and appeals or references on matters of law from certain tribunals including the Lands Tribunal.

court of first instance The court in which legal proceedings are initiated or where a case is first tried, eg in civil law in England and Wales the county court or the High Court.

court of last resort The final court from which no further appeal can be made, ie in the UK generally the House of Lords (but sometimes in England and Wales the Court of Appeal) or the European Court.

Court of Protection The court which administers the property and protects the interests of persons of unsound mind. It is headed by a "Master".

court of record Any court whose proceedings and acts are permanently recorded. Such courts have power to punish for contempt of court and their judgments and decisions create precedents, binding upon inferior courts.

Court of Session The Scottish court corresponding to the Supreme Court of Judicature and comprising an Outer House (equivalent to the High Court) and an Inner House (equivalent to the Court of Appeal).

covenant **1.** Strictly, an obligation undertaken by a party and effected by deed, eg in a lease, obligations of the landlord or tenant. *See* EXPRESS COVENANT; IMPLIED COVENANT; POSITIVE COVENANT; RESTRICTIVE COVENANT. **2.** A subjective assessment of the character and quality of a tenant in terms of being able and willing to comply with the terms and conditions of the lease. In valuations the quality of the covenant will normally influence the yield adopted. A tenant of sound standing is often referred to as a "good covenant".

covenant value That part of the capital value of an investment property which is attributable to the fact that it is let to a particular tenant.

cover **1.** The protection against perils offered under an insurance contract. *See* RISK. **2.** A Stock Exchange term for collateral which is deposited as security against an open position. **3.** The amount of money available for distribution by a company as dividend divided by the amount actually paid. If the quotient is 1 or more, the dividend is covered that number of times; if less, the dividend is uncovered. **4.** In futures trading the purchase of futures to offset a previous transaction.

"Crawley" costs The actual and reasonable expenses which the owner of premises who is dispossessed by compulsory purchase incurs in searching for new premises. The name originates from the case of *Harvey* v *Crawley Development Corporation* (1957), where the dispossessed owner of a house was held by the Court of Appeal to be entitled to reimbursement, in a claim for disturbance, of her legal costs, surveyors' fees and travelling expenses incurred in seeking another house, including abortive expenditure where an unfavourable survey report had resulted in her not proceeding with a proposed purchase. Sometimes known as "Harvey" costs.

created ground rent A rent for land which is paid under a lease for a site upon which one or more buildings have already been erected. It is often the result of a leaseback transaction and the normal characteristic is that at the date it is created the rent is more than the ground rental value of the land on the assumption that the buildings did not exist but significantly less than the rack-rental value of the property including the buildings. *Cf* IMPROVED GROUND RENT.

criterion rate A generic term used for the discount rate selected in carrying out a discounted cash flow appraisal by the net present value method; the rate adopted will be chosen by reference to the cost of money and/or alternative investments. *See* OPPORTUNITY COST OF MONEY RATE; TARGET RATE.

critical path analysis A management technique (especially in project management) whereby a project is analysed, and its activities and events (an activity taking place between two events) are portrayed as a network. The network may be used to demonstrate the project's duration and the sequence of activities which must not be extended if delay is to be avoided (the critical path).

crop yield In a given period the quantity of a crop produced per unit of land area. *Cf* YIELD PER HEAD.

cross-easements Mutual easements annexed to two adjoining tenements, eg mutual rights of support between two contiguous buildings in different ownership.

cross-hatching In plan-making, sets of parallel lines drawn diagonally across another set. *See* HATCHING (HACHURES).

cross option A reciprocal form of put and/or take option, being exercisable by either party to a contract.

Crown Agent (Scotland) The solicitor to the Lord Advocate's Department and, as such the chief Crown solicitor in criminal matters.

Crown Estate The hereditary landed estate of the monarch in right of the Crown administered by the Crown Estate Commissioners. The estate currently includes a wide range of commercial, residential and agricultural property throughout Great Britain as well as most of the foreshore and seabed and the rights to mine gold and silver. Revenue from the estate is surrendered to the Treasury by the monarch in exchange for the Civil List and capital receipts are reinvested in land or held in government securities.

Crown Estate Commissioners A board consisting of the First Commissioner, who is the chairman, and the Second Commissioner, who is the secretary and the permanent senior official of the Crown Estate Office, and also a number of part-time commissioners. Their function is to administer the Crown Estate as empowered under the Crown Estate Act 1961 and their powers include the sale of freeholds and the grant of leases.

Crown land A general term, not used in statute, for any land in which an interest belongs to the monarch in right of the Crown or of the Duchy of Lancaster or of the Duchy of Cornwall or belongs to a government department or is held in trust for the monarch but occupied for the purposes of a government department. *See* BONA VACANTIA.

cruising waterway Under section 104 of the Transport Act 1968, a narrow canal or inland waterway designated as suitable for cruising, fishing and other recreational purposes.

cubic content The volume of a building or structure. For statutory purposes, eg planning, compensation and taxation, it is ascertained by external measurement. *See* CODE OF MEASURING PRACTICE.

cubing Calculation of the volume of a building in cubic feet or cubic metres.

cubing code A code for measuring the cubic content of buildings and structures, particularly prepared for planning compensation or taxation. The current (1988) cubing code for taxation purposes is that agreed in 1976 between the Inland Revenue and representatives of the RICS and RIBA for cubing buildings under the Finance Act 1974. It is reproduced in full in the *Code of Measuring Practice* published jointly by the Royal Institution of Chartered Surveyors and the Incorporated Society of Valuers and Auctioneers.

cujus est solum ejus est usque ad coelum et ad inferos Whose is the soil, his also is that which is above and that which is below the surface (to the heavens and the underworld). This is the theoretical rule that ownership of land includes the airspace above and the substrata. Under Part IV of the Civil Aviation Act 1949 the rule has, however, been breached in that no action can lie in trespass or nuisance in respect of aircraft flying at a reasonable height. According to Griffiths J in *Bernstein of Leigh (Baron)* v *Skyviews & General Ltd* (1978), "The academic writers speak with one voice in rejecting the uncritical and literal application of the maxim."

cullery A tenancy in Carlisle.

cum Latin for "with".

***cum* cap** A Stock Exchange expression indicating that a buyer of securities may participate in a known forthcoming capitalisation issue of the company concerned.

***cum* dividend (*cum* div)** A Stock Exchange term indicating that the price currently quoted for a particular security is on the basis that the purchaser is entitled to receive all future benefits such as dividends, bonuses or rights issues. *Cf* EX DIVIDEND.

***cum* pref** A popular abbreviation for cumulative preference share.

***cum* rights** A Stock Exchange term indicating that a buyer of securities is entitled to participate in a known forthcoming rights issue of the company concerned.

cumulative preference share A preference share carrying the additional right, as a priority over ordinary shareholdings, of being paid any arrears of dividends from previous years out of the profits of the following year(s). *See* PREFERENCE SHARE.

cumulo value The total gross value or net annual value of a particular statutory undertaking which may extend over two or more rating areas. The mechanics of calculation in accordance with the statutory formulae are both complex and expedient, reflecting in any year such matters as the standard amount first payable, adjusted by movements in the national rate poundage, volume of business activity by the specific undertaking, eg in the case of railways the number of passenger journeys, freight tonnage and other relevant factors.

currency linked bond A bond expressed in terms of one currency, but repayable in another on a basis agreed at the outset, eg 1 million of sterling lent for use in France at a time when it is worth 10 million francs will be repaid by the number of francs needed to buy 1 million of sterling at the date of repayment.

current cost accounting A method of preparing a company's accounts in which the fixed assets are stated at their value to the business having regard to current rather than historic costs. The net current replacement cost is generally used, ie the present cost of acquiring a replacement asset that will provide the same service and output.

current rate The present rate of interest on a security which has a variable rate.

current tenancy In relation to business tenancies, this is defined by section 26 of the Landlord and Tenant Act 1954 (tenant's request for a new tenancy) as one "granted for a term of years certain exceeding one year, whether or not continued by section 24 of this Act, or granted for a term of years certain and thereafter from year to year."

current use value (CUV) Under the Development Land Tax Act 1976 this was defined as the market value of an interest in land on the assumption that (with certain exceptions) planning permission would be granted for any development of a class specified in Schedule 8 to the Town and Country Planning Act 1971 (or Schedule 6 to the Town and Country Planning (Scotland) Act 1972) and that it was, and would remain, unlawful to carry out any material development of the land not already begun. If appropriate, the valuer could have regard to any value attributable to the prospect of carrying out activities listed in Part II of Schedule 4 to the 1976 Act. There is a broadly similar definition of CUV (but excluding the positive planning assumption) in the Finance Act 1974, Schedule 3, Part I, and this still applies for certain capital gains tax purposes under the Capital Gains Tax Act 1979, Schedule 5, Part II.

current yield The remunerative rate of interest which is, or would be, appropriate at the date of valuation, assuming the property to be let at its full rental value. It will be the same as the reversion yield where the reversion is to full rental value, and the same as the term yield where the rent receivable under the lease is the full rental value. *See* ALL RISKS YIELD.

curtilage Described in *Sinclair-Lockhart's Trustees* v *Central Land Board* (1950) as "the ground which is used for comfortable enjoyment of a house or other building . . .", such being "regarded in law as being within the curtilage of that house or building and thereby is an integral part of the same although it has not been marked off or enclosed in any way". It is enough that it serves the purpose of the house or building in some necessary or reasonably useful way.

curved line depreciation Depreciation which assumes a progressive decrease in the value of a property or other asset over a given period, so producing a curved line when plotted as a graph, eg depreciation in the cost of a lease for capital gains tax purposes. *Cf* REDUCING BALANCE DEPRECIATION; STRAIGHT LINE DEPRECIATION.

custodian trustee A trustee having custody and care of trust property.

custom A practice which by long-established usage in a particular locality has come to be accepted as part of the local law.

cut-off date **1.** The date on which an agreement or clause in an agreement ceases to have effect. **2.** The last day of a period for calculating a certain payment or cost relating to an agreement.

cy-près As near as.

cy-près doctrine The principle which enables effect to be given as near as possible to the intention of a settlor or testator where it cannot be carried out precisely as directed by him.

D

damage feasant Destruction of crops and/or property caused by another's animals straying and trespassing on one's land.

damages **1.** Money recoverable by court action by one suffering a loss or injury resulting from breach of contract, breach of statutory duty, or under either statute or tort. *See* LIQUIDATED DAMAGES; UNLIQUIDATED DAMAGES. **2.** **(USA)** The loss in value of retained premises adjoining property taken in condemnation proceedings (in UK, compulsory purchase).

dangerous structure notice A notice issued by a local authority to a building owner requiring him to put a building into a safe condition. Most local authorities have the power to serve such notices under the Public Health Acts. Inner London boroughs have similar powers by virtue of the London Building Acts and some other major provincial towns and cities, such as Birmingham and Manchester, have similar powers under their own private Building Acts.

date of valuation (valuation date) In current practice the date on which a property is considered to be of the value stated, regardless of the signing date. Many valuations for statutory purposes will be based on values at a specific date, sometimes defined by statute, otherwise by practice or by judicial interpretation. *Cf* SIGNING DATE.

daylight code *See* SUNLIGHT AND DAYLIGHT CODE.

daylight exposure limit On the foreign exchange markets this describes the limits set by a bank for its dealings in any one day in a particular currency.

daylight factor An assessment of the natural light falling into a room either directly or indirectly. It is usually expressed as a ratio, or as a percentage of the light measured at the bottom of a window as against that three feet above floor level in the darkest area of the room. *See* WALDRAM DIAGRAM.

daywork contract A form of contract for relatively small-scale building works where payment is based on hours worked, cost of materials, use of plant, transport charges, and a percentage for the contractor's overheads and profit.

dead rent A base rent for mineral-bearing land, payable whether or not the land is worked, but which may be subsumed by the royalties when they total more than the dead rent. *See* MINERAL ROYALTY.

dealer in land A person who buys and sells (or buys, builds and sells) property for profit on a basis which may be identified as such under the "badges of trade". A dealer's profits are assessed for tax on income in accordance with Schedule D, Case I, of the Income and Corporation Taxes Act 1988. *Cf* INVESTOR IN LAND.

death duty Any tax which arises on death, eg the former estate duty and capital transfer tax and the present inheritance tax.

debenture Written acknowledgement or evidence of a debt, especially stock issued as security by a company for borrowed money.

decapitalisation The translation of a capital sum into its periodic, usually annual, equivalent by applying a suitable rate of interest. *Cf* CAPITALISATION.

decibel A unit of measurement of sound.

declaration **1.** A discretionary remedy in the High Court, especially in the Chancery Division, where a ruling on a question of law is given but this does not involve an enforceable judgment. **2.** An unsworn oral or written statement made out of court but which in certain circumstances may nevertheless be admissible as evidence, eg a declaration made by a person who has subsequently died and which, when he made it,

a he knew would be against his pecuniary or proprietary interest (declaration against interest),
b concerned the alleged existence of a public or general right (declaration concerning public or general rights), or
c was made in the course of his duty to record or report his acts (declaration in course of duty).

See ADMISSIBLE EVIDENCE.

declaration of trust A statement declaring that certain property is to be held on trust; it is often made when the intended trustee already possesses the property, which he is not entitled to hold for his own benefit. *See* TRUST.

declaratory judgment A judgment merely giving the court's opinion on a legal question or as to the parties' rights but lacking any provision for enforcement. *See* DECLARATION 1.

dedication The giving for public use by the owner of a private property of the whole or part of his interest therein, or a right over it, and its acceptance by the appropriate public authority, eg for highway purposes, or by some other body such as the National Trust.

deductions Under Schedule A, the amounts of payments made by a landlord which are allowable against the rent receivable in a computation to arrive at taxable income under leases in the United Kingdom, eg for maintenance, repairs, insurance, management, certain services, rent and rates, if appropriate. *See* SCHEDULES.

deed A document, being written evidence of a legal transaction, which has been signed, sealed and delivered to testify to the agreement of the parties concerned. *See* ESCROW; EXECUTION; SEAL; STAMP DUTY.

deed of gift A deed conveying a property (or properties) from the donor to the donee with no consideration passing.

deemed Assumed to have a certain attribute or to have taken place (of a notional event) for a specific purpose, eg development by a local authority, when authorised by a government department, is "deemed" to have planning permission. *See* DEEMED PLANNING PERMISSION.

deemed disposal Usually for taxation purposes, an assumed sale and re-acquisition of property at a particular time. An example was for capital gains tax purposes where a property was owned before, and sold on or after, April 6 1965 and an election was made to use the open market value at that date instead of the time-apportionment method for computing the tax.

deemed listing The treatment of an unlisted building as though it had been listed as of special architectural and historic interest, eg under section 54 (10) of the Town and Country Planning Act 1971, where the building had been subject to a building preservation order under Part II of the Town and Country Planning Act 1962, or under section 58(4) of the 1971 Act where a building is subject to a building preservation notice.

deemed planning permission Under the Town and Country Planning Acts, the situation in which planning permission is treated as having been granted without the need for the normal procedure. This applies in certain special cases, eg under section 40 of the 1971 Act, to development by local authorities and statutory undertakers may be deemed to have planning permission by direction of the government department whose authorisation of the development is required under statute. *Cf* GENERAL DEVELOPMENT ORDER; SIMPLIFIED PLANNING ZONE; SPECIAL DEVELOPMENT ORDER.

deemed premium Under the Taxes Act 1988, on the grant of a lease of a term of 50 years or less, a sum (not actual money) which is treated as a premium for income taxation purposes, eg the increase in value of the landlord's reversion immediately after the grant where the tenant has undertaken to carry out improvements to the property.

de facto In fact; as a matter of fact. Eg a trespasser may be in occupation of land *de facto* but not *de jure*. *Cf* DE JURE.

default The failure to do something required by law, eg a "judgment in default" in favour of one party, where the other fails to comply with the required legal procedure. For instance, one party may default by not attending a court hearing or not serving a particular notice or counternotice.

default notice A notice which has to be served on a party in alleged breach of contract stating the nature of the breach and requiring its remedy as a prerequisite of instituting legal proceedings for breach of contract.

defeasible When an estate or interest in property may be brought to an end by the operation of a condition subsequent or a conditional limitation.

defects liability period (retention period) An agreed period following practical completion of a building, engineering or other constructional operation during which the contractor is obliged to remedy any defects appearing in the building caused by the failure of materials or workmanship to meet the requirements of the building contract. Amounts specified in the contract will be withheld until such time as defects are remedied. *See* BUILDING CONTRACT CERTIFICATES; RETAINED SUM.

defender (Scotland) A person against whom legal action is brought. In England called a defendant.

deficit financing With a view to making a profit or receiving a profitable return, the funding of a project which has the inherent risk of the initial revenue being less than the total outgoings, including any interest or notional interest payable on money borrowed or otherwise procured.

definitive maps Maps of public paths and bridleways prepared by county councils under the National Parks and Access to the Countryside Act 1949 after survey, consultation and representation procedures. Under the Countryside Act 1968, they are subject to periodic review and special reviews. They should also show roads used as public paths, such as ancient tracks, green lanes and unmetalled roads.

dehors Outside of, eg dehors the contract means outside the scope of, or irrelevant to, the contract.

de jure By right; as a matter of law. *Cf* DE FACTO.

"Delaforce effect" In valuations to determine the price payable under section 9 of the Leasehold Reform Act 1967, an argument that a tenant anxious to enfranchise is more likely to increase his offer than is the landlord to reduce his quoted price in order to achieve a settlement. (From *Delaforce* v *Evans* (1970).)

delict (Scotland) A wilful wrong, ie a deliberate breach of a legal duty to another, other than a breach of contract or where there is strict liability. *See* TORT.

delivery In respect of a deed this means an act so done as to indicate an intention to be bound. Thus a deed may be delivered although it is retained by one of the parties, by his solicitor or, less usually, by a third party. *See* ESCROW.

de minimis A term applied to some act causing damage or injury, the degree of which is such that its effect is regarded in law as negligible and so may be disregarded for the purposes of enforcement of law. (From *de minimis non curat lex*— the law does not concern itself with trifles.)

demise **1.** Strictly speaking, this is synonymous with a lease and means the grant of a right to the exclusive possession of property for a term of less than that held by the grantor. **2.** Colloquially, used to signify the premises demised, ie the area of property the subject-matter of a lease (demised premises).

demolition The pulling down of a building or structure and, perhaps, the clearance of its site. Various enactments govern demolition, eg the Building Regulations under the Buildings Act 1984.

Demolition and Dismantling Industry Register (DDIR) A register of contractors who voluntarily meet proper performance and working criteria in demolition work.

Demolition Industry Group Training Association An industry-led education and training body for supervisors, operatives and others concerned with demolition.

demolition order An order which a local housing authority may make under section 205 of the Housing Act 1985 requiring a house which is unfit for human habitation, and which cannot be made fit at reasonable expense, to be demolished. Such an order may not be made in respect of a "listed building", and if a building subject to a demolition order becomes listed the order has to be terminated and a closing order made. Demolition orders not restricted to residential property can also be made by the court, under the Public Health Acts 1936-61 and the Health and Safety at Work etc. Act 1974.

density In town planning, a term applied to the number of units permitted per acre (or hectare), usually in relation to residential accommodation.

department store A, usually, multi-level retail property varying in size from one selling an extensive, but not comprehensive, variety of goods in at least 6,500 m^2 (70,000 sq ft) gross floorspace to one selling a full range of different lines requiring about 23,000 m^2 (250,000 sq ft) of gross floorspace. A distinctive feature of a department store is that it stocks a significant amount of clothing and household goods. Major department stores may have 55,000 m^2 (600,000 sq ft) or more of gross floorspace.

deposit **1.** A sum held in an account, eg a bank deposit account, to earn interest at a fixed or variable rate. **2.** *See* CONTRACT DEPOSIT. **3.** *See* PRE-CONTRACT DEPOSIT. **4.** The placement of the deeds of a mortgaged property with the mortgagee. **5.** An accumulation of mineral material laid down by natural processes, eg sedimentation, precipitation or volcanic action. *See* MINERAL RIGHTS; MINERAL ROYALTY; MINERALS.

deposit receipt **(Scotland)** A procedure for placing purchase money in a bank in the joint names of the parties, only to be released by agreement of the parties upon completion of the transaction.

depreciable amount In the valuation of land and buildings in accounting for depreciation ". . . that part of the open market value or cost of the whole property, at the time it was acquired or valued, which can be expressed as the value to the business at that time of the buildings on the land." (*RICS Guidance Notes on the Valuation of Assets*.) Such an amount is arrived at either:

a "By deducting from the cost or valuation of the asset the value of the land for its existing use at the relevant date . . ." or
b "By making an assessment of the net replacement cost of the buildings at the relevant date . . .".

This is an apportionment and does not represent the open market value of the buildings. *See* RESIDUAL AMOUNT.

depreciated replacement cost basis (DRC) A method of valuing properties of unusual character or location for which evidence of comparable transactions does not exist. This basis of valuation "requires an estimate of the open market value of the land in its existing use and an estimate of the new replacement cost of the buildings and other site works, from which deductions are then made to allow for the age, condition, functional obsolescence and other factors which result in the existing property being worth less than a new replacement. It is a method of using current replacement costs to arrive at the value to the business in occupation of the property as existing at the valuation date." (*RICS Guidance Notes on the Valuation of Assets*.) *Cf* CONTRACTOR'S BASIS/METHOD.

depreciated value *See* DEPRECIATION; WRITTEN-DOWN VALUE.

depreciating asset Under section 117(6) of the Capital Gains Tax Act 1979, a wasting asset or an asset which will become a wasting asset within 10 years, ie one having a life not exceeding 60 years.

depreciation 1. Decrease in the value of real property caused by obsolescence, deterioration in its condition, or other factors. 2. One or more deductions made for accounting (or taxation) purposes to allow for the actual or assumed reduction in the capital value (cost) of an asset over an assumed or prescribed period. *See* CAPITAL ALLOWANCES; CURVED LINE DEPRECIATION; REDUCING BALANCE DEPRECIATION; STRAIGHT LINE DEPRECIATION.

deprival value The value to a business of an asset, being the loss which would be suffered by the business if it were deprived of that asset. This may be equivalent to its net replacement cost.

depth factor (USA) A factor which represents the differing values, by percentage, of sections of a plot of land measured from a common frontage. If the value of the standard unit is taken as 100%, then the first 25% of its depth is worth 40% of the whole, the second 25% is worth 30%, and the third 25% is valued at 20%, and the remaining quarter at 10%. The principle is similar to halving back.

derating The total or partial exemption by statute from rates of a specific class or classes of property. The only example of total derating is that of agricultural hereditaments. There was partial relief for industrial hereditaments between 1929 and 1963.

derelict Property which has been abandoned and neglected, or descriptive of such property.

dereliction 1. Exposure of land when the sea recedes permanently. *Cf* ALLUVION. *See* ACCRETION. 2. The abandonment of a chattel by the owner.

derelict land grant A grant provided under statute for the reclamation or improvement of land which is derelict, eg under section 9 of the Local Government Act 1966, as amended by section 117 of the Local Government, Planning and Land Act 1980.

derogate To destroy, prejudice or diminish a grant to, or right of, another person. It is a rule of law that no man may derogate from his own grant, eg a vendor or landlord having conveyed premises intended to be used for purposes known to him, the vendor or landlord may not, by what he does on his adjoining land, make it impossible for the intended use to be carried on.

design and build contract (design and construct contract) An all-embracing package whereby a contractor undertakes building, engineering work and/or other constructional operations in accordance with a design, specification, and estimate of cost prepared by himself which are all accepted by the employer.

design guide A planning document which is not specific to any particular site but provides a general code of practice for the design of buildings, roads and other features of developments in a particular area, eg a county , published by a local planning authority or other body. *Cf* DEVELOPMENT BRIEF; PLANNING BRIEF.

designation order A ministerial order specifying that a particular area of land is to be used, developed or safeguarded for a statutory purpose, eg an order designating the site of a new town under section 1 of the New Towns Act 1981 or a national park under section 5 of the National Parks and Access to the Countryside Act 1949 or declaring an area to be of archaeological importance under section 33 of the Ancient Monuments and Archaeological Areas Act 1979. (In the latter instance local authorities have similar powers.)

designed for a purpose A structure is designed for a purpose if its physical appearance and layout are such that it is apparently intended for that purpose:

Belmont Farm Ltd v *MHLG* (1962). In *Wilson* v *West Sussex CC* (1963) the expression was held to mean "intended to be used for that purpose".

desk valuation An imprecise term indicating a valuation of a property by someone who has not made a physical inspection of a property for that purpose. Traditionally, many will believe that no property can be valued unless it has been inspected at that time; contemporary needs for frequent valuations and the possibly prohibitive cost of a full inspection and valuation make it essential to compromise.

determinable interest An interest which will automatically terminate on some specific event which may never happen, eg a settlement or devise of land to A so long as he remains of a specific faith but which will pass or revert to B if A changes his faith. *Cf.* CONDITIONAL INTEREST; CONTINGENT INTEREST.

devaluation **1.** In valuation practice, the analysis of a comparable to extract the unit of comparison or other comparative evidence, eg the yield. **2.** A reduction in the worth of a property. *See* END ALLOWANCE.

developer An entrepreneur who has an interest in a property, initiates its development and ensures that this is carried out (for occupation, investment or dealing) and from the outset accepts the ultimate responsibility for providing or procuring the funds needed to finance the whole project.

developer's budget method A cash flow appraisal of a proposed development project which breaks down the duration into periods, eg months, quarters or years, and allocates expenditures and receipts to those periods. Interest is also computed on a periodic basis. The method may be used to find profit (or loss), break-even, and periodic interest costs. *Cf* NET PRESENT VALUE METHOD.

developer's profit (or loss) The amount by which, on completion or partial completion of a development, the estimated value or the price realised on sale of a developer's interest exceeds (or is less than) the total outlay, including such figure for the land as is considered appropriate in the circumstances (including accrued interest). *See* DEVELOPER'S BUDGET METHOD.

developer's return *See* DEVELOPMENT RETURN.

developer's risk and profit In a residual valuation the amount which is allowed to cover both:

a an estimate of the sum needed to reflect the risk element between the valuation date and the completion of the development programme and
b an amount to meet the developer's requirement for profit on the venture.

Cf DEVELOPER'S PROFIT.

development Under section 22 of the Town and Country Planning Act 1971 this is defined as "the carrying out of building, engineering, mining or other operations in, on, over or under land, or the making of any material change in the use of any buildings or other land". Certain of these operations are excluded from the definition of "development", eg internal alterations to a building or structure which do not materially affect its appearance. *Cf* REFURBISHMENT.

development appraisal An assessment of the financial and practical aspects of a development either at its inception or during its progress. *See* FEASIBILITY STUDY.

Development Board for Rural Wales A government-sponsored organisation formed in 1977 under the Development of Rural Wales Act 1976 to promote the economic and social development of Mid Wales, which covers 40% of the land area of Wales — now known as Mid Wales Development. It is empowered to acquire land and develop property, including building houses, but it cannot engage in farming or forestry.

development brief A statement issued by the owner of a site giving detailed requirements for its proposed development, as guidance to would-be developers. It usually includes planning and development parameters, the procedures for the selection of the developer, the tenure being offered, and a request to prospective developers for details of their experience, status and proposed method of funding. *Cf* DESIGN GUIDE; PLANNING BRIEF.

development charge A charge formerly levied on developers under the Town and Country Planning Act 1947 and abolished by the Town and Country Planning Act 1952. The payment (at 100% of the development value) was required before work authorised by planning permission could commence. *Cf* BETTERMENT LEVY; DEVELOPMENT GAINS TAX; DEVELOPMENT LAND TAX.

development control The powers of a local planning authority under Parts III and IV of the Town and Country Planning Act 1971 (and related statutes) to control the development and use of land, by, *inter alia*,

- a the refusal or grant (with or without conditions) of planning permission;
- b the issue of enforcement notices;
- c the making of revocation, modification or discontinuance orders;
- d the grant or refusal of listed building consents;
- e the designation of conservation areas;
- f the making of tree preservation orders;
- g the enforcement of advertisement regulations.

development corporation A body corporate set up under statute to plan, develop and manage an area of land, eg a development corporation for a new town under the New Towns Act 1981 or an urban development corporation under the Local Government, Planning and Land Act 1980.

development expenditure The total cost to a developer in undertaking a development. This falls under two main headings:

- a the cost of land acquired, or the value of land already held, plus interest (actual or notional) during the building programme and
- b those costs directly related to the development processes, ie obtaining planning consent, demolition of any existing buildings, site preparation, construction, professional fees, legal expenses, together with interest on these items and an allowance for contingencies.

These components represent the total outlay which can be used, with due allowance for voids and other post-completion contingencies, for comparison with the value of the created asset. *See* DEVELOPMENT APPRAISAL; FEASIBILITY STUDY.

development gains tax (DGT) A former charge under Schedule D, Case VI which was introduced by the Finance Act 1974. It was largely superseded by development land tax but could arise, for example, on a first letting or occupation of a property following a project of material development which commenced on or after December 18 1973 but before May 18 1976. However, all such potential liability to the charge was abolished from March 19 1985 under the Finance Act 1985. Also known as development gains charge (DGC).

development land tax (DLT) A tax introduced by the Development Land Tax Act 1976 charged on the occasion of an actual, part or "deemed" disposal of an interest in land, subject to exemptions, reliefs and concessions. The tax was paid by the owner of the interest on the "realised development value", ie the amount (if any) by which the net proceeds of the disposal exceeded the highest of three alternative base values. DLT was abolished by the Finance Act 1985 for all disposals on or after March 19 1985.

development management *See* PROJECT MANAGEMENT.

development, material *See* MATERIAL DEVELOPMENT.

development notice A colloquial name for a notice published in a local paper by the local planning authority under section 28 (1) of the Town and Country Planning Act 1971. It gives details of a planning application for development which in their opinion is likely to affect the character or appearance of a conservation area.

development, permitted *See* PERMITTED DEVELOPMENT.

development plan Generally, a plan for an area, prepared by a local planning authority and indicating the manner in which the area should be developed. *See* DISTRICT PLAN; LOCAL PLAN; "OLD STYLE" DEVELOPMENT PLAN; STRUCTURE PLAN; UNITARY DEVELOPMENT PLAN.

development profit (or loss) *See* DEVELOPER'S PROFIT OR LOSS.

development return (developer's return) The yearly net rental income (or its equivalent) from a development project, expressed as a percentage of the development expenditure excluding

a any allowance for developer's risk and profit in the costs and
b an allowance for an annual sinking fund, if any.

development, speculative *See* SPECULATIVE DEVELOPMENT.

development value Generally, the amount by which the value of any property for development or redevelopment differs from the property's existing use value. *See* EXISTING USE VALUE 2.

development yield In a valuation to ascertain a ground rent, the rate at which costs are decapitalised to find the annual deduction from the occupation rents; it comprises:

a an investment yield,
b an annual allowance for developer's risk and profit and, in some instances,
c an annual sinking fund element.

devise A gift; to give or bequeath real property by will.

dictum A formal statement on a point of law made by a judge in the course of a judgment. *See* OBITER DICTUM; RATIO DECIDENDUM.

differential rating Former rating practice required that a general rate had to be made at a uniform amount per pound within a rating area and charged on each rateable value. However, rate demands now show three different rate poundages, one each for commercial, mixed and domestic hereditaments. This practice is known as "differential rating".

dilapidations Those items of disrepair which arise through breach of contract, especially by one of the parties to a lease, giving rise to a right to damages or remedial action. *See* SCHEDULE OF DILAPIDATIONS.

direct comparison method (Also known either as **comparative method** or **market value approach**.) A method of valuation by which the rental or capital value of a property is assessed having regard to the prices or rents recently achieved by other properties which are similar in such matters as location, size, character and accessibility and the extent to which appropriate adjustments can be made to reflect differences. *See* COMPARABLE; UNIT OF COMPARISON.

direct evidence *See* ORIGINAL EVIDENCE 1 AND 2.

direct mail The distribution by post or hand delivery of suitable letters and publications to a select list of recipients.

direct placement The placing of securities directly with a financial institution or other investor without the involvement of an underwriter.

director In a company, one of the persons who collectively comprise the board, having responsibility to run the company, ie conducting its affairs on a day-to-day basis and accounting to the shareholders from time to time. He may be an executive director employed, normally full time, by the company and paid a salary, or a part-time non-executive director remunerated by such fees as are approved by the company.

disability A term used in rating to describe a physical disadvantage (either permanent or temporary) suffered by a property in comparison with others of a similar class, eg a shop with a restricted or temporarily restricted access. Such a disability will, if proven, qualify for relief. *See* END ALLOWANCE.

disclaimer The renunciation of:

a a right or claim,

b an interest in property, eg the liquidator of a company may disclaim an onerous lease held by the company,

c a possible obligation or responsibility, eg in a survey report the renunciation of responsibility for the consequences of non-notification of defects in inaccessible parts of a building, or

d in estate agents' particulars, responsibility for any inaccuracy of information.

disclosure Making information available, especially to the public, as in the case of a quoted company producing and distributing a detailed and comprehensive report each year, or more frequently, which presents a true and fair picture of its financial position (capital and revenue) and of the activities undertaken during the period under review. Public opinion has over the years called for less secrecy, more accountability and more openness in the type, breadth and depth of information which is disclosed. The underlying reason is to minimise the risk of dishonest or otherwise improper conduct of business affairs.

discontinuance order An order made under section 51 of the Town and Country Planning Act 1971 by a local planning authority requiring the discontinuance of a lawful use of land or buildings and perhaps the removal or alteration of buildings. A claim for compensation may arise under section 170 of the Act, covering such matters as depreciation in the value of land, disturbance and expenditure in complying with the order (less the value to the claimant of any recoverable materials).

discount **1.** An allowance for prompt or early payment deducted either from a sale price or from a debt. **2.** A reduced price at which goods may be offered to special categories of buyer or on a special occasion.

discount broker One who sells securities at a lower rate of commission but offers no advice on investment.

discounted cash flow analysis (DCF) Techniques used in investment and development appraisal whereby future inflows and outflows of cash associated with a particular project are expressed in present-day terms by discounting. The most widely used forms of DCF are the internal rate of return (IRR) and the net present value (NPV). The techniques may be used for such purposes as the valuation of land and investments, the ranking of projects and evaluating the design of projects or their components. *See* INCREMENTAL YIELD ANALYSIS; COSTS IN USE.

discounted cash flow yield Another name for internal rate of return.

discounting A mathematical procedure by which sums due to be received or incurred at specific dates in the future are brought to their current value at the valuation date allowing for accumulated interest at a selected rate, which it is assumed would be earned during the intervening period. *See* PRESENT VALUE OF £1.

discount rate The rate, or rates, of interest selected when calculating the present value of some future cost or benefit. *See* DISCOUNTING; PRESENT VALUE OF £1.

discount store (discount warehouse) A retail outlet which, because it is one of many branches belonging to the same owner who is able to buy goods in bulk, can offer them at a relatively low price. Unlike the practice in traditional multiple shops, the price charged to retail customers reflects a proportion of the preferential discount available to the store owner. *Cf* RETAIL WAREHOUSE.

discount warehouse *See* DISCOUNT STORE.

discount yield Another term for internal rate of return.

discovery of documents The compulsory disclosure of relevant documents held by one party to the opposing party in a civil action or arbitration. Sometimes this is automatic and mutual, eg in High Court actions begun by writ, but otherwise it requires an order of the court, tribunal or arbitrator.

discretionary trust One in which the trustees have discretion over who (within a prescribed class of persons) shall receive any benefit under the trust and in what proportions.

disentailing deed A deed executed by a person who is of full age and entitled to possession of an entailed interest in property enlarging his entailed interest into a fee simple.

disentailment The act of disentailing or barring an entailed interest, thus enlarging the interest into a fee simple.

dispone (Scotland) A term used in the conveyance of land; literally to convey formally.

disposal (disposition) The transfer of land by, for instance, sale, assignment, grant of a lease, death, gift or exchange. For capital gains tax purposes it includes instances where certain capital sums are derived from assets, notwithstanding that no asset is acquired by the person paying the capital sum, eg a sum received under an insurance policy for fire damage to a building. *See* PART DISPOSAL.

disposition (Scotland) A unilateral deed by which property, heritable or movable, is alienated.

disregards Items which are ignored in valuations of property, eg in valuations for lease renewals under the Landlord and Tenant Act 1954 Part II and on rent review (where the lease so requires).

dissolution Formal termination, eg the formal dissolving of a company by winding up. *See* LIQUIDATION.

distress (distraint) The act of seizure of chattels without legal process to enforce satisfaction of a demand, performance of an obligation or redress of an injury; most commonly used today as a means of recovering arrears of rent. Only in the case of tenancies subject to the Rent Acts is a court order necessary.

distribution In an industrial/consumer economy the process of moving goods from a production plant, or a bulk storage area such as a warehouse, to another place which is nearer in the chain of movement to the ultimate user. Typically the transfer of products from a wholesaler to a retailer.

distribution in kind The process of giving to the shareholders of a company, in a form other than money, something to which they are entitled or as a result of a decision taken by the board of the company, eg an issue of shares in lieu of a dividend payment.

district plan In town and country planning a development plan, now known simply as a "local plan", for the general control of development and use of land, prepared by the local planning authority and covering that authority's area. *Cf* ACTION AREA; SUBJECT PLAN.

district shopping centre A group of shops including at least one supermarket, which acts as the anchor tenant. It is often supplementary to a main town shopping centre and usually has an emphasis on the sale of convenience goods, but also offers a limited range of comparison goods. Its size range is from 10,000 m^2 (100,000 sq ft) to 20,000 m^2 (200,000 sq ft) serving a catchment area of 10,000-75,000 people. *See* HIERARCHY OF SHOPPING CENTRES.

district valuer (DV) A professional valuer employed by the Board of Inland Revenue dealing with valuations for taxation, compulsory purchase and other purposes on behalf of government departments and some local authorities. The office of district valuer is now integrated with that of valuation officer.

disturbance Interference with the legal rights of an owner or occupier. Where such interference results from the exercise of a statutory power and causes loss or injury not directly affecting the value of the interest held, there is normally a separate item (or items) of compensation, eg on the compulsory purchase of occupied premises this may include removal expenses, loss of profits, the cost of adaptation of new premises, or permanent loss of goodwill. Where the disturbance is not authorised by statute the injured party will have a right of action for damages and/or an injunction.

disturbance payment Compensation paid by an authority in pursuance of one of its statutory powers, eg compulsory purchase or in the implementation of an improvement notice under Part VII of the Housing Act 1985, to an occupier of land who would otherwise not have a compensatable interest. Such payments are authorised by section 37 of the Land Compensation Act 1973, section 38 of which sets out the amount of the disturbance payment. *Cf* "CRAWLEY" COSTS.

diversification The strategy, in corporate business, portfolio investment and marketing, of putting effort into fields which differ substantially from the main activities hitherto undertaken.

dividend The periodic amount received by a shareholder of a company being the return received on his investment. It is usually an annual figure which is commonly assessed and paid in two instalments; the first, or interim, may be paid on the authority of the board of directors at some time during a year of account; the second, or final, is recommended by the board at the annual general meeting and if approved by an appropriate majority of the shareholders is then distributed to the shareholders. Payment is made out of the net income of the company after corporation tax or, if the income for the relevant period is insufficient, partly or wholly out of revenue reserves accumulated from past years' surpluses of profit.

dividend yield The dividend per share of a company expressed as a percentage of the current share price, eg a total dividend of 8p where the market share price is 160p giving a 5% yield.

divisible balance In a valuation using the profits basis to assess rent, rental value or rateable value, the amount found by deducting the tenant's proper working expenses, except rent and rates, from the estimated gross income.

Divisional Court A court comprising two or more judges of one of the divisions of the High Court, whose function is to hear appeals on certain matters prescribed in statutes and to supervise the inferior courts.

divorce value Additional value released by the subdivision of a property into two or more physical parts and/or interests. *See* BREAK-UP VALUE. *Cf* MARRIAGE VALUE.

DIY (do-it-yourself) store An outlet mainly supplying the retail buyer (usually a householder) with basic materials, components and goods to be used to do his own building, plumbing, furnishing, decorating etc. Often these outlets are located on the periphery of a town, with on-site parking space, and may be established in suitably adapted warehouses or other buildings with adequate clear space.

documentary evidence (written evidence) Evidence in written form. *Cf* ORAL EVIDENCE.

domestic fixtures *See* TENANT'S FIXTURES.

domestic hereditament A dwelling-house and specified subsidiary accommodation for a motor vehicle or private storage. Domestic and mixed hereditaments are entitled to domestic rate relief, scaled down for mixed hereditaments.

domicile For taxation purposes, the country which is regarded as an individual's present home and, therefore, the country assessing the tax payable by that person.

dominant tenement A parcel of land which benefits from an easement or some other incorporeal right such as a restrictive covenant. Thus, where an easement of way exists over parcel A for access to parcel B, parcel B is the dominant tenement: parcel A is the servient tenement. *See* TENEMENT 1.

***dominium directum* (Scotland)** The right to superiority. *See* FEU (SCOTLAND).

***dominium utile* (Scotland)** The right to property granted to and enjoyed by a vassal. *See* FEU (SCOTLAND).

Donaldson's Investment Tables A set of valuation tables compiled by Philip Marshall BSc FRICS and the investment department of Donaldson's, chartered surveyors, showing equated yields and unitisation yields for certain rates of growth of rent at given frequencies of rent reviews, equivalent yields and implied growth rates. *See* VALUATION TABLE.

double glazing/triple glazing Two/three panes of glass, one behind the other with cavities between them, which may be installed either as factory-made sealed units or as double/triple windows to provide noise insulation and/or to retain or exclude heat. Also known as secondary glazing.

double option A put and take option.

double sinking fund method A valuation approach for leaseholds devised to avoid the over-recoupment of capital when valuing variable profit rents by the dual rate method.

downside *See* UPSIDE AND DOWNSIDE.

downtown (USA) A colloquial expression used to indicate a central business district or shopping area of a city or large town. Evolution can produce more than one such area as, for example, in New York, ie Upper and Lower Manhattan. The word is also used in other countries.

drainage rate, occupier's *See* OCCUPIER'S DRAINAGE RATE.

drainage rate, owner's *See* OWNER'S DRAINAGE RATE.

draw down In development finance the withdrawing of part, or the whole, of a standing loan, usually for substantial sums over a long period. *See* TENDER PANEL FACILITY; TRANCHE.

driftway *See* BRIDLEPATH.

drop lock loan A form of loan in which interest payable begins by being at a variable rate but, if a selected rate of interest used as a reference falls to or below an agreed level, then the interest payable is thereafter fixed or "locked" at a rate, calculated according to the terms of the agreement.

drove road *See* BRIDLEWAY.

dual rate *See* DUAL RATE METHOD; YEARS' PURCHASE.

dual rate method A method of valuing terminable income flows, eg profit rents under a lease. Allowance is made for part of the net income to be notionally invested in a sinking fund at an accumulative rate to recoup initial outlay, with the remainder of the net income being capitalised at an appropriate remunerative rate of interest.

dual rate table A valuation table of years' purchase calculated on the basis of individually selected remunerative and accumulative rates of interest. *Cf* SINGLE RATE TABLE.

dual rate years' purchase *See* DUAL RATE TABLE.

dubitante Doubting; eg in a note on a law case th reference may be, "Held, Smith LJ and Jones J (Brown LJ *dubitante*) . . .".

dumpy level In land surveying, an instrument used to measure comparative levels, comprising a telescope, capable of rotating through 360 degrees in a horizontal plane about a vertical axis.

Dutch auction An auction at which the proceedings commence with the auctioneer quoting a higher price than he might reasonably expect to receive. If he is unable to secure an acceptance at that figure he will reduce the figure by stages until someone accepts. The acceptor is then legally obliged to proceed with the purchase.

dwelling In general parlance, self-contained living accommodation. The term includes flats and maisonettes, or possibly similar accommodation which is not completely self-contained, ie having some shared facilities. More specifically, statutory definitions include:

a Rent Act 1977, sections 19 (8), 85 (1) and 107: "a house or part of a house";

b Housing Act 1985, section 343: "premises used or suitable for use as a separate dwelling;

c Landlord and Tenant Act 1985 section 38: "a building or part of a building occupied or intended to be occupied as a separate dwelling, together with any yard, garden, outhouses and appurtenances belonging to it or usually enjoyed with it."

dwelling-house A dwelling, being a structure of a permanent nature. For the purposes of Part III of the Housing Act 1985 (dealing with secure tenancies) it "may be a house or a part of a house," while land let together with a dwelling is also treated as part of the dwelling-house, unless the land is agricultural land exceeding 2 acres.

E

earnest money A sum deposited, before an agreement is binding in law, by one of the parties with the other as an indication of his good faith and his intention to honour the terms of the agreement, eg a pre-contract deposit.

earnings yield The earnings of a share in a company, derived from profits net of corporation tax, expressed as a percentage of the share price, ie the reciprocal of price/earnings ratio. *Cf* DIVIDEND YIELD.

easement A right appurtenant to a parcel of land entitling the dominant owner to use the land of the servient owner in a particular manner, or constraining the legal rights otherwise enjoyed by the servient owner, eg a right of way, right to light, right of support. Strictly speaking, easements cannot exist "in gross", ie personal and unattached to the ownership of land, but rights similar to easements can be created by statute, usually for the benefit of public utility undertakings, and these are commonly referred to as "statutory easements", eg oversail.

easement of light *See* LIGHT AND AIR EASEMENTS.

eavesdrop (Scotland) A servitude, also known as stillicide, which imposes on a servient tenement the burden of receiving the drippings from the eaves of a dominant tenement.

eaves height Defined in the *RICS/ISVA Code of Measuring Practice* as "(a) Internal: The height between the floor surface and the underside of the roof covering, supporting purlins or underlining (whichever is the lower) at the eaves on the internal wall face. (b) External: The height between the ground surface and the exterior of the roof covering at the eaves on the external wall face, ignoring any parapet".

economic approach (USA) US term for investment method.

economic life The period during which the value of a site and buildings in any possible use is greater than the value of the site for any other feasible purposes including redevelopment. *Cf* PHYSICAL LIFE.

economic rent *See* COST RENT.

EEC grants and loans for industrial buildings Grant assistance of varying degrees available through the European Regional Development Fund for qualifying businesses. Loans currently (1988) of up to 50% of the fixed asset cost are also available through the European Coal and Steel Community for any manufacturing industry located in specified areas or where the coal or steel industry is running down. Further, the European Investment Bank may provide medium-term loans (at a fixed rate of interest), at present not exceeding 50% of the cost of a project, to firms which further the development of the assisted areas in Great Britain and Northern Ireland.

effective capital value In valuations for rating purposes using the contractor's basis, the capital amount, being the aggregate of the land value and depreciated replacement building cost. From this the appropriate annual value is determined by decapitalisation at a rate of simple interest.

effective floor area *See* NET INTERNAL AREA.

effective rate of interest The annual rate of interest equivalent to the terms applying to a specific financial arrangement, where interest is payable at intervals other than yearly, and there may be other special provisions, eg rolled-up interest. In considering the alternatives available for the use of money it is essential to have a common denominator for the purposes of direct comparison and this is provided by the effective rate of interest.

eighth schedule development One, or more, of the classes of development under Schedule 8 to the Town and Country Planning Act 1971. These do not constitute "new development". For most purposes when assessing statutory compensation, one can assume that planning permission for 8th Schedule development would be granted and any element of value attributed thereto is included in the compensation. Moreover, certain taxation legislation has allowed valuations to include the notional right to undertake 8th Schedule development, eg in assessing current use value for development land tax.

ejusdem generis Of the same kind or nature. The term is used where a list of particular words is followed by general words, the latter being limited to the same kind as the particular words. For example, in the expression "cattle, sheep, goats, pigs and other animals" the words "other animals" would be construed as *ejusdem generis* with the preceding words, ie as farm animals.

electromagnetic distance measurement (EDM) In land surveying, the measurement of distance by instruments which use electromagnetic waves, eg infra red, laser, light, polarised light, or radio. The time taken by these waves to travel between two points enables their distance apart to be calculated. *See* GEODIMETER; TELLUROMETER.

eligible objects For inheritance tax, tangible objects in respect of which there is available an exemption or a relief from the tax.

emblements Annual crops cultivated by labour or the profits from such crops. Traditionally, in certain circumstances, these could be harvested by an outgoing tenant farmer after his tenancy had expired. Likewise, a tenant for life of settled land, if his interest ceases for some reason other than his own act, is entitled to emblements. If the estate is limited to the tenant's own life, his personal representative(s) can harvest the crops. Today the term "holdover" is more often used instead of "emblements".

empty rate *See* UNOCCUPIED RATE.

enabling Act/enabling statute The Act which authorises the use by local and public authorities and/or by government departments of powers of compulsory purchase to acquire land for purposes of a particular kind, eg the Highways Act 1980, which authorises the taking of land for highway construction or improvement.

enactment *See* ACT OF PARLIAMENT.

encroachment Unauthorised extension of the boundaries of a piece of land over adjoining land which belongs to another.

encumbrance (incumbrance) In strict property terms a debt or charge legally secured over land, thus encumbering it. In general parlance, however, it is used to include legal rights or interests in or over someone else's land, eg easements or restrictive covenants.

end allowance A deduction made in a valuation for rating to reflect some disability in a particular hereditament when compared with others of a similar type. *Cf* QUANTITY ALLOWANCE.

endowment The placing of funds or property into trust for a specific purpose, eg the maintenance of a charitable institution, or for the benefit of some person(s).

endowment assurance policy A life assurance contract providing for the accumulation of capital payable at the end of a specified term or on death, whichever is the earlier.

endowment trust A fund or portfolio set up and held in trust for the repair, maintenance and upkeep of heritage property.

energy management A systematic approach to the provision and use of energy in a building or other structure. Its essence is the conservation of energy output for a determined level of need, being based on an energy plan and budget. Careful monitoring is carried out to ensure that necessary changes are made to improve efficiency.

enforcement notice A notice served by a local planning authority under the Town and Country Planning Act 1971 requiring a breach of planning control to be remedied. There is a right of appeal to the Secretary of State, but failure to comply with the notice, if unopposed or confirmed on appeal, is a criminal offence.

enfranchisement *See* LEASEHOLD ENFRANCHISEMENT.

English rose *See* PEPPERCORN RENT.

engrossment The formal and final version of a property document prepared by a solicitor in readiness for signing and sealing following agreement of the final draft between the parties.

enhancement expenditure Under section 32(1)(*b*) of the Capital Gains Tax Act 1979, expenditure reflected in the state or nature of the asset at the time of disposal and incurred for the purpose of enhancing the value of the asset. It is an allowable deduction in computing a gain or loss.

enlarge In property law this means to acquire rights which increase an estate or an interest in land to a greater estate or interest, eg enlarging a lease into a superior lease or freehold by acquiring the reversion, or converting an entailed interest into a fee simple by barring the entail *See* DISENTAILMENT; LEASEHOLD ENFRANCHISEMENT.

entail A special form of equitable interest which provides for the transfer of real estate on death, eg under the rules of primogeniture. *See* ENTAILED INTEREST.

entail, barring the *See* DISENTAILMENT.

entailed interest An equitable interest in land where ownership is restricted to the life of a person and the lives of the "heirs of his body" either generally or of a specific category, eg limited to male offspring. If and when there are no qualifying heirs, the land passes to the remainderman (if any) nominated in the settlement or to the reversioner, ie the original settlor or his lawful sucessor.

enterprise zone Under section 179 of and Schedule 32 to the Local Government, Planning and Land Act 1980 (as amended by the Housing and Planning Act 1986), an area designated by the Secretary of State as requiring special planning, fiscal and economic development treatment, thus generating its renewal. Among the special advantages of such designation are simplified planning procedures, exemption from rates for industrial and commercial properties and the availability of 100% capital allowances for income taxation. *Cf* SIMPLIFIED PLANNING ZONE.

enterprise zone allowance A capital allowance for the construction within an enterprise zone of an industrial building, hotel, commercial building or other qualifying structure if constructed within 10 years of the designation of the zone.

entirety value In valuations under the Leasehold Reform Act 1967, the capital value of a house in good condition and with vacant possession including any element of additional value attributable to the development potential of its site. *See* CLEARED SITE APPROACH; MODERN GROUND RENT; NEW-FOR-OLD APPROACH; STANDING HOUSE APPROACH.

entry *See* NOTICE OF ENTRY; RIGHT OF ENTRY.

envelope **1.** The enclosing parts of a building or structure, eg walls, roof, doors and windows, which together form its external shape. **2.** Land outlined on a plan which is regarded by the planning authority as the physical extent of a village or small urban area for the purposes of planning control.

envelope ratio The ratio of the costs of alternative envelopes (or of their components) to the floor area so enclosed. Such ratios may then be used to compare various designs. *See* ENVELOPE 1.

equalisation fund A form of sinking fund which is set aside each year to provide financial resources for items of repair or renewal which are likely to be undertaken at intervals of more than one year, eg external decoration or renewing parts of heating boilers. These allowances are needed to ensure that yearly accounts reflect the total cost of maintaining a property. If any item relates to an installation having a particularly long life, separate finance may not be required if a sinking fund has been set up and has matured for replacement of the entire building.

equated rent Given the rental value on a normal rent review pattern, the rent resulting from an adjustment to reflect a variation from the norm. For instance, where a property is to be let on a rent review pattern which is longer than usual in such cases, a higher rent (equated rent) will offset the fact that the lessor cannot enjoy the higher rental income at the normal frequency, whereas the tenant benefits, from anticipated rental growth, during the intervening period. The variables needed to determine the equated rent are the growth rate expected, the different review patterns and the all-risk yield, together with the rent on the usual pattern of reviews. *See* CONSTANT RENT; UPLIFTED RENT.

equated yield In valuing an investment property the internal rate of return, being the discount rate which needs to be applied to the flow of income expected during the life of the investment so that the total amount of income so discounted at this rate equals the capital outlay. Rents at review, lease renewal or reletting take account of expected future rental changes due to variations in the value of money, ie the calculation reflects the valuer's views on the impact of inflation (or, if he so thinks, deflation) as well as his views on rental changes due to other factors. *Cf* EQUIVALENT YIELD. (*See* Appendix IV.)

equitable Originally describing a right or legal concept valid only in the former Court of Chancery and not recognised by common or statute law, this now means recognised under the rules of equity which, since the merger of law and equity under the Judicature Acts 1873-75, can apply in all courts of law.

equitable charge A form of security in equity where specific property is charged with a debt or other obligation but there is no actual transfer (or formal agreement to the transfer) of ownership or possession. *See* EQUITABLE MORTGAGE.

equitable easement Any easement other than one created by deed, prescription or statute and held in fee simple absolute in possession or on a term of years absolute, eg an easement lasting for life or one created by contract not under seal.

equitable estate Originally a property right recognised by the former Court of Chancery, as opposed to a legal estate. The term is now obsolete but is sometimes erroneously used for "equitable interest".

equitable estoppel (quasi-estoppel) The extension of the common law doctrine of estoppel to include promises as well as statements of fact by the person making the representation.

equitable interest **1.** An interest enforceable against anyone other than a bona fide purchaser for valuable consideration who does not in law have direct or implied "notice" of its existence. For this purpose, "notice" now means a registration prior to the purchase under the Land Charges or Land Registration Acts. *See* LAND CHARGE; LAND REGISTRATION. **2.** Any interest in, or a charge on, land other than a legal estate.

equitable lease (informal lease) An agreement for grant of a lease or tenancy which does not satisfy the formal requirements to create a legal lease but otherwise contains the essential terms, eg a written agreement not under seal for a term exceeding three years. This may take effect as an agreement for lease in respect of which the court may order specific performance, but the agreement will only be enforceable against a third party acquiring another interest for value from the landlord if it has been registered as an estate contract.

equitable lien A right to enforce a claim for the performance of an obligation with the security of a property, but not possession thereof, until the obligation is discharged. It is therefore analogous to a charge. It includes the right, authorised by the court, to recover the amount of a debt from the proceeds of a sale of the security.

equitable mortgage A mortgage which is not a legal mortgage, taking, for example, the form of:
a an equitable charge;
b the mere deposit of title deeds with the mortgagee; or
c the mortgage of an equitable interest.

equitable remedies Those remedies which were originally available only in the former Court of Chancery to supplement the legal remedies under the common law. Since the fusion of law and equity they have been available in all divisions of the High Court at the court's discretion. They include, *inter alia*, injunctions, specific performance, rescission, rectification and the appointment of a receiver.

equitable rights All rights recognised by equity. *See* EQUITABLE; EQUITABLE INTEREST; EQUITABLE REMEDIES.

equitable waste Waste by act of commission, being wanton destruction causing serious damage to the demised premises. Thus it is a flagrant example of voluntary waste.

equity **1.** That part of the law in England and Wales originally administered by the Lord Chancellor and subsequently by the former Court of Chancery, recognising concepts and doctrines and granting remedies not acknowledged by the common law. Under the Judicature Acts 1873-75 the common law and equity were "fused" and administered by all the courts, but where the rules of law and equity conflict the latter prevail. **2.** An equitable right or claim. *See* EQUITABLE INTEREST. **3.** An underlying right to share in the profit from some development or other commercial venture. **4.** An ordinary share, or stock, in a limited company entitling the holder to such dividends as are distributed from the attributable earnings of the company. In a winding-up the equity shareholders rank last for any distribution after payment of all other indebtedness of the company.

equity capital The risk capital, usually of a corporate body, being in the form of ordinary shares. These only qualify for income by way of dividend paid from the attributable profit, or accumulated revenue reserves, of the company. In terms of capital as distinct from revenue, the equity is equated to the worth of the company's assets after deducting all liabilities. *See* EQUITY 4; RISK CAPITAL; VENTURE CAPITAL.

equity finance Money in the form of a loan made available to a company, generally for a specific venture such as a development where the lender, as part of the bargain, becomes entitled to a share of any profit, whether or not in receipt of interest.

equity linked mortgage (equity participation mortgage) A mortgage whereby the interest on the principal in part or in whole is calculated, usually yearly, by reference to changes in the annual equity return on the security, eg it may reflect annual increases, or possibly decreases, in the annual return on, or the value of, the property on which the mortgage is secured.

equity of redemption The mortgagor's right to redeem, ie repay, the mortgage at the end of the mortgage period or at some earlier agreed date(s). *See* CLOG ON EQUITY OF REDEMPTION.

equity-sharing lease A lease granted at less than rack rental value, thereby entitling the tenant to an equity share, being a proportion of the full value. At a rent review date, the tenant is usually entitled to reflect in the new rent a deduction from full rental value based on his equity share at the outset. *See* GEARING.

equivalence, principle of *See* PRINCIPLE OF EQUIVALENCE.

equivalent annual cost The equivalent on a yearly basis of those sums which pay for items of cost which occur at intervals of more or less than 12 months. *Cf* COSTS IN USE. *See* EQUALISATION FUND; VIRTUAL RENT.

equivalent reinstatement A basis of compensation for compulsory acquisition being the "reasonable cost" of providing an equivalent property on a suitable site as a substitute. Under rule (5) of section 5 of the Land Compensation Act 1961 a claimant is entitled to adopt this basis, subject to the discretion of the Lands Tribunal, where, but for compulsory purchase, the land would continue to be devoted to a purpose of such a nature that there is no general demand or market for land for that purpose, eg for hospitals, churches or schools, and provided reinstatement is bona fide intended.

equivalent yield In valuing an investment property, the internal rate of return, being the discount rate which needs to be applied to the flow of income expected during the life of the investment so that the total amount of income so discounted at this rate equals the capital outlay. Rents at review, lease renewal or reletting are taken at values current at the date of valuation except to the extent that they reflect any future changes in value anticipated by the valuer caused by factors other than his view on the impact of inflation or deflation. *Cf* EQUATED YIELD. (*See* Appendix IV.)

escalator clause A clause in a contract or a lease providing for an adjustment (up or down) in the financial terms to reflect some change in specified but external factor(s), eg a change in the Retail Price Index.

escheat *See* BONA VACANTIA.

escrow A deed which is signed, sealed and conditionally delivered but does not become operative until the condition has been fulfilled. In the meantime it is usually held by a third party.

established claim A claim made by an owner of land for the loss of development value arising from the provisions of the former Town and Country Planning Act 1947. Also called a Part VI claim. Outstanding claims are now embodied in the "unexpended balance of established development value" (UXB or UBED).

established use A use of property which was:

a begun without planning permission before 1964 and has continued ever since;
b begun with a conditional planning permission before 1964 but one or more of the conditions have not been complied with since the end of 1963; or
c begun after 1963 as a result of a change of use not requiring planning permission at that time.

In all such cases one can obtain an "established use certificate".

established use certificate A certificate granted by a local planning authority (or by the Secretary of State on appeal) under section 94 (or section 95) of the Town and Country Planning Act 1971 confirming that a particular use of land or a building is "established" for planning purposes and, as such, does not require planning permission for its continuance. *See* ESTABLISHED USE.

estate **1.** The right to some form of ownership in land. In strict law all real property belongs to, and is held from, the Crown and what one owns is an estate or an interest in the land, eg a freehold or a leasehold. *See* EQUITABLE INTEREST; LEGAL ESTATE. **2.** An area of land usually in one ownership or recognised as having been in one ownership which, to the public at large, is regarded as of such significance as to justify being identified as an entity in its own right. Typical examples lie in landed estates and residential or industrial estates. **3.** For inheritance tax purposes, a deceased individual's property, both real and personal, comprising everything (other than "excluded property" as defined by the Inheritance Tax Act 1984) to which he was beneficially entitled. In some instances this will extend to cover properties over which he had general powers of disposal.

estate agency work Defined by section 1 of the Estate Agents Act 1979 as (with certain exceptions) things done by a person in the course of business (including one in which he is employed) pursuant to instructions received from a client who wishes to dispose of or acquire an interest in land:

a to effect the introduction to the client of a third person wishing to acquire or dispose of such an interest; and
b after the introduction to secure the disposal or acquisition of that interest.

Among the exceptions excluded from the definition are work done by a practising solicitor (or his employee) in the course of his profession; credit or insurance brokerage; surveys or valuations under contracts separate from estate agency work; planning applications and other work under the Planning Acts; acquisitions or disposals on behalf of employers, in the course of one's employment, or on behalf of employees (past, present or future) by reason of their employment; things done in relation to any interest in a property subject to a mortgage by a receiver of the income.

estate agent One who acts for, and usually advises, a principal in respect of transactions involving real estate, eg sales, purchases, lettings, mortgages. *See* ESTATE AGENCY WORK; EXCLUSIVE AGENT; RETAINED AGENT; SOLE AGENT; SUB-AGENT.

estate contract A contract by a landowner undertaking to create or convey the right of ownership of a legal estate to a third party. Such a contract establishes an equitable interest which the purchaser can enforce against third parties if it has been registered as a land charge (for unregistered land) or protected by registration in the charges register at the Land Registry (for registered land).

estate duty A former tax which was charged on a person's estate on death. It was replaced in 1975 by capital transfer tax, which was itself superseded in 1986 by inheritance tax.

estate owner The owner of a legal estate (as opposed to an equitable interest) in land.

estate pur (or per) autre vie An interest in property lasting during the lifetime of another. (Strictly this cannot now be a legal estate.) *See* LIFE TENANCY; TENANCY PUR (OR PER) AUTRE VIE.

estate terrier An information system sufficient for the effective and efficient day-to-day running of an estate. It includes:

a estate boundaries and plans;
b abstracts of title and leases;
c details of lettings;
d details of easements and other rights and obligations affecting the estate.

estoppel A legal rule based upon the principle that it is unjust for a person to break a promise or to act in a way inconsistent with a previous declaration (either express or implied) if another party is led to believe that he may act, and does indeed act, on the strength of that promise or statement. This rule prevents the promiser from reopening the matter by denying the truth of his statement or breaking his promise, eg a landlord who promises his tenant he will not enforce an absolute covenant against assignment is unlikely to be allowed to change his mind once the tenant has entered into a commitment with a prospective assignee.

estovers The right (dating from feudal times) of a lessee or tenant for life to take timber for immediate and essential purposes from his own holding. This ancient right to take timber from land outside a person's holding is usually enjoyed with others and is then known as "common in estovers". The equivalent Saxon word was "bote".

Eurobond A form of bond, issued by a government or corporate body, denominated in the domestic currency of the issuers and made available, usually by a syndicate of bankers, in international financial markets situated in countries other than that of the issuers.

European Court (Court of Justice of the European Communities) The court of the EEC and the other European Communities, which sits in Luxembourg and has the following primary functions:

a interpretation of the treaties establishing the Communities;
b ruling on the validity and interpretation of EEC legislation;
c determining whether acts or omissions by the Commission, the Council of Ministers or any member states are violations of the treaties.

The court consists of 13 judges assisted by six advocates general, all of whom are appointed by the member states acting collectively.

evasion In relation to taxation, an illegal act or omission (and therefore a criminal offence) resulting from the production of false information or the deliberate failure to disclose relevant information in order to reduce or escape taxation which is properly due. *Cf* AVOIDANCE.

evict To expel or eject someone from property whether lawfully or not. Force need not necessarily be used in the process. The eviction of a residential occupier is a criminal offence unless resulting from successful court proceedings (Protection from Eviction Act 1977).

evidence Information tending to prove or disprove the existence of some fact. *See* CIRCUMSTANTIAL; CONCLUSIVE; DIRECT; DOCUMENTARY; EXTRINSIC; HEARSAY; OPINION; ORAL; ORIGINAL; PRIMA FACIE; PRIMARY; REAL; SECONDARY.

evidenced in writing Supported by documentary evidence: a prerequisite for the enforceability of certain classes of contract, eg under section 40 of the Law of Property Act 1925 contracts for the sale of land are unenforceable unless the contract is in writing or evidenced by a memorandum duly signed.

excambion (Scotland) A contract under the terms of which one piece of land is exchanged for another.

excepted rate Under section 115 of the General Rate Act 1967 any of those rates which are not included in the general rate, namely:

a any rate for commission of sewers, drainage, walls, embankments or other works,
b any church rate, tithe rate or rector's rate,
c any rate leviable by conservators of a common,
d any water rate and
e any garden rate or square rate (not levied by a rating authority).

exception A corporeal part of a property excluded from a sale or tenancy, eg the exception of minerals or timber. *Cf* RESERVATION.

excess charge A charge made by a landlord at the end of the year for the amounts due and legally recoverable from the tenant, under the terms of the relevant lease, on account of services provided for that tenant during the year, where the payments already made have proved to be inadequate.

exchange of contracts The first formal and legally enforceable step in the disposal of real property, ie when the parties duly sign and exchange copies of a document embodying the terms of the deal.

excluded property For the purposes of inheritance tax defined by section 6 of the Inheritance Tax Act 1984 as "Property situated outside the United Kingdom . . .

if the person beneficially entitled to it is an individual domiciled outside the United Kingdom . . .", together with certain other specific categories of property.

excluded services For value added tax purposes, the services of an architect, surveyor or other person acting as a consultant or in a supervisory capacity: Value Added Tax Act 1983, Schedule 5 Group 8A — Protected Buildings — Note (2). *See* TAXABLE PERSON.

exclusive agent *See* SOLE AGENT; EXCLUSIVE AGENT.

exclusive rent (exclusive rental) **1.** Originally a rent payable under the terms of a lease which imposed upon the tenant an obligation to pay the rates. **2.** More commonly today, a rent under a clear lease which makes the tenant responsible for payment of rates, cost of services and other outgoings. *Cf* INCLUSIVE RENT.

ex dividend (ex div or xd) A Stock Exchange term indicating that the price currently quoted for a particular security is on the basis that the purchaser is not entitled to any dividend declared for payment by the Company but not yet paid. When paid, the dividend belongs to the original shareholder who sold ex dividend. *Cf* CUM DIVIDEND.

executed trust (completely constituted or perfect trust) A trust which is complete and enforceable by the beneficiaries without any further action by the settlor or some third party. *Cf* EXECUTORY TRUST.

execution The act of signing a document in such a way as to make it legally enforceable. In the case of a deed this is achieved in the time-honoured way of signing (in the presence of witnesses), sealing and delivering.

executor(s) One or more persons named in a will whose responsibility it is to obtain probate, settle tax and other liabilities (if any), collect moneys owing to the deceased and then distribute the net estate in accordance with the provisions of the will.

executory trust (incompletely constituted or imperfect trust) A trust which is incomplete because it cannot be enforced by the beneficiaries until some further act is done by the settlor or a third party. *Cf* EXECUTED TRUST.

exempt lease A lease exempted from the security of tenure provisions of Part II of the Landlord and Tenant Act 1954 following a joint application to court by the landlord and the tenant under section 38(4) of that Act (as amended by the Law of Property Act 1969).

exemption A provision which removes financial liability or other legal obligation imposed by statute, regulation, byelaw, contract or common law, eg the exemption from rating of properties occupied by the Crown or foreign sovereigns, or the exemption from most taxes of properties used by charities for their own purposes. *Cf* RELIEF. *See* EXTRA-STATUTORY CONCESSION.

exempt supply A supply of goods or services, as specified in Schedule 6 to the Value Added Tax Act 1983, upon which there is no charge to VAT. *Cf* STANDARD RATED SUPPLY; ZERO-RATED SUPPLY.

ex gratia As of favour, ie something done without legal obligation or admission of liability.

***ex gratia* payment** A discretionary payment, usually one made by a public body to a payee who has no strict entitlement to compensation. For instance, section 63(2) of the Housing Act 1985 enables a local authority using clearance area powers to make, at its discretion, a payment to a shopkeeper whose trade is adversely affected by the resulting decline in population.

exhibit *See* REAL EVIDENCE.

ex interest (xi) A Stock Exchange term indicating that a purchaser of a security is not entitled to receive an interest payment already due but not yet paid.

existing use rights A colloquial expression which, in broad terms, signifies all those uses of property which do not need planning permission. Such uses include changes in use either within a particular class of the Use Classes Order or permitted under the General Development Order, plus any uses specified in an established use certificate.

existing use value **1.** A colloquial expression broadly signifying the open market value of an interest in land disregarding any element of value attributable to a use, or a new development, other than one within the existing use rights, the latter including *inter alia*:

a the unexpended balance of established development value,

b the rights under Schedule 8 to the Town and Country Planning Act 1971, and

c the General Development Order.

See EXISTING USE RIGHTS. **2.** For the particular purpose of compensation when the Secretary of State declines to confirm a purchase notice and instead directs that planning permission should be granted for some other development, there is a statutory definition under section 187(5) of the Town and Country Planning Act 1971, with similar effect to 1. above but excluding GDO rights. **3.** For the valuation of assets which are owner-occupied and used for a relevant business, the term is defined in the *RICS Guidance Notes on the Valuation of Assets* as "... open market value but with the added assumption that the property will continue as owner-occupied in its existing use, and thus ignores any possible alternative use of the property, any element of hope value, any value attributable to goodwill and any possible increase in value due to special investment or financial transactions such as sale and leaseback which would leave the company with a different interest from one which is to be valued. Open market value for existing use would, however, include the possibilities of extensions or further buildings on undeveloped land or redevelopment of existing buildings provided such construction can be undertaken without major interruption to the continuing business ..."

ex officio Descriptive of a position held on a board, council, committee or similar body by virtue of office, eg where a chairman of a council is automatically a member of its committees.

ex parte Literally on behalf of one side only, eg an *ex parte* application is one made in judicial proceedings either by a person who is interested therein but is not a party thereto, or by one party thereto in the absence of the other.

expected value The average value derived from a number of separate valuations, each based on different assumptions or possibilities. The likelihood of each assumption proving to be correct is weighted according to degrees of probability to enable the average to be calculated.

expert A person having special experience, knowledge and skills in a particular subject. *See* EXPERT WITNESS.

expert, independent *See* INDEPENDENT EXPERT.

expert witness A person with special experience, knowledge of or skills in a subject whom a court will accept as such and allow to attest to facts and give an opinion.

exposure **1.** The degree to which a property for sale or letting is brought to the attention of potential buyers or tenants through such means as advertising and multiple listing groups. **2.** The aspect, ie the direction in which a property faces.

express covenant A covenant, eg in a lease, specifically included in the relevant document. *Cf* IMPLIED COVENANT.

express trust A trust which is expressly created by the settlor, either by formal document or by clear intention from a written document or oral statement(s) by the settlor. *Cf* IMPLIED TRUST (RESULTING TRUST).

extended lease *See* LEASEHOLD REFORM.

external valuer For the purpose of asset valuations a ". . . qualified valuer who is not an internal valuer and where neither he nor any of his partners or co-directors are directors or employees of the company or of another company within a group of companies or have a significant financial interest in the company or group, or where neither the company nor the group has a significant financial interest in the valuer's firm or company. 'Company' includes any other form of organisation, eg a Trust." (*RICS Guidance Notes on the Valuation of Assets*.) *See* INDEPENDENT VALUER 2; INTERNAL VALUER; QUALIFIED VALUER 2.

extinguishment The ending of a right or obligation (such as a debt) or interest in land, eg the forfeiture of a lease.

extrapolation forecasting The analysis and study of historic trends and their projection, reflecting present circumstances, as a means of predicting future market conditions.

extras In a building contract, those items of work carried out which, although not specified or otherwise described in any contract document or on any plans embodied in the contract, are found to be necessary or required to be done, authorised by the employer or his representative and costed in accordance with the provisions of the contract.

extra-statutory concession An exemption or relief from tax which is not statute based but may be granted in a particular and defined set of circumstances at the discretion of the Inland Revenue. A list of concessions currently allowable is available from the Board of Inland Revenue. *Cf* EXEMPTION; TAX RELIEF.

extrinsic evidence Evidence on matters not mentioned in a document produced in evidence in order to explain, vary or contradict its apparent meaning.

F

facade The face of a building, more especially the front elevation.

face value The stated, or ostensible, value of a security or coin when issued, but which does not usually equal its market value. *See* PAR VALUE.

facilities management The co-ordination of many specialist disciplines to create the optimum working environment for staff.

facility letter A letter from a lender to a borrower setting out the terms and conditions which govern the financial arrangements made between them. Often the implementation is a matter of honour between the parties, but sometimes such a letter can be legally enforceable.

factory Defined by the Factories Act 1961 section 175(1) as ". . . any premises in which, or within the close or curtilage or precincts of which, persons are employed in manual labour in any process for or incidental to any of . . ." the purposes as listed in the section. These include: "(a) the making of any article or of part of any article; or (b) the altering, repairing, ornamenting, finishing, cleaning, or washing or the breaking up or demolition of any article; or (c) the adapting for sale of any article; . . .".

NB Since this Act is designed to protect employed persons it is important for anyone wishing to know the full extent of its application to read the relevant section, because it applies to some premises in which activities are undertaken which may not generally be regarded as "industrial", eg slaughter houses and gasometers. *Cf* INDUSTRIAL BUILDING.

factory outlet A retail outlet attached to a factory where goods may be sold. Depending on the circumstances, the prices will be either at a level not exceeding the manufacturer's recommended minimum or at a special lower level.

faculty (Scotland) A power reserved by or conferred upon a person to dispose (wholly or partially) of property for his own or another's benefit.

fag end A colloquial term for a lease having only a short time to run and normally of nominal value only.

fair rent The rent determined by a rent officer (or, on appeal, by a rent assessment committee) under a regulated tenancy and registered as such under the Rent Acts in respect of certain dwelling-houses. The basis of determining a fair rent is set out in section 70 of the Rent Act 1977, as amended, under which *inter alia* any scarcity element for that type of dwelling-house in the locality has to be disregarded. *See* REGISTERED RENT.

fair value A sum which may be considered to be the fair and reasonable worth of a specific interest in property.

fair wear and tear (reasonable wear and tear) Dilapidations caused by the normal action of the weather and ordinary use, assuming reasonable conduct by the party concerned. In a lease, liability under a repairing covenant is sometimes restricted, so that the party in question (usually, but not necessarily, the tenant) is not responsible for such dilapidations. *Cf* WASTE.

fall-back figure **1.** The minimum figure acceptable to someone offering his property for sale, lease or hire. **2.** Sometimes used to mean "forced sale value".

Family Expenditure Survey An annual government survey giving information about householders' spending on goods and services. It is a source of data for feasibility studies for proposed shopping developments.

fascia board **1.** A lengthwise on-edge board attached to a wall or to the ends of rafters or beams, usually for aesthetic reasons. **2.** A board, usually extending over the whole or the major part of a shop window, displaying the name of the business.

fast-food shop Retail premises for the sale, often under franchise, of light, fast-cooked food for eating on the premises or taking away. *See* TAKE-AWAY SHOP.

feasibility study A study of a proposed scheme or development, including the practicality of its achievement and its projected financial outcome.

fee **1.** An estate capable of inheritance. **2. (Scotland)** The full right of property in heritage, in contrast to a liferent. **3.** The remuneration payable to an agent or professional adviser for services performed. *See* SCALE FEES.

fee farm rent *See* RENTCHARGE.

fee, procuration *See* PROCURATION FEE.

fee simple **1.** The highest form of freehold land tenure under English law, in which "fee" signifies heritability of the tenancy and "simple" that there is no qualification as to the heirs who may succeed to it. In legal theory a tenancy in fee simple is held from the Crown. **2.** Commonly, though wrongly, used as a synonym for freehold tenure, which has a wider meaning in law. *Cf* FEE TAIL. *See* FEE SIMPLE ABSOLUTE IN POSSESSION.

fee simple absolute in possession The only form of freehold ownership which can exist as a legal estate under the Law of Property Act 1925. "Fee" and "simple" are both explained under "fee simple"; "absolute" means that it will last for ever, ie it is not determinable, except that the land will revert to the Crown as *bona vacantia* if the owner dies intestate and without heirs; "in possession" indicates either physical possession or the right to take rents and profits, eg the rent payable by a tenant under a lease. *Cf* TERM OF YEARS ABSOLUTE.

fee tail The old (pre-1926) term for land granted as an entailed interest whereby succession to heirs is limited, eg to the heirs of the grantee's body or to the heirs male of the grantee. If there are no surviving special heirs the estate reverts to the grantor or passes in "remainder" to such person or heirs as have been nominated in the grant. *Cf* FEE SIMPLE.

felling direction A directive issued by the Forestry Commission under section 18 of the Forestry Act 1967 to the owner of afforested land requiring him to fell particular trees so as to allow better growth to others, thus improving overall productivity.

felling licence A licence required from the Forestry Commission under section 9 of the Forestry Act 1967, except in emergency, to fell trees over 4 inches in diameter.

fellow A full, or senior, member of a professional body who enjoys the maximum privileges of membership.

Ferrous Foundry Industry Scheme A government scheme providing finance for companies in the iron and steel foundry industry. It includes financial support for new buildings and improvements in working arrangements. It was set up under section 8 of the Industry Act 1972.

feu (Scotland) A feudal holding. To feu is strictly to give out land upon a feudal arrangement whereby the vassal holds land of a superior landowner. He is then virtually owner of the land so long as he pays rent and observes any conditions. Feu is the equivalent of fee in England and Wales, originally a grant of land made by a sovereign as a reward for services rendered. A piece of land thus feued is sometimes referred to as a feu. *See* DOMINIUM DIRECTUM; DOMINIUM UTILE.

feuar (Scotland) The person who has possession and use of ground in return for a feu duty.

feu charter (Scotland) A unilateral document signed by a superior which sets up the relationship of superior and vassal. It specifies the boundaries of the feu, the purposes for which the ground is feued, the conditions attaching to the grant and the feu duty payable.

feu contract (Scotland) A contract between a superior and his vassal regarding the giving of land in feu.

feudal superior (Scotland) *See* SUPERIOR.

feu disposition (Scotland) A unilateral deed signed by a superior, the contents of which are in a feu charter, except that the feuar pays down a lump sum or "grassum" and the feu duty stipulated to be paid is often nominal only.

feu duty (Scotland) An annual payment comparable to a perpetual rentcharge south of the border. New feu duties are now prohibited. In certain circumstances existing duties can or must be redeemed.

feu farm (Scotland) Feu duty normally payable yearly or half-yearly in perpetuity.

FIABCI The International Real Estate Federation, which was originally called Fédération Internationale des Administrateurs de Bien Conseils et Immobiliers, but now the Fédération Internationale des Professions Immobilières, although the old initials are retained.

fiar (Scotland) The owner of a fee. *See* FEE 2.

fiduciary **1.** Descriptive of a relationship in which a person is bound to exercise rights and powers in good faith for the benefit of another, eg trustee and beneficiary. **2.** A person so bound.

fief Territory held in fee, ie by a subordinate from a superior who could be his sovereign. A feudal benefice or an estate under the feudal system.

FIG Fédération Internationale des Geomètres, the international title of the International Federation of Surveyors.

final account The finally agreed statement of the total sum to be paid as calculated at the end of a contract. The figure includes all interim payments and retentions, and the payment due thereunder is the amount outstanding.

final certificate A document recording the completion of a building contract. In straightforward cases, this is issued coincidentally with the certificate of making good defects. Sometimes, however, adjustment to work during the building programme may justify either claims for "extras" or reductions in the contract price. These have to be agreed between the quantity surveyor and the contractor before the architect can issue the final certificate. *See* BUILDING CONTRACT CERTIFICATES.

financial year **1.** Generally, when used for statutes referring to finance (other than taxation), the 12 calendar months from April 1 to March 31. **2.** For the accounts of companies and other bodies, the 12 consecutive calendar months commencing on a fixed date of their choice. *Cf* CALENDAR YEAR; FISCAL YEAR.

finder's fee **1. (UK)** A fee paid to someone who, though not instructed to do so, finds a buyer, a property or a source of finance for a potential client. *See* RUNNER. **2. (USA)** A term sometimes used to signify a payment to an unlicensed person, but generally a finder's fee is considered a commission and may be paid only to one who holds a real estate licence (or similar qualification) and is instrumental in finding a suitable property or finance for a buyer or a prospective purchaser for an owner wishing to sell a property.

fine **1.** A monetary penalty for a criminal offence. **2.** A capital payment by a tenant to the landlord on the grant or renewal of a lease in lieu of or to reduce the rent. *See* PREMIUM.

finishes Coverings, mostly internal, and not forming part of the structural framework of a building.

firebote (fuelbote) Timber that a tenant for life, or for a term of years, may take from the land to keep his house warm.

fire certificate A certificate covering matters of safety required under the Fire Precautions Act 1971 for hotels, boarding houses, factories, offices, shops and railway premises, excluding those buildings containing less than a minimum number of employees (the list being subject to revision by the Secretary of State). In order to obtain a fire certificate, one must apply to a fire officer, who then inspects the building and issues a list of requirements (eg fire doors). Once the fire officer is satisfied that those requirements have been met he will issue the fire certificate. It enables fire officers, in the event of an emergency, to have prior knowledge *inter alia* of the permitted number of people on each floor; it also informs officials of any authorised inflammable/explosive materials on the premises.

fire extinguishing appliances warranty An undertaking by an insured to provide fire extinguishing appliances in the building(s) to which the insurance policy refers, in accordance with specifications laid down by the insurer. If the insured makes such a warranty, a discount may be negotiated in the premium.

fire insurance Insurance against loss or damage to property by fire and which may also cover certain allied risks. The policy can be on a basis of "reinstatement" or "indemnity".

fire officer An official of the local authority, usually a fireman, empowered to inspect buildings to check means of escape arrangements and fire precautions.

Fire Offices Committee A committee appointed by the insurance companies to regulate standards of construction of new buildings or adaptation of existing buildings. The premiums required for insurance cover are calculated accordingly.

fire-resisting construction Work complying with the regulations and standards laid down by the Fire Offices Committee for the construction of new buildings or adaptation of existing buildings.

fire wall A fire-resistant wall built with the object of preventing or delaying the spread of fire from one building, or part of a building, to another.

firm A collective noun for persons who are grouped together in a business partnership. In Scottish law, as distinct from the law in England and Wales, a firm is a legal persona separate and distinct from the partners, who are nevertheless jointly and severally liable for the acts or omissions of the firm as in English law. *Cf* COMPANY.

first floor **1. (UK)** Usually, a complete floor which is immediately above a ground level (floor). *Cf* MEZZANINE. **2. (USA)** Usually, a complete floor at ground level.

first-year allowance *See* CAPITAL ALLOWANCES a.

fiscal year (tax year) The year of assessment for income tax, capital gains tax and inheritance tax. It is the 12 calendar months from April 6 to April 5. *Cf* CALENDAR YEAR; FINANCIAL YEAR.

fish farming Under paragraph 9 of Schedule 5 to the Local Government Finance Act 1988, the breeding or rearing of fish, or the cultivation of shellfish, for the purposes of (or for purposes which include) transferring them to other waters or producing food for human consumption. (Shellfish includes crustaceans and molluscs of any description.) *See* AQUACULTURE; MARICULTURE.

fittings *See* FIXTURES.

fixed assets Tangible but immovable assets, eg land, buildings and heavy plant, which when in use are necessary for the operation of a business, as opposed to current or liquid assets, eg cash or trading stock.

fixed charge A charge where the lender has security for a loan on a particular asset of the borrower. If the borrower defaults the asset can be realised and the proceeds applied to discharge the outstanding debt. *Cf* FLOATING CHARGE.

fixed price contract A building contract in which the total price is fixed at the outset usually subject only to changes due to subsequent variations in statutory undertakers' charges.

fixed rent A rent which cannot be changed during the entire period of a lease or, at the date when the lease is being valued, will be unaltered for such a length of time that no change in capital value would be attributed to the prospect of a different rent during the remainder of the lease. *Cf* VARIABLE RENT.

fixtures Chattels (or in Scotland "movables") which are so affixed or "annexed" to land or a building as to become in fact part thereof, thereby losing their character as chattels (or movables) and passing with the ownership of the land. Whether or not a chattel or movable has become a fixture depends on both the degree and object of annexation. For example, if the article cannot be removed without serious damage to itself or to the land or building to which it is attached, *prima facie* it will be a fixture; however, if the purpose of affixation is to enjoy the article (eg fixing a valuable tapestry to a wall) rather than to benefit the use of the land or building, it may not have become a fixture. Those fixtures which are commonly regarded as easily removable are often described as "fittings"; hence the expression "fixtures and fittings". *See* TENANT'S FIXTURES.

flat A separate set of premises, normally all on the same floor, forming part of a building, divided horizontally from some other part of the building, constructed or adapted for the purposes of a private dwelling and occupied wholly or mainly as a private dwelling.

flat yield *See* APPENDIX IV.

flatted factory An industrial building of more than one storey, usually with two or more goods lifts, and constructed or converted for multiple occupation. The building is sub-divided into small, separately occupied units which are used for manufacturing, assembly and associated storage.

flit (Scotland) The act of a tenant removing himself from a property.

float *See* FLOTATION.

floating charge A charge where the lender has security for a loan spread over all, or a defined class of, the borrower's assets. *Cf* FIXED CHARGE.

flooded market clause A colloquial term for various statutory provisions, particularly for capital taxation, eg Inheritance Tax Act 1984, section 160, which states that in determining open market value the price shall not be assumed to be reduced on the ground that all of the property, eg a sizeable estate, is to be placed on the market at one and the same time. *See* PRUDENT LOTTING.

floor In a building or structure, generally a plane surface, usually horizontal but sometimes inclined, eg in a theatre, which carries furniture, equipment and the like for use by the occupiers. The numbering of floors in a building is not the same in all countries. *See* FIRST FLOOR.

floor area The aggregate superficial area of a building, taking each floor into account. The *RICS/ISVA Code of Measuring Practice* distinguishes the following categories and should be consulted for full details: **1.** Gross external area (GEA) (formerly referred to as "reduced covered area" or "gross floor space"). **2.** Gross internal area (GIA). **3.** Net internal area (NIA).

floor load The live or superimposed load on a floor, usually expressed in pounds per square foot (lb/sq ft) or kilo Newtons per square metre (kN/m^2) (British Standard Code of Practice No 3, Chapter 5, Part I).

floor plan A plan showing the layout of a building, or part of a building, and including particularly the size and disposition of rooms and usually their actual or intended use.

floorspace *See* FLOOR AREA.

floor space index An index introduced to assist in controlling the density of new buildings in a particular area through a ratio of gross floor space to site area plus half the width of any roads which border the property. *Cf* FLOOR AREA; PLOT RATIO.

flotation The first issue to the public of shares by a company in order to raise capital, after which they are quoted on the Stock Exchange and are available for sale/purchase. At least 25% must be issued for an official listing and at least 10% for the Unlisted Securities Market. *See* YELLOW BOOK.

flying freehold A colloquial term for a separate freehold interest in some upper part or parts of a building. (Such interests are rare in England and Wales.)

folly A building or structure erected at the whim of an owner, often at great expense and usually serving no practical purpose.

fooler (USA) A free flow of shoppers which does not result in a high retail turnover and high shop rentals. This phenomenon usually occurs where the pedestrians may otherwise be in a shopping frame of mind but are deterred by such features as inadequate pavements, traffic congestion or, for example, they are passing through a shopping area located between a large car park or bus station and a more attractive pedestrianised shopping precinct. *Cf* RABBIT RUN.

footpath Defined under the Highways Act 1980 as "a highway over which the public have a right of way on foot only, not being a footway . . .".

foot super A unit of measurement commonly used in the building trade when calculating surface (ie superficial) areas of a building, being synonymous with square foot.

footway Defined under the Highways Act 1980 to mean a way comprised in a highway which also comprises a carriageway, being a way over which the public have a right of way on foot only; in other words, a footpath or pavement alongside a public road.

force majeure A force which cannot be resisted: in other words, something beyond the control of the parties involved. It includes acts of God and acts of man, eg riots, strikes, arson. In many contracts, eg building contracts and insurance policies, specific provision is made for damage or injury arising from force majeure. For example, the financial liability of a building contractor for failure to complete by a specified date may be relieved to the extent it was caused by force majeure.

forced sale value Defined in the *RICS Guidance Notes on the Valuation of Assets* as open market value, but with the proviso that the vendor has imposed a time-limit for completion which cannot be regarded as a reasonable period in which to negotiate the sale, taking into account the nature of the property and the state of the market. *See* OPEN MARKET VALUE 2.

foreclose down Where there are two or more mortgages of the same property, the legal principle that a mortgagee bringing an action for foreclosure must make all subsequent mortgagees and the ultimate mortgagor parties to the action and give them the opportunity to redeem the mortgage(s). If they fail to do so by the date prescribed in the court order, all the mortgages concerned are foreclosed. *Cf* "REDEEM UP, FORECLOSE DOWN".

foreclosure 1. (UK) The mortgagee's restricted power to extinguish the mortgagor's right of redemption by transferring the mortgagor's interest in the property to himself, if the mortgagor defaults in paying his dues or in complying with any other terms of the mortgage deed. **2. (USA)** The legal process by which a mortgagee can sell the mortgagor's interest in the property to satisfy the debt: also called "foreclosure sale". Also applied to the extinguishment of a mortgagor's right of redemption. *See* EQUITY OF REDEMPTION.

forecourt An area of land in front of a building or buildings and used for such purposes as retail display, car parking and/or the sale of petrol.

foreshore That part of the sea-shore lying between mean high and mean low tide lines (except in Scotland, where spring tides apply). The presumption is that the foreshore is owned by the Crown, but this may be rebutted by proof of an earlier grant by the Crown. In the Duchies of Cornwall and Lancaster the Crown interest vests in the Duchy concerned.

Forestry Commission A government body, established in 1919, whose principal activities are the development and improvement of afforestation, the production of timber and the promotion of the interests of the forestry industries.

forestry land For capital allowances against income taxation, this means woodlands in the United Kingdom where the profits of occupation are assessed under Schedule D by virtue of the Taxes Act 1988, and any houses or other buildings occupied together with, and wholly or mainly for the purposes of, such woodlands. *See* SCHEDULES.

forfeiture The right of a landlord to retake physical possession of the premises and thus put an end to a lease following the tenant's failure to remedy a breach of covenant. This right may be contained within the lease or the landlord may have it by operation of law. (The lessee has certain rights in equity and under statute to claim relief from forfeiture.) *See* RE-ENTRY.

formal tender A bid made by completing and submitting a tender document. *Cf* INFORMAL TENDER.

formula method A method of valuing gas, electricity or water undertakings for rating purposes: applicable only when statute so prescribes.

forward commitment In property development, an arrangement having the following features:

a an undertaking to make money available to the developer (or other type of entrepreneur) at a determinable future date;
b repayment at the determinable date of debts incurred by the developer in the interim on a specific project; and
c the grant to the provider of the money of either a long-term mortgage secured on the completed project or of an interest therein. *See* FORWARD LETTING/FORWARD SALE; FUNDING.

forward finance Commonly signifies a forward commitment where the money made available, plus accrued interest or agreed charges, is repaid relatively shortly thereafter from the proceeds of sale of either the completed project or an interest therein to a third party. *See* FORWARD LETTING/FORWARD SALE.

forward funding Commonly signifies a forward commitment where the last stage is the grant of a long term mortgage.

forward letting/forward sale An agreement to take a lease of or purchase a new property, or part thereof, made in advance of completion of the development or works on an existing building. Such an arrangement usually eases the securing of finance. (Sometimes called pre-letting or pre-sale.) *See* PRE-LET.

franchise A business in which a franchisor licenses a franchisee to undertake certain business activities, usually under the name of the franchisor. The franchisor may provide:

a initial services, which may include selection of site and premises, fittings, staff training and sales promotion, and
b running services such as bulk purchase of stock.

The franchisee undertakes to pay a capital sum or royalties or both.

franked investment income A revenue distribution which has already been subject to a tax deduction, eg dividends received by one company from another, bearing the appropriate tax credit, both companies being resident in the UK.

fraudulent preference Either the payment of money or the transfer of property by a debtor to one or more of his creditors with a view to putting the recipient(s) in a position of advantage compared with other creditors. If an individual debtor is made bankrupt or a debtor company is liquidated within six months of such a payment or transfer, the transaction is void and the trustee in bankruptcy or the liquidator can recover the money or property.

free and clear Having no liens, ie unencumbered title to real property against which there are no claims, mortgages, voluntary liens or other burdens.

freehold In general parlance this is used as shorthand for the tenure of an estate in fee simple absolute in possession. Strictly speaking, however, freehold includes fee simple, entailed interests (formerly "fee tail") and tenancies for life.

free house A public house where the licensee is free to buy his goods from whomsoever he chooses. *Cf* TIED HOUSE.

free issue *See* CAPITALISATION OF RESERVES.

freeport An enclave within the boundaries of a particular state but treated as being outside the customs territory of that state. Goods may be manufactured, processed and stored within a freeport and subsequently exported without payment of customs duty. In the event of their crossing the boundary of the state, customs duty and other internal taxes are payable.

Friends of the Historic Houses Association A body comprising those (other than owner members) who support the Historic Houses Association; benefits include admission to over 200 historic houses without charge.

front money Money, or drawing rights, made available as initial short-term finance for the development of land. If provided by an institution which is later to provide long-term finance, interest on the front money may be "rolled up" or "warehoused" during development.

frontage (line) The full length of a plot of land or a building measured alongside the road on to which the plot or building fronts. In the case of contiguous buildings individual frontages are usually measured to the middle of any party wall(s). *Cf* BUILDING LINE. *See* RETURN FRONTAGE; SHOP WINDOW DISPLAY.

frontage method A system for valuing land or buildings based upon the length of frontage to a road, street or footpath. *Cf* DIRECT COMPARISON METHOD.

frontager A person who owns or occupies land which abuts a highway, a river or the sea.

froth income A colloquial term for that part (if any) of an income which is above the open market rental value of a property at a particular time.

frustrated contract A contract which will be terminated because of some unforeseen change in circumstances that goes to the root of the agreement and therefore makes satisfactory performance of the contract impossible, eg a contract for the sale of land abroad which is rendered incapable of performance through the outbreak of war.

frustration of contract The ending of a contract by some unforeseen occurrence which makes it impossible (or illegal) to perform or to achieve its main purpose. The frustrating event will normally discharge the contract. Sums already paid can be recovered and those due will cease to be payable, except where a party has already received some valuable benefit from the contract, in which event he must pay a reasonable sum for this.

fuel, feal and divot (Scotland) A servitude giving a right to cut and remove peat for fuel and turf for fences.

full age The age at which a minor reaches majority and becomes an adult in law. As from January 1 1970 this has been 18 years.

full management An arrangement whereby all functions of property management are delegated to a managing agent. It frequently applies to a building or buildings in multiple occupation. *Cf* ACTIVE MANAGEMENT.

full rent **1.** *See* RACK-RENT. **2.** For income taxation (Schedule A, under the Taxes Act 1988, section 24(7)) a rent which ". . . is sufficient, taking one year with another, to defray the costs to the lessor of fulfilling his obligations under the lease and of meeting any expenses of maintenance, repairs, insurance and management of the premises . . . which fall to be borne by him".

full rental value (FRV) The best possible rental that might reasonably be expected in the open market for a particular property at a given time, having regard to the terms of the actual or notional lease, eg responsibility for repairs, rights of assignment or subletting, or basis of review.

full repairing (and insuring) lease (FRI lease) A lease under which the lessee is responsible for the whole cost of repairing and maintaining (and insuring) the property.

funding Although strictly synonymous with financing, this term is usually applied to either of the following arrangements:

a a lender advances part or the whole of the total development costs, ie land and construction costs, fees, etc, and grants a long-term loan secured on the property following its completion or at such date as is determined by reference to the initial agreement, eg when the property has been let or substantially let, or a specific time has elapsed following completion; or

b a potential purchaser similarly advances part or the whole of the total development costs but upon completion, or such other date as is determined by the original agreement, acquires the property at a price calculated by reference to such formula as was embodied therein.

There are variations of this principle, but in all cases the interim finance bears interest at an agreed rate. This may be paid during progress of the development or "rolled up". In the case of an outright purchase, a balancing payment is made to the developer, being the difference between the total sums already advanced (including accrued interest if not paid previously) and the investment value. *See* ROLLED-UP INTEREST; SALE AND LEASE-BACK.

fund in modic (Scotland) Property being the subject of multiple poinding.

furth (Scotland) Beyond the boundaries of; outside.

future estate *See* FUTURE INTEREST.

future interest A right to property not taking immediate effect, eg a reversion or remainder. Under the Law of Property Act 1925, all future interests other than future leases can now exist only as equitable interests.

future lease A lease granting possession to the tenant only from some future date. Under the Law of Property Act 1925 this can qualify as a legal estate but must take effect within 21 years of the date of the lease, or agreement for lease; otherwise it is void. *See* FUTURE INTEREST.

G

gablet *See* GAMBREL ROOF 2.

gale **1.** A periodical payment of rent, from "gavel", a rent or duty. **2.** Grant of a right to work a particular vein of coal or iron in a specific location in the Forest of Dean.

gales of rent *See* GALE 1.

gambrel roof **1. (USA)** A ridged roof,

each side having two slopes, the lower of which is the more steeply inclined. An alternative name for mansard roof. **2. (UK)** A roof having a normal pitch on both sides of a ridge. At each gable end there is a sloping section running up towards the ridge but stopping short of it and becoming a vertical wall. The vertical section is called a gablet or little gable.

game Variously defined in different Acts of Parliament. For example, under the Game Act 1831 the definition encompasses hares, pheasants, partridges, grouse, heath or moor game and black game. There are other definitions in the Night Poaching Act 1828, the Poaching Prevention Act 1862 and the Game Licences Act 1860. *Cf* GROUND GAME. *See* GAME BIRD.

game bird Under section 27 of the Wildlife and Countryside Act 1981: ". . . any pheasant, partridge, grouse (or moor game), black (or heath) game or ptarmigan". For most purposes, game birds are excluded from the definition of "wild birds" under that Act.

garden city A town developed at a relatively low density, intended to combine the advantages of both urban and rural living, self-sufficient in employment, with its own industry, commerce, shops and agriculture, being one of a number of such satellite towns grouped around a central city. The term was first used, by Ebenezer Howard, in 1898 and the concept was first implemented in Letchworth Garden City from 1903.

garden rate (square rate) An additional rate levied by a rating authority (or other person) for the upkeep of a central garden. It is raised from ratepayers of certain properties which overlook that garden.

gavel **1.** A rent or duty. **2.** An auctioneer's hammer.

gavelkind An obsolete tenure, formerly common in Kent and rare elsewhere, by which lands upon intestacy descended from the father to all the sons (or if there were no sons, to all the daughters) in equal portions and not to the eldest child as in primogeniture. There were special provisions for passing half of the estate to a widow for life, so long as she remained chaste and unmarried.

gazebo (belvedere) A light building or structure like a summer house in a garden or attached to a building. The original gazebo was built to provide a small room well above ground level, with a good view of the landscape and sometimes enabling advance warning to be given of approaching stage coaches.

gazumping A situation in which a vendor, having agreed to sell property at a certain price subject to contract, breaks his word and either seeks a higher price from the purchaser on the grounds of having received a higher offer from another or accepts a higher offer from another. *Cf* REVERSE GAZUMPING.

geared leaseback The disposal by a freehold or leasehold owner of his interest in a property in return for an inferior leasehold interest where the rent payable is geared to a fixed percentage of some variable, often rack-rental value.

geared rent A rent which is calculated as a given proportion of:

a the rental value of, or the actual rent(s) received from, the subject property or

b the rental value of a broadly similar property or, less usually, one of a different kind.

The purpose of gearing is often to reflect any capital contribution made by the tenant but may be for some other reason, eg lack of evidence of rents of properties similar in all respects to the subject property, in which event method b will be used.

gearing **1.** Traditionally, the use of borrowed money at fixed rates of interest to improve the annual yield on the equity cash contribution (or equivalent) made by the borrower in an investment. In the case of a property, if the net rental income provides an initial remunerative rate of return higher than the interest paid on borrowed money, the net cash return to the borrower on his own financial contribution is increased above the remunerative rate. When prices for property reflect anticipated growth of rental income, the initial yield (remunerative rate of return) may become lower than the fixed rate of interest payable on borrowed money. A favourably geared investment, based on anticipated future growth of rental value due to inflation, will always be easier to finance if the lending market is reflecting inflation. *Cf* ADVERSE GEARING. **2.** A form of gearing arises in the case of an underleasehold interest where the lessor pays a fixed rent to his landlord for a period longer than that during which the underlessee also pays a fixed rent. When the underlessee's interest terminates, or his rent is subject to review, assuming the rental value has increased, the lessor will be able to secure a higher rent. Thus his net income becomes advantageously geared until such time as the lessor's interest terminates or a rent review becomes operative. A similar outcome arises if the lessor pays his landlord a percentage of the initial rental value but is entitled, on receipt of future rental increases, to retain a higher share of such increases than he receives from the initial rents. **3.** For companies, the ratio between loan capital (eg debentures, mortgages) and equity capital (eg ordinary share stock), usually expressed as a percentage of loan capital to total net asset value. In forecasting the future gearing of a company, regard will be had to the likelihood or otherwise of any rights being exercised to convert loan stock etc into ordinary shares.

Note: Gearing can operate in both directions, ie in a rising market the equity-holder's share rises faster than the market, but in a falling market the reverse happens and the equity-holder suffers. At such time the position of the equity-holder may be safeguarded by degearing where practicable, eg by buying in the loan capital in the market or by an arrangement with the holder of the loan capital. *See* LEVERAGE.

general agent One with authority to act for his principal in all matters of a specified kind or one acting in the course of the agent's usual business or profession. *Cf* SPECIAL AGENT.

General Commissioners Persons appointed by the Lord Chancellor (for England and Wales) or by the Secretary of State for Scotland, with powers conferred on them by the Taxes Act relating to appeals or other matters. *Cf* COMMISSIONERS OF INLAND REVENUE. *See* SPECIAL COMMISSIONERS.

general development order (GDO) A statutory instrument under the Town and Country Planning Acts granting permitted development rights for various specified types of development and setting out certain planning procedures for the control of development *See* PERMITTED DEVELOPMENT.

general improvement area (GIA) An area defined and declared as such by a local authority under section 253 of the Housing Act 1985, and which must be predominantly residential but cannot include — although it may surround — a housing action area. The purpose is to effect or assist in the improvement of the amenities and/or dwellings with a view to environmental development and improvement of the area as a whole.

general rate A charge levied by a rating authority, for the general services provided, on the rateable value of each hereditament in the rating area (other than those specifically exempted). It includes any sums payable collected on behalf of, and paid to, other authorities under precepts issued by them. A rating authority is required to declare a general rate for each rating period, commencing on April 1 or October 1. *See* DIFFERENTIAL RATING.

general vesting declaration A legal procedure used in connection with compulsory purchase whereby an acquiring authority, having obtained a compulsory purchase order, is able to obtain possession and ownership of the land. This is a procedure for the speedy acquisition of land and normal conveyancing practice does not have to be adopted.

gentleman's (gentlemen's) agreement An agreement not legally enforceable but intended to rest on the honour of the parties. Such an agreement cannot create a tenancy (*Rhodes* v *Dalby* (1971)).

gentrification The rehabilitation of a run-down residential area, usually an inner-city area, as a result of better-off people, often young professionals, moving into the area and improving their properties. The term refers both to the physical improvement and to the "upward" change in social mix.

geodimeter An instrument from which readings are taken for the measurement of distance by projecting a light or laser beam to a reflector.

geometrical zoning (arbitrary or arithmetical zoning) A zoning method for the purpose of valuations where the depth of each zone of a shop is determined by convention, based upon the experience of valuers, and applied generally to the shops in an area. *Cf* NATURAL ZONING. *See* HALVING BACK.

gift over A provision in a will or settlement for an interest in property to come about on the termination of an earlier interest.

gilts (gilt-edged securities) Securities where the government guarantees both the interest and the nominal capital sum payable upon redemption. *Cf* BLUE CHIP.

glazing The use of glass as a building material, usually in windows (where the transparent or translucent qualities are essential).

glebe (land) Land attached to a parish church.

global cover The financial protection available under an insurance contract arranged on a "global" basis, whereby insurers will grant cover on all properties owned, leased or occupied by an insured anywhere in the UK (and sometimes extended to other countries), subject to an agreed maximum sum insured.

Goade plans Plans showing the area of a town devoted to retail uses. They contain the names of each retailer and describe the use of each shop unit as well as giving street names, one-way streets, pedestrian areas, service roads and car parks, location of banks, building societies and hotels, road distance from London, details of new developments, vacant properties and sites. They cover most shopping areas in the UK, the Republic of Ireland and parts of France. Produced by and available from C E Goade Ltd, Old Hatfield, Herts.

godown A term used in Asia, particularly in Hong Kong, for a building broadly similar to a flatted factory, ie a multi-storey building subdivided into small units which are used for either manufacturing or storage. Godowns are usually old and rarely, if ever, served by lifts.

going concern value The total value of a business as carried on, with all its assets and liabilities, goodwill and potentialities. If the premises used are owned by the business, they form part of the going concern value on the basis of their value to the business.

gold clause A clause in a lease which provides for the rent to be reviewed by reference to the price of gold.

good consideration (meritorious consideration) In legal terms this generally signifies consideration of an intangible nature, eg natural love and affection or a moral duty. It is insufficient to establish an enforceable contract. *Cf* VALUABLE CONSIDERATION.

good covenant *See* COVENANT 2.

good leasehold title In registered leasehold land, the equivalent of absolute title, except that the landlord's right to grant the lease is not guaranteed, usually because the landlord's title is unregistered.

good marketable title A title entirely free of encumbrances.

good title A title supported by adequate evidence. *See* ROOT OF TITLE.

goodwill In property terms an intangible but marketable asset founded on the probability that customers will continue to resort to the same premises where business is carried on under a particular name, or where goods are sold or services provided under a trade name, with the consequence that there is likely to be a continuing prospect of earning an acceptable profit. However, in some cases goodwill may be wholly or largely personal, depending on the character of the proprietor. Although its value to him may be substantial, if he retires or dies or, on moving, is unable to set up again in the same locality, that value may be lost. On a sale of the premises in such circumstances the goodwill element will be extinguished, except in so far as his customers can be successfully recommended to another person. *Cf* KEY MONEY.

grant deed (USA) A type of deed used to transfer real property where the grantor warrants against having made prior conveyances or encumbrances. When title insurance is purchased, such warranties in a deed may be of little practical significance.

grassum (Scotland) A single payment made in addition to a periodic payment such as rent or feu duty. In England and Wales this would normally be referred to as a premium.

gravity model A mathematical model, often used by retail planners, to estimate turnover at several shopping centres having regard to the fact that all of them are simultaneously giving a choice to prospective customers. Retail spending in a number of residential zones is allocated to centres on the basis of their relative attraction and distance from the residential zones, using a formula analogous to that for gravity in physics. *See* CATCHMENT AREA; REILLY'S LAW OF RETAIL GRAVITATION.

green belt For planning purposes, the name given to an area of rural land surrounding a town, city or conurbation in which development is discouraged, with the object of preserving the rural environment by checking further urban growth and sprawl or the coalescence of adjoining urban areas.

green field site An area of land, usually on the edge of a town or city or away from substantial urban areas, hitherto undeveloped but for which development is now proposed.

Green Paper A paper issued by a government department setting out preliminary proposals on a particular subject and seeking opinions thereon. It is normally made available to the general public through the HMSO and is often the first in a sequence of consultation stages, followed by Yellow Papers and White Papers, prior to the possibility of legislation.

green wedges Areas of agricultural land, woodland or recreational land left or created as part of a planning policy to separate urban neighbourhoods or districts. *Cf* GREEN BELT.

grey property (grey land) A term commonly applied to property surrounded by or adjoining a clearance area, whose acquisition is reasonably necessary for the satisfactory development or use of the cleared area. The special basis of compensation for the acquisition of unfit houses does not apply to such property, which is normally coloured grey on the relevant local authority plans. *Cf* PINK-HATCHED-YELLOW LAND; PINK LAND.

gross *See* IN GROSS.

gross development value (gross realisation) In a residual valuation, the value of the proposed development as though completed at the time of the valuation. *See* RESIDUAL METHOD.

gross external area (GEA) (formerly referred to as "reduced covered area" or "gross floorspace") The aggregate superficial area of a building taking each floor into account. As described in the RICS/ISVA Code of Measuring Practice this includes: external walls and projections; internal walls and partitions; columns, piers, chimney-breasts, stairwells, and lift wells; tank and plant rooms, fuel stores whether or not above main roof level (except for Scotland, where for rating purposes these are excluded); and open-sided covered areas and enclosed car-parking areas; but excludes: open balconies; open fire escapes; open covered ways or minor canopies; open vehicle-parking areas, terraces etc; domestic outside wcs and coalhouses. In calculating GEA, party walls are measured to their centre line, while areas with a headroom of less than 1.5m (5 ft) are excluded and quoted separately.

gross floorspace *See* GROSS EXTERNAL AREA.

gross fund A funding institution not paying corporation tax or any other type of tax on income or capital gains, eg pension funds, friendly societies and registered trade unions, or those unit trusts which restrict the purchase of units to tax-exempt funds.

gross income Income before deduction of any outgoings, for which the recipient is liable, eg for property such items as repairs, insurance and management.

gross internal area (GIA) Measurement of a building on the same basis as gross external area, but excluding external wall thicknesses.

gross leasable area A term sometimes used in relation to managed shopping schemes to correspond broadly with the definition of gross internal area in the RICS/ISVA Code of Measuring Practice.

gross lease A lease which obliges the lessor to meet all or part of the expenses of the leased property, such as taxes, insurances, maintenance, utilities.

gross realisation *See* GROSS DEVELOPMENT VALUE.

gross redemption yield *See* INTERNAL RATE OF RETURN; REDEMPTION YIELD.

gross rent Actual or estimated rent before deduction of outgoings. *Cf* NET INCOME; NET RENT.

gross replacement cost In the valuation of land and buildings in accounting for depreciation this is ". . . the estimated cost of erecting the building or a modern substitute building having the same gross internal area as that existing at prices current at the relevant date. This figure may include fees, finance charges appropriate to the construction period and other associated expenses directly related to the construction of the building". *(RICS Guidance Notes on the Valuation of Assets). See* DEPRECIABLE AMOUNT; NET REPLACEMENT COST.

gross trading profit The total annual turnover or receipts less purchases (adjusted for stock changes as appropriate).

gross value **1.** In rating, defined by section 19(6) of the General Rate Act 1967 as "the rent at which a hereditament might reasonably be expected to let from year to year if the tenant undertook to pay all usual tenant's rates and taxes and the landlord undertook to bear the cost of the repairs and insurance and other expenses, if any, necessary to maintain the hereditament in a state to command that rent". *Cf* NET ANNUAL VALUE; RATEABLE VALUE. **2.** The capital value of a property before making adjustment for acquisition costs.

ground annual (Scotland) An annual payment secured on land. It is akin to a rentcharge in England.

ground game Defined under the Ground Game Act 1880 as meaning hares and rabbits. *Cf* GAME.

ground lease A long lease granted at a ground rent, ie a rent disregarding the value of any buildings on the land but reflecting any right to develop the land with buildings. The tenant may

a be obliged to erect buildings, or
b be permitted (but not required) to erect buildings thereon, or
c be debarred from so doing.

ground rent Rent paid for vacant land which is suitable for development. If the property is improved, ground rent is that portion attributable to the land only but may reflect a right to undertake certain building operations. *Note:* Modern ground leases normally incorporate periodic rent reviews and often the basis of review is an agreed proportion of the rack-rental value (or of rack-rents received) at the date of review. In such circumstances the rent payable on review can be significantly different from the ground rental value of the land for a new development. *See* MODERN GROUND RENT; SECURED GROUND RENT; UNSECURED GROUND RENT.

growth area An area of planned or spontaneous expansion of population over the years ahead.

growth rate The rate at which rents or capital values in a particular market have increased (or declined, "negative growth rate") in the past or are predicted to change in the future. It may be due either to actual or expected changes in supply and demand, ie real change, or to inflation (or deflation) and is usually expressed as an annual percentage from some given time and, probably, over a stated period of years. *See* IMPLIED GROWTH RATE.

guarantee, guaranty An agreement to pay a debt or perform the obligation of another in the event of the debt or action not being paid or performed. There must be a failure to pay or perform before the guarantee can be said to take effect. *Cf* WARRANTY.

guarantor A third party to a contractual relationship who guarantees certain undertakings by a party to the contract, eg that rent will be paid and tenant's covenants performed under the terms of a lease. *See* SURETY.

Gunter's chain A 66-foot chain of 100 links used traditionally by surveyors for measuring land. Invented by Edmund Gunter (1581-1626), the surveyor's chain is now largely superseded by other measuring devices. *See* CHAIN.

H

habendum The clause in a deed, eg of a conveyance or a lease, which follows the granting clause and defines the nature and duration of the estate of the grantee.

hachures *See* HATCHING.

ha-ha A sunken bank or ditch, usually separating a formal garden from surrounding parkland without interrupting the view. Its use is to prevent grazing animals from encroaching on the garden.

Most commonly the level of the garden is above that of the parkland.

half a year In a lease this signifies a fixed term beginning on a quarter day and ending two quarter days later.

halving back A method of applying a unit of rent to the zones of the area of a shop for rental valuation purposes, usually confined to the ground-floor area. The principle is that the most valuable area of a traditional shop is to be found at the front, ie the display area, and that the value then declines with increasing depth. The shop is divided into zones, usually of equal depth, with the value of the first, ie the front zone, being x per annum per sq ft or m^2. Each successive zone is then "halved-back" in value, ie $\frac{x}{2}$, $\frac{x}{4}$, and so on, but where the depth is considerable a large rear zone ("remainder zone") may be valued at a flat rate per sq ft or m^2 without further halving back. If there is a rear or return frontage with direct access and possibly with window displays giving the prospect of additional custom, the value in relation to zoning will be modified. *See* ZONE A VALUE; ZONING METHOD.

harassment Use of violence, abuse, threats and similar behaviour to obtain possession from a tenant. Under the Rent Acts harassment, whether or not followed by unlawful eviction, is a criminal offence.

hardcore method (layer method) A method of valuing (by reference to the hardcore rent) a freehold or other superior interest in property which is subject to a lease (or underlease) followed by a reversion. The hardcore rent, which is relatively secure, can be capitalised into perpetuity (or for the length of the lease) at a lower rate than any "marginal" rent, ie an anticipated or estimated increase in rent upon review, a fixed increase, or reversion. *Cf* TERM AND REVERSION METHOD.

hardcore rent A rent or part of a rent receivable from a property, which is sufficiently secure in relation to rental value to be judged by a valuer as assured. It is therefore reliably predicted to continue for the duration of the interest being valued despite any provision for it to be adjusted at given intervals, eg under a rent review clause. *See* BASE RENT; HARDCORE METHOD.

"Harvey" costs *See* "CRAWLEY" COSTS.

hatching (hachures) Parallel lines, usually drawn at an angle, used in plan-making to delineate specific areas or other features. *See* CROSS HATCHING.

head lease A leasehold interest held directly from the freeholder and subject to one or more underleases in the whole of, or part of, the property. *See* SUBLEASE.

head rent The rent paid by a head lessee to his freeholder.

headroom The minimum uninterrupted space below a ceiling, door lintel or a bridge. It may be measured to the underlying floor, road or general surface or to the top of any plant or other equipment, whether fixed or movable, which is below the ceiling, lintel or bridge.

heads of claim The several categories or titles under which claims may be made, eg in the case of compulsory purchase claims under section 4(2) of the Land Compensation Act 1961, the amounts under such headings as the value of land taken, disturbance and injurious affection.

heads of terms Fundamental points of an agreement intended to form the basis of a formal contract. In a letting these usually include duration of the lease, the initial rent and obligations and rights of the respective parties, such as rights of assignment, subletting, maintenance, insurance and use.

hearsay evidence (second-hand evidence) Evidence originating from the statements (oral or written) of a person other than the witness testifying. Although there is a general rule against the admissibility of hearsay evidence, there are numerous exceptions to this principle, eg in civil cases under the Civil Evidence Acts 1968-72. *Cf* ORIGINAL EVIDENCE.

heave Vertical or lateral movement of the soil. This may be caused by, among other things, geological disturbance, frost, increased moisture content, eg when trees are felled, or by chemical changes. *Cf* SETTLEMENT 3.

hedge Investment with the characteristic that the investor's capital and/or income are to varying degrees protected from loss due to inflation or other causes of price movement from inflationary effects. As with a natural hedge, which reduces the impact of wind and provides shelter, it cannot act as a complete barrier in gale force conditions. The financial crisis throughout the world in the early 1970s uprooted many financial "hedges", as did the one in 1987.

hereditament **1.** Real property. **2.** Under section 115 of the General Rate Act 1967, property which is, or may become, liable to a rate, or a unit of such property which is, or would fall to be, shown as a separate item in the valuation list. *See* CORPOREAL HEREDITAMENT; INCORPOREAL HEREDITAMENT.

hereditament, mixed *See* MIXED HEREDITAMENT.

hereditament, rateable *See* RATEABLE HEREDITAMENT.

heritage body Any of the bodies listed in Schedule 3 to the Inheritance Tax Act 1984, as amended, eg the National Trust, the Historic Churches Preservation Trust and the Nature Conservancy Council. A gift to a heritage body is an exempt transfer of value for inheritance tax purposes.

heritage coast A stretch of coastline which is designated as such jointly by the Countryside Commission (formerly National Parks Commission) and the relevant local planning authority in accordance with the recommendations of DOE Circular 12/72. Subsequently it is subject to conditions of control as part of a long-term national policy for selected coastal areas of outstanding natural beauty. The stewardship of heritage coasts and hinterlands involves careful planning and use of land and requires the co-operation of landowners, farmers, residents, visitors and amenity groups. Currently (March 1988) 37 areas are protected under this scheme and others are planned.

heritage property Property designated as such by the Inland Revenue under section 30 of the Inheritance Tax Act 1984 and including

a pictures, prints, books, manuscripts, works of art, scientific collections and other things not yielding income which appear to the Inland Revenue to be of national, scientific, historic or artistic interest;

b any land of outstanding scenic, historic or scientific interest (in the opinion of the Inland Revenue);

c any building needing special steps for preservation because of its outstanding historic or architectural interest (in the opinion of the Inland Revenue);

d any area of land essential (in the opinion of the Inland Revenue) to protect the character and architecture of a building in category (c);

e any object which in the opinion of the Inland Revenue is historically associated with a building in category (c).

Transfers of all such properties are potentially exempt from inheritance tax, while capital gains tax may be deferred in certain circumstances.

hide **1.** In old English law, a measure of area of land sufficient to support a household being, according to its location, anything from 60 acres to 120 acres in extent. **2.** A structure or place providing concealment for one or more persons from which to observe birds, game or other creatures in their natural habitat.

hierarchy of shopping centres The ranking of centres according to the volume of their retail trade, eg community, neighbourhood, district, subregional and regional shopping centres.

High Court of Justice (Usually abbreviated to the "High Court"). The highest tier of courts of first instance (ie before which an action is first tried). It was created by the Judicature Acts 1873-75 but now derives its constitution from the Supreme Court Act 1981 and is part of the Supreme Court of England and Wales. It is subdivided into three divisions: Queen's Bench, Chancery and Family. Decisions of the High Court are binding on inferior courts but not on the High Court itself and from those decisions appeal lies to the Court of Appeal. *See* PUISNE JUDGE.

high point loading A concentration of abnormally heavy floor-loading at one or more particular places in a building or other structure where extra support may be required.

high-rise building A building of outstanding height compared with the average in one locality. Blocks of flats of five storeys or more have been regarded as "high rise". *Cf* TOWER BLOCK. *See* MULTI-STOREY.

highway Surprisingly, despite the more colloquial meaning of this word as a "main road", it is legally a strip of land over which the general public have a right of passage for those purposes permitted in the particular case. It may be a footpath, bridleway, driftway or carriageway (not necessarily for all forms of vehicle). Ownership of the sub-soil is usually unchanged by the dedication of the surface as a highway. *See* DEDICATION.

highway easement (USA) A right granted, or taken, for the construction, maintenance and operation of a highway. Ordinarily, in the case of a public thoroughfare, the holders of abutting land are assumed to own the underlying land to the centre of the right of way.

Historic Buildings and Monuments Commission for England Popularly known as English Heritage, this body, established under the National Heritage Act 1983, is responsible for securing the preservation of England's architectural and archaeological heritage. It also promotes and manages over 350 monuments and buildings originally maintained by the Secretary of State for the Environment. The commission is largely funded by the government.

Historic Houses Association (HHA) A body which provides its owner-members with advice, services and meetings on the management, insurance, taxation, repair, maintenance and running of their historic houses, gardens and similar properties. *See* FRIENDS OF THE HISTORIC HOUSES ASSOCIATION.

historical cost accounting The traditional accounting convention for the compilation of financial statements on the basis of costs actually incurred by the current owner. Its use can lead to accounts being prepared which do not reflect the underlying value of the assets at the date of the annual accounts. *Cf* CURRENT COST ACCOUNTING.

hi-tech building (high-technology building) Primarily a modern industrial building or easily adaptable older building which is particularly suited to the flexible uses and space needs of business organisations engaged in modern technologies. Such activities usually require more office or laboratory space than a traditional factory and also more sophisticated and adaptable installations for services and communications.

holding 1. The area of land demised to a tenant. 2. The extent of land and/or building(s) occupied by a tenant for the purposes of his business and for which he has security of tenure under Part II of the Landlord and Tenant Act 1954.

holding over Where a tenant remains in possession after the expiration or determination of his tenancy. He first becomes a tenant on sufferance, then a trespasser if he fails to leave on being requested to do so. However, he becomes a tenant at will if the landlord agrees to his remaining in possession and usually becomes a periodic tenant if he offers rent which is accepted. The term cannot be applied to a tenant having security of tenure under Part II of the Landlord and Tenant Act 1954 (business premises), the Rent Acts (residential) or the Agricultural Holdings Acts.

holding period (USA) The period during which a taxpayer owns a capital asset, thereby determining whether there has been a long-term or short-term capital gain for taxation purposes.

holdover *See* EMBLEMENTS

holograph A document, eg a deed or a will, wholly in the handwriting of the person from whom it is issued.

home loss payment Additional compensation to persons displaced from their dwellings as a result of compulsory acquisition. Such persons must qualify for payment under section 29 of the Land Compensation Act 1973 by having occupied the house as their principal residence for at least five years.

hope value The element of open market value of a property in excess of the existing use value, reflecting the prospect of some more valuable future use or development. It takes account of the uncertain nature or extent of such prospects, including the time which would elapse before one could expect planning permission to be obtained or any relevant constraints overcome, so as to enable the more valuable use to be implemented. *See* DEVELOPMENT VALUE; LATENT VALUE.

horizontal slice A term applied where an additional rent is payable to a landlord or each of a legal sequence of landlords, eg freeholder, intermediate lessor, sublessor, if the net rental income from a property is in excess of a sum stated. In such cases a base rent will be paid under the terms of the leases(s) with traditional covenants (other than for rent payments) and the additional rent is usually calculated as some proportion of the extra income. It is also called top slice income. *Cf* VERTICAL SLICE.

"Horn" principle *See* PRINCIPLE OF EQUIVALENCE.

Hoskold factor (USA) A multiplier used to capitalise terminable income, introduced by a Mr Hoskold in the late 19th century, as a basis for undertaking an early system of dual rate valuations.

housebote An allowance of timber which may be cut from a lord's wood for the repair of a house or tenement. It is a common right to a lessee for years or for life. *Cf* ESTOVERS.

House of Lords In its judicial capacity, this is the final court of appeal throughout the UK in both civil and criminal matters. The members of the two appellate committees are known as Lords of Appeal in Ordinary and are presided over by the Lord Chancellor.

housing action area A residential area declared by a housing authority under section 239 of the Housing Act 1985 because living conditions there are unsatisfactory, having regard to social conditions and the physical state of the properties, with the aim of improvement within a five-year period. The authorities are empowered to acquire land, provide, improve or repair housing accommodation and improve the environment with financial assistance from the government.

housing association Defined by section 1(1) of the Housing Associations Act 1985 and section 5(1) of the Housing Act 1985 as "... a society, body of trustees or company — (a) which is established for the purpose of, or amongst whose objects or powers are included those of providing, constructing, improving or managing, or facilitating or encouraging the construction or improvement of, housing accommodation, and (b) which does not trade for profit or whose constitution or rules prohibit the issue of capital with interest or dividend exceeding such rate as may be prescribed by the Treasury, whether with or without differentiation as between share and loan capital ...". *Cf* HOUSING SOCIETY; HOUSING TRUST. *See* HOUSING CORPORATION; SELF-BUILD SOCIETY.

housing authority Defined by section 4 of the Housing Act 1985 as "... a local housing authority, a new town corporation or the Development Board for Rural Wales ...".

housing co-operative Defined by section 27(2) of the Housing Act 1985 as "... a society, company or body of trustees for the time being approved by the Secretary of State for the purposes of this section ...", the latter empowering a local housing authority, with the approval of the Secretary of State, to make agreements for such co-operatives to perform any of the housing authority's duties relating to the provision of housing accommodation on land owned by the authority.

Housing Corporation A body first established by Parliament in 1964 which promotes voluntary, non-profit-making housing associations to provide homes for people most in need. It registers housing associations so that they may receive public funds to build new homes or to renovate older property. It then supervises and controls them to ensure that those funds are properly accounted for and effectively used.

housing society A society registered under the Industrial and Provident Societies Act 1893 which (a) does not trade for profit and (b) is established for the purpose of constructing, improving or managing houses. Generally such houses are to be kept available for letting, but the rules of the society may enable its members to rent or occupy houses provided or managed by the society.

housing trust Defined by both section 2 of the Housing Associations Act 1985 and section 6 of the Housing Act 1985 as "... a corporation or body of persons which — (a) is required by the terms of its constituent instrument to use the whole of its funds, including any surplus which may arise from its operations, for the purpose of providing housing accommodation, or (b) is required by the terms of its constituent instrument to devote the whole, or substantially the whole, of its funds for charitable purposes and in fact uses the whole, or substantially the whole, of its funds for the purpose of providing housing accommodation.". *Cf* HOUSING ASSOCIATION.

humidifier A unit, often part of a heating or air-conditioning system, which raises the relative humidity in a room or building by the emission of water vapour into the air.

hundred per cent location A colloquial appraisal term used particularly in connection with retail property and referring to either land of the highest value in an area or land best suited to a specific use. (Like all superlatives it should be treated with caution — subjective judgments can be wrong and the best today is not necessarily the best tomorrow.)

hypermarket A self-service store (usually single-level) selling a wide range of food and non-food goods with at least 5,000 m^2 trading floorspace, together with ample car-parking facilities. *Cf* SUPERMARKET; SUPERSTORE.

hypothec (Scotland) A right in security over the effects of a debtor valid without possession by the creditor, eg hypothec for rent and feu duty.

hypothetical tenancy An imaginary tenancy which has to be assumed in certain cases in order to ascertain the notional terms and conditions under which premises would be let in order to determine the gross or net annual value for rating purposes or the rent on a rent review.

hypothetical tenant The fictitious tenant holding a hypothetical tenancy or the fictitious assignee of an actual or hypothetical tenancy.

hypothetical use A use, not being the actual use, which is assumed for the purpose of ascertaining the rental value of a property, eg on a rent review.

I

immediate landlord In a chain of interests, eg freeholder, head lessee and occupying tenant, the interest immediately above that of a particular tenant. *See* COMPETENT LANDLORD; INTERMEDIATE LANDLORD; SUPERIOR LANDLORD.

implied covenant A covenant assumed in law to be in a lease even though not expressly included, eg that the tenant of the building maintains it in a tenant-like and proper manner. *Cf* EXPRESS COVENANT.

implied growth rate The annual percentage rate at which the rental income from a specific rack-rented property investment will have to increase (at the relevant dates of rent reviews and reversions) to ensure that the investment matches a selected gross redemption yield (target GRY), thereby justifying the return appropriate at the date of disposal or valuation. For property investment, the yield offered by long-dated, high-coupon, gilt-edged stock is usually taken as the basis for the target GRY. Owing to the inherent disadvantages of property as an investment, eg illiquidity and obsolescence, the target GRY may be, say, 2% above gilts. Different review patterns are reflected by altering the rate, eg if a property is on a seven-year rather than a five-year review pattern, the implied growth rate must be greater in order to match a year-by-year target GRY.

implied notice *See* CONSTRUCTIVE NOTICE.

implied trust (resulting trust) A trust arising either from the presumed (but unexpressed) intention of the settlor or by operation of equity. The term "resulting trust" is more appropriate where this is for the benefit of the original settlor or his estate.

improved ground rent A rent not exceeding the full rental value of the land itself, but greater than the ground rent previously payable under a lease, since the grant of which land values have increased. The term is also applied where the original ground lessee (or his successor):

a creates a ground underlease at a higher rent for development (rather than developing the property himself); or
b wishes to vary covenants or to undertake some work which would otherwise be prohibited by the terms of the lease, thus giving the landlord a right to substitute a higher ground rent reflecting the additional value of the change he permits. *Cf* CREATED GROUND RENT.

improved land (USA) Land having either on-site improvements, off-site improvements or both. *See* IMPROVEMENTS.

improved value (USA) An appraisal term encompassing the total value of land and improvements, eg buildings, rather than the separate value of each.

improvement line A line on a map or plan, prescribed under section 73 of the Highways Act 1980, alongside a street but some distance from it. No buildings may be erected or extended, nor any permanent excavation made, between the improvement line and the highway. The purpose is to provide for eventual road widening. Compensation may be claimed for any injurious affection to property by the prescription of the line. *Cf* BUILDING LINE.

improvement notice A notice issued by a local housing authority under Part VII of the Housing Act 1985 requiring that a dwelling which is below a defined standard is brought up to an acceptable standard. The formal procedure provides that the authority may serve a provisional notice which in default may be followed by an improvement notice with powers of enforcement or the right to undertake the work at the owner's expense. This procedure can be adopted only if the dwelling:

a is in a general improvement area or a housing action area or, failing that,
b having been built or converted before October 3 1961, is the subject of representations by the occupying tenant and the authority agree that it is below the required standard.

improvements Generally, physical changes which enhance the capital value of land or buildings. These may include additional buildings, extensions to existing buildings, installation of new services, eg central heating and air conditioning and infrastructure works. On the other hand, mere replacement by a modern equivalent of something worn out would normally be regarded as a repair rather than an improvement. The distinction has legal and taxation consequences. *Cf* REFURBISHMENT. *See* ON-SITE IMPROVEMENTS; OFF-SITE IMPROVEMENTS; TENANT'S IMPROVEMENTS.

imputed notice Notice given to an agent, when acting as such, and which is therefore "imputed" to his principal. For example, where a purchaser employs a solicitor, any actual or constructive (implied) notice which the solicitor receives relating to the property in question is regarded as having been received by the purchaser.

incentive fee *See* CONTINGENCY FEE.

inclusive rent In essence, and traditionally, a rent payable where the landlord has an obligation to pay the rates. In modern leases, where a landlord is legally responsible for the provision of services paid for by himself, the cost — or part thereof — may be recovered from the tenant either as part of the "rent" or as a separate sum expressed in the lease to be recoverable as "rent". Either way the total sum paid by the tenant has been described as an "inclusive rent", but it is more sensible to confine the use of these words to those cases where the landlord meets the cost throughout the term with no right to adjust the sum he can recover regardless of his proper expenditure. *Cf* EXCLUSIVE RENT.

income (revenue) Earnings received during a given period, eg rents, less outgoings from property, or sales from trade, less expenses. The amounts attributable to each period frequently differ. To the extent that income is not spent on consumable goods or recurring items of expenditure for living purposes, eg rent or rates, the surplus or part thereof may be invested in permanent or durable assets, thus being translated into capital. *Cf* CAPITAL.

income tax An annual or periodic tax assessed on personal incomes derived from one or more sources. The principal Act by which the charges to income tax are established is the Income and Corporation Taxes Act 1988 (amended by the current Finance Act). *See* SCHEDULES.

income tax year *See* YEAR OF ASSESSMENT.

income, terminable *See* TERMINABLE INCOME.

Incorporated Association of Architects and Surveyors (IAAS) This body was established in 1925 to register the professional interests of its members, each of whom was practising as an architect and/or surveyor. One of its objects is to unite, in one body, architects, surveyors and allied professions. Its creation followed a need made apparent by the merger of the RIBA with the Society of Architects and a proposed statutory requirement for registration of the landed professions such as architects and surveyors. Members are required to qualify by examination and to conform to a code of conduct.

Incorporated Society of Valuers and Auctioneers (ISVA) Formed in 1967 by an amalgamation of the Valuers' Institution and the Incorporated Society of Auctioneers and Landed Property Agents, it commenced operations in its present form in April 1968. Membership consists of estate agents, valuers and surveyors and represents a cross-section of persons employed in the profession of the land. Corporate membership is awarded as the result of success in examinations set by the society, coupled with relevant professional experience.

incorporeal hereditament An intangible right over land that does not give the owner present or future physical possession, eg easements, profits à prendre and restrictive covenants.

incremental yield In an incremental yield analysis this is the internal rate of return calculated on the relationship between the present value of both the individual capital inputs and cash flows of the projects under consideration. *See* DISCOUNTED CASH FLOW ANALYSIS.

incremental yield analysis An analytical method in discounted cash flow techniques used to compare the potential of alternative projects. It involves subtracting the present value of anticipated expenditure as discounted according to the risk factor on a smaller project from that of a larger, thereby enabling the incremental return on the difference between the two to be calculated. If this yield exceeds the investor's opportunity cost of capital, then the larger scheme would appear to be the more favourable. *See* DISCOUNTED CASH FLOW ANALYSIS; OPPORTUNITY COST.

incubator building (USA) **1.** A building constructed for the purpose of testing new materials and/or techniques of construction and use. **2.** A building providing low-rent space for manufacturing or other businesses which are in their early stages or with limited operating capital. *See* NURSERY UNIT.

incumbrance *See* ENCUMBRANCE.

indemnity insurance The protection offered by an insurance contract (policy) whereby, on the occurrence of the risk insured against, eg a fire, the insurer will make a payment sufficient to reimburse the financial loss incurred by the insured. Thus the insured party cannot treat insurance as a possible means of securing profit. *Cf* CONTINGENCY INSURANCE.

indemnity period The period under an insurance policy during which the policy holder is entitled to receive compensation for loss, injury or damage arising from an event defined in the policy. *See* CONSEQUENTIAL LOSS OF RENT.

indenture A deed between two or more parties, each party having his own copy. Originally copies were all included on a single document from which each copy was torn or cut along a wavy (indented) line.

independent expert Someone with relevant specialist knowledge who is appointed to resolve a difference between parties, eg as to a rent review or the interpretation of a clause in a lease. He uses his own specialist knowledge in addition to any evidence presented to him. His decision is final and binding on the parties but, unless his contract of appointment provides otherwise, he can be sued by an aggrieved party if his decision is manifestly negligent. *Cf* ARBITRATOR.

independent retail outlet A retail outlet operated by an individual retailer, or by an organisation with fewer than ten branches. *Cf* MULTIPLE RETAIL OUTLET.

independent surveyor An impartial surveyor appointed to resolve a dispute. He may act either as an arbitrator or as an expert, depending upon the terms, express or implied, of the appointment or as implied from the circumstances.

independent valuer **1.** One chosen to make a valuation because it is considered that he can and will act impartially, so that his decision can be relied upon to be unbiased. He may be called upon to adjudicate between parties in dispute or to provide an independent opinion required by, for example, the owner or some other interested person(s). **2.** For the specific purpose of asset valuations, ". . . an External Valuer who has no other recent or foreseeable potential fee earning relationship concerning the subject property apart from the valuation fee and who has disclosed any past or present relationship with any of the interested parties or any previous involvement with the subject property" (*RICS Guidance Notes on the Valuation of Assets*). *Cf* INTERNAL VALUER.

indexation An automatic adjustment to a rate, price or payment in line with variations in a specific index, eg by adjusting the income receivable by reference to the retail price index in order to protect the value of an asset from loss due to the effect of inflation.

indexation allowance A tax relief applicable to capital gains introduced by the Finance Act 1982, as amended by the Finance Act 1985. In effect this gives an owner the benefit of the base value of an asset being adjusted by reference to the retail price index, thereby ensuring he is taxed only on real gains. The allowance applies only since March 1982. Although gains before April 1982 are now exempt from capital gains tax for all disposals on or after 6th (or 1st) April 1988, the indexation allowance is unchanged.

indirect construction costs Costs of a building or works additional to those of labour, machinery and materials. They include the costs of administration, financing, taxes and insurance, loss of interest on money invested and professional fees. *Cf* ON-COSTS.

indirect evidence *See* CIRCUMSTANTIAL EVIDENCE.

industrial building **1.** Defined by the Town and Country Planning (Use Classes for Third Schedule Purposes) Order 1948 in terms now adopted in the definition of "industrial process" in the Use Classes Order 1987 (though the latter includes film, video and sound recording). **2.** In everyday parlance, the meaning is somewhat wider than for planning and extends to buildings used for quarrying and mining and, perhaps, for storage and other uses ancillary to industrial processes. **3.** For the purpose of capital allowances for income taxation, "industrial building or structure" is defined by the Capital Allowances Act 1968, as amended, to mean mills, buildings and structures used for a wide range of activities, including factories; transport, docks, inland navigation, water and electricity undertakings; for the purposes of a "tunnel undertaking" or a "bridge undertaking"; for the storage of goods or materials to be used for the manufacture of other goods or materials, finished goods or materials awaiting delivery; mines, oil wells, etc; or for certain agricultural or fishing purposes.

industrial building allowance (IBA) *See* CAPITAL ALLOWANCES.

industrial development certificate (IDC) A certificate which was issued by the Secretary of State for Trade and Industry under the Town and Country Planning Act 1971 certifying that certain forms of development, broadly speaking the erection of an industrial building of a prescribed class or a change of use of premises from non-industrial to industrial, could be carried out consistently with the proper distribution of industry. These provisions were suspended in 1982, but have now been formally repealed by the Housing and Planning Act 1986, section 48, which came into force on January 7 1987.

industrial improvement area Normally an older industrial or commercial area, declared to be such by a local authority under section 4 of the Schedule to the Inner Urban Areas Act 1978, in which, by making loans and grants, the authority seeks to secure improved amenities and the conversion or improvement of buildings for industrial or commercial purposes.

industrial process Defined by the Town and Country Planning (Use Classes) Order 1987 as meaning: "a process for or incidental to any of the following purposes:

(a) the making of any article (including a ship or vessel, or a film, video or sound recording);
(b) the altering, repairing, maintaining, ornamenting, finishing, cleaning, washing, packing, canning, adapting for sale, breaking up or demolition of any article; or
(c) the getting, dressing or treatment of minerals;

in the course of any trade or business other than agriculture, and other than a use carried out in or adjacent to a mine or quarry;". *See* INDUSTRIAL BUILDING.

inferior court Any court subordinate to the superior courts and whose jurisdiction is limited to a specific area of the country and/or to claims not exceeding a specified size or cases of a specific nature. In England and Wales the inferior civil and criminal courts are the county courts and the magistrates' courts respectively. *Cf* SUPERIOR COURT.

inferior interest Any interest (whether immediate or otherwise) granted out of an interest in land. *Cf* SUPERIOR INTEREST.

inflation-prone yield On an investment, a rate of return which is vulnerable to the effects of inflation. *Cf* INFLATION-RISK-FREE YIELD.

inflation-risk-free yield On an investment, a rate of return which the issuer guarantees or assures will be adjusted upwards at the due dates of payment if, and to the degree that, inflation has reduced the value of money. The extent to which payment is "free" of risk will depend on the status and reliability of the issuer, eg a Government-issued index-linked fund would be virtually risk-free. *Cf* INFLATION-PRONE YIELD.

informal tender Any tender lacking one or more of the characteristics of a formal tender, eg one not based upon a formal tender document. *See* LIMITED TENDER; PRIVATE TENDER.

infrastructure Buildings, structures and apparatus by which services essential to the development and use of land are provided by developers and/or statutory authorities, eg railways, roads, bridges, electricity, gas, water, sewerage and telephone installations.

***in gremio* (Scotland)** In the body of. Any clause or condition or restriction set forth in a deed is said to be *in gremio* of it.

in gross Descriptive of a right which exists independently of land, ie not appendant or appurtenant to it, eg shooting rights or rentcharges.

inherent defect A defect within the structure of a building which was inadvertently "built-in" at the time of design or construction or both.

inheritance tax A duty charged on the property of a deceased person and introduced by section 100 of the Finance Act 1986 to replace capital transfer tax, to which it is broadly similar (except in relation to gifts). NB As from July 2 1986 the Capital Transfer Tax Act 1984 is known as the Inheritance Tax Act 1984. *Cf* ESTATE DUTY.

inhibition One of the means of protecting "minor interests" in land registration, involving an order of the court or Registrar which forbids any dealings with the land, either absolutely or until a certain time or event, and subject to such terms or conditions as the court or Registrar thinks fit. *Cf* CAUTION; RESTRICTION.

initial return (initial yield) In an investment analysis, the initial net income at the date of purchase expressed as a percentage of the purchase price. *Cf* TERM YIELD. *See* REVERSIONARY RETURN.

injunction An order by a court preventing a person from acting or restraining someone from doing or continuing to do some act ("prohibitory injunction"), or directing some positive action ("mandatory injunction"). *See* INTERLOCUTORY INJUNCTION; PERPETUAL INJUNCTION.

injurious affection The diminution in value (actual or anticipated) of an interest in land resulting from the use of statutory powers; this may but need not give entitlement to compensation. Examples of entitlement to compensation include:

a under section 7 of the Compulsory Purchase Act 1965, as amended by section 44 of the Land Compensation Act 1973, compensation is payable where part of the land of an owner is compulsorily acquired and the part not acquired is depreciated in value by what is proposed to be done by way of works on, or use of, the part acquired and to some extent works on land adjoining that acquired;

b under section 10 of the Compulsory Purchase Act 1965, compensation may be payable when no part of the affected land is acquired for the scheme, provided the case comes within the "McCarthy Rules"; and

c under Part I of the 1973 Act, compensation for depreciation in existing use value caused by the use of public works may be claimed, provided this results from one or more of the "physical factors" set out in section 1(2) of the Act. *See* EXISTING USE VALUE.

Inns of Court Situated in London, these are the four self-regulating legal societies: Inner Temple, Middle Temple, Lincoln's Inn and Gray's Inn, to one of which every barrister-at-law must belong. The Inns are governed by "benchers" who enjoy the privilege of confirming admissions to the profession which are necessary for members to practise as advocates or counsel in courts of law. *See* RATING AUTHORITIES.

in personam Against the person. Descriptive of an action against, or a right enforceable against, a specific person or persons, eg the right of a beneficiary against his trustee(s). *Cf* IN REM.

input tax For a taxable person:

a the value added tax charged on the supply to him of any goods or services; and

b the value added tax paid or payable by him on the importation of any goods. *Cf* OUTPUT TAX.

in rem Against the thing. Descriptive of an action or right available against the world at large, eg a right of ownership in property. *Cf* IN PERSONAM.

insider dealing Briefly, where an individual who is connected with a company uses unpublished price-sensitive information in buying or selling shares, either on his own or another's account, to make a profit or to avoid a loss. (Dealing in this way may constitute a criminal offence under the Company Securities (Insider Dealing) Act 1985, as amended.)

insolvency The state of a company or person unable to meet debts at, or within an acceptable time of, the date they are due. Unless wound up or made bankrupt, such company or person may survive with the help of creditors, if they believe that their potential loss can be eliminated or reduced by the business continuing — probably with representatives of the creditors being in charge or alongside the management. *See* RECEIVER.

inspection This has been defined by the RICS (in the context of building society valuations) as: "A visit to, and examination of, a property for the purpose of obtaining information prior to expressing a professional opinion as to its value, state of repair or any other aspect. The extent of the inspection will depend upon its purpose." *See* RE-INSPECTION.

inspector of taxes An officer of the Department of Inland Revenue responsible for making assessments for taxes and investigating irregularities.

institutional investors These are generally taken to include banks, pension funds, insurance companies, unit trusts and investment trusts, which are together commonly referred to in the investment field as the "institutions". *See* FUNDING.

insurable interest A property interest likely to be adversely affected by damage to the property, thereby causing some loss to the owner. Only a person with such an interest may take out an insurance policy on the property, eg owner, purchaser, mortgagee, bailee or trustee.

insurable value (USA) Value of property for insurance purposes. For fire insurance this is based on the value of the property less indestructible parts (land). For title insurance the sale price (market value) is used.

insurance The process whereby one party (the insurer) indemnifies the other party (the insured) against the financial consequences, in whole or in part, of any loss by way of damage or injury suffered by the insured on the occurrence of certain specified perils. *Cf* ASSURANCE. *See* INSURANCE CONTRACT.

insurance contract An agreement between the insurer and the insured specifying the risk(s) against which the insured is protected, the terms upon which the agreement can be enforced, the amount of consideration payable (the premium) and the duration of the policy.

insurance rent A payment equivalent to rent which is made to the landlord under an insurance policy for a specified period during which rent is not recoverable under a lease following partial or total destruction of the demised premises. *See* RENT CESSER CLAUSE.

insurance value An estimate of the sum of money that would normally indemnify the owner if a building or structure is damaged or destroyed. It is usually the cost of reinstatement, allowing for all professional fees and possibly also inflation and other factors, but may be the open market value of the property less the site value.

insured A person who is protected under a policy of insurance.

insurer The individual or corporate body providing protection under an insurance contract.

intensification of use An increase in the degree of use of land or buildings amounting to a material change of use for planning purposes. This may give rise to the need for planning permission or, in the absence of such permission, may result in enforcement action by the local planning authority. If the use falls within a "use class", intensification of that use will not normally involve development requiring planning permission.

interaction of taxes Statutory provisions whereby a taxpayer enjoys relief from double taxation where more than one UK tax arises on the same property transaction or series of transactions. An example may arise on the grant of a short lease at a premium, where there may be an assessment for both revenue and capital gain, in the case of a company by way of corporation tax and in the case of an individual by way of income tax and capital gains tax.

interdict (Scotland) The judicial prohibition issued by a Scottish court, comparable with the English injunction. In an emergency *interim interdict* can be obtained on application *ex parte*.

interest (in property) A right of ownership or some right over land in another's ownership. The term embraces legal estates and legal and equitable interests.

interest, equitable *See* EQUITABLE INTEREST.

interest, legal *See* LEGAL INTEREST.

interest on unpaid compensation In compulsory purchase, the interest that an acquiring authority pays on any outstanding compensation from the date of possession until completion of the conveyance, as provided by section 38 of the Land Compensation Act 1961. The rate of interest is prescribed by the Treasury from time to time.

interim certificate A signed statement (usually one of a series issued periodically, eg monthly) by an architect, surveyor or supervising officer to a contractor for presentation to the client certifying the work carried out under the building contract during the relevant period and requesting payment (less any retention). *See* BUILDING CONTRACT CERTIFICATES.

interim finance rate The rate of interest levied on development costs and expenses (which may or may not include the purchase cost of the land) where finance is made available during the building programme. *Cf* BRIDGING FINANCE.

interim rent Under the Landlord and Tenant Act 1954 Part II, as amended by the Law of Property Act 1969, a temporary rent payable from the date of expiry of the current tenancy (or the application for an interim rent, if later) up to the commencement of the new lease or cessation of possession

interlocutor (Scotland) Strictly, an order or decision of the court short of the final judgment, but in practice applied to any order of the court.

interlocutory injunction A temporary injunction granted by the court to safeguard the plaintiff, pending hearing of the main action. *Cf* PERPETUAL INJUNCTION.

intermediate landlord A lessee who creates a sub-interest in the whole or part of the land or premises demised and to that extent holds an interest between the freeholder or the superior landlord and his own subtenant.

internal drainage board A corporate body comprising elected members drawn from local landowners and occupiers formed to supervise, maintain and improve the drainage of the area. They have extensive powers to effect the works necessary, including compulsory purchase and their right to levy drainage rates from occupiers and owners of land within their district. Their authority is defined in the Land Drainage Acts 1930-1971. *See* OCCUPIERS' DRAINAGE RATE; OWNERS' DRAINAGE RATE.

internal rate of return (IRR) (money weighted rate of return) **1.** The rate of interest (expressed as a percentage) at which all future cash flows (positive and negative) must be discounted in order that the net present value of those cash flows should be equal to zero. It is found by trial and error by applying present values at different rates of interest in turn to the net cash flow. It is sometimes called the discounted cash flow rate of return. **2.** An alternative explanation might be: the highest rate of interest (expressed as a percentage) at which an investment can be funded if the cash flow generated is to be sufficient to repay the original outlay at the end of the project life. *See* REDEMPTION YIELD; OPPORTUNITY COST.

internal repairing lease A lease under which all or some internal (but no external) repairs are the responsibility of the tenant. The extent to which external repairs are the responsibility of the landlord depends upon the wording of the lease. *Cf* FULL REPAIRING (AND INSURING) LEASE.

internal valuer In asset valuations, a "... qualified valuer who is a director (or equivalent status thereto) or an employee and who has no significant financial interest in the company or organisation" (*RICS Guidance Notes on the Valuation of Assets*). *Cf* EXTERNAL VALUER; INDEPENDENT VALUER 2.

International Council of Shopping Centers (ICSC) A non-profit-making trade association, based in New York, which represents and promotes the activities of shopping centres in over 40 countries. Its membership comprises shopping centre owners, surveyors, developers and managers, as well as architects, attorneys, contractors and others. It publishes a monthly magazine and organises conferences worldwide.

International Real Estate Federation (Fédération Internationale des Professions Immobilières) Commonly called FIABCI, being the initials of its original title: "Fédération Internationale des Administrateurs de Biens Conseils Immobiliers", it was founded in 1951 in Paris and now (1988) has 44 member countries, each with a national chapter, and 17 corresponding countries. A British Chapter was founded in 1962 and is sponsored by the RICS. The federation's objects are:

- a to promote the competence, professional conduct and organisation of the real estate profession;
- b to collect and disseminate information of professional interest;
- c to consider the major problems confronting the profession in the various countries, with a view to finding broad solutions; and
- d to safeguard the interests of members and to strengthen and extend the influence of the profession.

inter vivos Between living persons.

intestacy, rules of *See* RULES OF INTESTACY.

intestate **1.** Not having made a valid will. **2.** Not disposed of by will. **3.** A person who dies without making a will. *See* RULES OF INTESTACY.

in the market **1.** Property (or other commodity) which is currently for sale or to let (or hire). **2.** Descriptive of a person wishing to buy or rent a certain type of property.

intra vires Literally "within the powers". Descriptive of a company, public authority or other body acting within the powers granted to it by memorandum of association, statute or other enabling document. *Cf* ULTRA VIRES.

inverse condemnation (USA) A procedure for claiming compensation for loss of value to a property resulting from works or activities carried out by a public authority. The property is condemned to the extent of such loss and just compensation must be paid to its owners. *Cf* INJURIOUS AFFECTION.

investment **1.** Using a capital sum, other than for the purpose of trade, to acquire an asset which will, hopefully, produce an acceptable flow of income and/or appreciate in capital value. **2.** An asset acquired by the process described in 1. above. *Cf* TRADE. *See* BADGES OF TRADE.

investment company Defined for tax purposes in section 103 of the Taxes Act 1988 as meaning: ". . . any company whose business consists wholly or mainly in the making of investments and the principal part of whose income is derived therefrom, but includes any savings bank or other bank for savings except any which, for the purposes of the Trustee Savings Bank Act 1985, is a successor or a further successor to a trustee savings bank." *Cf* TRADING COMPANY. *See* BADGES OF TRADE; INVESTMENT PROPERTY.

investment method The determination of the value of an interest in land by the capitalisation of actual or estimated net rental income. The choice of yield is made by comparison with such other investments as bear the nearest relationship in such matters as the physical characteristics, use, degree of risk and life of the investment. *See* YEARS' PURCHASE.

investment property Generally, any property purchased with the primary intention of retaining it and enjoying the total return, ie income and/or capital appreciation, over the life of the interest acquired. The net income from investment property is subject to income tax or corporation tax under Schedule A or Schedule D Case VI. *Cf* DEALER IN LAND. *See* BADGES OF TRADE; INVESTMENT COMPANY.

investment trust company A public corporate body registered under the Companies Acts and having for its main purpose the investment of shareholders' funds in the shares of other companies, to that extent being unique. Thus investors with small cash resources can spread their risks over a considerable range of shares, knowing the entire portfolio is under specialist management. Before such a trust company can be established, the Inland Revenue must be satisfied that:

a it is resident in the United Kingdom and must not be a "close" company;
b its income is derived wholly or mainly from shares and securities;
c it does not invest more than 15% of its assets in the shares and securities of any one company, but investment in other approved investment trusts is not restricted;
d all its ordinary share capital is quoted on the UK Stock Exchange;
e its articles prohibit the distribution by way of dividend of any surplus realised on the sale of assets; and
f it does not retain more than 15% of the income received each year from its investment in shares and securities.

The practical application of these requirements is affected by a number of important qualifications and interpretations. Unlike a unit trust, which is open-ended, an investment trust company is a closed-end fund, ie the ordinary capital is fixed to the same extent as any other public limited company. The investment trust company is exempt from paying tax on the capital gains made within its funds. The shares of such trusts offer those who invest small amounts a chance to benefit from the lower risks associated with larger investment portfolios.

investment yield The annual percentage return which is considered to be appropriate for a specific valuation or an investment, being expressed as the ratio of annual net income (actual or estimated) to the capital value. It is therefore a measure of an investor's opinion about the prospects and risks attached to that investment. The better the prospects and the lower the risks, the lower the expected yield and thus the greater the capital value. The required yield from an investment is estimated in the light of such factors as:

a the security in real terms of the capital invested;
b the security in real terms and regularity of the income;
c the ability to adjust the income to reflect market conditions;
d the complexity and cost of management;
e the ease and likely cost of realising the capital; and
f the tax position.

Cf RETURN (ON CAPITAL).

investor in land A person who acquires land with the view to holding it indefinitely for a return in the form of rent and/or long term capital appreciation. *Cf* DEALER IN LAND. *See* BADGES OF TRADE.

irritancy (Scotland) A right to terminate a contractual relationship in consequence of neglect or contravention. It may be *legal* (implied by law) or *conventional* (result of agreement).

ish (Scotland) The termination, usually of a lease.

isochrone A line on a plan joining points from which it will take an equal time to reach a shopping (or other) centre on foot or by use of a given mode of transport. The usefulness of such lines depends on the skill of the originator in choosing points at suitable and doubtless variable intervals ensuring that, by and large, people living or working between the line and the centre can reach the centre within the time stated.

isoval On a plan or map, a line which passes over land or properties of equal value. When a plan of this nature is completed the isovals drawn thereon will resemble contour lines on an Ordnance Survey plan. It is essential to know the base of values selected for the isovals on these "value maps", eg land value, net rental value or rateable value; each being calculated according to a stated unit of area of land or building.

iter (Scotland) An easement which allows one to pass over another's land.

J

JCT Contract A standard form of building contract created and published by the Joint Contracts Tribunal, not however being a statutory document but the most widely used of several "standard" forms of building contract.

joint agent One of two or more agents jointly instructed by a principal to act on his behalf. In the case of estate agents this is normally on the basis that if any one of the agents effects the sale, letting or other disposition of the property, being the subject of the principal's instructions, the other joint agent(s) will share the remuneration in agreed proportions. None of these agents would be entitled to a commission if the transaction is concluded as a result of someone else's introduction. *Cf* JOINT SOLE AGENT.

joint and several obligation An obligation entered into by two or more persons under which each person is liable severally (individually), as well as jointly with the others. *Cf* JOINT OBLIGATION.

joint board A board representing two or more bodies, eg local authorities; such boards may be created under statute by order of a Minister. They may be concerned with planning, education, public health functions, burial or other matters.

Joint Contracts Tribunal A group of people representing various interested professionals, including contractors, architects, surveyors and representatives of local government, in order to publish a standard form of building contract. *See* JCT CONTRACT.

joint development company A company formed by two or more parties to develop or redevelop a site for their mutual benefit as shareholders of the company. *See* JOINT VENTURE.

jointly and severally *See* JOINT AND SEVERAL OBLIGATION.

joint mortgage **1.** A mortgage undertaken by two or more mortgagors, being a joint obligation of all of them. **2.** Less commonly, another term for a syndicated loan, ie where there are two or more mortgagees.

joint obligation An obligation entered into by two or more persons so that in the event of litigation all must sue or be sued together. *Cf* JOINT AND SEVERAL OBLIGATION.

joint ownership *See* CO-OWNERSHIP.

joint planning board Constituted under section 1 of and Schedule 1 to the Town and Country Planning Act 1971, the special local planning authority for parts of the areas of two or more local planning authorities, where considered expedient by the Secretary of State. Joint planning boards in England are currently (1988) the Peak Park Joint Planning Board and the Lake District Special Planning Board.

joint sole agent One of two or more agents jointly instructed as the only agents entitled to represent the principal. It is customary for the joint agents to share any commission earned on an agreed basis, irrespective of which agent effects the sale or letting. *Cf* JOINT AGENT. *See* SOLE AGENT.

joint tenancy A form of joint ownership having four requisites (known as the "four unities") namely:

a possession, each tenant being entitled to the whole land;
b interest, each having the same estate or interest;
c title, each holding under the same instrument and
d time, each holding for the same duration of the estate or interest.

On the death of a tenant his share passes to the surviving tenants until eventually all the shares are vested in the sole surviving tenant. Joint tenants take equal shares of the rents and profits of the land. *Cf* TENANCY IN COMMON. *See* JOINTURE; SURVIVORSHIP.

jointure Originally a term referring to the holding of an estate by a husband and wife as joint tenants under a grant made before the marriage but currently meaning provision for the maintenance of a widow, eg an annuity secured on heritable property as a provision for a wife against her widowhood.

joint valuers Generally and, in particular, for asset valuations, where ". . . two (or more) valuers are jointly (and severally) appointed to provide a valuation". (*RICS Guidance Notes on the Valuation of Assets*.)

joint venture An association of two or more individuals or bodies to carry on a single business enterprise for profit, for which purpose they contribute property, money, effects, skill and/or knowledge. *See* JOINT DEVELOPMENT COMPANY.

judge A public officer appointed to hear and adjudicate on causes in a court of justice. The following abbreviations are used in law reporting in England and Wales: Lord Chancellor — LC; Lord of Appeal in Ordinary — Lord X; Lord Chief Justice — CJ; Master of the Rolls — MR; President (of the Family Division of the High Court) — P; Vice-Chancellor — V-C; Lord Justice of Appeal — LJ, plural LJJ; Judge of the High Court — J, plural JJ. Northern Ireland has its own Lord Chief Justice, Lord Justices of Appeal and Judges of the High Court; the same abbreviations are used. Scotland's most senior judges are the Lord President and Lord Justice General (one post) and Lord Justice-Clerk. Abbreviations are not used in Scottish law reporting.

judicial foreclosure (USA) Foreclosure through court action rather than by a power of sale. Judicial foreclosure is sometimes necessary to remove certain tax liens.

judicial sale (USA) Sale of real property pursuant to a court order in a foreclosure proceeding, with the proceeds going to satisfy a mortgage debt and any balance being returned to the owner.

judicial trustee A trustee appointed by the court under the Judicial Trustee Act 1906 as sole or co-trustee, being an officer of the court and subject to its control.

junior mortgage (USA) A second or subsequent mortgage, where the mortgagee, on default of the mortgagor, ranks after more senior mortgagees and takes repayment out of the residue after the senior mortgagees have been satisfied.

jurat **1. (USA)** The certificate of an officer, such as a public notary, before whom a statement in writing was sworn to. **2.** That part of an affidavit stating where, when and before whom the affidavit was sworn.

jurisdiction **1.** A court or tribunal's power to hear and decide an action, dispute or issue. **2.** The geographical area within which their judgments or orders may be enforced.

jus quaesitum tertio **(Scotland)** The right of a third party to sue arising out of a contract between two other parties.

K

Kelly's Post Office Directories Annual directories including street-by-street guides to businesses and professional occupiers in London and some other major towns.

key money **1.** That part of the capital price obtained for the freehold or lease of a shop excluding the value of any goodwill but which is additional to the sum of the capitalised value of the estimated profit rental and of the value of any shopfittings of use to the ingoing occupier. **2.** The term also applies to certain payments unlawfully demanded from incoming tenants by outgoing tenants or by landlords of residential property protected by the Rent Acts. *Cf* PREMIUM.

key property In land assembly, a property which is required in order to achieve the optimum development scheme, eg land which provides access to back-land, so unlocking the latter's development potential.

key tenant *See* ANCHOR TENANT(S).

key trader *See* ANCHOR TENANT(S).

key worker A person whose skill and experience is so essential to a business that he cannot readily be replaced. In the compulsory purchase of premises involving the relocation of a business employing key workers, the reasonable cost of their removal and other expenses incurred as a result of the move may form a valid item of claim.

kiosk A small enclosed retail outlet, normally without toilet facilities and occupying less than 15 m^2 of retail floorspace, frequently located on a public concourse or other place where it may remain open only during peak times and be closed securely when there are no customers. Kiosks are now sometimes included in managed shopping schemes.

kissing gate Seemingly romantic, but merely a swing gate without a latch hung within a U- or V-shaped aperture in a fence or wall; designed to exclude animals and vehicles.

knacker In a property context, a dealer who buys old houses for the materials which he can sell-on.

knock-out agreement *See* RING.

know-how **1.** Under section 533(7) of the Income and Corporation Taxes Act 1988, ". . . any industrial information and techniques likely to assist in the manufacture or processing of goods or materials, or in the working of a mine, oil well or other source of mineral deposits (including the searching for, discovery, or testing of deposits or the winning of access thereto), or in the carrying out of any agricultural, forestry or fishing operations." The cost of acquisition of know-how may be eligible for a writing-down allowance. *See* CAPITAL ALLOWANCES. **2.** Generally, knowledge acquired by education, training and experience, thus enabling more reliable decisions to be taken.

L

laches Negligence or unreasonable delay in enforcing a right. An equitable remedy may be refused in the case of a stale demand where a party has "slept on his rights" and thereby acquiesced in the infringement thereof for what is considered by the court to be an excessive length of time. (The word is singular, not plural.)

Lady Day The Feast of the Annunciation: March 25, an English quarter day.

Lammas August 1, a Scottish quarter day.

land assembly The process of forming a single site from a number of parcels of land, usually for eventual development or redevelopment. This will include acquisition of the individual interests, removal or discharge of any restrictive covenants or other encumbrances and obtaining physical possession, when required, from occupiers.

Land Authority for Wales Originally set up under the Community Land Act 1975, a body empowered by Part XII of the Local Government, Planning and Land Act 1980 to acquire land in Wales suitable for development, to execute infrastructure works and to dispose of the land to other persons for development by them.

land availability study A study carried out to discover land available, eg for development. It may be made by developers, surveyors, local planning authorities or other interested parties. Strictly speaking only land which is currently available, and where no obstacles or impediments to the proposed use or development exist, should be considered. However, the term is also used for studies aiming to identify land which may become available within a predetermined period, and these usually describe any action required to make the land available with vacant possession, with advice, where appropriate, upon the likelihood of securing planning and other approvals.

land bank A stock of land held by a builder or developer for future development.

land certificate A certificate issued by the Land Registry to the proprietor of a parcel of land as proof of ownership and containing full details of the registered title. *Cf* TITLE DEEDS.

land charge A burden imposed upon land which creates a third party right or interest in the land, especially one which has to be registered prior to the disposal of the servient (ie affected) land in order to be enforceable against a purchaser for value of that land. Examples of registrable charges are mortgages, contracts to buy or lease land, restrictive covenants and equitable easements. Registration where appropriate should be in:

a the *land charges register* under the Land Charges Act 1972 (for unregistered land);
b the *charges register* of the Land Registry (for registered land);
c the *local land charges register* (for both unregistered and registered land) in respect of local land charges, ie those in favour of a local authority using its statutory powers.

land charges register A register for those land charges imposed upon unregistered land. It is one of the registers maintained by the Land Charges Department of the Land Registry under the Land Charges Act 1972. It should therefore be inspected by or on behalf of an intending purchaser of such land before completion. *Cf* LAND REGISTER.

Land Commission A body created by the Land Commission Act 1967, but abolished in 1971, to acquire, manage and dispose of land on behalf of the community where it was felt that the community had contributed to the value of the land and should benefit from its profits.

land drainage Any system installed in land with a view to draining it of surface or underground water. *See* OCCUPIER'S DRAINAGE RATE; OWNER'S DRAINAGE RATE.

Land Improvement Company Formed by Act of Parliament in 1853, this company exists to provide long-term loans for capital improvements to estates and farms, subject to the approval of the Ministry of Agriculture, Fisheries and Food.

landlord The owner of an interest in land who, in consideration of a rent or other payment (eg a premium), grants the right to exclusive possession of the whole or part of his land to another person for a specific or determinable period by way of a lease or tenancy. *See* TENANT.

landlord's fixtures Chattels attached to premises in such a manner as to become legally part of the freehold. They may not be removed by the tenant. *Cf* TENANT'S FIXTURES. *See* FIXTURES.

landlord's improvements Any work of a capital nature, ie other than maintenance or repair, undertaken by the landlord, or by the tenant at the landlord's expense, which increases the value of the landlord's interest in a property. *See* IMPROVEMENTS.

land register **1.** The register of land interests and title which is kept by the Land Registry. It is in three parts: the property register; the proprietorship register and the charges register. Access to individual entries on the register is currently restricted to the owner of the land concerned or someone authorised by him but under the Land Registration Act 1988 the register is to be open to viewing by members of the public as from a date to be appointed. *Cf* LAND CHARGES REGISTER. **2.** A record of specified details of publicly owned sites which are not being used for the purposes of the performance of any public body's functions or the carrying on of their undertaking. There are restrictions on areas of land to be registered and provision for the authority to explain the reasons why the land is lying idle and its future expected use. A register is prepared by the Secretary of State for the Environment for each district or London Borough which he has designated for this purpose under Part X of the Local Government, Planning and Land Act 1980.

land registration The process of recording details of land and its ownership on a register. The system of registration of title in England and Wales, originally introduced on a voluntary basis, has been varied to the extent that it is now compulsory in many areas, whilst the voluntary system was continued in others but has been suspended. The intention is that registration will become compulsory throughout both countries before the end of the century.

Land Registry The government body, first set up in 1862, to simplify conveyancing by maintaining a "land register" recording details of interests in land and guaranteeing the validity of the titles registered. Its organisation comprises a head office in London and a number of regional offices. *See* LAND CHARGE.

Lands Tribunal A tribunal for England and Wales set up under the Lands Tribunal Act 1949 and proceeding in accordance with rules made by the Lord Chancellor. Its jurisdiction includes adjudication on disputed compensation for the compulsory acquisition of land, compensation for injury and loss for which entitlement accrues under the Town and Country Planning Act 1971, certain capital assessments of land made by the Commissioners of Inland Revenue, rating appeals from local valuation courts, leasehold reform appeals from leasehold valuation tribunals, discharge or modification of restrictive covenants and registration of notional obstruction of light. The tribunal comprises the President (who must be a barrister or have held judicial office) and members who are all either legally qualified or experienced in valuation. The tribunal also deals with references by agreement involving the valuation of land. A similar tribunal has been established for each of Scotland and Northern Ireland.

latent damage In the property sense, damage to a building or structure which exists at the time a person acquired an interest therein, and is of such a nature that it cannot be known to the person concerned, or his adviser, by the normal process of inspection and examination. Eg a purchaser who could not be expected to realise the damage existed, whether with the help of expert advice or not, may in certain circumstances have a right to claim damages from a previous owner or from the party responsible for the damage if negligence can be proved. Rights to pursue any action for negligence in such cases are governed by the provisions of the Latent Damage Act 1986.

latent defect A hidden or concealed defect inherent in the design or construction of a building, which could not be discovered by inspection, despite reasonable care.

latent value An increment of value which is realisable in full only on some future event such as the marriage of sites, grant of planning permission, provision of infrastructure, or securing vacant possession.

law agent (Scotland) A term once commonly used for solicitor or writer. The English word "solicitor" is now generally used.

law day (USA) **1.** The day (date) in a note, mortgage etc, when the debt is to be paid. **2.** A holiday honouring the law and legal profession.

lawful use A use of land which:

a was begun with the benefit of planning permission (either express or deemed) and continues to accord with the terms of that permission;

b was begun before July 1 1948 and has since continued without abandonment or extinguishment;

c was the normal use before July 1 1948, where the land was temporarily used for another purpose at the date but the normal use was resumed before December 6 1968;

d was the last use of the land before July 1 1948, where the land was unoccupied at that date but the use was resumed before December 6 1968;

e is a use resumed following the implementation and subsequent expiry of a temporary planning permission for a material change of use;

f is a use resumed following the implementation of a permission granted by a development order subject to a limitation;

g is a formerly lawful use resumed following enforcement action.

law report A report of a court case regarded as of general or special interest and containing a reference to the relevant facts and a summary of the judgment and sometimes also the verbatim judgment. (A list of the principal published reports concerning property matters is contained in Appendix III.)

layer method *See* HARDCORE METHOD.

layout **1.** The external and/or internal arrangement of a building or group of buildings or other structures. **2.** The plans (drawings) showing such an arrangement, possibly including roads, paths and other physical features.

leap year A calendar year of 366 days occurring once every four years (except for the last year in each century, eg the year 2000).

lease **1.** The grant, subject to consideration, of a right to the exclusive possession of land for a definite period (or one capable of definition) which is less than that held by the grantor. **2.** The right so granted, ie the leasehold estate. **3.** The document granting the right. In practice, the term "lease" is usually reserved for a lease under seal (a statutory requirement for a term of more than three years from the date of the grant). *Cf* LICENCE. *See* TENANCY AGREEMENT.

lease, occupational *See* OCCUPATIONAL LEASE.

lease, participating *See* SIDE BY SIDE LEASE.

leaseback *See* SALE AND LEASEBACK.

lease for life A lease under which land is held for the life of the lessee or another. *See* LIFE TENANCY.

leasehold An estate in land held for a "term certain" or on a periodic tenancy. *See* LEASE.

leasehold enfranchisement **1.** The act of a lessee in acquiring one or more superior interests, principally the freehold estate. **2.** The statutory power of a qualified residential lessee under the Leasehold Reform Act 1967 to acquire the freehold and intermediate interests in the house occupied.

leasehold improvements (USA) Improvements made by the lessee. *See* TENANT'S IMPROVEMENTS.

leasehold reform This term includes the statutory right of a qualified lessee both to enfranchisement and to an extended lease at a modern ground rent under the Leasehold Reform Act 1967. *See* LEASEHOLD ENFRANCHISEMENT 2.

leasehold valuation tribunal One of the tribunals set up under the Housing Act 1980 to decide on the following matters under the Leasehold Reform Act 1967 where landlord and tenant cannot agree: the price payable where the property is enfranchised (section 9); the amount of rent payable under an extended lease (section 15(2)), and the amount of any compensation payable to a tenant whose landlord exercises overriding rights (sections 17 and 18). The members of a tribunal are drawn from the local rent assessment panel. There is a right of appeal to the Lands Tribunal.

legal charge A statutory form of legal mortgage, first created under the Law of Property Act 1925, and of a simpler and shorter nature than a mortgage by demise. There is no conveyance of estate to the mortgagee under such a charge.

legal estate Under the Law of Property Act 1925, this means either a fee simple absolute in possession or a term of years absolute. No other legal estates can now subsist.

legal interest Often, although erroneously, used synonymously with legal estate but should be confined to one of those rights over another's land which are held either for a fee simple absolute in possession or for a term of years absolute, eg easements, rentcharges and charges by way of legal mortgage. *Cf* EQUITABLE INTEREST.

legal memory For the purpose of legal evidence, eg for the establishment of such matters as lawful ownership or rights, the earliest date to which "memory" can be applied. In 1275 this was arbitrarily fixed at the date of the accession of Richard I in 1189, and has never been changed. *Cf* LIVING MEMORY; TIME IMMEMORIAL.

legal mortgage A mortgage created either:

a by a "charge by way of legal mortgage", or
b by demise, ie the grant of a lease, eg for 3,000 years, for freehold property or, in the case of leaseholds, by a sublease for a term slightly shorter than that held by the mortgagor.

Cf EQUITABLE MORTGAGE.

legal remedies Those remedies available under the common law for redressing a wrong by judicial process, eg damages. *Cf* EQUITABLE REMEDIES.

lessee The grantee of a lease. *See* TENANT.

lessor The grantor of a lease. *See* LANDLORD.

let **1.** To grant a lease or tenancy, especially a short tenancy. **2.** To award a building contract.

letter of attornment On the sale of property, a letter from the vendor or his agent to the tenants advising them of the sale and directing that from a given date rent and other charges due be paid to the purchaser or such other person as may be stated in the notice. *See* ATTORNMENT.

letter of comfort A letter from a third party to one of the parties to a contract giving an assurance that the recipient may expect the other party to, for example, honour some specified undertaking given in the contract, behave in a manner consistent with the understanding between the parties, be in a position to finance the deal or continue in existence as a subsidiary of the author. In property terms, in particular, such a letter may be written by a bank or other financial institution on behalf of a prospective developer, purchaser or lessee. The purpose is to give confidence to the recipient that the other party will have the resources to complete the contract or in other respects may be relied upon to act in accordance with what is promised. Whether such a letter will be legally binding as distinct from giving the author a moral responsibility depends upon the circumstances of each case. There are no general rules which can be applied. *Cf* LETTER OF INTENT.

letter of intent A term similar to but distinguishable from a letter of comfort — with which it is often confused — in that it is written by one party to a contract to the other party as a type of "side letter". *Cf* LETTER OF COMFORT.

letting value **1.** Rental value. **2.** For the purposes of section 15(2) of the Leasehold Reform Act 1967, the value of the relevant site at a given time ". . . (without including anything for the value of buildings on the site) for the uses to which the house and premises have been put since the commencement of the existing tenancy . . ." with certain exceptions.

leverage (USA) The use of borrowed money at a rate of interest below the remunerative rate enabling the borrower to achieve an initial return on the residual equity which is larger than it would otherwise be, plus the hopeful prospect of a disproportionately high participation in growth income over the years ahead. The borrower accepts the risks involved if his forecast is incorrect, since the security is primarily for the benefit of and to protect the lender. *See* GEARING.

lex loci The law of the place.

lex loci actus The law of the place where a legal act takes place.

lex loci contractus The law of the place where a contract is made.

lex loci rei sitae (lex loci situs) The law of the place where the asset in question happens to be. This is relevant in circumstances such as the succession to immovable property on intestacy, when the law applicable will be that of the country in which the property is located even if the deceased owner was living outside the jurisdiction of that country.

lex loci solutionis The law of the place where a contract is to be performed.

ley Farmland on which grass is grown temporarily. Where this is alternated with other crops, it is known as ley farming.

LIBID (London interbank bid rate) The rate a bank will receive if it goes to the market with funds for deposit overnight. *Cf* LIBOR.

LIBOR (London interbank offer(ed) rate) The rate of interest at which the first-class banks in London lend to one another in the open market. The rate will be influenced by the duration of the loan. *Cf* LIBID.

licence The lawful grant of a right to do something which would otherwise be illegal or wrongful. It may be gratuitous, contractual or coupled with an interest in land. The grantor of a licence is the licensor and the grantee is the licensee. A gratuitous ("mere" or "bare") licence can always be revoked (ie cancelled), but revocability of a contractual licence depends on the terms of the contract. A licence coupled with an interest in land may be irrevocable and, unlike the other two categories, may be binding on successors in title of the licensor. One example of a licence is permission, usually required in writing, given specifically by an owner to a tenant, enabling something to be done which otherwise would be in breach of a term of the lease. A licence does not of itself transfer any interest in the land but may authorise the licensee to enter the licensor's land for some specific purpose, eg market trading. It differs from a tenancy in that the licensee does not have paramount control of the land and may only enter thereupon for the purposes of the licence; the licensor may enter the land and use it in any way not inconsistent with the rights of the licensee. However, a landlord may authorise by licence some act or omission by a tenant which would otherwise be a breach of the terms of the lease.

licensee *See* LICENCE.

licensor *See* LICENCE.

lien In common law a right to hold the property of another as security for the performance of an obligation, usually the payment of a debt, eg a vendor's lien under a contract of sale is a right to retain the property until payment of the purchase price. A common law lien lapses as soon as possession is given up. An equitable lien is a right to enforce a claim for the performance of an obligation with, until the obligation is discharged, the security of a property but not possession thereof. It is therefore analogous to a charge. It includes the right, authorised by the court, to recover the amount of a debt from the proceeds of a sale of the security.

life beneficiary One who receives payments or other benefits from a trust for his lifetime.

life-cycle cost(ing) A discounted cash flow technique which measures the total cost or annual equivalent cost of a building. It will have regard to such matters as cost of construction, running costs, repair and renewals of components or parts of the building, and, possibly, the cost of the way in which activities are conducted in a building by the occupiers. *See* COSTS IN USE.

life interest An interest in property for the remaining life of the owner or for the life of another. *Cf* LIFE TENANCY.

liferent (Scotland) An easement which entitles a man for the remainder of his life to the use of another's property. The liferenter's right is similar to that of an owner for life.

life tenancy Historically, a lease granted at a fine or rent for a life or lives. The Law of Property Act 1925 converted such interests into terms for 90 years certain but determinable following the death(s) of the person(s) concerned. *Cf* LIFE TENANCY UNDER A SETTLEMENT. *See* LEASE FOR LIFE.

life tenancy under a settlement A life interest created for the lifetime of a beneficiary under a settlement where no fine or rent is paid; it is an interest in equity and the beneficiary is a tenant for his life. *Cf* LIFE TENANCY. *See* LIFE INTEREST.

light and air easements Those easements which entitle an owner of property to receive adequate light and air. In practice they are sometimes conveniently dealt with together in a light and air agreement, the obstruction of one also obstructing the other. An easement of light can exist only in relation to a defined aperture in a building or structure which has become part of the land. An easement of air can exist only in relation to a defined channel on the servient tenement or a defined aperture on the dominant tenement. Ingress of other light and air can be protected by restrictive covenants prohibiting or limiting obstructive erections (on other land). There is no easement of prospect and a view can be protected only by acquiring the land on which an obstruction might be erected or by negotiating restrictive covenants with the owners of such land. *See* ANCIENT LIGHTS.

limitation of actions The statutory restriction of the period within which legal actions seeking remedy or restitution must be brought in relation to the cause of the action. Currently (1988) the principal Limitation Acts are those of 1939 and 1980. In relation to property, these are now amended by the Latent Damage Act 1986.

limited company A public or private company, incorporated under the Companies Act, where the financial liability of shareholders for the debts of the company are limited to the value of their shareholding, including any amount unpaid on such shares when they have been issued only partly paid. Technically it includes a company limited by guarantee. *Cf* UNLIMITED COMPANY.

limited liability The extent to which the debts of a company are the legal responsibility of the shareholders. In a company with limited liability the shareholders' responsibility for the debts of the company is restricted to their capital commitment to the business. *Cf* PUBLIC LIMITED COMPANY (PLC); UNLIMITED COMPANY.

limited liability company A company with limited liability. *Cf* PUBLIC LIMITED COMPANY (PLC); UNLIMITED COMPANY.

limited tender A type of tender where the invitation to bid is restricted to a specific group or class of tenderers.

limits of deviation Boundaries laid down under powers of compulsory acquisition within which alterations may be made to an approved route for a motorway or railway or similar construction works without the necessity of seeking a variation in power. These are intended to allow some flexibility when meeting unforeseen geographical or other physical problems. The limits are usually lateral but may be vertical, as in the construction of a tunnel.

linear interpolation A term used in mathematics for the estimation of a value at any point on a straight line joining two given values, assuming the difference between the two values to be spread evenly along the line. Sometimes used to find the internal rate of return instead of either plotting yields graphically against net present values or continuing to calculate by trial and error.

line of credit A form of credit on which a borrower is entitled to draw a specified amount of money over a given period of time from a bank or other lender on terms agreed at the outset.

lines only *See* OVERSAIL.

liquidated damages A predetermined sum of money payable to a party in the event of a breach of contract by another party; the amount concerned, or the method of calculating it, and other provisions are specified in the contract. *Cf* PENALTY; UNLIQUIDATED DAMAGES.

liquidation **1.** The clearing up of financial affairs of a business by getting in what was owed, selling assets to meet liabilities and distributing any surpluses to those entitled, eg creditors or shareholders. The liquidation of a company is an essential step preceding its being wound up and finally dissolved by its being struck off the register. **2.** The conversion of the assets of a business or individual to cash or similar. *See* WINDING-UP.

liquidator A person appointed by the court (in a compulsory liquidation) or by the creditors of a company (in a creditors' voluntary winding-up) or by the members of the company (in a members' voluntary winding-up) for the purpose of effecting the liquidation.

liquidity The degree to which a company or individual can meet immediate or foreseeable financial commitments.

listed building A building of special architectural or historic interest included on a list compiled and kept by the Secretary of State for the Environment under the Town and Country Planning Act 1971. There are three Grades of listed buildings: I, II* and II, Grade I being regarded as of exceptional interest. Grade II buildings are of special interest which warrants every effort being made to preserve them. Grade II* are particularly important Grade II buildings. The owner and occupier must be informed (but need not be consulted beforehand) if a building is listed and he may not alter, extend or demolish it without listed building consent.

listed building consent Written permission granted by a local planning authority, or by the Secretary of State on appeal, for the demolition, alteration or extension of a listed building. Currently (1988) the local planning authority must refer applications relating to Grades I and II* buildings to the Secretary of State for the Environment for guidance before consent can be granted. A local authority which itself wishes to demolish a listed building must apply to the Department of the Environment.

listed company A quoted company. *See* LISTING 2.

listing **1.** The inclusion or addition of one or more buildings to the list of buildings of special architectural or historic interest. *See* LISTED BUILDING. **2.** The obtaining of a right to have a company's shares or other securities quoted on a particular Stock Exchange. *See* YELLOW BOOK.

living memory A phrase indicating the period of recollection of a living person for the admission of evidence in the courts. *Cf* LEGAL MEMORY.

load bearing The capacity of an element in a building structure to support a weight in addition to its own, whether vertically or laterally. Thus a load-bearing wall is one which supports part of the structure in addition to its own weight. *Cf* FLOOR LOAD.

local authority An elected corporate body which is responsible for the administration of specific public services to the community in a defined area. These bodies include county councils, district councils, parish (England) or community (Wales) councils and, in the City of London, the Common Council. Where there is no parish council, parish trustees perform the same function. In many Acts of Parliament there is a special definition of "local authority" for the purposes of the Act, eg parish councils may be excluded.

Local Enterprise Development Unit (Northern Ireland) The small business agency for Northern Ireland, being a limited company sponsored by the Province's Department of Economic Development. Its aim is to encourage the establishment of new small firms and the expansion of existing businesses in providing new job opportunities in Northern Ireland.

local land charges Various charges for securing money recoverable from owners or occupiers of property by local authorities (eg for the maintenance of sewers and drains) or restrictions or obligations relating to the use of land imposed by a local authority, Minister of the Crown or a government department, eg enforcement notices and section 52 agreements. They are recorded in a local land charges register kept by the district council under the Local Land Charges Act 1975. These charges differ from those recorded in the Land Registry, as they are:

a registered against the land, not the name of the estate owner,
b related to both registered and unregistered land, and
c of a public nature, with one exception, ie rights to light.

local land charges register *See* LOCAL LAND CHARGES.

local non-domestic rating list Under section 41 of the Local Government Finance Act 1988 a list of non-domestic hereditaments compiled and maintained by the valuation officer for a charging authority. The first list must be compiled on April 1 1990 and on April 1 of every fifth year thereafter. *See* QUINQUENNIAL.

local plan A plan drawn up by a local planning authority under the Town and Country Planning Act 1971. Local plans cover individual districts within a local planning authority's area. They have to be consistent with the provisions of the structure plan drawn up by the county planning authority and interpret its objectives. *Cf* UNITARY DEVELOPMENT PLAN.

local planning authority Either a county council or a district council, but a joint planning board may be established for the whole or parts of the area of two or more of these authorities. The allocation of functions between county planning authorities and district planning authorities varies considerably and is complex, but broadly the county is responsible for structure plans while the district is responsible for local plans and for most development control matters.

local taxation Generally descriptive of the system of raising revenues by local authorities, eg rates, community charge. *Cf* NATIONAL TAXATION.

local user restriction In planning a condition imposed on a planning permission to restrict the use or occupation of a property to a user or occupier already within the local area. Frequently used to give preference to local companies already established, operating in the area and needing more space. *See* USER.

local valuation court A tribunal which hears appeals against existing entries on the valuation list — or against proposals to amend it. The appeal may be made by the valuation officer or by an "aggrieved person" (eg generally the occupier and/ or owner of the property or the rating authority). From a local valuation court decision there is right of appeal to the Lands Tribunal. A local valuation court consists of members selected from a local valuation panel constituted, generally for county areas, under the General Rate Act 1967. *See* HEREDITAMENT.

location plan A plan which, for clarity of interpretation, is of a large scale (eg 1:1,250 or 1:2,500) to show the position of a specific property in relation to its surroundings. *Cf* BLOCK PLAN; SITE PLAN.

lock-up shop A shop of modest size, without living accommodation attached, usually one of several in a row and run by an individual or family.

locus poenitentiae **1.** The power of drawing back from a bargain before anything has occurred which might confirm it in law. The term also means a place in which there is an opportunity for repentance; a penitentiary. **2.** (Scotland) The opportunity to withdraw from a "contract" which is not binding on account of its informality; this right is cancelled by some form of personal bar, eg *rei interventus*, or by homologation, ie validation of the defective contract.

London Interbank Bid Rate *See* LIBID.

London Interbank Offer(ed) Rate *See* LIBOR.

long tenancy In residential legislation (Landlord and Tenant Act 1954 Part 1, Leasehold Reform Act 1967 and Rent Act 1977) this means a lease for a term certain exceeding 21 years. *Cf* SHORT LEASE.

long-term agreement In insurance this means an agreement whereby someone undertakes to insure with the same insurer for a specified number of years. In return a discount in the premium is made, normally 5% for an undertaking of three years.

loss adjuster A professional person experienced in quantifying a loss entitlement under an insurance claim who acts for insurers but not in the capacity of an employee. His duties include satisfying himself that a claim is valid, assessing the sums properly due and agreeing a fair and proper settlement with the insured.

loss assessor An experienced person who in the event of an insurance loss arising is instructed by the claimant to assist in establishing the amount of damage incurred and to negotiate the best financial settlement possible on behalf of his client.

loss of profits, temporary *See* TEMPORARY LOSS OF PROFITS.

loss-leader An article sold substantially below the normal mark-up price and often below cost in order to attract customers into a shop.

lot A property or chattel (or a group of properties or chattels) which is offered for sale, particularly by auction, as a single and separate entity. *See* LOTTING.

lotting For a disposal, especially by auction, the division of property into parts, each of which is capable of being sold separately in a way which is thought likely to result in a more favourable total price than the property would fetch if sold as a whole. In the case of chattels offered at auction it may consist of the grouping of a number of (possibly disparate) items to form lots of a practicable and convenient size. *See* PRUDENT LOTTING; FLOODED MARKET CLAUSE.

lump A casual workforce in the building industry, characterised by special arrangements for collecting income tax on earnings. Historically this has been "more honoured in the breach than in the observance".

lump sum (building) contract A contract placed with a builder at a fixed price.

lunar month At common law a period of 28 days. Astronomically a period of about 29.5 days, being the time taken by the moon to make one revolution of the earth.

lux A term quantifying the intensity of lighting at a given point, particularly relevant in building design. There are recommended criteria for different applications. Formerly the term "lumen", which was approximately one-tenth of a lux, was used.

M

made land Land reclaimed by enclosing an area of water and then draining and/or pumping out from the enclosure. As a result the land may become physically suitable for agriculture, horticulture, building or other development. A classic example of pumped-out land is the polders of Holland. *Cf* MADE-UP LAND.

made-up land Land, initially unsuitable for building, which has been contoured or levelled by tipping non-toxic and otherwise environmentally acceptable waste materials and covering them with soil to a satisfactory depth. Such land may become suitable for building after the lapse of a period sufficient for the particular waste to become consolidated. *Cf* MADE LAND.

magnet store (magnet trader) A large store operated by retailers who are known or expected to be effective in attracting the shopping public, eg a department store or supermarket. In the process this enables other shops en route or in the vicinity to trade profitably. In practice the term is mainly used to describe a store in a shopping centre development.

mail or maill (Scotland) An old word meaning rent.

maintain Continue to keep something in a particular condition. In property terms it refers specifically to the upkeep of, for example, a building or other structure, plant and equipment, landscaping or roads. In a lease covenant, "to maintain" means to keep substantially in the same condition as when the lease was granted. *Cf* REPAIR.

maintenance In property parlance, the keeping of a building, structure or other physical feature in a specified, eg wind and weather tight, condition. The approved cost of maintenance may be deductible for income taxation under Schedule A or Schedule D Cases I, II or VI. *See* CAPITAL EXPENDITURE; MAINTAIN; REPAIR.

maintenance period Another term for defects liability period.

maintenance trust fund A fund set up in a trust which can be used only in maintaining a building to the extent defined by the trust deed, thereby benefiting the occupiers. Usually it is for a single building in multi-occupation to ensure that cash is available when required. *See* RENEWAL FUND.

maisonette A separate dwelling forming a part of a building but usually on more than one floor (distinguishing it from a "flat"). Although originally found in converted houses or above shops, today there are instances where whole buildings have been purposely designed to provide maisonettes or a mixture of maisonettes and flats. (Colloquially, but incorrectly, the term is sometimes applied to two-storey buildings subdivided into flats.)

major interest For value added tax purposes, a freehold interest or a lease for a term exceeding 21 years.

mala fide In bad faith. *Cf* BONA FIDE.

malfeasance The doing of an unlawful act. *Cf* MISFEASANCE; NON-FEASANCE.

mall Historically, a wide and perhaps sheltered promenade; more recently in property terms, describing a wide walkway through or in a shopping centre.

managed fund A fund managed by a specific body, eg an insurance company, on behalf of a number of investors, each having a stake according to his contribution. The fund, investing the large sums of money raised, is able to acquire a spread of property investments, enabling the individual investors to have a wider interest in the market sector than they could otherwise achieve. *Cf* PROPERTY BOND; PROPERTY INVESTMENT TRUST; PROPERTY UNIT TRUST.

managed shopping scheme A retail or mixed development in which thc retail element is planned, developed, owned and managed as a single entity and contains at least 5,000 m^2 (55,000 sq ft) of gross floorspace (gross leasable area), comprising three or more retail units.

management *See* PROPERTY MANAGEMENT.

management, active *See* ACTIVE MANAGEMENT.

management, full *See* FULL MANAGEMENT.

management, property portfolio *See* PROPERTY PORTFOLIO MANAGEMENT.

managing agent An agent undertaking all, or some, property management functions on behalf of a landlord.

managing trustee A trustee having responsibility to manage trust property.

mandamus Literally "we command". Originally a writ but subsequently a prerogative order of the Queen's Bench Divisional Court commanding a person, body or inferior court to perform some public duty. Under the Supreme Court Act 1981 and Rules of the Supreme Court, Order 53, it is one of the means whereby an aggrieved party can obtain a legal remedy by the process of judicial review. *Cf* CERTIORARI; PROHIBITION.

man of straw A person who is unable or unlikely to fulfil a financial obligation owing to lack of resources.

mansard roof Named after a French architect, François Mansard, a roof which, on one or more sides, has two slopes of different degree, with a steep lower slope and a flatter upper slope. It was designed to give more attic space when municipal law in 17th-century Paris limited the height of front walls of buildings.

map A drawing representing the features of an area of land but not wholly to scale, eg an Ordnance Survey sheet to a scale smaller than 1:2500. *Cf* PLAN.

march An archaic term used (often in the plural) to describe the border lands between England and Wales and between England and Scotland. In this sense used as a verb, it means "to border upon" and is more commonly used in this sense in Scotland than in England.

marginal rate An opportunity cost of money rate based on an organisation's marginal cost of raising money for a project, eg the cost of a new equity issue, a debenture or other security.

marginal rent *See* HARDCORE METHOD.

marginal yield In the hardcore method of valuation, the rate at which the top layer of income is discounted.

mariculture The farming of sea fish, using intensive methods.

market **1.** A situation in which buyers and sellers of a particular commodity or service are in sufficient numbers to create the opportunity of comparing prices and quality, thereby enabling the forces of supply and demand to operate. *See* IN THE MARKET. **2.** A large open or covered area in which a variety of traders offer goods for sale, usually displayed at stalls, to members of the public, either during normal shopping hours for the locality or, more unusually, on certain specified days only.

marketable title *See* GOOD MARKETABLE TITLE.

market capitalisation The value of a quoted public company at a given time, as evidenced by multiplying the total shares on issue by their individual price in the market.

market forces Those forces which affect the speed and price at which property changes hands, ie supply and demand. These in turn are influenced by:

a such matters as the location, type, quality, size and character of the property in relation to current requirements;
b the cost of money, having regard to the price; and
c the relative attraction of other forms of investment.

market price The sum realised on the disposal of a property in a given market. Commonly, but incorrectly, used interchangeably with "market value". *Cf* ASKING PRICE; RESERVE; SELLING PRICE.

market value The same as open market value. *Cf* MARKET PRICE.

market value approach *See* DIRECT COMPARISON METHOD.

market yield *See* ALL RISKS YIELD.

marriage value Latent value which is or would be released by the merger of two or more interests in land. For example, two adjoining parcels may be worth more as one property than the aggregate of their separate values. Similarly, two interests in the same property may have a greater value when merged than the sum of their individual values.

Martinmas November 11, the feast of St Martin the Bishop of Tours. One of the term days in Scotland. *See* QUARTER DAYS.

material change of use A change in the use of a property which is so significant as to be regarded as development under section 22 of the Town and Country Planning Act 1971 and thus require planning permission, eg (i) where the uses fall within different use classes; (ii) where one or more of the uses is or are *sui generis*; (iii) where there is an intensification of a *sui generis* use.

material detriment The degree of real and substantial injury or damage to land occurring if part only of a "house, building or manufactory" is to be compulsorily acquired, such that the claimant may require the whole to be acquired under section 8 of the Compulsory Purchase Act 1965. Where disputed, this is determined by the Lands Tribunal. *Cf* INJURIOUS AFFECTION.

material development Defined by paragraph 6 of Schedule 3 to the Finance Act 1974 in relation to any land as meaning "the making of any change in the state, nature or use of the land" but excluding anything listed in paragraph 7 of the Schedule. These are, for example, works of maintenance, improvement, enlargement to a building not extending the cubic content of the original building by more than one-tenth, rebuilding any building existing within the previous 10 years within similar limits and certain specified uses or change of use. The only current (1988) relevance of the definition is in relation to the bases of assessing capital gains tax of properties held in April 1965 and disposed of prior to April 1988. (This definition was also relevant to assessments for development gains tax, while there were other definitions for betterment levy and development land tax, all these taxes now being obsolete.)

maximum compensation *See* CEILING VALUE.

McCarthy rules The popular name for the principles (enunciated in

Metropolitan Board of Works v *McCarthy* (1874)) governing the right to claim compensation for injurious affection where no part of the claimant's land is acquired. In summary these are (i) that the injurious affection must be the consequence of a lawful exercise of statutory powers, (ii) that it arises from something which, if done without statutory authority, would give rise to a cause of action, (iii) that the value of the interest in land must be affected by physical interference with some legal right enjoyed by the claimant in connection with the property and (iv) that the damage arises from the execution of the works, not from their authorised use.

meliorating waste *See* AMELIORATING WASTE.

memorandum of association In respect of every incorporated company whether with limited or unlimited liability, a document drawn up by the founders as a statutory requirement under the Companies Act stating *inter alia* the name of the company, its registered address and its objectives. *Cf* ARTICLES OF ASSOCIATION. *See* INTRA VIRES; ULTRA VIRES.

merger of interests The amalgamation of a superior interest with one or more immediately inferior interests in the same property, thereby amalgamating several titles into one, eg the purchase by a freeholder of his lessee's interest, usually extinguishing the latter. *See* MARRIAGE VALUE.

mesne Intermediate. Originally descriptive of the Lord of the Manor, holding from the monarch and granting a tenancy or tenancies to a third party or parties. Similarly, today, where there are a head lessor, head lessee and underlessee, the head lessee is the mesne.

mesne profits **1.** The amount a tenant must pay, if he has remained unlawfully in possession of his landlord's premises, for the period of unlawful occupation. **2.** Where a landowner suffers trespass on his land, he is not only entitled to claim damages for such action but can also claim compensation for being deprived of the use and occupation of the land. This claim (mesne profits) is assessed according to the current rental value of the land.

messuage A dwelling-house with its outbuildings, curtilage and garden.

mezzanine In a building of several storeys, an intermediate floor extending to a lesser area than the main floors, usually between the ground and first floors.

Michaelmas September 29, the feast of St Michael. One of the quarter days. Traditionally the day when a landlord fed his tenants with roast goose.

Midsummer Day June 24, the feast of St John the Baptist. One of the quarter days.

mineral rights The right to extract and dispose of minerals naturally occurring in, on or under the ground. The owner of the land may dispose of or reserve the mineral rights, but various statutes for particular minerals have extinguished some of these private rights and vested them in the state or the Crown, as in the case of coal, natural gas, petroleum, gold and silver.

mineral royalty A sum which is payable to a landowner by a mineral operator under the terms of his mining lease; it is calculated at a specified sum for each defined quantum of mineral extracted, eg £x per ton.

minerals Four types of mineral substances won from the earth:

a metalliferous (or metallic), eg gold, copper, iron;
b industrial (non-metallic), eg gypsum, china clay, salt;
c bulk (or aggregates), eg sand, gravel, rock or stone; and
d hydrocarbons, eg coal, petroleum.

minimum compensation The basis of compensation prescribed by section 117 of the Town and Country Planning Act 1971 where a local authority is acquiring compulsorily a listed building which has been deliberately allowed to fall into disrepair for the purpose of justifying its demolition and the development or redevelopment of the site or any adjoining site.

minimum lending rate The successor to the "bank rate", being the rate of interest at which the Bank of England would lend to discount houses, ie the keenest rate of interest as between the highest rank of lender and the highest rank of borrower. *Cf* BASE RATE.

minimum rent A rent below which a variable rent will not fall, eg (i) a stated rent payable for the whole or part of the duration of a lease containing a formula for a possibly higher rent on review; (ii) a dead rent under a mining lease; and (iii) a base rent under a turnover lease. *See* DEAD RENT.

mining lease Not strictly a lease, but a contractual agreement which gives a mining operator the mineral rights from a specified area of land. Defined in the Landlord and Tenant Act 1927 as "a lease for any mining purpose or purposes connected therewith . . .". *See* MINERAL ROYALTY.

mining operations Defined for the purposes of the Town and Country Planning (Minerals) Regulations 1971 as "the winning and working of minerals other than excepted minerals in or under land, whether by surface or underground working". (There are, however, other definitions, eg in the Town and Country Planning General Development Order 1977 and the Town and Country Planning (Minerals) Act 1981.)

minor interest Any one of the (third party) rights and interests in land which are not registered on the Land Register under the Land Registration Acts and are not overriding interests. Some (but not all) minor interests may be protected by a notice, caution, inhibition or restriction.

minor superior tenancy Defined in the Leasehold Reform Act 1967, Schedule 1, as amended, as a "superior tenancy having an expectation of possession of not more than one month and in respect of which the profit rent is not more than £5.00 per year".

minor tenancy Defined in the Compulsory Purchase (Vesting Declarations) Act 1981 as a "tenancy for a year or from year to year, or any lesser interest". *See* GENERAL VESTING DECLARATION.

misfeasance Improper performance of a lawful act. *Cf* MALFEASANCE; NONFEASANCE.

misrepresentation A false or misleading statement of fact, made by or on behalf of one contracting party to another, which, although not forming part of the contract, induces the other party to enter into the contract. If the misleading statement is made by an agent acting within his express or implied authority, legal liability attaches to the principal alone and not to the agent. The remedies available for misrepresentation are rescission of the affected contract and/or damages for loss suffered. The extent to which the court allows either or both of these remedies will depend upon whether the offending statement was made

a fraudulently, ie with knowledge that it was untrue;
b negligently, ie honestly but without reasonable grounds for believing it; or
c innocently, ie honestly and reasonably.

missives Informal and preliminary writings exchanged by parties negotiating for a contract as an indication of intent, which in Scotland, unlike England, may be lawfully binding according to the nature of the contract. *See* MISSIVES OF SALE.

missives of sale (Scotland) An offer to sell and an acceptance of the offer, in written form. In order to be binding, the documents must show full and complete agreement as to the subject, price and other relevant details. They must be probative or holograph of either parties or agents. To constitute agreement, missives (which can also cover leases) may be an exchange of letters between agents, adopted as holograph.

mitigation of loss The duty of a plaintiff or claimant seeking a legal remedy or compensation to take any reasonable steps open to him to reduce or avoid the loss.

mixed development A development which has buildings in two or more uses, eg a shopping centre with leisure facilities or with residential units. *Cf* MIXED HEREDITAMENT.

mixed hereditament A part residential, part commercial hereditament of which the proportion of the rateable value attributable to the part used as a residential hereditament exceeds one-eighth: see the General Rate Act 1967, section 48 as amended by the Local Government, Planning and Land Act 1980, section 33.

mode or category of occupation Generally in the valuation of a hereditament for rating purposes, the assumption that the hypothetical tenant occupies the premises for the same purpose as the actual or potential occupier. However, this broad principle does not apply in every specific case, eg a shop must be valued as a shop (but not any particular kind of shop). *See* REBUS SIC STANTIBUS.

model clauses (repair regulations) A colloquial term for the Agriculture (Maintenance, Repair and Insurance of Fixed Equipment) Regulations 1973 (SI 1973, No 1473), which, in the absence of agreement between the parties to an agricultural tenancy, provide standard terms and conditions on the maintenance, repair and insurance of certain items of fixed equipment.

model rent review clause A rent review clause published as a standard in the drafting of leases. A number of such model clauses are published by the RICS jointly with the Law Society and by the ISVA.

modern ground rent A rent for an extended lease, being the "letting value" of the site of a house, as determined under section 15 of the Leasehold Reform Act 1967 as amended.

modernisation Changes made to the interior and/or exterior of a building structure and/or its service installations for the purpose of reflecting contemporary developments of function, design or possibly decoration.

modification order An order, made by a local planning authority under section 45 of the Town and Country Planning Act 1971, modifying a planning permission. It may give rise to compensation under section 164 of the Act. *Cf* REVOCATION ORDER.

moiety A half share. Often used to describe a commission payment by one agent to another where they have both acted on the same side in a transaction and agreed to share equally any fee earned and paid.

money weighted rate of return *See* INTERNAL RATE OF RETURN.

Monte Carlo simulation A method of development appraisal analysis which involves the generation of random numbers (hence "Monte Carlo") in the selection of the variables used in an appraisal, eg rental value, yield, costs of construction. It seeks to assist in the assessment of the risk involved in a project.

monument *See* ANCIENT MONUMENT.

mortgage The conveyance of a legal or equitable interest in freehold or leasehold property as security for a loan and with provision for redemption on repayment of the loan. The lender (mortgagee) has powers of recovery in the event of default by the borrower (mortgagor). A mortgage is a form of land charge and can be either legal or equitable. There can be more than one mortgage on the same property. *See* EQUITY-LINKED MORTGAGE; PRIORITY OF MORTGAGES.

mortgage broker An agent who advises on and procures loans by way of mortgage for borrowers.

mortgage, first, second ... *See* PRIORITY OF MORTGAGES.

mortgage, joint *See* JOINT MORTGAGE.

mortgagee *See* MORTGAGE.

mortgagee's powers/remedies On default of the borrower, the powers which the lender may use to restore his position, ie: (i) sue on the personal covenant; (ii) take possession of the relevant property; (iii) appoint a receiver; (iv) exercise a power of sale, ie the right to sell the property, any surplus being paid to the mortgagor after redeeming any subsequent mortgages; (v) foreclose.

mortgagor *See* MORTGAGE.

mortis causa On account of death. A *mortis causa* writing or deed is one which takes effect on the death of the grantor. A *mortis causa* gift (or *donatio mortis causa*) is a gift made in contemplation of the donor's death. It has certain of the qualities of a legacy and is revocable in the event of the donor's recovery.

multiple agency The appointment of two or more agents to dispose of the same property independently of one another on the basis that only the successful agent is entitled to a commission. *Cf* JOINT AGENT; JOINT SOLE AGENT; SOLE AGENT.

multiple poinding (Scotland) An action taken to determine the disposal of property to which conflicting claims are made. *See* FUND IN MODIC.

multiple position A prime trading location in a shopping area at which multiple retailers are or may be represented. *See* MULTIPLE RETAIL OUTLET.

multiple regression analysis A statistical technique which quantifies the relationship between one variable (the dependent variable) and a number of other variables (independent variables). It is used in property performance analysis.

multiple retail outlet A retail outlet operated by an organisation with 10 or more branches. *Cf* INDEPENDENT RETAIL OUTLET.

multi-storey Descriptive of a building of five or more storeys, either above or below ground level. *Cf* TOWER BLOCK.

mutual option An option exercisable by either party to a contract in the event of some specific happening or on specified dates, eg where at a date for the review of the rent under a lease, each party has the option to determine the lease rather than pay or accept the new rent.

N

naked trust *See* BARE TRUST.

National Association of Estate Agents (NAEA) A body set up in 1962 to represent and protect the interests and reputation of those practising as estate agents.

National Grid Two series of lines, one drawn parallel to the central meridian of the Ordnance Survey and the other at right angles to it, so forming a grid over a map. This enables any point covered by this grid to be referenced and expressed by its co-ordinates.

national park An area of land designated as such under the National Parks and Access to the Countryside Act 1949 by the Countryside Commission (formerly the National Parks Commission). Defined as an extensive tract of country which, by reason of its natural beauty and the opportunities afforded for open-air recreation, should, in the opinion of the Commission, be preserved and its natural beauty enhanced for the purpose of promoting its enjoyment by the public.

national taxation Generally descriptive of the system of raising revenues by central government, covering such charges as personal income and corporation taxes; capital gains tax; inheritance tax; consumer taxation, eg value added tax and, perhaps, national insurance contributions. *Cf* LOCAL TAXATION.

National Water Authority Currently (1988) this is a proposed public body to take over certain regulatory functions of the water authorities once they become privatised.

natural right A common law right to some benefit attaching to the ownership of land in its natural state, eg the right of support to one's land by a neighbour's land, as distinct from a right of support to a building, which has to be the subject of an express, implied or presumed grant. *Cf* EASEMENT.

natural right of support A common law right attached to land (unless temporarily suspended by formal agreement) which prohibits the owner of an adjoining property from doing any act which endangers the stability of the surface and substrata of the land enjoying the right, or neglecting to do something which is needed to maintain its stability. Note: There is no natural right of support to a building. *See* RIGHT OF SUPPORT.

natural zoning The determination of the number and depth of the zones of a shop, where the physical features of the building or site make it impracticable to use the geometrical method. The depth of each zone is then determined by analysis of the actual depths of nearby shops. *Cf* GEOMETRICAL ZONING (ARBITRARY OR ARITHMETICAL ZONING).

nec vi, nec clam, nec precario *See* VI, CLAM OR PRECARIO.

negative covenant *See* RESTRICTIVE COVENANT.

negative development value Development value which is negative, ie where the existing use value is greater than the value of the property for development or redevelopment.

negative premium *See* REVERSE PREMIUM (NEGATIVE PREMIUM).

negative prescription (extinctive prescription) (Scotland) The extinguishment of a right or obligation by lapse of time. Under the Prescription and Limitation (Scotland) Act 1973, there are now only two such prescriptions, the "quinquennial" (five years) and the "long" (20 years).

negative value The value of an asset which is a liability to its owner and can be disposed of only by means of a payment to the purchaser; the "value" to the owner is therefore a minus quantity.

negligence **1.** A breach of contract or a tort, committed either carelessly or inadvertently, rather than deliberately. **2.** An independent tort comprising a breach of a legal duty of care, owed to an individual or class of persons, eg the common law duty to exercise due care owed by persons using a highway to others on that highway.

negotiation Discussion, written or otherwise, between two or more parties on different sides, the aim being to reach a common agreement.

negotiator Someone who conducts negotiations, usually as an agent, with a view to reaching agreement with another party or parties, or their agents, in a property transaction, eg sale, purchase, letting or rent review.

neighbourhood shopping centre A small shopping centre, smaller than a district shopping centre, usually based on a supermarket, offering a range of convenience goods as well as some personal services, such as laundry, dry cleaning and confectioner/newsagent/tobacconist (CNT). It normally has an area of some 5,000 m^2 and serves a catchment area of 5,000 to 10,000 people. *See* HIERARCHY OF SHOPPING CENTRES.

net annual value For rating purposes this is defined in section 19(3) of the General Rate Act 1967 as "the rent at which it is estimated the hereditament might reasonably be expected to let from year to year if the tenant undertook to pay all usual tenant's rates and taxes and to bear the cost of repairs and insurance and other expenses, if any, necessary to maintain the hereditament in a state to command that rent". *Cf* GROSS VALUE. *See* RATEABLE VALUE.

net income **1.** For property income taxation purposes, generally gross rent less allowable deductions, ie actual outgoings. **2.** For property valuation purposes this corresponds with net rental. *Cf* TRUE NET INCOME.

net internal area (NIA) (Formerly sometimes referred to as "effective floor area".) The usable space within a building measured to the internal finish of structural, external or party walls, but excluding toilets, lift and plant rooms, stairs and lift-wells, common entrance halls, lobbies and corridors, internal structural walls and car-parking areas.

net lettable area *See* RENTABLE AREA.

net present value (NPV) The result of applying the net present value method of appraisal.

net present value method A method used in discounted cash flow analysis to find the sum of money representing the difference between the present value of all inflows and all outflows of cash associated with the project by discounting each at a target yield. *Cf* INTERNAL RATE OF RETURN.

net redemption yield *See* REDEMPTION YIELD.

net rent Income from property after deduction of all outgoings, including repairs (with a yearly provision for repairs likely to be required at longer intervals, eg lift repairs, major decorations), insurance and management costs to be met by the recipient but excluding taxes payable by the recipient. *Cf* GROSS RENT.

net replacement cost In the valuation of land and buildings in accounting for depreciation, this is ". . . the gross replacement cost reduced to reflect the physical and functional obsolescence and environmental factors so as to arrive at the value of the building to the business at the relevant date". (*RICS Guidance Notes on the Valuation of Assets.*) *See* DEPRECIABLE AMOUNT; GROSS REPLACEMENT COST.

net retail floorspace (trading floorspace) A term used by retail management to define the internal floor area of a department store occupied by the selling and service departments. It includes the floor area to which customers have access, counter space, checkouts, fitting rooms, space immediately behind counters and circulation space forming an integral part of the department. It excludes lobbies, staircases, plant rooms, cloakrooms and other amenity rooms, together with floorspace serving more than one department such as line checkouts and window display space. It is measured from the internal faces of walls and partitions and the centre of aisles to adjoining departments.

net sales area The area in a retail store open to the public where the goods are displayed and sold. It excludes service areas, eg toilets, passageways, lifts and staircases.

net trading profit (NTP) Gross trading profit less working expenses (some being incurred each year, others being the annual equivalent of any estimated expenditure likely to be incurred at longer intervals).

network analysis Descriptive of such techniques as critical path analysis (CPA), programme evaluation review techniques (PERT) and precedence techniques.

net yield *See* TRUE NET YIELD.

new-for-old approach A method of valuation under section 9 of the Leasehold Reform Act 1967 which involves carrying out a valuation of the site by the residual method by reference to the value of a new house, when completed, and the total cost of building it. *Cf* CLEARED SITE APPROACH; STANDING HOUSE APPROACH.

new town A town developed (or in the course of development) on land designated as such under one of the New Towns Acts, now (1988) consolidated in the New Towns Act 1981. After such designation, subsequent development is under the control of a development corporation, who also administer and manage the whole or part of the new town area. *See* NEW TOWN DEVELOPMENT CORPORATION.

new town development corporation Under the New Towns Act 1981, a quasi-autonomous body established by and responsible to the Secretary of State for the Environment (or for Scotland or for Wales) for the creation and management during development of a particular new town. In practice, emphasis is placed upon the need to consult with local authorities on major issues to obtain their understanding and agreement to proposals, even though this does not prejudice the right of the development corporation to make the decisions. The local authority may refer their views on some issues to the Secretary of State for consideration before the development corporation's decision is implemented. *See* COMMISSION FOR THE NEW TOWNS; NEW TOWN.

New Towns Commission *See* COMMISSION FOR THE NEW TOWNS.

nil value The value of an interest in property which has no worth for a particular purpose or, alternatively, for any purpose.

nominal consideration Consideration in name only and having either insignificant monetary value or at least one so small that it is token in relation to the market value of a property. *See* PEPPERCORN RENT.

nominal rate The percentage rate of interest stated on the face of a bond or gilt-edged stock, eg undated 3.5% War Loan. (The real rate of interest will be different where the market value of the stock is not at its face value.) *Cf* REAL RATE. *See* NOMINAL VALUE 1.

nominal value **1.** The par or face value, as distinct from the market value, of an asset, eg of a share in a company. **2.** A negligible capital sum paid for an asset, eg £1, or a negligible annual sum for rent, ie a peppercorn rent.

non-catastrophic perils (wet perils) A group of fortuitous events which may result in damage to property — by storm, tempest, flood, bursting or overflowing of water tanks, apparatus or pipes, or impact by any road vehicle, horses or cattle. In consideration of the payment of an appropriate premium an insurance company may, under the contract, subject to special conditions, extend the cover under a policy to include such destruction or damage. *Cf* CATASTROPHIC PERILS.

non-conforming use The use of a property which does not conform to the allocation of the area for planning purposes. Such a property may have been built in conformity with the planning requirement at the time and a policy change ensued; more usually, the property was constructed before planning control was introduced.

non-feasance Failure to perform a legal duty. *Cf* MALFEASANCE; MISFEASANCE.

non-loadbearing wall (partition wall) A wall used to form a division between areas of a building and carrying only its own weight and not a superimposed load.

non-recourse loan A type of loan where the terms provide that the lender's only security is the property offered to support the loan.

non-recurring expense Expenditure, usually of a nature which is unlikely to be repeated, such as works needed to comply with a statutory requirement, eg installation of a fire escape.

non-tariff insurers Insurance companies which are not members of the Fire Offices Committee.

normal wear and tear *See* FAIR WEAR AND TEAR.

north point A sign on a plan or map denoting the direction of either geographic or, less usually, magnetic north.

no-scheme world In compulsory purchase, the state of affairs which would have subsisted at the valuation date with respect to the land being acquired and other land if the scheme had not existed, so that no development would have been or would be carried out thereunder and the planning background would not have been affected by it.

notice of compliance A formal notice, issued by a rating or precepting authority, indicating that they accept the rate capping restraints placed upon them by the Secretary of State for the Environment.

notice of entry A notice served on the owner and occupier(s) of a property by an authority possessing compulsory purchase powers requiring possession to be given by a date prescribed in the notice. A minimum of 14 days' notice must be given. *See* NOTICE TO TREAT.

notice to complete Notice served by a vendor on a purchaser or vice versa requiring the other party to complete the transaction by a given date. *Cf* COMPLETION NOTICE; PRACTICAL COMPLETION CERTIFICATE.

notice to quit A certain and reasonable notice required by law, custom, special agreement or statute, enabling either the landlord or the tenant or the assignees or representatives of either of them, without the consent of the other, to determine a tenancy from year to year or other periodic tenancy. *Cf* NOTICE TO TERMINATE.

notice to terminate A formal notice served by the competent landlord on a tenant of business premises under section 25 of the Landlord and Tenant Act 1954 terminating the current tenancy as from the date stated on the notice. *Cf* NOTICE TO QUIT.

notice to treat A notice served on owners, lessees and mortgagees by an authority with compulsory purchase powers to acquire land. The notice gives particulars of the property to be acquired, demands details of the recipient's interest in the land and his claim for compensation and states that the authority are willing to treat for the purchase of the land. *See* COMPULSORY PURCHASE ORDER; NOTICE OF ENTRY.

nuisance A use of property which interferes with the lawful rights of and enjoyment by the occupier(s) of other property or members of the public, eg by excessive noise, odours, fumes or other harmful or unpleasant emissions. *See* PRIVATE NUISANCE; PUBLIC NUISANCE.

nursery unit The UK equivalent of an incubator building in the USA. *See* INCUBATOR BUILDING 2.

O

obiter dictum A judge's expression of opinion on a point of law which is not essential to his decision on the matter at issue (*ratio decidendum*) and does not, therefore, have binding authority. *See* DICTUM.

occupation Physical use and control of property. *Cf* POSSESSION. *See* MODE OR CATEGORY OF OCCUPATION.

occupational lease A lease under which the lessee occupies the land or premises demised rather than grants a further interest to a sublessee.

occupation(al) rent A rent paid by the occupier of land or building(s).

occupier, rateable *See* RATEABLE OCCUPIER.

occupier's drainage rate A rate charged by an internal drainage board on the occupier of an agricultural property to meet the cost of maintaining drainage works. *Cf* OWNER'S DRAINAGE RATE.

offer A presentation or proposal, the acceptance of which may, in certain circumstances, create a contract. To be legally binding when accepted, an offer must be definite as to the parties, the subject-matter and the consideration. In addition, in the case of property transactions, section 40 of the Law of Property Act 1925 provides that to be enforceable the contract must be evidenced in writing. If made "subject to contract", it does not normally bind the parties involved, but in Scotland it does.

Official List Under the auspices of the International Stock Exchange, the principal market in the securities of public limited companies, ie with relatively large and mature companies. *Cf* THIRD MARKET; UNLISTED SECURITIES MARKET. *See* YELLOW BOOK.

off licence **1.** A licence generally issued by magistrates allowing the licensee to sell alcoholic beverages for consumption off the premises. **2.** Premises which are so licensed. *Cf* ON LICENCE.

off price centre (USA) A shopping centre, usually in a fringe location, with retail stores buying direct from manufacturers and offering goods for sale at discount prices.

off-site improvements Works carried out on land to make other land (with or without existing buildings) suitable for development or improvement, eg roads, pavements, water mains or sewers. *See* INFRASTRUCTURE.

"old-style" development plan One of the original types of development plan first introduced under the Town and Country Planning Act 1947, prepared in great detail for urban areas and all subject to ministerial approval. Although under the Town and Country Planning Act 1971 these plans were intended to be replaced by structure and local plans, they have not yet been entirely superseded in some areas, to the extent that a local plan has not yet been prepared, is incomplete or does not cover some part of the area covered by the "old style" development plan.

on-costs The additional expenditure likely to be incurred when planning or undertaking an activity involving a basic cost. In a development it includes the incidental costs of professional services prior to the start of the scheme and the costs associated with the development, such as fees, legal charges, insurance and finance, when the basic cost will be the consideration for the land and payment under the building contract. *See* DEVELOPMENT EXPENDITURE.

one-hour door A fire-resistant door, usually self-closing, which will hold back a fire for a minimum of one hour.

one-stop shopping A system of retailing in which the purchaser can buy under one roof all the merchandise he requires falling within a product group, eg DIY or food.

on licence A licence generally issued by magistrates which allows the licensee to sell alcoholic beverages for consumption either on or off the premises. *Cf* OFF LICENCE.

on-site improvements Structures erected, or works undertaken, for permanent use on a site, such as buildings, roads, landscaping and fences; often just called "site improvements." *Cf* OFF-SITE IMPROVEMENTS.

open-ended Descriptive of any vehicle for investment which from time to time can vary the amount of equity funds raised from shareholders or subscribers, eg a unit trust where every time a subscriber puts money in, the number of units issued is increased (or decreased if money is taken out).

open market value **1.** The best price which might reasonably be expected to be obtained at arm's length for an interest in a property at the date of valuation, subject to any statutory assumptions which may be required. **2.** For the purpose of asset valuations this is defined by the *RICS Guidance Notes on the Valuation of Assets* as the best price which might reasonably be expected to be obtained for an interest in a property at the date of valuation assuming:

a a willing seller;
b a reasonable period in which to negotiate the sale;
c that values will remain static during that period;
d that the property will be freely exposed to the market; and
e that no account will be taken of any higher price that might be paid by a person with a special interest.

"open position" A colloquial expression applied to a situation where a short-term trader in the stock market buys securities in the hope and expectation that he will resell them at a profit within the same account, thereby closing his position.

open rent review Where notice for the relevant rent review may be served after the date specified in the lease, even though no action has been taken at the "due" date. The date to which the calculation of rent is then related and the date from which it becomes payable will depend on the terms of the lease.

***opera citato* (*op cit*)** In a book, article or other written matter, a second or further reference to a work which has been previously referred to or cited.

opinion evidence Evidence by a witness of his opinion, as distinct from evidence of fact(s) of which he has personal knowledge. Although generally inadmissible in a court of law, there are numerous exceptions, eg expert witnesses may give evidence of their opinion on questions within their particular field.

opportunity cost The return or other benefit forgone in pursuing one particular investment opportunity rather than another. This enables a comparative judgment to be made with knowledge of their relative advantages or disadvantages.

opportunity cost of money rate A type of criterion rate, based upon the cost of money, used in the net present value method. It may be one of the following: the marginal rate, target rate or weighted rate. *Cf* INTERNAL RATE OF RETURN.

option A unilateral right, created by contract, enabling one of the parties, if he so wishes and if the circumstances are covered by the terms of the contract, to exercise a right to do something or require the other party to do (or refrain from doing) something in the future. *Cf* MUTUAL OPTION.

oral evidence (parol evidence) Evidence spoken by a witness in court, normally on oath or affirmation. *Cf* DOCUMENTARY EVIDENCE (WRITTEN EVIDENCE).

ordinary share The risk-bearing share in a corporate body, ie the ordinary shareholders collectively own the equity capital in a company. *See* EQUITY CAPITAL.

Ordnance Survey Founded in 1791 to produce maps for military purposes, its first offices were in the Tower of London. It is now a Civil Service department of 2,000 people based in Southampton. Ordnance Survey is responsible for surveying and topographic mapping in Britain, including geodetic surveys and scientific work. There are also about 1,000 local surveyors in offices around the country. The main national commitment is to update and publish maps at three different scales: for mountain and moorland areas the largest scale maps published are those to 1:10,000 (approx 6 in to 1 mile), the largest scale plans for other rural areas are 1:2,500 (approx 25 in to 1 mile) and for urban areas 1:1,250 (approx 50 in to 1 mile).

original evidence **1.** A statement by a witness in court as proof of a fact in issue. *Cf* HEARSAY EVIDENCE. **2.** Testimony by a witness that he was aware of a fact in issue through one of his senses, or a statement that he was in some particular mental or physical state. *Cf* CIRCUMSTANTIAL EVIDENCE. **3.** Evidence of a statement made by someone other than the witness but offered to prove the statement was made (rather than to verify it). *Cf* HEARSAY EVIDENCE.

ornamental fixtures *See* TENANT'S FIXTURES.

outgoings Costs incurred by the owner of an interest in property, usually calculated on a yearly basis, eg management, repairs, rates, insurance and rent payable to the holder of a superior interest, as appropriate to his contractual or other liabilities. It is prudent to make annual provision for future items involving expenditure at intervals of more than one year. *See* EQUALISATION FUND.

outline planning application Application for outline planning permission.

outline planning permission Formal consent in principle to a proposed development of a property, subject to subsequent approval of "reserved matters". NB This applies only to development comprising building and/or engineering works, not to a material change of use.

out-of-town shopping centre A shopping centre located away from an urban area. The principal features for success include ready access to a good road system, a large catchment area of potential shoppers and substantial car parking facilities. *Cf* HYPERMARKET.

output tax For value added tax, the tax charged on goods or services supplied by a taxable person. *Cf* INPUT TAX.

overage (income or rent) That part of the income receivable in excess of a base rent and calculated by a formula, such as one related to turnover and/or profit. (The term is derived from practice in the US, where this method of rent calculation was first used.) *See* OVERRIDE 2; PERCENTAGE LEASE; PERCENTAGE RENT.

overall yield A generic term for the internal rate of return, whether or not calculated as an equated or equivalent yield.

overreach In the conveyance of land held on trust, to transfer a beneficiary's rights from the land to the proceeds of sale, enabling the land to be sold free from the trust.

override **1.** To invalidate some legal right. **2.** (USA) A form of overage calculated by reference to the quantity of goods sold by a tenant, eg the number of gallons of gasoline sold from a petrol station.

overriding interest An interest in registered land which is not itself registrable but is nevertheless binding upon the registered proprietor and any purchaser (whether known to him or not). Examples include legal easements, the rights of persons in actual occupation of the land (unless on inquiry they failed to disclose their rights) and most leases. *Cf* MINOR INTEREST.

overriding lease An intermediate lease granted by the landlord to another party for a term longer than that of an existing lessee, thereby creating a landlord and tenant (but not a contractual) relationship between the new and old lessees. Thus there is privity of estate but not of contract. *See* CONCURRENT LEASE.

oversail (lines only; span only) A cable or wire crossing a parcel of land without support on that land, ie the land is crossed by lines only, with the supporting poles or pylons on adjoining properties.

Over-the-Counter Market Created by licensed dealers in shares, a market for shares in companies which are not floated under the auspices of the International Stock Exchange, ie outside the Official List, the Unlisted Securities Market and the Third Market.

owner Strictly speaking, in relation to landed property, this means the freeholder but generally also includes a leaseholder. There are varying definitions for statutory purposes and the relevant provisions of the particular statute should always be referred to, eg in the Town and Country Planning Act 1971 there are two different definitions, one applying to sections 27 and 29 and the other to the remainder of the Act. For rating purposes, it is defined by section 115 of the General Rate Act 1967 as: "person for the time being receiving or entitled to receive the rack-rent". There are circumstances, eg in the rating of empty property, where the owner is deemed to be the occupier and is therefore rated.

owner's drainage rate A rate charged by an internal drainage board on the owner of an agricultural property to meet the capital cost of new or improved drainage works.

P

PABX Private Automatic Branch Exchange. An automatic telephone system which accepts incoming calls and, via a switchboard operator, distributes them to the appropriate extensions. *Cf* PMBX.

package deal (building) contract *See* DESIGN AND BUILD CONTRACT.

Panel on Takeovers and Mergers A non-statutory body set up in 1968 as a "watchdog" empowered to regulate the conduct of takeovers and mergers of companies in the UK and some in the Republic of Ireland, so as to ensure fairness and "equality of treatment and opportunity for all shareholders" by ensuring that conduct is proper, honourable and ethical in accordance with rules established by the Panel and known as the City Code. Its members are drawn from the principal financial institutions.

parcel (of land) An area of land, separately identifiable and usually in one ownership. The term is most commonly used in legal documents such as deeds and conveyances.

park Under paragraph 15 of Schedule 5 to the Local Government Finance Act 1988, an area of land, which (i) has been provided by, or is under the management of, a relevant authority or two or more relevant authorities acting in conjunction and (ii) is available for free and unrestricted use by members of the public. It includes a recreation or pleasure ground, a public walk, an open space within the meaning of the Open Spaces Act 1906 and a playing field provided under the Physical Training and Recreation Act 1937.

parking ratio The relationship between the number of car-parking spaces and the amount of accommodation available for other uses within a building or group of buildings.

parol evidence *See* ORAL EVIDENCE.

Parry's Valuation Tables A set of valuation tables, first published in 1913, based on the assumption that income is receivable in arrears at the end of each year and that interest is also payable annually.

part disposal When part of an asset is the subject of a disposal and the remainder is retained by the owner. For capital gains tax and certain other purposes it may be either

a where part of the asset is disposed of, or

b where a separate interest or right is created, eg on the grant of a lease or easement.

partial completion certificate (partial possession certificate) Under a building contract, a signed statement issued by an architect, surveyor or supervising officer where an employer wishes to take possession of a completed part of a large building contract. In such cases consequential procedure has to be considered and agreed for the issue of a certificate of interim practical completion and a certificate of making good defects for the remainder of the project as well as a certificate of making good defects for the part taken into possession. *See* BUILDING CONTRACT CERTIFICATES.

participating lease (participation lease) *See* SIDE-BY-SIDE LEASE.

participators Those persons who take part in a joint venture and share the risks and ultimate profits/losses. The respective rights and obligations of the participants will depend on the terms of agreement entered into and will not necessarily be the same.

particulars Details of a property which is to be sold or let. They are usually prepared by an agent for distribution to those who, it is considered, might be interested, eg prospective buyers or tenants.

partnership **1.** Under the Partnership Act 1890, "a relationship between persons carrying on a business together with a view to profit". The legal rights and responsibilities of the partners are mainly governed by the Partnership Act with some derived from the Companies Acts and the relevant partnership agreement or agreements. **2.** The relationship between two or more parties in a joint venture, eg a development involving a developer, local authority and a funding institution, where the financial success of each "partner" is dependent on the profitable outcome of the development.

partnership area *See* SPECIAL AREA.

part performance Where a contract would otherwise only be enforceable if adequately evidenced in writing, a legal doctrine enabling one party to the contract to require its enforcement, despite the absence of written evidence, on the ground that something has been done which is tantamount to establishing that there must have been a contract: otherwise no such thing would have been done. For example, where someone claiming to be a purchaser enters and carries out alterations to a property with the knowledge and acquiescence of the owner, the court might hold this to be a sufficient act of part performance of an oral contract of sale.

part possession Where part of a property is occupied by the owner or is vacant, the remainder being subject to one or more tenancies.

Part VI claim *See* ESTABLISHED CLAIM.

party wall A wall separating the properties of two adjoining owners, each of whom has certain rights over the wall. Such a wall may legally be divided into two vertical slices, one belonging to each owner, with or without cross-easements of support, or it may belong entirely to one of the adjoining owners, subject to an easement in favour of the other to have it maintained as a dividing wall. In certain parts of the country, there are local Acts of Parliament which qualify the general law in the area affected, eg the London Building Acts 1930-1939. Thus in inner London the 1939 Act contains two definitions of "party wall", the more important being for Part VI, concerning the rights and obligations of building owners and adjoining owners. For this purpose section 44 defines a party wall as meaning both (i) a wall forming part of a building and standing on lands of different owners to a greater extent than the projection of its foundations and (ii) so much of any other wall as separates buildings belonging to different owners. A more general definition in section 4 of the 1939 Act and applying except in Part VI is: ". . . so much of a wall which forms part of a building as is used or constructed to be used for separating adjoining buildings belonging to different owners or occupied or constructed or adapted to be occupied by different persons together with the remainder (if any) of the wall vertically above . . .".

party wall agreement Generally outside inner London, a document setting out the respective rights of the owners of properties separated by a party wall. It is drawn up by solicitors and is enforceable against purchasers when registered as a land charge. *Cf* PARTY WALL AWARD.

party wall award In inner London, a document which has the force of law, drawn up by two surveyors (who appoint a third surveyor to resolve any disputes) under the London Building Acts 1930-1939, describing agreed work to be carried out to or adjacent to a party wall or structure. It sets out the rights and obligations of the parties. *Cf* PARTY WALL AGREEMENT.

par value The price which, for example, a share or stock in a company is stated to be worth "on the face of it". Each certificate of ownership will state a sum which is the issued price of each unit, eg £1 ordinary shares. According to market conditions and the financial standing of the issuing company, such securities may have an open market value equal to that stated price (par value), more than the price (above par) or less than the price (below par). *See* FACE VALUE.

passing rent The rent which is currently payable under the terms of a lease or tenancy agreement.

patent (USA) An instrument by which public land (federal or state government's) is conveyed to a person.

patent defect A defect which is plainly visible or would be discovered by the exercise of reasonable care. *Cf* LATENT DEFECT.

payback An imprecise measure of the relative worth of an investment or project whereby the number of years taken to repay the capital outlay out of income is estimated; the shorter the period, the better the proposal. The method fails to take account of income received after the period so calculated and it also ignores the time-value of money to be received. *See* NET PRESENT VALUE METHOD.

payment in kind Payment other than by money, eg the transfer of land or other assets by a taxpayer in lieu of inheritance tax.

payment on account An interim payment in partial satisfaction of a future liability, eg:

a an advance payment by a tenant towards the cost of services for which he will be liable when the final cost has been calculated or
b a payment to a builder during the progress of work.

penal rent A financial punishment of a tenant for failing to honour his obligation to pay rent at the proper time, taking the form of a vastly higher figure being payable during the period of default.

penalty A fine, custodial sentence, penal damages or other punishment imposed by a court or tribunal or by other means, eg under a contract, on a wrongdoer. If the "penalty" is imposed by the terms of a contract, it will not be enforced as such by the court. *Cf* LIQUIDATED DAMAGES. *See* PENAL RENT.

peppercorn rent A token rent payable as consideration to a landlord, being either of a nominal amount of money or, more imaginatively, an English rose or a peppercorn. In modern times this usually occurs where the tenant has paid a premium to the landlord.

percentage lease A lease, generally of a retail business property, which includes provision for the rent to be determined as an agreed percentage of a figure based on the tenant's trading performance, eg the tenant's gross sales. There is usually a base rent. *See* PERCENTAGE RENT; TURNOVER LEASE.

percentage rent (turnover rent) A rent which is calculated as a proportion of the annual turnover of the lessee's business. Usually, it does not fall below a base rent. More commonly used in the USA, although in recent years being applied with increasing frequency in the UK, especially in the case of the more profitable retail outlets. *See* OVERAGE (INCOME OR RENT).

performance bond A sum of money, usually 10% to 20% of the contract sum, guaranteed by a third party (insurance company or bank) available to be drawn upon by the employer if the contractor fails to carry out the terms of the contract. Arrangements for the bond will normally be made by the contractor.

peril A particular fortuitous event which may result in property being damaged or destroyed. Hazards such as these are usually the subject of insurance cover payable in respect of damage caused by them. *See* CATASTROPHIC PERILS; NON-CATASTROPHIC PERILS.

periodic tenancy A tenancy which continues by reference to an agreed period, eg weekly, monthly, quarterly, yearly, until terminated by either party serving notice to quit. *Cf* TERM OF YEARS.

permissive waste Waste resulting from a tenant's failure to maintain the demised premises and allowing them to deteriorate by act or omission. *Cf* VOLUNTARY WASTE.

permitted development Colloquially, development for which planning permission is deemed to exist without specific application being made, ie development for which permission is granted by a development order, either general or special (see the Town and Country Planning Act 1971, section 24). *Cf* ARTICLE 4 DIRECTION.

permitted development value In order to assess compensation payable where the Secretary of State directs that planning permission be granted for some alternative development (in lieu of his confirming a purchase notice), this is defined by section 187 (5) of the Town and Country Planning Act 1971 as the value of an interest in land having regard to his direction but assuming no other planning permission would be granted. *See* EXISTING USE VALUE 2.

permitted use Colloquially, either **1.** a use authorised by an actual grant of planning permission or **2.** a use allowed by the deemed grant of planning permission under the General Development Order.

perpetual injunction A final and permanent injunction. *Cf* INTERLOCUTORY INJUNCTION.

perpetuity **1.** The quality of continuing forever. **2.** Something having that quality, eg a freehold estate.

perpetuity period In real estate, a specified period of time by the end of which a future estate in land must become effective, eg following the duration of a life or lives in being plus 21 years.

personal bar (personal exception) (Scotland) Action based on the word or act of another which leads to the one who acts being prejudiced. *See* ESTOPPEL; LOCUS POENITENTIAE.

personal representative A person empowered to act as executor under a will or appointed as administrator on intestacy. *See* ADMINISTRATION 1 AND 2.

personalty (personal property) All property other than realty or real property, eg chattels and other movable property, but by a quirk of legal history personalty includes leaseholds. *See* REAL PROPERTY (REALTY).

photogrammetry The principles and practice of plan-making based upon the use of aerial photographs.

photo interpretation The practice of examining single or stereoscopic pairs of aerial photographs to understand the nature, extent and characteristics of features shown and then applying the knowledge acquired thereby in reporting, recommending or deciding on some matter, eg in planning, agriculture, forestry or archaeology.

physical factors Under the Land Compensation Act 1973, section 1(2), these are listed as noise, vibration, smell, fumes, smoke, artificial lighting and the discharge on to land of any solid or liquid substance. Compensation may be payable under Part I of the Act where the value of an interest in land is depreciated by any of these "physical factors", caused by the use of public works.

physical life The period during which a building or structure is capable of occupation and/or use having regard to such factors as its structural condition and whether it meets or is capable of meeting accepted standards and statutory requirements. *Cf* ECONOMIC LIFE.

pink-hatched-yellow land Land added to a clearance area because it contains badly arranged houses or narrow or badly arranged streets and shown on the definitive plan in pink and yellow hatching. *See* PINK LAND; GREY PROPERTY.

pink land On plans for clearance areas, land containing dwellings unfit for human habitation, which is shown coloured pink. *See* PINK-HATCHED-YELLOW LAND; GREY PROPERTY.

pitch In property parlance, this has two principal meanings, namely: **1.** the angle of slope of a roof; **2.** the relative position of retail properties by reference to potential business and profitability.

plan **1.** A drawing to scale of the layout and construction of a part of a building, whether existing or proposed, in horizontal section, eg of a particular floor or set of rooms, and showing details such as windows, doors and permanent partitions. *See* BLOCK PLAN. **2.** A drawing of a relatively small area of land, usually drawn to a large scale and including details of boundaries, buildings, structures, services and other man-made features of a relatively permanent nature in addition to physical features. **3.** A set of proposals for the performance of a task or undertaking in a controlled manner or in a series of predefined steps according to certain principles or rules. In the case of the future development of an area, it would probably embrace maps and written statements. *Cf* MAP. *See* DEVELOPMENT PLAN; LOCAL PLAN; LOCATION PLAN; STRUCTURE PLAN.

planimeter A mechanical device for measuring the superficial area of a parcel of land plotted to scale on paper.

planner (town planner) A person who advises on planning matters concerning development and use of land; usually qualified by professional experience and or academic study. *See* ROYAL TOWN PLANNING INSTITUTE.

planning appeal An appeal to the Secretary of State for the Environment against a local planning authority's refusal of planning permission or its grant subject to conditions.

planning application An application for planning permission. This may be an outline or a detailed application, the latter being supported by detailed plans and descriptions. (NB An outline application cannot be made for a material change of use.)

planning blight The adverse effect upon the value of property of proposals by some public authority, the implementation of which is likely to involve compulsory purchase and/or disturbance. In certain circumstances the public authority can be compelled to acquire, in advance of its requirements, a property so affected. *See* BLIGHT NOTICE.

planning brief Guidelines on planning matters for the future development of an area or site laid down by the local planning authority. *Cf* DEVELOPMENT BRIEF.

planning consent A colloquial term for planning permission.

planning gain A benefit to the public — either generally or in a particular locality — usually in connection with the grant of a planning permission. The term is usually applied when a developer offers, agrees, or is obliged to incur some expenditure, surrender some right or grant some concession which could not be embodied in a valid planning condition. Frequently, such a planning gain results from the implementation of an agreement which may be made under section 52 of the Town and Country Planning Act 1971 or a covenant entered into under section 33 of the Local Government (Miscellaneous Provisions) Act 1982. *See* CONDITION 3.

planning permission Formal approval by a local planning authority or by the Secretary of State (following an appeal or if he calls in an application) of a proposed development under the Town and Country Planning Act 1971. *See* CONDITIONAL PLANNING PERMISSION; OUTLINE PLANNING PERMISSION.

planning unit The unit of occupation for land and/or buildings. It is the subject of a body of case law.

planning zone An area which has been allocated by a local planning authority, eg in a development plan, local plan or unitary development plan, for particular land uses or activities.

plot ratio The ratio of the gross floorspace of a proposed or existing building to the site area. *See* FLOOR AREA.

PMBX Private Manual Branch Exchange. The old-fashioned plug-in-line method of receiving and transferring calls, plugging them into the appropriate extension and removing the line from the socket at the end of the conversation. *Cf* PABX.

"Pointe Gourde" principle In the assessment of compensation where land is acquired compulsorily, the case law doctrine, established in *Pointe Gourde Quarrying & Transport Ltd* v *Sub-Intendent of Crown Lands* (1947), that any increase or decrease in the value of the land taken resulting from the scheme underlying the acquisition shall be ignored. *See* NO-SCHEME WORLD.

policy (Scotland) Term applied to the park or grounds of a large country estate.

portfolio A collection of property or other investments held in one ownership. *Cf* LAND BANK. *See* DIVERSIFICATION.

portfolio management, property *See* PROPERTY PORTFOLIO MANAGEMENT.

positive covenant A covenant imposing on the covenantor a positive obligation to undertake some act, eg a covenant by a lessee to erect a building on the demised land. *Cf* RESTRICTIVE COVENANT.

possession Control over landed property either by occupation and use or, in the case of a landlord, the right to receive the rents, if any, and to exercise the rights and duties in connection with the lease.

possessory title **1.** A claim to ownership of land based on evidence which is inconclusive or non-existent and which, within a prescribed period, is challengeable by one who has a stronger claim. **2.** In registered land, a title subject to some qualification or exception stated in the register, eg a property held subject to some right or interest arising before a specified date.

post-tensioned concrete *See* POST-TENSIONING.

post-tensioning A method of constructing "pre-stressed" concrete whereby steel bars or wires are embedded in the concrete and stressed after the concrete has set, then being anchored at the ends. Any space which appears around the bars or wires may then be filled with cement grout. Typically, this method is used for larger structures and where several members are to be connected. *Cf* PRE-TENSIONING.

poundage In rating, the amount payable by a ratepayer for every £1 of rateable value, ie it is the rate in the £.

power of appointment A power given by the owner of a property (the donor of the power) to another (the donee or appointee) to dispose of (appoint) the property to a third party (the appointee) chosen by the appointer within any limits prescribed by the donor. Such a power may be:

a general, ie the appointment may be made to anyone,
b special, ie the appointment is to be only within a class selected by the donor or
c hybrid, ie the appointment can be to anyone except a small class.

practical completion certificate Under a building contract, a signed statement issued by the architect, surveyor or supervising officer at the time that the building is complete in virtually all respects and ready for occupation. This certificate authorises the release of an agreed percentage of any retention money, begins the period of defects maintenance, and takes a new building out of the contractor's insurance and on to the building owner's insurance. *See* BUILDING CONTRACT CERTIFICATES; TRANCHE.

prairie value A colloquial term for the value of woodlands, as assessed under Schedule B in the Taxes Act 1988, excluding the value of the timber, the land being assumed to be in its natural and unimproved state.

precedence technique The use of procedure diagrams to show the dependency and priority of individual tasks or activities needed to perform a complex procedure or project. *See* NETWORK ANALYSIS.

precept The amount demanded from rating authorities by a precepting authority such as county or parish councils. The demands are to cover the financial needs of the precepting authorities not covered by other means, and the amount is expressed as a part of the general rate.

precepting authority Under section 144(1) of the Local Government Finance Act 1988, one of the following: a county council, a metropolitan county police authority, the Northumbria Police

Authority, a metropolitan county fire and civil defence authority, the London Fire and Civil Defence Authority, the Receiver for the Metropolitan Police District, the sub-treasurer of the Inner Temple, the under-treasurer of the Middle Temple, a parish or community council, the chairman of a parish meeting and "charter trustees".

precinct, shopping *See* SHOPPING PRECINCT.

pre-contract deposit A sum paid in advance of a contract as an earnest of good faith and usually held by a third party, eg an agent or solicitor. Such a deposit acts as part payment on completion of the contract but it does not create a legally binding agreement meanwhile. If the purchaser repudiates the contract without good reason he may forfeit the deposit depending upon the terms of the agreement, express or implied, made between the parties. There is a statutory definition of "pre-contract deposit" in section 12(3) of the Estate Agents Act 1979. *Cf* CONTRACT DEPOSIT.

pre-emption A right of first refusal, eg where a vendor may, at a time of his choosing, decide to dispose of a property but is then required to offer it first to the holder of the right. *Cf* OPTION.

preference share A share in a company giving the holder an entitlement to a fixed rate of interest by way of dividend plus a priority over ordinary shareholders to receive that entitlement out of profits before anything can be paid to them. A preference shareholder also has priority over ordinary shareholders in the event of a capital repayment. *See* CUMULATIVE PREFERENCE SHARE.

pre-funding The long-term financing of a development project arranged prior to the commencement of building operations.

prelet Colloquial term for a legally enforceable agreement for a letting to take effect at a future date, eg on practical completion of building operations.

premises **1.** That wording at the beginning of a conveyance or lease giving the date and naming the parties and the words of conveyance, including the description of the land(s) (with or without buildings) the subject of the document. **2.** Land alone or a building or part of a building, eg a flat, together with its land (if any).

premium **1.** The price paid by an actual or prospective lessee to a lessor, usually in consideration for the rent's being reduced to below what otherwise would be payable. *Cf* REVERSE PREMIUM. **2.** Incorrectly but commonly, the price paid for the purchase of (usually) a leasehold interest. It may represent a capital payment to reflect that the rent payable is below market value or, alternatively, recognise a special value to the purchaser above market value. *Cf* KEY MONEY. **3.** The periodic amount payable to an insurer by the insured as consideration for the insurance policy.

premium rent **1.** A rent above the level which a property could reasonably be expected to command in the open market on normal terms. Such rents may be justified in instances where the tenant receives a present or future benefit against the market, eg in inflationary conditions where upward-only rent reviews are normally required at five-yearly intervals, the tenant may be prepared to pay a higher rent if fixed for a longer period of, say, 10 years. *See* UPLIFTED RENT. **2.** A rent which is higher than would reasonably be expected because the tenant is particularly anxious to secure the property. *Cf* KEY MONEY 1.

prerogative order One of the three orders issued by a Divisional Court in supervising the conduct of the inferior courts, administrative tribunals and certain other bodies having judicial — or quasi-judicial — functions. The prerogative orders (formerly known as prerogative writs) are certiorari, mandamus and prohibition. They are obtained by means of a successful action for judicial review.

prescription The acquisition or establishment of a right after unrestricted and continuous enjoyment over a minimum period, eg for a right of way after 20 or 40 years, these being the periods for establishing respectively *prima facie* or absolute rights under the Prescription Act 1832.

present value The future worth of a property or a sum of money discounted to its present-day equivalent, taking account of all relevant circumstances, including, for example, inflation or taxation. *See* DISCOUNTING.

present value of £1 At a particular date, the worth of £1 receivable in a given number of years discounted at a selected rate of interest. It is the reciprocal of the amount of £1.

present value of £1 per annum Today's worth, as a capital sum, of the right to receive £1 per annum for a given number of years, when each yearly receipt has been discounted at a selected rate of interest and their individual present values aggregated. It is synonymous with years' purchase.

press relations Maintaining contact with the press and the issue of suitable information (press releases) about a product, service or firm for publication as editorial matter. There is no charge and inclusion should not depend upon the taking of advertising space. *Cf* PUBLIC RELATIONS. *See* PUBLICITY.

pre-stressed concrete A type of reinforced concrete in which all or some of the ordinary steel reinforcement is replaced by high-tensile steel bars or wires which are tensioned by "pre-tensioning" or "post-tensioning". The number and positioning of wires or tendons can be arranged to eliminate all tension in the concrete, thereby preventing cracking and so rendering the concrete water-tight and gas-tight as well as increasing its durability. Pre-stressed concrete structures can achieve greater spans and carry higher loading.

presumptive evidence *See* PRIMA FACIE EVIDENCE.

pre-tensioning A method of constructing concrete slabs or beams, usually factory-made floor and roof slabs, in which high-tensile steel bars or wires are stressed in a mould before the concrete is poured in. *Cf* POST-TENSIONING. *See* PRE-STRESSED CONCRETE.

price/earnings ratio (P/E ratio) A Stock Exchange term indicating the relationship between the total value of a company's shares at the price per share quoted in the market and the earnings, after tax paid, of the company concerned, eg if the price gives a capitalisation value of 100 and the post-tax earnings are 5 the ratio is 100 divided by 5 equals 20.

price payable The sum to be paid by the lessee of a dwelling-house who is enfranchising under the Leasehold Reform Act 1967 as amended. Section 9 gives the assumptions to be taken into account by the valuer; they will differ according to the rateable value of the dwelling-house.

***prima facie* evidence (presumptive evidence)** **1.** Evidence sufficient to discharge the burden of proof unless evidence in rebuttal is offered. **2.** Evidence of a fact sufficient to justify a reasonable inference of its existence but not amounting to conclusive evidence.

primary evidence Evidence which, by its nature, suggests that no better evidence is available, eg the original of a document. *Cf* SECONDARY EVIDENCE.

primary use In town planning terms, the main permitted use of a planning unit comprising the whole, or part, of a property. *Cf* ANCILLARY USE.

prime cost contract A form of building contract where the contractor's remuneration is calculated on the actual costs of materials, labour and plant (the prime costs) plus an agreed figure or percentage for administration, overheads and profit. Particularly used where it is difficult, at the estimating stage, to ascertain the extent of the works required, eg in the restoration of historic buildings. *See* COST-PLUS CONTRACT.

prime property **1.** Generally: The best property from a particular person's viewpoint. **2.** Investment: A property of a particular type which commands the maximum years' purchase in relation to rent for that type of property when calculating capital value at a given date. *See* PRIME TRADING LOCATION.

prime tenant A tenant whose reputation is such that there is no doubt he will fulfil his obligations under any lease he enters into.

prime trading location A shopping area where one has, and can expect to retain, the best quality of tenant and which has the best forecast of rental growth.

prime yield Descriptive of the current yield used in the valuation of property let at full market value and which — for the class of property concerned — is of the best physical quality, in the best location, and with the best tenant's covenant and contemporary lease terms. *See* COVENANT 2; CURRENT YIELD.

primogeniture The right of succession of an eldest son to an estate on the owner's death (to the exclusion of all other claimants). *Cf* GAVELKIND.

principal **1.** The amount of a loan or mortgage (as distinct from the interest payable thereon). **2.** The client on whose behalf an agent acts.

principle of equivalence The duty of an authority acquiring land or buildings compulsorily to compensate the claimant so as to leave him in the same financial position as he enjoyed prior to the acquisition.

priority of mortgages Where there are two or more mortgages secured on a property, the order in which they are discharged by repayment to the extent of any funds available on default by the mortgagor.

priority yields In financial agreements for development projects, the selected rate(s) of interest for ascertaining the tranche(s) of income reserved firstly to the funding institution and secondly to the developer. In effect, each tranche is a percentage of the capital invested or the value attributed to the developer's expertise and contribution. The agreements usually provide for any income over the "priority" tranche(s) to be shared, in agreed proportions, between the parties.

private Act An Act of Parliament passed as a result of a privately petitioned bill which has been approved by the legislature. It differs from a public Act to the extent that it is generally of interest only to specific individuals or is applicable only in specified local areas rather than of effect in a national sense.

private company A company where the shares are owned by a few people, often being members of a family, and not available for purchase by any member of the public. *Cf* QUOTED COMPANY.

private nuisance The unauthorised use of a property in such a way as to cause damage to or interference with the enjoyment of another's property and giving rise to a civil claim (in tort). *Cf* PUBLIC NUISANCE.

private street works code A procedure, contained in sections 205 to 218 of the Highways Act 1980, whereby a "street works authority" (a county council or, in Greater London, a London borough) may resolve to make up a private street and recover the cost from the owners of the land fronting, adjoining or abutting the street. Objections to the proposals are determined in a magistrates' court. Once the street has been made up, it may be adopted under section 28 as a public highway unless the majority in number of owners object (and their objection is not overruled by the magistrates' court). The highway must be adopted if the majority in rateable value of the owners so request. *Cf* STREET WORKS CODE.

private tender (closed tender) A tender restricted to named parties.

private treaty The most common method of disposal of real property, in which negotiations are carried out between the vendor and prospective purchasers (or their respective agents) privately and in comparative secrecy, normally without any limit on the time within which they must be completed before contracts are exchanged. *Cf* AUCTION; TENDER.

privity of contract The direct relationship between two parties to an agreement which, for each of them, is legally enforceable, eg the relationship between an original lessor and the original lessee that persists throughout the entire term of the lease (and any extension thereof under an option), even after the assignment of either's interest in the property. *Cf* PRIVITY OF ESTATE.

privity of estate The relationship in tenure of landlord and tenant between the two parties, who may or may not be the original landlord or tenant. *Cf* PRIVITY OF CONTRACT.

procedure diagram A pictorial represention of the tasks and activities needed to perform a process, procedure or project. International standards exist for the symbols used in such diagrams. *See* CRITICAL PATH ANALYSIS; PROGRAMME EVALUATION REVIEW TECHNIQUES.

procuration fee A payment, usually in money, to a person who has, by his efforts, brought about something required by his principal, eg a fee payable to an agent who has arranged a loan by way of mortgage on behalf of his principal as borrower.

professional negligence A term often applied to the failure to meet the higher standard of care owed by "professional" advisers or other skilled persons to their clients or third parties by virtue of the special skill and experience which they hold themselves out to possess. Such is not strictly a special branch of the law of negligence but demonstrates that the standard of care — and thus the question whether there has been negligence — will depend upon the circumstances of the particular case, including the knowledge, skill and experience of the person concerned.

profit à prendre A right to take some produce for one's own benefit from the land of another, eg rights to shoot game, graze cattle or extract minerals. Such a right may exist in gross or appurtenant to neighbouring land. *Cf* EASEMENT. *See* RIGHT OF COMMON; TURBARY.

profit rent In valuing a lessee's interest(s), the sum of the rent(s) received from any subtenant(s) and the rental value of any space occupied by the lessee and of any unlet accommodation, less the total rent(s) payable to the immediate landlord(s), with appropriate adjustments for differences in the terms of the leases.

profits basis (profits method) **1.** A method adopted in the valuation of such properties as hotels, theatres, cinemas and caravan parks based upon the accounts of the business conducted on the premises. From the total earnings are deducted all proper annual costs such as working expenses, cost of borrowed money and depreciation; the balance is divided between "tenant's share" and rental value. The capital value (if required) can then be calculated using the investment method. **2.** In rating, "profits basis" is defined in section 115 of the General Rate Act 1967 as the "ascertainment of the value of [a] hereditament by reference to the accounts, receipts or profits of an undertaking carried on therein". This method has evolved from the need of valuers to ascertain the net annual value (rent) as a share of the profit that the hypothetical tenant would make for a property which is rarely, if ever, let.

programme area *See* SPECIAL AREA (PARTNERSHIP AREA).

programme (project) evaluation (and) review technique (PERT) One of several techniques of network analysis. It has the particular feature that the user provides estimated optimistic and pessimistic durations of activities as well as the most likely durations. It, therefore, gives a range of outcomes. *See* CRITICAL PATH ANALYSIS; PROCEDURE DIAGRAM.

prohibition Originally a writ but subsequently a prerogative order of the Queen's Bench Divisional Court restraining an inferior court or tribunal or a public authority from exceeding its jurisdiction or acting contrary to law. *Cf* CERTIORARI; MANDAMUS.

prohibition notice A notice served under section 22 of the Health and Safety at Work etc Act 1974, by an inspector appointed under section 19 of that Act, stating that the inspector is of the opinion that certain activities by persons at work involve or will involve a risk of serious personal injury, specifying the matters giving rise to the risk, stating any alleged contravention of statutory provisions and directing that the activities concerned shall not be carried on by or under the control of the person on whom the notice is served unless the matters specified are rectified. The notice has immediate effect, if so declared, or comes into force at the end of the period specified in the notice. There is a right of appeal to an industrial tribunal.

prohibitory injunction *See* INJUNCTION.

pro indiviso **(Scotland)** Descriptive of property which is jointly owned.

project management (development management) The leadership role which plans, budgets, co-ordinates, monitors and controls the operational contributions of property professionals, and others, in a project involving the development of land in accordance with a client's objectives in terms of quality, cost and time.

proof of evidence A documentary record of the evidence to be given by a witness who is to testify in court, at an arbitration, public inquiry or before some other tribunal. Originally the document was intended solely as an "aide-memoire" for the counsel conducting the case, but now it is customary for expert witnesses to be allowed to read from or refer to their proofs of evidence even in civil court proceedings.

property That which is capable of being owned; it is classified as personalty and realty.

property asset management A comprehensive form of management, similar to property portfolio management except that the managers have a wider degree of discretion to realise property, if thought fit, and retain the cash proceeds or transfer them to other types of investment pending an expected opportunity to reinvest in property on more favourable terms. The primary objective is to maximise overall financial performance. *Cf* PROPERTY MANAGEMENT.

property bond An investment, being a life assurance policy, in the form of units in a property investment fund owned and managed by a life assurance company. They become the property of the insured upon payment of a single premium. There are tax concessions both on capital growth in value and on permitted withdrawals of the total invested at the outset.

property in action The right to recover property by judicial proceedings. *Cf* CHOSE IN ACTION.

property investment trust A public company, having certain tax advantages and complying with rules applicable to its operation and investment activities, managed by a professional specialist team and established for the purpose of acquiring mainly shares in property companies — public or private. To such an extent as is permitted legally, without prejudicing its beneficial tax treatment, it may invest in other securities, own property directly or undertake development. It provides shareholders with an interest in a wide-ranging portfolio and the reassuring knowledge that investment policy is in the hands of experts. *Cf* PROPERTY BOND; PROPERTY UNIT TRUST.

property management The range of functions concerned with looking after buildings, including collection of rents, payment of outgoings, maintenance including repair, provision of services, insurance and supervision of staff employed for services, together with negotiations with tenants or prospective tenants. The extent of and responsibility for management between landlord and tenant depend on the terms of the lease(s). The landlord may delegate some or all of these functions to managing agents. *Cf* FACILITIES MANAGEMENT; PROJECT MANAGEMENT. *See* ACTIVE MANAGEMENT; FULL MANAGEMENT; PROPERTY PORTFOLIO MANAGEMENT.

property management agreement The contract between an owner and property manager. *See* PROPERTY MANAGEMENT.

property owners' public liability insurance An insurance contract which indemnifies the insured property owner against any damages agreed or awarded to third parties arising from his negligent acts or omissions as owner.

property portfolio management The unified management of a group of properties which are held in one ownership. Decisions taken in respect of any issue are reached on the basis of achieving the maximum benefit for the owners, having regard to the effect on the portfolio as a whole rather than on an individual property. *See* PROPERTY MANAGEMENT; PROPERTY ASSET MANAGEMENT.

property register One of the three parts into which the register of each individual title to land is divided under the Land Registration Rules 1925. It contains a description of the land and the relevant interest together with a reference to a filed plan or general map based on the Ordnance Survey map. Notes on any easements, rights, privileges, conditions and covenants benefiting the land are also included. *Cf* PROPRIETORSHIP REGISTER. *See* CHARGES REGISTER.

Property Services Agency (PSA) A body within the Department of the Environment, created by the reorganisation of existing offices in 1972 to provide government departments with estate and property management, building construction, maintenance and supply services.

property unit trust A unit trust, approved by the Department of Trade and Industry, having the object of investing in property.

proper valuation Under regulation 37 of the Insurance Companies Regulations 1981 (SI 1981, No 1654) this ". . . means, in relation to land, a valuation made by a qualified valuer, not more than three years before the relevant date which determined the amount which would be realised at the time of the valuation on an open market sale of the land free from any mortgage or charge."

proposal Under the General Rate Act 1967, a formal procedure by which an aggrieved person or the Valuation Officer may seek to alter the valuation list by having a new entry included (by the Valuation Officer) or an existing entry amended or deleted (by the Valuation Officer or another).

proprietorship register One of the three parts into which the register of each individual title to land is divided under the Land Registration Rules 1925. It contains the name and address of the proprietor and the nature of his title (ie absolute, good leasehold, qualified or possessory) and notes any cautions, inhibitions and restrictions that may affect his right of disposing of the land. *Cf* PROPERTY REGISTER. *See* CHARGES REGISTER; LAND REGISTRY.

prospectus The document prepared in accordance with the Yellow Book and relevant statutes for the flotation of a company. It provides particulars of all the information which may be regarded as necessary in order to understand and evaluate the terms upon which the flotation is proposed.

protected building For value added tax purposes, a listed building or any ancient monument (to which certain works may be eligible for zero rating, eg changes other than repair and maintenance), as described in Schedule 5, Group 8A, to the Value Added Tax Act 1983.

protected monument A "scheduled monument" or any monument which is under the ownership or guardianship of the appropriate Secretary of State for environmental matters or a local authority by virtue of the Ancient Monuments and Archaeological Areas Act 1979. The term is used solely in the context of the offence under the Act of damaging or destroying a monument (section 28(3)). *Cf* ANCIENT MONUMENT.

protected shorthold tenancy Under section 52 of the Housing Act 1980, a protected tenancy granted for a term of not less than one year and not more than five years, subject to conditions relating to termination, prior notification of its nature and the registration of rent. *See* ASSURED SHORTHOLD TENANCY.

protected tenancy Under section 1 of the Rent Act 1977, the contractual tenancy of a separate dwelling-house which benefits from the Act in such matters as security of tenure and rent regulation, and which is not a tenancy excluded under sections 4 to 16A of the Act, eg it is not a holiday letting or an agricultural tenancy.

protective trust *See* ALIMENTARY TRUST.

prudent lotting For valuation purposes, the principle of dividing, if appropriate, an estate into two or more units which are considered as likely to attract the best possible price, eg for capital taxation such as inheritance tax.

public Act Any Act of Parliament other than a private Act. Unlike the latter, a public Act is "judicially noticed" and its existence does not therefore have to be proved in legal proceedings.

publicity A term covering all forms and methods of publicising a product, service or firm. These include press advertising; direct mail; press and public relations; brochures; specifications; display boards and sponsoring.

public limited company (plc) A limited company whose shares are offered for sale to the public on the Official List, the Unlisted Securities Market, the Third Market or the Over-the-Counter Market. *See* QUOTED COMPANY.

public nuisance An act or omission adversely affecting the public, or some section of it, and usually contrary to statute law, eg the Public Health Act 1936. Such an act is usually a criminal offence but may also give rise to civil claims by individuals particularly affected. *Cf* PRIVATE NUISANCE.

public relations The systematic organisation of events, eg conferences, cocktail parties and displays, or the presentation of gifts, or any other activity which serves to impress and remind clients and potential clients of the host's capabilities. It covers the planned development of good relationships with clients, suppliers, government and local authority departments, competitors and, in some cases, the public. *Cf* PRESS RELATIONS; PUBLICITY.

public tender (open tender) A tender open to any member of the public who is able to fulfil the requirements specified in the tender document, the tender being advertised for this purpose. *Cf* PRIVATE TENDER.

public trust A trust for the benefit of the public and which may (but need not) be a charitable trust.

Public Trustee A public officer, appointed by the Lord Chancellor under the Public Trustee Act 1906, who may act as an ordinary, custodian or judicial trustee and with a duty to administer in particular small estates.

puffing **1.** At auction sales, the practice of bidding ostensibly as or on behalf of a genuine prospective purchaser but in reality on behalf of the vendor in order to stimulate bidding and enhance the price. **2.** The extolling or exaggeration of a property's good points, especially by an auctioneer or estate agent, in describing the property.

puisne judge A judge of the High Court not having a distinctive title.

purchase notice A notice served by a qualified owner of a property on a local authority requiring it to purchase his interest. Such a notice can be served, for example, following the refusal of planning permission or its grant, subject to unacceptable conditions, if the owner can show that the property is incapable of reasonably beneficial use in its existing state.

put and take option (put and call option) A contract whereby one party has the right to exercise, at his discretion, either a put option or a call option. *Cf* PRE-EMPTION. *See* CALL OPTION; PUT OPTION.

put option **1.** A contract whereby one party has the option to sell his interest in a property to the second party, usually within a specified time at a stated or calculable price and/or in defined circumstances. It is binding against a third party only if registered as an estate contract. **2.** The stock exchange term for a bargain entitling an owner of securities to sell them at a specific time in the future at a defined price. *Cf* CALL OPTION. *See* PUT AND TAKE OPTION.

Q

qualified covenant A restriction contained in a legal document which limits the rights of a person having an interest in the land but, by its wording, envisages the possibility of removing the limitation on terms agreed between the parties, eg a covenant by a lessee not to assign or sublet without the landlord's written consent. In certain cases, such as the one quoted, statute law strengthens the applicant's position by importing such words as "such consent not to be unreasonably withheld". *Cf* ABSOLUTE COVENANT.

qualified title In registered land, a title subject to some qualification or exception stated in the register, eg a property held subject to some right or interest arising before a specified date.

qualified valuer **1.** One with an appropriate academic or professional qualification and suitable experience in valuing land or chattels. **2.** For the purpose of asset valuations, ". . . a Corporate Member of the Royal Institution of Chartered Surveyors, or the Incorporated Society of Valuers and Auctioneers, or the Rating and Valuation Association, with appropriate post-qualification experience and with knowledge of valuing land in the location and of the category of the asset" (*RICS Guidance Notes on the Valuation of Assets*). A somewhat lengthier definition is to be found in Regulation 37 of the Insurance Companies Regulations 1981 (SI 1981, No 1654).

quantity allowance (quantum allowance) In a valuation of a relatively large property when appropriate in market terms, an end deduction from the rental or capital value, which has been calculated by reference to comparable smaller properties; its purpose is to reflect the greater size of the subject of the valuation. *Cf* END ALLOWANCE.

quantum meruit As much as it is worth: an expression used especially in relation to fees for services (in the absence of any other arrangement), based upon the time involved and the quality of the services provided.

quarter of a year 91 days as distinct from three months.

quarter days (term days)
English
Lady Day — March 25
Midsummer — June 24
Michaelmas — September 29
Christmas Day — December 25
Scottish
Candlemas — February 2
Whitsunday — May 15
Lammas — August 1
Martinmas — November 11

quasi-easement A right or privilege enjoyed by the owner of land over adjoining land he also owns and which, if the latter were in separate ownership, would be an easement. On conveyance of the "dominant" land to another party, the quasi-easement will normally become a true easement unless the conveyance provides otherwise. *See* DOMINANT TENEMENT; SERVIENT TENEMENT.

Queen's Bench Division The division of the High Court whose principal function is to hear civil actions in contract or tort but which also hears appeals from magistrates' courts and from a number of tribunals and supervises all the inferior courts.

Queen's warehouse Any place provided by the Crown or appointed by the Commissioners of Customs and Excise for the deposit of goods for security thereof and for the duties chargeable thereon. *See* WAREHOUSE.

quicquid plantatur solo, solo cedit Whatever is attached to the soil becomes part of the soil. A legal rule underlying the principle that fixtures attached to the land belong to the freehold owner of the land.

quiet enjoyment The express or implied right of a tenant to be given possession of the entire property and his entitlement to recover damages if there is substantial physical interference by acts of the lessor or someone claiming under the lessor.

quinquennial Intervals of five years; commonly used for the periodic inspection of heritage and other property and, in principle, for rating revaluation.

quitclaim deed (USA) A form of conveyance whereby the grantor conveys to the grantee without warranty of title whatever interest he possesses in the property.

quit rent A rent payable by the freeholder of a manor to the lord, by which he was released ("quit") from having to perform such services as ploughing the lord's demesne land or attending him in time of war. Quit rents were abolished on January 1 1936.

quoted company (listed company) A public limited company, the shares of which are listed on a recognised stock exchange. *Cf* PRIVATE COMPANY. *See* LISTING 2.

R

rabbit run A colloquial expression for the route most frequented by shoppers on foot and the areas where shoppers browse, thus tending to become prime locations. *Cf* FOOLER.

rack-rent A rent representing the full, or nearly the full, letting value of a property on a given set of terms and conditions. *See* BEST RENT.

rateable hereditament Under section 115 of the General Rate Act 1967, property which is, or may become, liable to a rate, or a unit of such property which is, or would fall to be, shown as a separate item in the valuation list.

rateable occupation Occupation giving rise to a liability to pay rates; determined by reference to case law and having criteria based on beneficial occupation and actual, permanent and exclusive possession.

rateable occupier An occupier who fulfils the criteria for rateable occupation, not being exempt from rates.

rateable plant and machinery Plant and machinery which is deemed to be part of a hereditament and liable to be assessed either as a part or as a separate item. Items qualifying are identified in section 21 of the General Rate Act 1967 and the Plant and Machinery (Rating) Orders.

rateable property A property for which the occupier is liable to be rated and which is shown in section 16 of the General Rate Act 1967 as comprising lands, houses, coal mines, certain other mines and sporting rights.

rateable value (net annual value) The figure upon which rate poundage is charged. Under section 19 of the General Rate Act 1967, it is either

a for those properties assessed direct to net annual value, "an amount equal to the rent at which it is estimated the hereditament might reasonably be expected to let from year to year if the tenant undertook to pay all usual tenant's rates and taxes and to bear the cost of the repairs and insurance and the other expenses, if any, necessary to maintain the hereditament in a state to command that rent", or
b the gross value less the statutory deductions. For the purpose of the new local non-domestic rating lists due to come into force on April 1 1990 in England and Wales (and April 1 1989 in Scotland), gross value becomes obsolete.

For all material purposes, rateable value and net annual value are now identical.

rate capping Under the Rates Act 1984, the power of the Secretary of State for the Environment to limit (or "rate cap") the expenditure of a rating or precepting authority which, in his view, is exceeding an acceptable level of expenditure. *See* PRECEPT.

rate demand The formal document issued by the rating authority to a ratepayer requiring payment of rates due on a hereditament.

rate, excepted *See* EXCEPTED RATE.

rate, garden or square *See* GARDEN RATE (SQUARE RATE).

rate, general *See* GENERAL RATE.

rate (of interest) The ratio of interest to principal, expressed as a percentage. *See* PRINCIPAL 1. Refer to Appendix IV.

rate of return *Cf* INVESTMENT YIELD. *See* RETURN (ON CAPITAL).

rate period Under the General Rate Act 1967, a year or part of a year for which a rate is made.

rate precept *See* PRECEPT.

rate, rector's *See* RECTOR'S RATE.

rates Generally that part of a local authority's funds raised by charges based on the occupation of land and buildings within their area. *See* GENERAL RATE; RATING AUTHORITIES.

Rating and Valuation Association (RVA) Founded in 1882, a body whose membership consists of persons engaged in rating assessments, revenue collection, valuation and allied spheres of activity. The association conducts its own examinations, and admission procedure. Full corporate membership is by examination, but there are exceptions.

rating areas As defined in section 1(1) of the General Rate Act 1967, these are the boroughs and districts of every county, the City of London, the Inner Temple and the Middle Temple.

rating authorities Under section 1(1) of the General Rate Act 1967, these are each borough or district council, the Common Council of the City of London, the Sub-Treasurer of the Inner Temple and the Under-Treasurer of the Middle Temple.

rating officer The officer of a rating authority responsible for rating matters.

rating surcharge Under section 17A of the General Rate Act 1967, rating authorities who had resolved under section 17 to charge empty rates were also empowered to charge a progressive surcharge on empty commercial property. This surcharge was suspended (but not abolished) from April 1 1981.

Rating Surveyors' Association A body founded in 1909 with a membership consisting of surveyors who specialise in rating. It acts broadly in conjunction with, but independently of, the RICS in promoting the interests of rating surveyors.

rating year For rating purposes, a period of 12 months beginning April 1. *Cf* RATE PERIOD.

ratio analysis In accounting and appraisal, a technique to assess the performance and efficiency of a business organisation or of the management of a building, estate or project. It is arrived at by calculating ratios between particular items in the accounts and comparing them with the ratios pertinent to a comparable activity.

ratio decidendum In a legal judgment, the essential reason(s) or rule(s) of law determining the judge's decision on the matter at issue. *Cf* OBITER DICTUM.

ratione soli By reason of (ownership of) the soil.

ratione solis By reason only.

rat run A colloquial term for a route, off principal roads, which is taken by drivers who are endeavouring to avoid traffic congestion.

re In the matter of, or with reference to.

real estate investment trust (REIT) (USA) A legally constituted organisation (entitled to preferential tax treatment) which enables investors to own and transfer shares of an interest in a property or properties; the shares can be dealt with in a manner similar to corporate stock. In order to qualify, a trust must, among other requirements, be owned by at least 100 shareholders and invest most of its capital in real estate loans or properties and receive income from them. The special feature is that such a trust reduces its own taxable income by a distribution to shareholders with no tax deducted, but this is taxable income in the hands of shareholders according to their own tax status. To maintain the trust's right to gross distributions these must, in aggregate, be equal to a minimum of 90% of the total trust income.

real evidence Evidence consisting of one or more tangible objects. These are known as "exhibits" once they are admitted in evidence.

realised development value (RDV) Under the Development Land Tax Act 1976 (now repealed), the amount (if any) by which the net proceeds of disposal of an interest in land exceeded the relevant base value, ie the highest of the three alternative base values of that interest, calculated according to rules laid down in the Act.

real property (realty) Freehold land, but not leaseholds; the latter are classified as personalty or personal property.

real rate At a particular time, the actual return on an investment in stocks and shares. It will be different from the nominal rate unless, exceptionally, the market value is the same as the nominal value.

realtor (USA) A broker or agent in real estate who is a member of a real estate board affiliated to the American National Association of Realtors.

realty *See* REAL PROPERTY.

reasonable period In the definition of "open market value" contained in the "*RICS Guidance Notes on the Valuation of Assets*", the period within which it would be reasonable to expect to sell a property at that value, having regard to the nature of the property and the state of the market. *Cf* FORCED SALE VALUE.

reasonable wear and tear *See* FAIR WEAR AND TEAR.

reasonably beneficial use The standard by which the Secretary of State determines whether circumstances exist, following an adverse planning decision, to justify confirmation of a purchase notice served by the owner of an interest in the land under section 180 of the Town and Country Planning Act 1971. The land has to be shown to be incapable of reasonably beneficial use in its existing state — or for any use likely to be permitted — as a result of the refusal of planning permission or certain other adverse planning decisions. Among the factors to be taken into account in deciding whether a use is reasonably beneficial are the physical state of the land, its size, shape and surroundings and the general pattern of land use in the area.

rebuild To reconstruct either an entire building or part of a building, restoring the building or the part substantially to its original form.

rebuilding clause A clause in a lease which imposes an obligation on either the lessor or the lessee to rebuild the demised premises in certain circumstances, eg in the event of the property's being destroyed by fire. *See* RENT CESSER CLAUSE.

rebus sic stantibus In its existing state; the term is applied to valuations for rating purposes. *See* MODE OR CATEGORY OF OCCUPATION.

receiver A person appointed by a court or by a mortgagee under statutory powers to safeguard property at risk and/or to collect rents or debts on behalf of debenture holders, mortgagees or other creditors. Following the appointment of a receiver, the circumstances may nevertheless justify obtaining a court order for the sale of the property or the bankruptcy or liquidation of the insolvent individual or company owning the asset(s). *Cf* LIQUIDATOR.

recital In a legal document the facts stated, usually before any reference to the transaction recorded therein, eg in a lease, the reference to the parties involved and any previous lease surrendered.

reconstruct *See* REBUILD.

recovery of land The regaining of possession of land by legal action against an unlawful occupier.

rectification The formal correction and amendment by the court of a mistake in a written contract which misrepresents the real intention of the parties to the contract. Essentials for rectification include:
a complete agreement prior to the written instrument to be rectified;
b intention of both parties that the exact terms be recorded in writing;
c clear evidence of a mistake common to both parties (or a unilateral mistake, of which the other party was aware, from which he would benefit and which he failed to draw to the attention of the mistaken party); and
d a literal fault so that the parties' intention is wrongly expressed.

rector's rate (church rate) The right of a parish priest to raise a rate for parish purposes but without power to enforce payment.

reddendum That part of a lease specifying the rent to be paid or the basis of calculating it.

redeem up, foreclose down Where there are two or more mortgages of the same property, the legal principle that a second or subsequent mortgagee wishing to redeem a superior mortgage by action in the court must make all (prior) intermediate and subsequent mortgagees, as well as the ultimate mortgagor, parties to the action and must redeem all (prior) intermediate mortgages and foreclose all subsequent mortgages, unless one or other of the mortgagors has redeemed the mortgage(s) before the date prescribed in the court order. *Cf* FORECLOSE DOWN.

redemption The cancellation of a mortgage (or other burden on land) by the repayment of the outstanding sum then due. *See* EQUITY OF REDEMPTION.

redemption date The date when a repayable security is due for encashment at its face value; it may be a finite date or a range of dates giving the borrower the option of repaying at any time within that range.

redemption period The period during which a mortgagor is empowered by agreement or by statute to redeem a mortgage.

redemption yield Usually related to government stock, the internal rate of return on an investment, making allowance for the annual income and for any capital gain (or loss). It may be expressed as gross or net of taxation, ie gross redemption yield or net redemption yield.

redevelopment Development of land which entails or follows the removal of all or most of the buildings or structures already existing thereon. In the USA the term usually signifies the development or improvement of land in an urban renewal project.

redevelopment clause A clause in a lease providing for the redevelopment of the property by one or other of the parties at or after a given date or dates. The term is also loosely, and incorrectly, applied to a lessor's option to terminate the lease for redevelopment.

reducing balance depreciation Depreciation calculated as a fixed percentage of the latest written down value. *Cf* CURVED LINE DEPRECIATION; STRAIGHT LINE DEPRECIATION.

re-entry A lessor's right to reclaim title to a property where rent due has not been paid, or some other significant breach of the lessee's covenants has not been remedied, within a period specified in the lease, eg 21 days for arrears of rent. In view of the rights to relief in equity, the landlord cannot normally enforce a right of re-entry without recourse to the courts. *See* FORFEITURE.

reference **1.** A formal request to the Lands Tribunal for the determination of a matter, such as one of the following:
(i) compensation on:
a compulsory purchase of land;
b injurious affection where no land is taken;
c blight and purchase notices;
d injury from land drainage works;
e revocation and other planning orders;
f mining subsidence; or
(ii) valuations for taxation, eg capital gains tax.
2. In written work, a note which may include details of the author, title, edition, publisher, date and page of any other publication used to support a point made. *See* OPERA CITATO (OP CIT).

referencing Measuring and recording the dimensions and details of a property.

refurbishment Improvement and modernisation of a building falling short of rebuilding or redevelopment and thus not normally requiring planning permission (other than for alterations to the external appearance), except in the case of listed buildings. *Cf* REBUILD; REDEVELOPMENT.

regeneration Under section 136 of the Local Government, Planning and Land Act 1980, "bringing land and buildings into effective use, encouraging the development of existing and new industry and commerce, creating an attractive environment and ensuring that housing and social facilities are available to encourage people to live and work in the area". *See* URBAN DEVELOPMENT AREA; URBAN DEVELOPMENT CORPORATION.

regional incentives Various central government grants and subsidies differentially available in certain areas to encourage regional development.

regional shopping centre Essentially a trading centre for comparison goods, visited on a special or occasional shopping trip to buy goods such as fashion items, shoes, furniture and electrical equipment where comparison is important. Such a centre has a trading area of at least 30,000 m^2 and draws on a population upwards of 150,000 within a radius of approximately 10 miles. *See* HIERARCHY OF SHOPPING CENTRES.

registered bonds Securities mainly in the form of fixed interest loans, the owners of which (in contrast to those of bearer bonds) are recorded by the issuing government or corporate body in an appropriate register.

registered land Land, the title to which has been registered at the Land Registry.

registered rent A fair rent under a regulated tenancy, recorded in the register kept for this purpose by the rent officer on its determination by him or, on appeal, by a rent assessment committee.

registered supplier A person whose turnover is sufficiently high to require notification and hence registration as one who must charge VAT on goods and services supplied which are not zero-rated or exempt.

register of available land *See* LAND REGISTER 2.

Register of Sasines (Scotland) A register instituted in 1617 and containing records of all titles and security deeds relating to land in Scotland, giving a purchaser ready access to information as to the last registered proprietor and whether the land is subject to any undischarged loan or other charge.

registration A procedure whereby prescribed property details are recorded and maintained for a given purpose at appropriate offices, eg the registration of fair rents, land title, or planning decisions.

regression analysis One of a set of statistical techniques whose purpose it is to quantify the relationship between two or more groups of data, generally known as variables. The object of this is usually to permit quantitative predictions or forecasting of one of the dependent variables.

regulated tenancy Under section 18 of the Rent Act 1977, a tenancy which is either a protected tenancy or a statutory tenancy.

rei interventus **(Scotland)** A doctrine whereby a party cannot withdraw from an informal agreement in writing or a verbal agreement capable of proof; this arises where action has followed the agreement and the other party has altered his position or incurred expenses, either to the knowledge of the first party or where such action or expenses were the normal and probable result of the agreement. *Cf* ESTOPPEL. *See* PERSONAL BAR; LOCUS POENITENTIAE.

Reilly's law of retail gravitation A formula prepared in 1929 which asserted that the distance of a retail catchment boundary from its centre depended on the distance from that centre to the next competing one and their relative attractiveness (usually expressed in terms of town population or shopping area). Subsequently developed into the retail gravity model.

reinspection **1.** During the course of a building contract, a return visit to the site to ascertain that work seen to be necessary during an earlier visit has been carried out. **2.** A further visit to a property which has been the subject of a previous inspection, particularly in the context of valuations for mortgage purposes. The reinspection is usually limited to a specific area of concern to establish whether certain conditions still exist or have been remedied.

reinstatement The act of putting a part or the whole of a building or structure back into the condition which existed at some relevant previous date.

reinstatement basis of insurance A method of assessing the sum insured or the loss under an insurance policy, whereby the amount payable is based on the cost of the insured property being repaired, if damaged, or rebuilt, if destroyed. The sum is calculated to include such matters as demolition of ruins, construction costs, professional fees and finance, together with an allowance for inflation for the period of reinstatement, on the assumption that the building is destroyed on the last day of the term of the policy. *Cf* INDEMNITY INSURANCE.

reinstatement value The result of applying the reinstatement basis of insurance.

reinsurance Where an insurer insures the risk, or part of the risk, with another insurer. *See* COLLECTIVE INSURANCE.

reiteration One of the badges of trade, being the evidence of a repeated procedure or process, eg the repeated buying and selling of properties. *See* TRADE.

relevant evidence Testimony of facts so related, whether directly or indirectly, to a fact in issue before a court or other tribunal as to prove or tend to prove or disprove the fact in issue. *Cf* ADMISSIBLE EVIDENCE.

relief **1.** (Rating) A statutory reduction in a liability to pay rates due to (i) the status of the occupier, eg a charity, or (ii) the special circumstances pertaining to the occupant's status, eg an agricultural dwelling or a dwelling altered to meet the needs of a person who is disabled. **2.** (Taxation) A statutory reduction in liability for a tax, which would otherwise be due in full. *Cf* EXEMPTION. *See* EXTRA-STATUTORY CONCESSION.

remainder A future interest in land which will take effect after expiry of an existing estate or interest, eg after a life tenancy comes to an end by the death of the life tenant. *Cf* REVERSION. *See* FEE TAIL.

remainder waterway Under the Transport Act 1968, a canal or inland waterway not designated as commercial or cruising: generally not suitable for navigation, although from time to time such waterways are restored for recreational purposes.

remainder zone For valuation purposes, any area left after the application of zoning, ie which does not warrant further subdivision. *See* HALVING BACK.

remeasurement contract (building contract) A form of building contract whereby payments are made during progress of the work at predetermined stages and the amounts paid are calculated at agreed rates on the nature and, as quantified by an approximate method, the extent of work done. Following completion, the final price of the contract work is established by an accurate measurement of the works with a consequential adjustment to reconcile that price with the sum already paid.

remunerative rate For valuation purposes, the selected yield at which the income, after allowing for any amortisation, from an investment property is capitalised, reflecting the risks inherent in that type of property. *Cf* ACCUMULATIVE RATE. *See* ALL RISKS YIELD; YEARS' PURCHASE.

renewal As distinct from repair, this is "reconstruction of the entirety meaning . . . not necessarily the whole but substantially the whole subject matter". (Lord Justice Buckley in *Lurcott* v *Wakely and Wheeler* (1911)). *See* REBUILD.

renewal fund An accumulation of periodic payments into a fund in order to meet future liabilities, eg for the eventual replacement of lifts, boilers and the like and sometimes including redecoration and similar works. *See* MAINTENANCE TRUST FUND; SINKING FUND.

renovation The act of making a building look like new, or restoring it to good condition by repainting, decorating, cleaning and undertaking minor repairs. *Cf* MODERNISATION.

rent Under a lease or tenancy, a periodic payment by the tenant to the landlord for the use of land. Although usually a sum of money, rent can take other forms, eg payment in products or in services. However, the payment must be certain or capable of being ascertained. *See* PEPPERCORN RENT.

rentable area The area of floorspace for which rent is calculated even though other areas, either within or outside the demise, are lawfully used by the tenant. For example, in an office building it is customary to exclude from the direct calculation of rent the space used for corridors, lobbies, stairways, lifts and toilets. *See* NET INTERNAL AREA.

rental value The rent that a property might reasonably be expected to command in the open market at a given time, subject to the terms of the relevant lease. *Cf* CAPITAL VALUE.

rent assessment committee A tribunal consisting of a chairman and normally either one or two members drawn from a rent assessment panel and charged under the Rent Acts with the duty of hearing and determining an appeal against a rent officer's assessment of a fair rent for a regulated tenancy of a dwelling-house.

rent assessment panel A body of persons (appointed for a particular area by the Lord Chancellor and the Secretary of State for the Environment) from whom are drawn the members of leasehold valuations tribunals, rent assessment committees and rent tribunals.

rent cesser clause A provision in a lease which allows the tenant to cease paying rent during a given period, such as during rebuilding after destruction by fire. *See* INSURANCE RENT.

rentcharge A payment not being rent but supported by a power of distress and charged upon land, although the relationship of landlord and tenant does not exist between the recipient and the payer. The Rentcharges Act 1977 provides for the voluntary redemption of existing rentcharges, the eventual extinguishment of all rentcharges and generally prohibits the creation of new rentcharges. Chief rents, fee farm rents and quit rents are examples of rentcharges. *Cf* RENT SECK.

rent-free period An agreed period, usually for several weeks or months, during which a lessee is allowed to occupy the demised premises without payment of rent:

a in consideration for the tenant incurring expenditure on such matters as fitting out the premises or carrying out repairs or improvements;

b to reflect market conditions which favour tenants, eg where the space available for letting exceeds the total tenant demand in that area; or

c by virtue of both a and b.

rent officer An officer appointed by, but independent of, the local authority who, by virtue of the Rent Acts, determines and registers fair rents following an application by the landlord or the tenant, or both, under a regulated tenancy of a dwelling-house.

rent passing *See* PASSING RENT.

rent review A provision in a lease whereby the amount of the rent is to be reconsidered at stated intervals, eg every 5 or 7 years, or on specified dates. The method and procedure for reviewing the rent are outlined in the lease. Failing agreement between the parties, there is normally provision for reference to a third party, ie an arbitrator or independent expert.

rent roll **1.** The sum of the rents payable under the tenancies of an estate. **2.** A document, card index or other information system which provides details relating to the rents from the tenancies of an estate.

rent seck A payment analogous to a rentcharge but which at common law was not supported by a power of distress. However, such a power was granted by statute in the 18th and 19th centuries.

rent tribunal A body, being a rent assessment committee sitting as a rent tribunal, with jurisdiction to determine rents for restricted contracts under the Rent Acts, as amended by the Housing Act 1980.

repair To make good by restoring to sound condition part or parts of a building or structure (or article). "Repair is restoration or renewal by replacement of subsidiary parts of a whole". (Lord Justice Buckley in *Lurcott* v *Wakely and Wheeler* (1911)).

repairs notice **1.** A notice which the local housing authority may serve under section 189 of the Housing Act 1985 requiring the execution of works to render an unfit house reasonably fit for human habitation, provided they are satisfied that such can be achieved at reasonable expense. **2.** Under section 115 of the Town and Country Planning Act 1971, a notice specifying works required for the proper preservation of a listed building. The notice explains that failure to carry out these works within the specified period may result in compulsory purchase and, in certain circumstances, "minimum" compensation.

replacement value The cost of replacing damaged items with new items. It will often be greater than the value of the original items before damage occurred. In the case of valuable antiques, replacement may be impracticable regardless of cost.

reporter (Scotland) A suitably qualified person appointed by the Secretary of State for Scotland to hold a public inquiry, eg for planning, and to make a report thereon to the Secretary of State or other authority by whom the inquiry was instructed. In certain cases, specified in orders made under statute, the appointed person assumes the Secretary of State's responsibility and will issue a reasoned decision letter.

requisition **1.** An application for an official search of the Land Registry, the land charges register or a local authority's records for a certificate disclosing encumbrances on the land. **2.** A list of queries related to title and submitted by a purchaser's or mortgagee's solicitors requesting information relating to title. **3.** The appropriation of property by military authorities in times of emergency.

rescission The cancellation of a contract, eg by the innocent party following a fraudulent misrepresentation. Rescission can be effected only if the parties can be restored substantially to their original positions.

reservation A right or interest which is created and retained by an owner of land when disposing of part or the whole of his interest, eg the retention of a right of way over land sold or leased. *Cf* EXCEPTION.

reserve At auction, an amount specified by the vendor below which the lot will not be sold. The reserve is not usually disclosed publicly although the catalogue or particulars should state that a reserve price has been fixed.

reserved matters In relation to an outline planning permission (or application), those outstanding matters for which details have not been given in the planning application. They may include siting, design, external appearance, means of access or the landscaping of the site.

reserve fund *See* RENEWAL FUND.

residence **1.** A place of abode used more or less indefinitely by an individual or family. **2.** The act of living in a place.

residual amount. In the valuation of land and buildings in accounting for depreciation, the land element left after deducting the depreciable amount.

residual method (residual valuation) A method of determining the value of a property which has potential for development, redevelopment or refurbishment. The estimated total cost of the work, including fees and other associated expenditure, plus an allowance for interest, developer's risk and profit, is deducted from the gross value of the completed project. The resultant figure is then adjusted back to the date of valuation to give the residual value. *See* DEVELOPMENT EXPENDITURE

residual value The value determined by a residual valuation. *Cf* SCRAP VALUE.

res nullius Something which has no owner.

restricted contract Under the Rent Acts a contract, which is not a regulated tenancy, granting a right of occupation of a dwelling-house, usually for a rent which includes payment for the use of furniture and/or services or where, for example, the accommodation is shared with a resident landlord. The rent, if disputed, is determined by a rent tribunal and is recorded in a register maintained by the president of the local rent assessment panel.

restriction An entry in the land register preventing dealings in registered land until compliance with specified conditions or requirements. A restriction can be entered only with the concurrence of the proprietor or at the instance of the Registrar. This is, therefore, a "friendly" entry, unlike a caution or an inhibition.

restrictive covenant (negative covenant) An obligation contained in a deed whereby the covenantor undertakes to refrain from some act affecting the land of the covenantee. The covenant may be stated in positive form, eg to use the property for some defined purpose only, ie to refrain from using it for any other purpose. *Cf* POSITIVE COVENANT.

resulting trust *See* IMPLIED TRUST.

retail The sale of goods to the final consumer, essentially in small amounts. *See* RETAIL TURNOVER.

retail gravity model *See* GRAVITY MODEL.

retail money market The financial market based upon deposits made by individuals and other customers with banks, building societies and certain other institutions. *Cf* WHOLESALE MONEY MARKET.

retail price index (RPI) An index recording the monthly changes in the cost, to the average UK consumer, of a selection of over 500 goods and services the composition of which has been changed from time to time. In its present form, the first base of 100 was introduced in 1956 and currently (1988) the latest in January 1987. When the base is changed the end-of-year figure has been represented in the following year as a new base of 100; therefore comparisons over the long term must reflect these adjustments. NB The Chancellor of the Exchequer is considering a change in the basis of the index (December 1988).

retail turnover (retail sales) Total trading receipts made both through retail outlets and by any special forms of trading (mail order, party plan and automatic vending machines), after deduction of all discounts, credits and deferred rebates to customers or staff. Hire purchase and other credit transactions are included at their cash value plus any charge made for credit provided by the retailer. It includes receipts from repairs, rentals and other services provided by retail outlets, but excludes receipts from non-retail establishments such as motor showrooms, public houses, restaurants, clubs and theatres.

retail warehouse A single-level retail store selling non-food goods with at least 1,000 m^2 gross floorspace, occupying a warehouse, purpose-built or industrial-type building with substantial car-parking facilities.

retained agent An agent instructed to represent his principal in selling, letting or seeking property, his entitlement to fees normally being dependent upon performance of the service.

retained sum (retained amount) Under a building contract, the agreed percentage of the contract price which is to be retained by the employer for an agreed period and paid only as and when any specified defects have been satisfactorily remedied. *See* DEFECTS LIABILITY PERIOD.

retaining wall A wall built to prevent encroachment by earth, water or other materials on to land.

retention period *See* DEFECTS LIABILITY PERIOD.

retirement relief The relief from tax available under section 124 of the Capital Gains Tax Act 1979 for a person who has reached the age of 60 years and who disposes of a business on retirement. Such relief is at an annual *pro rata* rate of gain for a maximum of five years, together with some marginal relief.

return (on capital) The ratio of annual net income to capital derived from analysis of a transaction and expressed as a percentage. (An analysis of a sufficient number of actual returns and a review of factors affecting investment policy will produce a pattern of yields.) *Cf* INVESTMENT YIELD. Refer to Appendix IV.

return (rate of) *See* RETURN (ON CAPITAL).

return for risk and profit A percentage of costs to allow for the developer's annual risk and profit in a valuation to determine a ground rent by deductions from actual or estimated occupation rent(s). *See* DEVELOPMENT YIELD.

return frontage The frontage of a site or building to a side road or footway, as distinguished from the main frontage which is normally along a more important highway.

revaluation **1.** A valuation carried out after and related to a date later than a previous valuation. **2.** The procedures and practices of reassessing all hereditaments to a prescribed date for the purposes of rating, so creating a new valuation list for each rating area. (Currently (1988) the Valuation Office is revaluing all commercial hereditaments in England and Wales to April 1 1988 for the new lists to come into force on April 1 1990.)

reverse gazumping A term sometimes applied to a situation in which a purchaser breaks his word and fails to enter into a contract which fairly reflects the terms agreed, possibly being willing to proceed with the original purchase at a lower price. This is more likely to happen in a falling market, when the purchaser can acquire another property on better terms. *Cf* GAZUMPING.

reverse premium (negative premium) **1.** A payment by the holder of a superior interest to a lessee in consideration of some benefit, eg an improvement in the terms of the lease from the landlord's point of view. **2.** Commonly, but incorrectly, a payment by the owner of a leasehold interest of negative value to an assignee in consideration for relieving him of the liablity.

reverse yield gap **1.** The difference between the yield from equities and the yield on gilt-edged (or fixed-interest) securities, where the yield from the former is exceeded by the yield from the latter. **2.** The difference in yields where a low-yielding investment is funded by a loan at a higher rate of interest.

reversion **1.** That part of a grantor's estate or interest in property left after the grant of some lesser interest, eg the interest of a landlord after granting a lease. **2.** Loosely applied to the future right to receive a substantial financial benefit, whether by way of capital or income.

reversion yield In a valuation for a term and reversion, the discount rate applied to the reversionary income. *Cf* REVERSIONARY RETURN. *See* TERM YIELD.

reversionary estate/reversionary interest *See* REVERSION 1.

reversionary income A potential change in income, especially that which will arise following a rent review or renewal of a lease or a reletting of a property.

reversionary investment A (property) investment, where a substantial part of the capital value is attributable to the prospect of a reversionary increase in rent.

reversionary return (reversionary yield) The income on reversion from a property expressed as a percentage of the purchase price. *Cf* REVERSION YIELD. *See* INITIAL RETURN.

revocation order An order under section 45 of the Town and Country Planning Act 1971 cancelling a planning permission, subject to confirmation by the Secretary of State unless all those affected notify the planning authority that they do not oppose the order. Compensation may be payable for abortive expenditure, or other loss or damage directly attributable to the revocation. *Cf* MODIFICATION ORDER.

RICS/ISVA Code of Measuring Practice *See* CODE OF MEASURING PRACTICE.

right of common The right enjoyed by one or more persons to enter land owned by another (common land) for a defined purpose. The right, which is a profit à prendre may be:

a appurtenant to other land,
b in gross (ie regardless of land ownership); or
c enjoyed by the residents of a particular location, eg the right to pasture their cattle on the common land.

right of entry The right of an authorised person or authority to enter land (including buildings). This may be:
a by express or implied agreement, eg the right of a landlord to enter the premises leased by him to check the state of repair;
b under statutory powers, eg the right of a local authority to inspect under the Housing or Public Health Acts; or
c to take possession under an approved compulsory purchase order, following a notice of entry.

right of light An easement entitling the owner of the dominant tenement to adequate daylight to a window or other aperture from the adjoining servient land. *See* ANCIENT LIGHTS; LIGHT AND AIR EASEMENTS; WALDRAM DIAGRAM.

right of support An easement attached to a property which extends the natural right of support so that the owner of adjoining property cannot do anything which impairs the stability of a specific building. *See* EASEMENT; NATURAL RIGHT OF SUPPORT.

right of way A right given to one or more persons to pass over another's land by way of a defined path. It may be
a an easement attached to the ownership of land;
b a licence, being a purely personal arrangement; or
c a right enjoyed by members of the public.

In each case the right may be limited in one or more of the following ways: (i) in relation to the time in which the right may be exercised, eg to go along a path on Sundays only; (ii) the purpose for which it is available, eg to give access to a garage across a neighbour's driveway; (iii) the method of passage allowed, eg on foot, on horseback or by vehicle; (iv) the means of identifying persons entitled to avail themselves of the right.

rights issue A procedure whereby the issued capital of a company is increased by offering new shares to existing shareholders at a price which is regarded as somewhat favourable to the shareholders. *Cf* CAPITALISATION OF RESERVES.

ring (bidding agreement; knock-out agreement) At auction, an arrangement whereby a group of prospective purchasers, in an endeavour to purchase a property more cheaply, conspire not to bid against each other in the room. One of their number may be nominated to bid and, if he is successful, the group hold a private auction subsequently. The surplus realised from the private auction is distributed amongst the members of the ring. This practice is illegal under the terms of the Auctions (Bidding Agreements) Acts 1927 and 1969.

riparian Descriptive of property to the extent that it is alongside a river or stream.

riparian rights Rights held by a person owning a property abutting a non-tidal watercourse. The rights may relate to the water itself, the bed of the watercourse or both and may extend to such matters as taking water for traditional domestic and agricultural purposes. for navigation or fishing.

rising rent A rent which will increase by predetermined amounts at given times during the term of a lease. *Cf* UPWARD-ONLY RENT REVIEW.

risk In insurance terms, the item(s) or subject(s) against which the protection is provided.

risk capital Cash or cash equivalent subscribed to support a commercial venture such that the whole or part of it may be lost if the venture fails, and if it succeeds the subscriber becomes entitled to his share of the profits, whether by way of income and/or capital appreciation, eg an ordinary share in a company. The degree of risk as estimated is reflected in the yield expected if the venture succeeds. *See* EQUITY 3 AND 4; EQUITY CAPITAL; VENTURE CAPITAL.

rolled-up interest A percentage by way of interest which is not paid at customary intervals but instead is added to the principal amount of a loan as it accrues. In effect it is converted into capital on which interest continues to accrue, thereby increasing the amount of debt outstanding which latter sum is repayable at a predetermined date. *See* FRONT MONEY.

rollover relief A right to postpone the payment of capital gains tax in cases where the proceeds or part of the proceeds of a disposal of business assets are used to acquire other assets.

root of title In conveyancing of unregistered land, a document which forms a solid basis to establish the title to the land. It must go back at least 15 years, sufficiently for identification, showing a disposition of the whole interest contracted to be sold and containing nothing throwing any doubt on the title.

Rose's Constant Rent Tables A set of valuation tables compiled by Jack Rose MPhil FSVA, based on the assumption that income is to be received quarterly in advance and interest is paid annually.

roup An alternative term for auction, particularly in Scotland and northern England.

royal assent The consent given on behalf of the sovereign to a parliamentary Bill, which has been passed by both Houses of Parliament. Such consent converts the Bill into an Act of Parliament.

Royal Institute of British Architects, The (RIBA) The principal professional body in the British Isles concerned with architecture. Founded in 1834, the purposes of the RIBA were expressed in the Royal Charter, granted in 1837, as the general advancement of civil architecture and for promoting and facilitating the acquirement of the knowledge of the various arts and sciences connected therewith. The RIBA now has more than 27,000 members, of which some 5,800 are overseas members.

Royal Institution of Chartered Surveyors, The (RICS) The principal professional body in the British Isles concerned with surveying. It was founded in 1868 by the amalgamation of three surveyors' clubs and has since been joined by, among a number of bodies, the Chartered Land Agents' Society, the Chartered Auctioneers' and Estate Agents' Institute (both in 1970), and the Institute of Quantity Surveyors (1982). The institution was granted a Royal Charter in 1881 and now (1988) has over 80,000 members, including overseas members, in seven divisions. The present divisions are Building Surveyors; General Practice; Land Agency and Agriculture; Land Surveyors; Minerals; Planning and Development; and Quantity Surveyors.

Royal Town Planning Institute, The The professional body in the UK chartered to promote the art and science of town planning. Established in 1914, it had by 1988 a membership of over 14,000. Members work in local government, central government, in private practice, or as academics in planning education or research.

royalty method A method of valuing mineral bearing land by which the royalties likely to be derived from extracting minerals over the life of the workings are estimated and capitalised.

royalty, mineral *See* MINERAL ROYALTY.

rules of intestacy Statutory provisions whereby certain relatives or dependants of an intestate are entitled to specific shares of the deceased's estate. If there are no beneficiaries under these rules, the estate passes to the Crown under escheat.

rules of succession On death the rules governing the distribution of the estate (real and personal) to beneficiaries under a will or on intestacy. *See* RULES OF INTESTACY.

runner **1.** A non-retained agent who makes his business from obtaining advance information on propositions and introducing them to other agents ahead of formal marketing. The intention is to establish a position entitling him to a share of any fee subsequently earned by any one of those agents in respect of such propositions. *See* FINDER'S FEE. **2.** A prospective purchaser for a property.

running yield (straight yield) The present income from a property expressed as a percentage of the present market value.

Ryde's scale A scale of valuers' fees for work done in preparing claims for compensation and negotiating their settlement following the compulsory acquisition of land. The scale was originally drawn up during the railway boom in mid-Victorian times by Edward Ryde, one of the founders of the Royal Institution of Chartered Surveyors and its president in 1880-83. For many years the scale was one of the official RICS scales of professional charges (Scale 5), but as a result of the abandonment of most of these scales in 1982 responsibility for it was taken over by the Chief Valuer, Valuation Office, Inland Revenue, who issued the present revised scale in 1984.

S

sale and leaseback An arrangement whereby a freeholder or a lessee sells his interest in a property for an agreed sum and takes back a lease on the whole or part of the property from the purchaser, generally either at a rack rent or at some lesser rent related to the price paid.

sale price The sum realised on the disposal of a property, whether offered in a recognised market or not, and probably after negotiation. *Cf* ASKING PRICE; SELLING PRICE. *See* MARKET PRICE.

scale fees A schedule of charges authorised as appropriate by the relevant professional or other body for specific professional work. Legally, they may no longer be taken as minimum fees, except in certain limited cases. *See* RYDE'S SCALE.

scarcity value The additional realisable value of a property in a market where there are more prospective purchasers/tenants than suitable and similar properties, so that its value exceeds what would be achievable if supply and demand were in balance. It is an element which has to be disregarded in assessing rents in two statutory contexts, namely rental determinations, including arbitrations under Schedule 2 to the Agricultural Holdings Act 1986 and the fair rent determinations under the Rent Act 1977.

Schedule A *See* SCHEDULES.

scheduled monument A monument which is included in a schedule of monuments compiled and maintained by the appropriate Secretary of State under the Ancient Monuments and Archaeological Areas Act 1979 (section 1(1) and (2)). *Cf* ANCIENT MONUMENT. *See* HISTORIC BUILDINGS AND MONUMENTS COMMISSION FOR ENGLAND.

schedule of condition A statement describing the physical state of a building;

used, for instance, where possession is taken and demolition is to be carried out in advance of the assessment of compensation under compulsory purchase.

schedule of dilapidations A list of the requirements of repair and maintenance which a tenant (or landlord) is obliged to make good under the terms of a lease or tenancy of a property. This can be in the form of either an interim schedule prepared and submitted during the lease or tenancy or a terminal (final) schedule on expiry of the lease or tenancy. In the latter case, the tenant's obligation is usually discharged by a cash payment based upon an agreed estimate of the cost of the relevant repairs or, if lower, the loss in value (if any) of the landlord's interest resulting from the disrepair.

Schedules Under the Tax Acts, the provisions for basic computations for income taxation of source(s) of income; they are Schedules A to F. The principal property Schedules are A, B and D, Cases I and VI:
Schedule A The provisions for the assessment of income from leases in the UK and premiums paid to landlords under short leases.
Schedule B The provisions for the assessment of income from woodlands managed on a commercial basis with a view to the realisation of profit.
Schedule D Case I The provisions for the assessment of income from a trade, eg that of a housebuilder or a property dealer.
Schedule D Case VI The provisions for the assessment of income from a number of sources, including furnished lettings, anti-avoidance under section 776 of the Taxes Act and certain holiday lettings.

scheme world In compulsory purchase, the physical and actual state of affairs at the valuation date and all incidents then affecting the reference land and other land, both in respect of physical characteristics and planning circumstances, including the existence of the scheme for which the land is acquired. *Cf* NO-SCHEME WORLD.

science park A development of an industrial nature suited to accommodate high technology, with supporting amenities, which is associated on site with or is close to a higher educational research establishment to provide cross-fertilisation of ideas between entrepreneurs and researchers for the purpose of enabling academic knowledge to be applied to effective commercial use. *Cf* BUSINESS PARK. *See* HI-TECH BUILDING.

scientific research For the purposes of capital and income taxation allowances, any activities in the fields of natural or applied science for the extension of knowledge.

Scottish Development Agency A government-sponsored organisation set up in 1976 under the Scottish Development Agency Act 1975. Its objectives are to help build a strong economy and a better quality of life in Scotland. A property development division established in 1984 works in partnership with the private sector to bring to the market industrial, commercial and residential property projects.

Scott schedule Named after a former official referee, a schedule, formerly known as an Official Referee's Schedule, which is required as pleadings from a tenant in an action for damages for breach of covenant to repair heard by the court, in particular in proceedings under section 18 of the Landlord and Tenant Act 1927. The schedule, which is usually prepared by a surveyor, sets out the tenant's answer to each item listed in the landlord's priced schedule of dilapidations, stating whether liability is admitted or denied and his view of the price claimed. The object is to have a single document detailing the issues between the parties, so as to reduce time at the trial and legal costs.

scrambled merchandising The selling of a variety, but limited range, of goods from one point.

scrap value For capital gains tax purposes, briefly, the predictable value, if any, which a wasting asset will have at the end of its predictable life, as known or ascertainable at the time when the asset was acquired or provided by the person making the disposal.

scrip issue *See* BONUS ISSUE; CAPITALISATION OF RESERVES.

seal Originally a waxed seal on which, whilst warm and soft, a design peculiar to each of the signatories was impressed. Its purpose was to prove the authenticity of the document. Deeds still have to be "signed sealed and delivered". Nowadays authentication is usually by a red paper wafer affixed by the solicitor and the signature on a deed is sufficient acknowledgment of the seal (the old formal procedure was for a signatory to place a finger on the seal and say: "I deliver this my act and deed"). The "seal" may even be the word "seal" written on the document, usually in a circle.

sealed bid An offer, usually in the form of a tender, submitted in a sealed package on the understanding that it will be opened simultaneously with other competitive offers at a stated time and place. In some circumstances tenderers are permitted to be present when the bids are opened.

sealed offer In proceedings before the Lands Tribunal, eg in connection with compulsory purchase or rating appeals, an unconditional offer which having previously been made by one party but rejected by the other party is then put in a sealed cover, sent to the Registrar of the Tribunal and opened after the Tribunal has made its decision. The amount of the sealed offer relative to the award has an important bearing on any decision by the Tribunal on costs.

search *See* REQUISITION 1.

sea wall **1.** A structure erected along a coastline where there is a risk of tidal seawater rising to such a level that might otherwise flood the coastal area. It may be constructed of stone blocks, banks of shingle, pebbles, reinforced concrete or earth banks of sufficient height to contain the highest water level. **2.** For taxation purposes (capital allowances), defined in section 30(1) of the Taxes Act 1988 as an embankment ". . . necessary for the preservation or protection of the premises against the encroachment or overflowing of the sea or any tidal river".

secondary evidence Evidence which, by its nature, suggests the existence of better evidence but is normally admissible if there is a satisfactory explanation for the absence of the primary evidence.

second-hand evidence *See* HEARSAY EVIDENCE.

second mortgage *See* PRIORITY OF MORTGAGES.

secret trust A trust, the existence of which is not disclosed in the document transferring the property to the intended trustee. It usually arises when the property has been given by a testator (less often by a settlor) to a person who has separately expressly or impliedly agreed to hold the property on trust for a third party.

section 4 grant Under section 4 of the Development of Tourism Act 1969, a capital grant made by a tourist board towards the cost of a tourist project.

section 40 agreement An agreement between a developer and the local highway authority under section 40 of the Highways Act 1980 whereby the authority will adopt one or more roads to be constructed by the developer.

section 52 agreement A legally enforceable agreement between the local planning authority and the owner of any land in their area made under section 52 of the

Town and Country Planning Act 1971. It restricts and/or regulates the development or use of land: eg the owner, in connection with a planning permission, may undertake to carry out works for the benefit of the community. *Cf* CONDITION 3. *See* PLANNING GAIN.

section 776 An abbreviation for section 776 of the Taxes Act 1988 (formerly section 488 of the Taxes Act 1970), which is intended "to prevent the avoidance of tax by persons concerned with land or the development of land." Assessments under this section are made by reference to Schedule D Case VI. *See* SCHEDULES.

secured ground rent A ground rent, payable to a superior landlord, usually the freeholder, related to the underlying value of land which, being developed, provides an additional security to the extent that the development enhances the value of the property. It is, therefore, a ground rent having a reduced risk of irrecoverability in part or in whole should there be default on the part of the ground lessee. *Cf* UNSECURED GROUND RENT.

secured loan A debt where, on default by the borrower, the lender has a legal right to sell something (the security) which is likely to command a price in the market sufficient to cover the debt and all costs incurred in recovering the amount of the debt, together with any accrued or unpaid interest and costs of disposal. This reduces the risk of loss by the lender in default of repayment.

secured rent A rent having a reduced risk of irrecoverability in part or whole by virtue of the relevant property's:

a producing a higher rent than the secured rent payable;
b having a higher rental value in the market; or
c being the subject of a rental guarantee by a third party of substance.

secure tenancy Defined by section 79 of the Housing Act 1985 as a tenancy under which a dwelling-house is let when satisfying the conditions described in sections 80 and 81 of that Act. Under section 80 the landlord must be one of a list of bodies, including a local authority, a new town or urban development corporation, a charitable housing trust and certain classes of housing association, whilst under section 81 the tenant (or each of joint tenants) must occupy the dwelling-house as his only or principal home.

security **1.** In property ownership, the policy and practice of protecting a building, its contents and its occupiers against those who enter it for illicit purposes. **2.** A certificate in the form of a share or stock in a company, showing right of ownership. Also, colloquially, extended to mean the investment itself. **3.** An asset which is legally nominated to be available to a lender for realisation and recovery of money owing following default by the borrower. *See* SECURED LOAN.

security of tenure **1.** The right of a tenant to remain in possession of demised premises in accordance with the terms of the tenancy. **2.** The statutory right of certain classes of tenant to remain in occupation of demised premises beyond the expiry date stipulated in their existing lease or tenancy. The three principal classes of tenant who enjoy such security are those who occupy certain residential, agricultural or business premises. The rules, constraints, exceptions and conditions applicable to these classes are contained in the specific legislation, ie the Rent Acts, the Agricultural Holdings Acts or Part II of the Landlord and Tenant Act 1954, respectively.

seisin In feudal times a person was seised of land or had the seisin thereof when he was in possession of it. The expression is now reserved for possession by a freeholder.

self-build society Defined by section 1(3) of the Housing Associations Act 1985 as "a housing association whose object is to provide for sale to or occupation by its members' dwellings built or improved principally with the use of its members' own labour''.

seller's market A market in any property or commodity where the circumstances are such that the seller has an advantage over a potential buyer to the extent that he can command a higher price than otherwise would be obtainable. In a classic situation this arises when there are more potential buyers than sellers. *Cf* BUYER'S MARKET.

selling price The sum which a vendor states that he is prepared to accept whether or not it is the price he eventually accepts. *Cf* SALE PRICE.

sensitivity analysis A series of calculations in a financial appraisal or forecast involving one or more variables, eg future rates of inflation or deflation and cost estimates, which are modified in turn to show the differing results.

service charge The amount payable by a tenant on account of services provided by his landlord. In the specific case of residential flats, as defined for the purpose of sections 18 to 30 of the Landlord and Tenant Act 1985, this means an amount payable by a tenant as part of, or in addition to, rent for services, repairs, maintenance or insurance or the landlord's costs of management, the amount varying with the relevant costs (including overheads).

serviced accommodation Suites of offices or rooms where the landlord provides a range of services within the individual demised premises extending beyond the traditional ones associated with the maintenance and management of the building itself or the operation and maintenance of the installation or plant therein, eg furniture, telephone, fax machine, room cleaning, and/or provides centralised special services, such as a receptionist and secretarial and communication facilities.

service occupancy A type of occupancy, usually of residential premises, which is granted by an employer to an employee as a condition of his employment for the better execution of his duties and which continues only during the period of employment. Following cessation of his employment, the occupier may be able to claim protection under the Rent Acts, where the ex-employer cannot satisfy the court that he has a justifiable need for the accommodation to house another employee. *Cf* SERVICE TENANCY.

service tenancy A tenancy where the tenant is an employee of the landlord, the employment having been the motive for the grant of the tenancy. In most cases the contracted tenancy is determinable if the employment ceases but may be automatically succeeded by a protected statutory tenancy under the Rent Acts. The distinction between ''service tenancy'' and ''service occupancy'' is often blurred, but the latter term should be confined to cases where no true tenancy exists.

service trade A business which, rather than selling goods, offers a service as its principal activity, eg dry cleaning, shoe repairing, travel agency. It should be noted that service trades may fall within Class A1, A2 or B1 of the Use Classes Order 1987; for example, a travel agency is classed as a shop (Class A1), whereas an estate agency is either financial and professional services (Class A2) or business (Class B1).

services **1.** The plant, machinery and other equipment installed in a property for the provision of water, drainage, heating, power, air-conditioning, lifts, fire protection and the like. **2.** The provision of facilities and the operating systems, such as hot water, central heating, air-conditioning, lifts and the like, and/or the availability of gardeners, porterage, caretaker or security guards, especially in a multi-occupied building. *See* SERVICE CHARGE.

servient tenement A parcel of land which is burdened by an easement or other incorporeal right such as a right of access or passage. *Cf* DOMINANT TENEMENT.

set-off 1. In litigation, a financial cross-claim by a defendant which, if both parties are successful, ie in claim and cross-claim, will be offset against the damages awarded to the plaintiff, the costs normally being calculated by reference to the net sum. 2. In the compulsory purchase of land, a reduction in the compensation payable to the claimant to reflect some financial benefit to him resulting from the scheme. *Cf* BETTERMENT 1.

setting out In construction or civil engineering projects, the preliminary stage of marking on the ground with pegs the lines of walls and corners of proposed buildings, the centre lines of roads or other features of a project, thereby establishing clear points of reference which should ensure that the building or structure is in fact built precisely where intended.

settled land Land which is the subject of a settlement under the Settled Land Act 1925. *See* SETTLEMENT 1.

settlement 1. A disposition of land or property by deed, will or possibly statute under which a trust is created by the settlor designating the beneficiaries and the terms upon which they are to benefit from the property, eg settlements under the Settled Land Act 1925, known as "strict settlements". 2. A negotiated agreement between parties in dispute, eg (i) in civil litigation or arbitration proceedings; (ii) in a claim for compensation arising from the exercise of statutory powers such as compulsory purchase. 3. Movement of the soil, eg where caused by subsidence to fill an underground void or by moisture extraction. 4. Movement of a building or structure where substrata are insufficiently firm to support the weight of the building or structure or the foundations are inadequate. *See* SUBSIDENCE.

settlor A person (individual or body) who makes a settlement or trust.

severance 1. The physical separation of land into two or more parcels, eg resulting from the exercise of compulsory purchase powers by an authorised authority on part of the land. 2. The right to compensation which may result from such separation, eg where a motorway is constructed through farmland, thereby making the running of the farm more costly. The right is provided under section 7 of the Compulsory Purchase Act 1965. *Cf* MATERIAL DETRIMENT.

SfB A classification system for components and materials used in building which was derived originally from a committee of representatives of the building industry in Sweden called Samarbetskommittén för Byggnadsfrågor, concerned with co-ordinating information.

shell construction (shell finish) A method of constructing a building whereby the developer completes the structure but leaves considerable work to be carried out, especially to the interior, before it can be occupied and used by a prospective tenant. It is common for retail property to be handed over in this form, leaving the tenant with the responsibility for the shop front and for covering rough concrete floors, unplastered walls and ceilings.

shophouse In South-east Asia, an historic or traditional form of building in which the ground floor is the family place of business and upstairs (one or more floors) is the family's living accommodation.

shopping arcade *See* ARCADE.

shopping centre A central location where shops are grouped together to serve a local or wider population. Centres are classified in hierarchical order by function and/or size, and by the area served. *See* HIERARCHY OF SHOPPING CENTRES.

shopping mall A group of retail outlets designed and built with ways for pedestrians on one or more levels to form a unified whole under one roof. *Cf* WALKWAY.

shopping precinct Usually an open, pedestrianised and possibly landscaped shopping area providing amenities for the public, such as sculptures, fountains, gardens with seating accommodation and children's play areas.

shop window display The overall width of glazing at the frontage of retail premises, which is designed to give passers-by a view of the shop itself or of goods or other things presented, for example usually on stands behind the glazing. It extends to include display windows and glazed entrance(s).

shortfall The amount by which receipts or reimbursements are less than sums paid out. Examples include:

a in insurance, the balance of money necessary to meet the cost of reinstatement of a damaged or destroyed property, after deduction of payments recoverable under the insurance policy;

b under service charge arrangements in leases, the difference between total expenditure which has to be borne by the landlord and some lesser amount recovered or recoverable from the tenant(s).

shorthold tenancy *See* ASSURED SHORTHOLD TENANCY; PROTECTED SHORTHOLD TENANCY.

short lease For the purpose of taxation of income or capital gains, a lease for a term of 50 years or less. *Cf* MAJOR INTEREST.

short tenancy In compulsory purchase, a tenancy for not more than a year to which the compensation provisions of section 20 of the Compulsory Purchase Act 1965 apply following notice of entry.

side-by-side lease A lease under which the net income received by the lessor is a predetermined proportion of the rents received by the lessee from sublettings, after deducting agreed expenses. Where the lessee himself occupies part of the property demised, this benefit should be reflected in the agreed proportions of net income to be shared between the parties, unless a notional rent is paid by the lessee for the part so occupied. Thus lessor and lessee are joint participants in the net income from the property.

side letter A letter accompanying a legal document, explaining the intention of the parties.

sight line On a plan, a line used as a means of establishing visibility standards at road junctions or access points on to public roads. The basic rule is that at eye-level (defined as 1.05 m above road level) there should be a clear view over a given area. *See* VISION SPLAY.

signing date The date on which a valuation certificate or report is signed. *Cf* DATE OF VALUATION.

simple trust *See* BARE TRUST.

simplified planning zone (SPZ) Under section 24A of the Town and Country Planning Act 1971, inserted by section 25(1) of the Housing and Planning Act 1986, "an area in respect of which a simplified planning zone scheme is in force". The adoption or approval of such a scheme has the effect of granting planning permission for development specified or of any class specified in the scheme. Every local planning authority has a power to prepare simplified planning zone schemes, with default powers reserved to the Secretary of State. *Cf* ENTERPRISE ZONE.

single rate method A method of valuing terminable income flows, calculated on the basis that the remunerative and accumulative rates of interest are identical. *Cf* DUAL RATE METHOD.

single rate table A valuation table of years' purchase calculated on the basis that the remunerative and accumulative rates of interest are identical. *Cf* DUAL RATE TABLE.

single rate years' purchase *See* SINGLE RATE TABLE.

sinking fund A sum of money set aside at regular intervals to earn interest on a compound basis either:

a to be set off against the diminution in value of a wasting asset, eg a lease, or
b to meet some future cash liability.

In property valuations it is usually assumed that the money will be invested at a "risk free" rate which is regarded as appropriate according to market conditions. The total amount calculated to accumulate by the sinking fund may be the same as the original investment or liability but possibly with an adjustment to reflect the view taken on future fluctuations in the value of money. *See* ANNUAL SINKING FUND.

site coverage The proportion of a site covered by buildings or structures. In the case of a complex design, the area of land covered by the building to the most extensive of its horizontal projections, which may be above ground level and/or on several different floors.

site finance *See* BRIDGING FINANCE.

site of special scientific interest (SSSI) A parcel of land designated by the Secretary of State for the Environment after consultation with the Nature Conservancy Council, under section 29 of the Wildlife and Countryside Act 1981, as requiring special protection to secure the survival in Great Britain of an animal or plant, or to comply with an international obligation or to conserve any of its flora, fauna, or geological or physiographical features. After the making of an order under the section, no person may carry out any operation on the land likely to be damaging or destructive without the prior written consent of the Nature Conservancy Council.

site plan A drawing of an area of land, on a horizontal plane, showing the boundaries and physical extent of the land included in a particular parcel. It may also show any existing buildings or the proposed layout of a development.

site value **1.** The value of undeveloped property as a site for development. **2.** That part of the value of a developed property attributable to the site. This may be calculated on the assumption:

a that the existing building(s) or structure(s) remain, or
b that they have been cleared away and the site is available for redevelopment.

3. For the purpose of assessing compensation under section 585 of the Housing Act 1985, for unfit houses beyond repair at reasonable cost or, with certain exceptions, for houses within a clearance area, this is defined as "the value at the time when the valuation is made of the site as a cleared site available for development in accordance with the requirements of the building regulations in force in the district" but not exceeding the ceiling value under section 589.

site value rating A system of local taxation adopted in some countries based upon the value of land, rather than the occupational value of the land with existing buildings, but including any element of value attributable to a potential for a use or development other than that existing at the relevant date.

sitting rent *See* VIRTUAL RENT.

sitting tenant The tenant who is either lawfully in physical possession or entitled to immediate physical possession of the demised premises. The expression is often employed in connection with the occupation of premises where the tenant is entitled to statutory protection upon expiry of the lease. *See* SITTING TENANT VALUE.

sitting tenant value The purchase price which might reasonably be expected to be paid in the open market at a given time by the tenant currently in possession of land.

"six rules" The rules set out in section 5 of the Land Compensation Act 1961 which govern the assessment of compensation on the acquisition of land by authorities possessing powers of compulsory purchase.

skill and care warranty A warranty to the effect that proper skill and care has been exercised in carrying out the planning, design and/or construction of a development. It is obtained by a developer, building owner or other party with an interest in a development project, who is not in a direct contractual relationship with the builders, architects or engineers. The warranty is given by such person as, having regard to the circumstances of the case, is competent to do so.

sleeping rent Another term for dead rent.

slice method *See* HARDCORE METHOD.

slum clearance The procedures for dealing with unfit buildings and other properties under the Housing Act 1985. *See* CLEARANCE AREA; DEMOLITION ORDER; SITE VALUE 3; UNFIT PROPERTY.

smallholding Land let by a smallholdings authority, ie a county council under the Agriculture Act 1970. To qualify, a unit of land must, when farmed under reasonably skilled management, be capable of providing full-time employment for not more than two men. In the early 1970s smallholdings authorities had to submit to the Ministry of Agriculture proposals for reorganising their smallholding estates and they cannot create any new smallholding unless already approved by the ministry in their proposals or given fresh ministry consent. The authorities have powers to acquire and manage land for the purposes of smallholdings and to let out surplus smallholding land. The minister has similar powers. Special rules apply to smallholdings which are agricultural holdings under the Agricultural Holdings Act 1986, eg the consent of the agricultural land tribunal to a notice to quit by a smallholdings authority is not normally required. *See* COTTAGE HOLDING.

smoke control area A totally, or largely, smokeless zone comprising the whole or part of a local authority district and established by means of a smoke control order. Within such an area, subject to any exemptions or limitations for the time being in force, it is an offence by the occupier of a building if smoke is emitted from its chimney(s), unless the smoke was caused only by an "authorised" fuel. *See* SMOKE CONTROL ORDER.

smoke control order An order under section 11 of the Clean Air Act 1956, made by a local authority but requiring ministerial confirmation, declaring the whole or any part of the local authority district to be a smoke control area.

sod fertility An additional item of claim by a tenant introduced into tenant-right valuations, by paragraph 12(1) of Schedule 1 to the Agriculture (Calculation of Value for Compensation) Regulations 1978 (SI 1978 No 809). This is in respect of long-term leys (established for three years or more) grown on a holding in an area where the growing of a succession of arable crops is normal practice. *See* SOD VALUE.

sod value The value of crops of clover, grass or lucerne of at least three years' duration planted for grazing or mowing purposes on what is normally arable land (long-term leys), either existing or ploughed out within the two years preceding the termination of an agricultural tenancy, calculated in accordance with paragraph 12(2) and (3) of Schedule 1 to the Agriculture (Calculation of Value for Compensation) Regulations 1978 (SI 1978 No 809). *See* SOD FERTILITY.

sole agent (exclusive agent) One who is the only agent entitled to represent his principal. In the absence of a specific contract to the contrary, such an arrangement does not entitle the agent to a fee if the principal effects a sale/purchase without the agent's help. *Cf* SOLE SELLING RIGHTS.

sole selling/letting rights The rights exercisable by an agent where the principal has contracted to convey wholly exclusive rights to sell/let the property, entitling the agent to commission even if the principal acts on his own behalf. *Cf* SOLE AGENT (EXCLUSIVE AGENT).

solum (Scotland) Ground on which a tenement is built.

solus agreement An agreement such as one between a petrol company and the occupier of a petrol filling station for the direct supply of petrol, diesel and oil on terms prohibiting the purchase of such products from any other supplier, usually in return for a loan and/or special price rebates.

special Act Defined by the Lands Clauses Consolidation Act 1845 as: ". . . any Act which shall be hereafter passed which shall authorise the taking of lands for the undertaking to which the same relates . . .", eg the Education Act 1944, which contains the power to acquire land for educational purposes.

special agent An agent authorised to act only for a special purpose or for a purpose not in the ordinary course of the agent's usual business or profession.

special area (partnership area) An area specified as such by a designated district authority under section 8 of the Inner Urban Areas Act 1978. It falls within the second level of designation (of areas of special social need), the first level being areas designated under section 1 of the Act and the third level the non-statutory designation of "programme areas".

Special Commissioners Persons of qualified legal standing appointed by the Lord Chancellor, after consultation with the Lord Advocate, "to perform such duties as are assigned to them by an enactment". They deal with special categories of tax appeals and (unlike General Commissioners) are salaried officials.

special development order (SDO) An order made under section 22(3) of the Town and Country Planning Act 1971 so as to modify the provisions of the general development order for specified areas or classes of area or to grant specific planning permission or greater freedom from control in certain areas. *Cf* SIMPLIFIED PLANNING ZONE.

speciality centre A shopping centre of a type first established in the USA, where specialist retailers (often individuals) provide high-quality and unusual goods and services in a setting which is attractive and interesting and has extensive refreshment and relaxation facilities. Such centres are generally intensively managed, are often in refurbished and conserved buildings of character, and attract a high proportion of tourist custom, eg Covent Garden, London.

special parliamentary procedure In compulsory acquisition, a parliamentary procedure (available after a compulsory purchase order has been confirmed by the appropriate minister) for special descriptions of land, eg:

a certain National Trust land; and,
b common, open space or fuel or field garden allotment land; and
c the site of an ancient monument or other subject of archaeological interest.

The procedure enables petitions of amendment and objection to be considered by a joint committee of both Houses of Parliament.

special purchaser A purchaser who has a particular reason for acquiring an interest in a property because of his own special circumstances, eg someone:

a who owns a different interest in the same property;
b who owns an adjoining property; or
c whose special needs can be satisfied only by the acquisition of that interest in that particular property.

In a and b there may be marriage value.

special purchaser value The price which might reasonably be expected to be paid by a special purchaser; this value will usually exceed that which might be paid by others who are in the open market. *Cf* MARRIAGE VALUE.

special suitability or adaptability In assessing compensation under compulsory purchase:

a the characteristics of a parcel of land which is specially suitable or adaptable for a purpose that can be achieved only under statutory powers or
b where there is no market for that purpose other than (i) for one special purchaser or (ii) for the requirements of an authority with compulsory powers.

Under rule (3) of section 5 of the Land Compensation Act 1961, any element of market value attributed to those characteristics has to be excluded.

specification A document which lists and describes all items of construction in a building or engineering project in sufficient detail to ensure that a contractor has enough information to enable the project to be carried out. The specification describes the materials, form of construction intended and the standard required in accordance with such plans and drawings as are provided.

specific performance Where damages would not be an adequate remedy, a court order requiring compliance with a contract by a person who is in default of his obligations, eg an order directing a defaulting vendor or purchaser to sell or buy a property, the subject of an agreement for sale.

speculative development The construction of a building or buildings where there is no known buyer or tenant at the outset but the scheme will be offered for sale or to let, usually at or near completion. Such schemes are commonly associated with dealers, but equally an investor may undertake such a development for retention within his portfolio. *See* DEALER IN LAND; INVESTOR IN LAND.

speculative funding The financing of a future development where there is a risk of not selling (or letting) the completed building at a figure exceeding, or even attaining, the development expenditure (or its annual equivalent). Nevertheless, the funding source forms a view at the outset that the development will be profitable, having regard to its own interpretation of the prospects. *See* UP-FRONT FUNDING.

speculator A person (usually a dealer) who undertakes a transaction in property in expectation of making a profit but with the risk of not doing so. *See* DEALER IN LAND; BADGES OF TRADE.

sporting rights Generally, rights of shooting, hunting or fishing. Such rights may be reserved to the landlord under a tenancy and will be defined in the agreement. The term is defined variously in statutes, eg in section 29(5) of the Taxes Act 1988 it "means rights of fowling, shooting or fishing, or of taking or killing game, deer or rabbits".

spot listing An emergency procedure, usually initiated by a local authority, for the addition of a building to the statutory list of buildings of special architectural or historic interest made under the Town and Country Planning Act 1971. The procedure is available where a building is under threat of demolition or fundamental change. *Cf* BUILDING PRESERVATION NOTICE. *See* LISTED BUILDING.

squatter A person in occupation of land without having any interest in the land or licence from the owner to be in possession thereof.

squatter's title The "title" to land acquired by 12 years' adverse possession against the person who had been lawfully entitled to possession.

stakeholder In property terms, an estate agent or solicitor holding a cash deposit paid by a prospective purchaser but having no right to transfer such deposit to his principal until the relevant transaction has been completed; meanwhile, the stakeholder is responsible to both parties for the sum's safe keeping.

stamp duty Under the Stamp Act 1891, as amended, a fixed or *ad valorem* tax chargeable on the execution of documents pertaining to certain transactions, eg leases, agreements for lease and conveyances. The duty is payable by the grantee, ie the lessee or purchaser, and the document cannot be adduced as evidence of the transaction unless adequately stamped.

Standard Industrial Classification (SIC) A document classifying for statistical purposes the economic activities carried on within the UK. It is produced by the Central Statistical Office and the latest revision, made in 1980, was primarily to examine and eliminate differences from the activity classification of the Statistical Office of the European Communities (SOEC). The SIC classifies activities into ten divisions, ranging from "Agricultural, forestry and fisheries" (Division 0) to "Other Services" (Division 9), each division being subdivided into classes, groups and individual activities.

standard rate **1.** The rate of value added tax which prevails at a particular time. *Cf* ZERO-RATED SUPPLY. **2.** The basic rate of income tax which applies in a particular tax year, eg 25% in 1988/89.

standard-rated supply For value added tax, a supply of goods or services where tax is charged at the standard rate. *Cf* EXEMPT SUPPLY; ZERO-RATED SUPPLY.

standard shop unit At a particular time, the most commonly demanded size for a retail outlet. In the 1970s this was approximately 20 ft frontage by 50 ft depth, but currently (1988) the requirement has increased and many multiples need 25 ft to 30 ft frontages and 100 ft depth; virtually all the space would be utilised for sales purposes.

standing house approach For the purpose of the Leasehold Reform Act 1967, a method of arriving at the site value, and hence the modern ground rent, by taking a proportion of the entirety value of the house. *See* CLEARED SITE APPROACH; NEW-FOR-OLD APPROACH.

starter homes Residential accommodation designed and built to suit the needs of first-time buyers. The design may permit the purchaser to enlarge or generally improve the facilities as additional financial resources become available.

starter housing The marketing mix of residential accommodation, furnishings and fittings therein, mortgage arrangements and other offerings which enable buyers to enter the housing market as owner-occupiers for the first time.

Statement of Standard Accounting Practice (SSAP) One of a series of documents about standard methods of accounting approved by the accountancy profession for application to financial accounts of companies and other bodies, with the intention of giving a true and fair view of their financial position. Each statement may contain limitations of general scope. The statements apply to the UK and the Republic of Ireland. Statements on a broader basis are issued by the International Accounting Standards Committees to promote worldwide harmonisation of accountancy standards, but they do not override UK or Irish law, or any SSAP.

statute law That part of the law which derives from legislation, ie Acts of Parliament. *Cf* CASE LAW; COMMON LAW.

statutory deductions ("stats") In rating, the amounts which are subtracted from the gross values of non-industrial properties to arrive at their net annual values. They are prescribed by the Valuation (Statutory Deductions) Orders 1962 and 1973. In the absence of gross values in the new local non-domestic rating lists to be prepared under the Local Government Finance Act 1988 they will become obsolete from April 1 1990 in England and Wales (and April 1 1989 in Scotland).

statutory formula Under the General Rate Act 1967, an arithmetical method of calculating the gross value or net annual value of certain hereditaments occupied by such statutory undertakers as gas, electricity, railway and water authorities.

statutory instrument (SI) A form of delegated legislation by which a minister supplements the broad provisions of an Act of Parliament by setting out details which can be varied from time to time. Some statutory instruments require positive resolutions of Parliament before coming into force, but others have to be laid before Parliament for 40 days and are liable to annulment by resolution of either House of Parliament during this period.

statutory tenancy Under section 2 of the Rent Act 1977, a tenancy of a separate dwelling-house which comes into existence under the Rent Acts, when the contractual tenancy is terminated by notice to quit or otherwise comes to an end.

statutory trust A trust created by statute when land is held by trustees on trust pending its sale, eg under the Law of Property Act 1925 beneficial joint tenants own land on a statutory trust for sale (as trustees for themselves). *See* JOINT TENANCY.

statutory undertakers Bodies or undertakings authorised by statute to construct and carry on operations which could not be constructed or carried on without statutory powers. In section 290 of the Town and Country Planning Act 1971, as amended, they are defined as those who are "authorised by any enactment to carry on any railway, light railway, tramway, road transport, water transport, canal, inland navigation, dock, harbour, pier or lighthouse undertaking, or any undertaking for the supply of electricity, hydraulic power or water".

stock-in-trade Products or property which a dealer holds in readiness to sell in the course of trade, eg trading stock or a property dealer's land and buildings. *See* DEALER IN LAND.

stop notice A notice served by a local planning authority under section 90 of the Town and Country Planning Act 1971 directing that an activity on land for which an enforcement notice has been served should stop, notwithstanding the enforcement notice has not yet come into effect. The notice may be served on any person who appears to have an interest in the land and wilful contravention is a criminal offence. However, compensation can be claimed for loss resulting from a stop notice, if the enforcement notice is quashed, varied or withdrawn otherwise than by the grant of planning permission (for a previously unlawful activity) or if the stop notice is withdrawn.

storage and preparation areas Those parts of a shop used for the storage and preparation of goods and for services, including stockrooms, bakeries and food preparation areas.

storey In a building or structure, any floor on one level. *See* FLATTED FACTORY; MULTI-STOREY.

straight-line depreciation Depreciation calculated as a fixed percentage of the original value which produces a straight line when plotted as a graph. *Cf* CURVED LINE DEPRECIATION; REDUCING BALANCE DEPRECIATION.

straight yield *See* RUNNING YIELD.

strata title Freehold title to a horizontal part of a building with other freehold titles above and/or below. Satisfactory arrangements for management usually involve a statutory obligation for the setting up of a management corporation with responsibility for the maintenance of common facilities and areas. Such titles are found, *inter alia*, in Singapore and New South Wales but not, so far, in England or Wales, because of the difficulty of enforcing positive covenants. *See* FLYING FREEHOLD.

street In general parlance this usually refers to a made-up road which has houses or other buildings on one or both sides. However, there are special definitions for statutory purposes, eg under the Highways Act 1980 section 329 (1) it "includes any highway and any road, lane, footpath, square, court, alley or passage, whether a thoroughfare or not and includes any part of a street . . .". There is a broadly similar (but longer) definition under the Public Utilities Street Works Act 1950 section 1(3). *See* STREET WORKS CODE.

street works authority *See* PRIVATE STREET WORKS CODE.

street works code A code under the Public Utilities Street Works Act 1950, as amended, governing the exercise of powers which include breaking up and tunnelling under a street, or breaking up and opening a sewer under a street. *Cf* PRIVATE STREET WORKS CODE.

strict settlement *See* SETTLEMENT 1.

structural survey *See* BUILDING SURVEY.

structure plan Under section 7 of the Town and Country Planning Act 1971, a written statement of the county planning authority's policy and proposals for land use and development of their area, containing such other matters and such diagrams as are prescribed by regulation. The plan has to be accompanied by an explanatory memorandum. *Cf* LOCAL PLAN; UNITARY DEVELOPMENT PLAN.

sub-agent A person who receives and acts upon instructions from an agent, rather than from the principal.

sub-contractor A contractor who undertakes part of a contract which is the overall responsibility of the main contractor and whose work is usually confined to a specialist skill, eg demolition, engineering installations or plastering.

subinfeudation (Scotland) The creation of a new feudal estate out of an existing one with a new vassal and superior relationship, so that the former vassal in occupation becomes the superior in the new estate but continues to hold the land from his own superior. *See* GROUND ANNUAL.

subjective value (value to the owner) An estimate of the worth attributed by an owner or prospective purchaser to an interest in property, taking into account his personal circumstances, eg sentiment or his tax situation.

subject plan A local plan linked to a specific class (or specific classes) of development or other use of the land to which it relates, eg mineral extraction.

subject to contract A phrase which qualifies a proposed agreement so that it is not legally enforceable in England and Wales until a formal contract has been entered into by the parties. (The position in Scotland is different.) *Cf* MISSIVES OF SALE (SCOTLAND).

sub judice Literally, under a judge. Descriptive of a case which is to be or is being heard by a court and of the rule against comment which may prejudice the outcome of the proceedings.

sublease (underlease) A lease held from a lessor who has a superior lease of or including the demised premises. *See* SUBTENANCY.

sublessee (underlessee) One who holds a sublease. *See* SUBTENANT.

sub-regional shopping centre Usually the retail centre of a large town which includes a selection of department stores and national durable multiples. It may have a gross floorspace in the order of 20,000 m^2 (200,000 sq ft) to 30,000 m^2 (300,000 sq ft) serving a catchment area of 75,000–150,000 people. *See* HIERARCHY OF SHOPPING CENTRES.

subrogation The process by which an insurer who has made payment against a loss takes over the rights of the insured. If the loss was partial, the insurer takes over the right to sue a third party for damages, which he may do in the name of the insured party; if the loss was total, the insurer takes over both the right to sue and the remains of the property itself. The insurer would not normally be entitled to retain more than the amount payable to the insured under the relevant policy (plus costs).

subscribing fund A financial body which contributes funds to make up a total cash requirement for a project, eg by taking up debentures or ordinary shares.

subsidence The sinking of land caused by the movement of sub-strata, eg as a result of mining operations. *See* SETTLEMENT 3 AND 4.

subtenancy A tenancy held from a landlord who has a superior tenancy of or including the demised premies. The term is synonymous with sublease where the demise is under seal but also includes an oral or a written agreement (not under seal).

subtenant One who holds a subtenancy. *See* SUBLESSEE.

sub-underwriter An individual or body, eg an insurance company or an issuing house, which accepts a delegated responsibility for a share of an underwriter's specific liability. *Cf* REINSURANCE.

succession, rules of *See* RULES OF SUCCESSION.

succession tenancy A tenancy to which apply the provisions of Part IV of the Agricultural Holdings Act 1986 relating to succession to agricultural holdings on retirement or death of the tenant.

sui generis Of its own kind, eg describing a property not in a use class.

sum insured The maximum limit of an insurer's liability under an insurance contract, normally for such sum either as was originally requested by the insured party or as adjusted to reflect changes in building costs, eg by indexation.

sunlight and daylight code Planning criteria concerned with the layout and design of proposed buildings (or structures) to ensure they will have adequate sunlight and daylight and, so far as possible, to safeguard similar rights for the adjoining land and buildings. *See* WALDRAM DIAGRAM.

superficial area A measure of a plane or surface, usually expressed as a square of a linear measure, eg square metres or square feet.

superior (Scotland) The grantor of land to a grantee who holds as a vassal and pays feu duty to the superior.

superior court Any of the higher courts of record whose decisions are binding as precedents on lower courts. In England and Wales the superior courts comprise the House of Lords, the Court of Appeal, the High Court and the Crown Court (and also the Restrictive Practices Court and the Judicial Committee of the Privy Council). *Cf* INFERIOR COURT. *See* SUPREME COURT OF ENGLAND AND WALES.

superior interest An interest in property out of which the owner has granted a lesser interest; the latter must have a terminal date or be capable of being determined before the terminal date (if any) of the superior interest. *Cf* INFERIOR INTEREST.

superior landlord The owner of a superior interest in property.

superior lease (superior tenancy) A superior interest which is not the freehold, eg a lease subject to an underlease.

superior tenancy *See* SUPERIOR LEASE.

supermarket A self-service store of between 400m^2 and 2,500 m^2 trading floorspace offering a wide range of food and with at least 80% of turnover from the sale of food and groceries. *Cf* HYPERMARKET; SUPERSTORE.

superstore A self-service store (usually single-level) selling a wide range of food, or food and non-food goods, with at least 2,500 m^2 trading floorspace and supported by car-parking facilities. Stores selling only non-food goods are excluded. *Cf* HYPERMARKET; SUPERMARKET.

supply For value added tax purposes, subject to exceptions, a provision of goods or services "but not anything done otherwise than for a consideration"; anything which is not a supply of goods but is done for a consideration is a supply of services.

support, right of *See* RIGHT OF SUPPORT.

Supreme Court of England and Wales Formerly called the Supreme Court of Judicature, which was created by the Judicature Acts 1873-75 (and replaced all the previous higher courts other than the House of Lords). It is constituted under the Supreme Court Act 1981 and comprises the Court of Appeal, the High Court of Justice and the Crown Court (for criminal matters). The president is the Lord Chancellor.

surety A person who offers security for payment of a debt, performance of an obligation, or the appearance of someone else in court. *See* GUARANTOR.

surrender (of lease or tenancy) Voluntary termination of a lease or tenancy by the tenant for years (or life) yielding up the balance of the term to the immediate landlord (or reversioner).

surrender clause A clause in a lease whereby the tenant is obliged to surrender — or offer to surrender — the lease to the landlord in stated circumstances, eg before seeking consent to assign. If the tenant holds a business tenancy protected under Part II of the Landlord and Tenant Act 1954, such a clause is void unless contained in an agreement endorsed by the court on the joint application of the parties under section 38(4). *Cf* BREAK CLAUSE.

surrender value **1.** The value of the unexpired portion of a lease if given up to the immediate landlord. *See* MARRIAGE VALUE. **2.** The sum which would be paid by an insurance company at a given time on the cancellation by agreement between the insured and insurer of a policy which has value.

survey A process of investigation into some subject involving measurement and/or assessment, eg building survey; land survey; land use survey; pedestrian survey.

surveyor A person professionally engaged in one or more branches of the landed profession of surveying. These include building; planning and development; estates; land; management; mining; quantity; valuation. *See* INCORPORATED SOCIETY OF VALUERS AND AUCTIONEERS; ROYAL INSTITUTION OF CHARTERED SURVEYORS.

survivorship On the death of a joint tenant, the right of the surviving joint tenant(s) to continued joint ownership of the interest in land concerned until there is only one survivor, who then becomes the sole owner.

suspended ceiling A ceiling, not being part of the structural framework of a building, installed below the level of the underside of the floor above or of the roof. Commonly used to provide space for services, eg cables, recessed lighting and piping; to reduce the cost of heating in a room; to improve the acoustics; or to produce more aesthetically pleasing proportions.

synallagmatic contract *See* BILATERAL CONTRACT.

system(s) built Descriptive of a building assembled mainly from mass-produced factory-made units and therefore capable of being repeated to a modular arrangement.

T

table *See* VALUATION TABLE.

tacit acceptance A failure to reject an offer which has legal consequences, eg acceptance of rent following a breach of covenant in a lease may constitute a waiver of the landlord's right to claim damages or to forfeit the lease for breach of covenant.

take-away shop A retail property for the preparation of meals which the customer purchases for consumption off the premises.

take-out An arrangement whereby repayment of an existing or continuing loan, eg short-term building finance, is secured by a legal obligation to redeem the debt from cash provided by a lender (of long-term finance) or a purchaser, either of whom has contractually agreed to make the funds available at the required future date.

Takeover Panel A popularly-used shortened name for the Panel on Takeovers and Mergers.

target rate A criterion rate selected in a particular instance to reflect the opportunity cost of money; often based on the equivalent yield of long-dated or undated government stock with a percentage addition or a discount to reflect the nature and characteristics of the project.

target redemption yield The redemption yield which is considered to be an appropriate objective for a specific project.

taxable person For value added tax purposes, defined by the Value Added Tax Act 1983 as a person who makes taxable supplies above a certain exemption limit and is registered or required to be registered thereunder.

taxable supply For value added tax purposes, supply of goods or services in the UK other than an exempt supply.

Tax Acts Defined by section 831(2) of the Income and Corporation Taxes Act 1988 as that Act plus ". . . all other provisions of the Income Tax Acts and the Corporation Tax Acts". *Cf* TAXES ACT; TAXES ACTS.

taxation of costs Where there are disputed costs of an action in a court, tribunal or public inquiry, the calculation by the relevant official (eg a taxing master in the Supreme Court or the Registrar of the Lands Tribunal) of charges recoverable by one of the parties from another.

tax-adjusted table In property terms, a valuation table containing figures which have taken taxation into account, eg in dual rate years' purchase tables where large allocations of annual income are needed to ensure that after taxation a sufficient sum is available for sinking fund purposes.

tax avoidance The arrangement of one's affairs within the law so as to make full use of exemptions, reliefs and other advantages to minimise taxation.

Taxes Act The Income and Corporation Taxes Act 1988. *Cf* TAX ACTS; TAXES ACTS.

Taxes Acts Defined by section 118(1) of the Taxes Management Act 1970 as that Act, plus the Tax Acts, the Capital Gains Tax Act 1979 and all other enactments relating to CGT (and DLT). *Cf* TAX ACTS; TAXES ACT.

tax evasion A criminal offence, being an effort to reduce or escape taxation which is lawfully due; usually by the production of false information or the deliberate failure to disclose relevant information.

tax relief *See* RELIEF 2.

tax year *See* FISCAL YEAR.

tellurometer In land surveying, an instrument for measuring long distances, eg up to 100 km, by sending and timing radio waves from a transmitter to a remote device.

temporary benchmark (TBM) In a survey of a site, a reference point having a relative height above a selected datum, which in turn is related to a permanent benchmark.

temporary loss of profits In a case of compulsory acquisition, the diminution in the level of profit suffered by a claimant for a relatively short period and justifying a claim for compensation under the heading of disturbance.

tenancy **1.** Strictly speaking, the interest of a person holding property by any right or title. **2.** More usually, an arrangement, whether by formal lease or informal agreement, whereby the owner (the landlord) allows another (the tenant) to take exclusive possession of land in consideration for rent, with or without a premium, either:

a for an agreed period or

b on a periodic basis until formally terminated.

3. Under the Landlord and Tenant Act 1954, section 69(1), this "means a tenancy created either immediately or derivatively out of the freehold, whether by a lease or underlease, by an agreement for a lease or underlease or by a tenancy agreement or in pursuance of any enactment (including this Act), but does not include a mortgage term or any interest arising in favour of a mortgagor by his attorning tenant to his mortgagee . . .".

tenancy agreement A lease for three years or less, not under seal.

tenancy at will A tenancy for no fixed term which continues so long as the landlord and tenant are willing that it should do so; it is an equitable interest and is created either by agreement or by implication of law. *Cf* TENANCY ON SUFFERANCE.

tenancy by estoppel A purported tenancy granted by someone who has no (or no adequate) estate or interest in the land. As between the grantor "landlord" and grantee "tenant" such a "tenancy" is binding and is converted into a true tenancy if the grantor subsequently acquires the requisite title to the land.

tenancy for life (or lives) A tenancy or lease lasting until the death of the tenant (or the last survivor of named lives). If it is for rent or in consideration for a fine it takes effect under section 149(6) of the Law of Property Act 1925 as a lease for 90 years, determinable on the death of the original tenant (or last survivor). However, all other life tenancies, ie those not at a rent or fine, are equitable interests arising under a settlement and governed by the Settled Land Act 1925. *Cf* TENANCY PUR (OR PER) AUTRE VIE. *See* LIFE INTEREST; TENANT FOR LIFE.

tenancy for years *See* TERM CERTAIN.

tenancy from year to year A periodic tenancy which continues by yearly intervals until terminated by notice to quit.

tenancy in common An undivided ownership in real estate by two or more persons whose shares need not be equal; each individual owner can freely dispose of his share by sale, gift or will. *Cf* JOINT TENANCY.

tenancy in fee tail (tenancy in tail) *See* ENTAILED INTEREST.

tenancy on sufferance In cases where there is no statutory protection, a tenancy created by implication of law when the tenant has remained in possession on expiry of his term and the landlord has not challenged the tenant's continued possession. *Cf* TENANCY AT WILL.

tenancy pur (or per) autre vie A tenancy which subsists for as long as the life of a person other than the tenant. *Cf* TENANCY FOR LIFE (OR LIVES).

tenant A person (or body of persons) holding a tenancy.

tenant for life (life tenant) **1.** A person holding a tenancy for life. **2.** Under section 19(1) of the Settled Land Act 1925: "The person of full age who is for the time being beneficially entitled under a settlement to possession of settled land for his life . . .". In addition, under section 20 of that Act, certain other persons are given the wide but specific powers of a "tenant for life", and are defined as such, eg a tenant in tail; a tenant for years determinable on death but not holding merely under a lease at a rent or fine.

tenant in fee simple The owner of an estate in fee simple, ie a form of freeholder.

tenant in fee tail The owner of an entailed interest.

tenant mix The range of trades and services represented in a shopping centre. The intention is that the mix will meet both the requirements of the catchment population and the centre management's objectives. *Cf* UNIT MIX.

tenant on sufferance The holder of a tenancy on sufferance.

tenant-right When an agricultural tenancy comes to an end, the outgoing tenant's entitlement to compensation under section 65 of the Agricultural Holdings Act 1986. The provisions for that compensation are set out in Part II of Schedule 8 to that Act covering growing and harvested crops, acts of cultivation, pasture laid down and other similar matters.

tenant's covenant *See* COVENANT.

tenant's fixtures Objects installed by a tenant which although strictly fixtures are, if capable of being removed without doing serious damage to the property, nevertheless lawfully removable by the tenant on vacating the premises. To qualify as such, they must be:

a trade fixtures, ie attached to a property for the purpose of the tenant's particular trade;

b ornamental and domestic fixtures, ie chattels or movables affixed to a house for ornament or the better enjoyment of the object itself, or

c agricultural fixtures, installed by a tenant farmer for the purpose of agricultural operations.

Cf LANDLORD'S FIXTURES.

tenant's improvements Improvements to land or buildings to meet the needs of — and carried out wholly or partly at the expense of — the tenant. When subsequently seeking a renewal of his lease, he may, under the Landlord and Tenant Act 1954, be entitled to the rent being assessed on the assumption that his improvements have not been carried out. If he vacates the premises he may become entitled to compensation under Part I of the Landlord and Tenant Act 1927; the basis of such compensation will reflect the extent to which his improvements have increased the rental value of the premises to the benefit of the landlord.

tenant's repairing lease A lease where the lessee is under an obligation to maintain and repair the whole, or substantially the whole, of the premises comprised in the lease. This meaning is also adopted for the purpose of Schedule A income taxation. *See* SCHEDULES.

tenant's share In a rental valuation of a property on the profits basis, an estimate of that part of the profit which the tenant is reasonably expected to retain. It is usually expressed as a percentage of gross receipts, tenant's capital or the divisible balance.

tender **1.** Strictly, an offer to supply land, goods or services which, if accepted, creates a contract. **2.** In the property market (but not an auction), the process or method whereby competitive bids are sought from a number of prospective or potential buyers/lessees/contractors. *See* FORMAL TENDER; INFORMAL TENDER; TENDERING PROCESS.

tender document One of the "identical documents" described in the definition of "tendering process".

tendering process The entire procedure of inviting bids by tender, receiving and considering them and usually accepting one of them. The features of a typical tendering process are:

a the preparation of identical documents, giving details of the subject of the bid,
b sending such documents to each proposed tenderer – the tenderers invited may be restricted in number and identity;
c the contents of each bid, which is usually sealed, are confidential until a date and time, specified at the outset, when tenders are opened;
d no tender or amendment is accepted after that date and time.

Both the bids and acceptances may be conditional or unconditional and, if the latter, the wording of the tender establishes a contract between the parties. The inviting party may reserve the right to accept any offer, not necessarily the best in financial terms, or accept none.

tender panel facility A method of raising relatively short-term money whereby a consortium of banks or other institutions agree to make available to a borrower a specific amount of cash; this is by way of a loan available to be drawn by instalments at calculable intervals, with the rate of interest payable usually being calculated by a formula agreed at the outset. However, at any major drawdowns of capital the members of the consortium may tender on other, more favourable, terms if they wish to increase their involvement. The concept is that the money is available at known costs but could be "fine tuned" if market pressures encourage this.

tender price indices A series of indices, published by the Building Cost Information Service of the RICS, relating to the level of prices likely to be quoted at a given time by contractors tendering for building work; ie it reflects the impact of market conditions on the tenderer's decision whether to bid at a high, low or average level relative to building costs. *See* BUILDING COST INDICES.

tenement **1.** Any property subject to tenure. **2.** Descriptive of a residential building, especially multi-storey, containing several dwellings.

tenets of rating An expression used to describe the four principal ingredients required for rateable occupation, ie occupation which is beneficial, actual, exclusive and sufficiently permanent.

tenure The basis upon which property is held, eg freehold or leasehold.

term **1.** The duration of a lease. The term commences from the date specified in the lease, which is not necessarily the date when the document is executed or registered. **2.** In a lease or other contract, one of the provisions expressing the agreement between the parties.

term and reversion method A traditional method of valuing a freehold or other superior interest in property which is subject to a lease (or underlease) and where the income is likely to change, eg on rent review and/or on reversion. It involves the valuation of the present rent receivable over the period of its duration together with the valuation of each subsequent different rent likely to be received on review or reversion for their separate estimated durations, each discounted to a present value. By aggregating the several values the total value of the property under consideration is obtained. *Cf* HARDCORE METHOD.

term certain A lease of fixed duration, such as a week or 10,000 years, which will expire, at common law, by effluxion of time at the end of the term granted. It includes also a periodic tenancy, which is initially a term certain.

term date The day on which a lease ends. *Cf* TERM DAY.

term day Another name for a quarter day.

terminable income An income which may be brought to an end permanently by the occurrence or non-occurrence of a specific act or event, eg the exercise of an option to determine a lease. *Cf* TERMINAL INCOME; TERMINATING INCOME.

terminal income A final payment by way of income, eg the rent payable for the last rental period of a lease. *Cf* TERMINABLE INCOME; TERMINATING INCOME.

terminating income An income which automatically ceases on a particular date or event, eg on the expiry of a lease or agreement. *Cf* TERMINABLE INCOME; TERMINAL INCOME.

termination The end of a lease, licence or franchise. Thus a lease commencing December 25 1900 for a term of 99 years terminates on December 24 1999.

term of years An interest in land subsisting for, or by reference to, a stated period, including both fixed-term leases and periodic tenancies.

term of years absolute The formal name for a leasehold estate in land (other than one terminable on the death of any person), which must be created by deed if for a term of three years or more.

term of years absolute in possession A term of years absolute where the lessor has physical possession and control of the property or the legal right to possession and control.

term yield In a valuation using the term and reversion method, the yield applied to the net income receivable under the lease to which the property is subject at the date of the revaluation. *Cf* INITIAL RETURN. *See* REVERSION YIELD.

terotechnology The management technology promoting the efficient installation and maintenance of equipment in buildings.

terrier *See* ESTATE TERRIER.

test of professional competence (TPC) An assessment of an individual's practical ability to practise as a chartered surveyor in his chosen specialisation. The test is taken by candidates who have obtained an exempting degree, or diploma or have passed the RICS professional examinations. A pass in the test entitles the successful candidate to apply for election as a professional associate of the Royal Institution of Chartered Surveyors.

theodolite An instrument used in land surveying for measuring angles in the horizontal and vertical planes.

thermal insulation A barrier of relatively non-heat-conducting materials. It may be incorporated in a building so as to reduce the loss or gain of heat between the interior and the exterior of the building (or between one part of the interior and another).

Third Market Under the auspices of the International Stock Exchange, a market for shares in companies which are unable to meet the requirements for the Official List or the Unlisted Securities Market, ie relatively young, immature companies with an initial low capitalisation. The object of the promoters may well be to qualify in due time for admission to one of the aforementioned markets. *See* YELLOW BOOK.

third surveyor In a party wall dispute in inner London, a surveyor appointed by the two surveyors representing the opposite parties, having the role of resolving differences between them. *See* PARTY WALL AWARD.

three-phase power A 415-volt electricity supply taken direct from the mains to provide the increased power necessary to drive heavy equipment within a property, such as lifts, boilers, plant and industrial machinery.

throughput method A method of valuation used to find the rental value of property based upon a unit of comparison applied to the quantity of goods sold over a given time, eg litres or gallons of fuel sold at a petrol filling station.

tied cottage A dwelling-house provided for the occupant as part of the terms of, and only during, his employment, especially in relation to agricultural work. *Cf* TIED HOUSE. *See* SERVICE OCCUPANCY.

tied house A public house, the licensee of which is bound under contract to obtain, usually all, his alcoholic and non-alcoholic drinks and other specified goods from the landlord brewer. *Cf* FREE HOUSE; TIED COTTAGE.

tied rent The rent payable where there is a commercial or employment relationship between the landlord and the tenant. Such rent is calculated by a method which reflects this special arrangement, as in the case of a tied house, where the lease requires the lessee to buy his goods from the landlord. *See* SOLUS AGREEMENT.

time apportionment Under Schedule 5, para 11, to the Capital Gains Tax Act 1979, as amended, for property acquired before April 6 1965 and disposed of after that date but before April 6 1988, the apportionment of the capital gain over the whole period of ownership as between the periods before and from April 6 1965, so as to find the gain since that date. (The use of market value at April 6 1965 in a computation was an alternative approach to finding the gain after that date.)

time immemorial A time or period of time which ended before the time of legal memory.

time of the essence The doctrine whereby a contract or term of a contract is enforceable only if the appropriate steps are taken within a stated or implied time-limit. Time is "of the essence" only if:

a stated to be so in the document concerned, or
b properly inferred from the nature or circumstances of the transaction.

timeshare Shared ownership of a property, primarily for holiday purposes, where each of the several owners owns the whole or part of the property for a particular period in each year for a number of years. Each owner has the right to occupy his property (or allow others to do so) for the particular periods.

Time-share Developers Association (TDA) An association of developers of time-share resorts who are concerned to maintain and enhance good standards for the development, management and marketing of timeshare projects.

time-value of money The recognition that a given sum of money in hand is more valuable than a right to the same sum in the future. In a valuation, regard is had to the moment when cash is receivable or payable in the future by discounting at a selected rate of interest. Thus a sum due at a future date has only a discounted value, ie a net present value. *Cf* PAYBACK. *See* INTERNAL RATE OF RETURN.

title The right to ownership of land. *See* ROOT OF TITLE.

title, abstract of *See* ABSTRACT OF TITLE.

title deeds Legal documents proving ownership of land and the terms on which it is owned. *See* ROOT OF TITLE.

title insurance Insurance against the consequences of defects in title.

tone of the list Under section 20 of the General Rate Act 1967, the statutory criterion used where a new or altered hereditament is valued for rating since the last general revaluation, so as to determine what value would have been ascribed to the property had it been in existence throughout the year before the valuation list came into force.

topping out The moment of time in the construction of a building when the structure and frame, including the roof, is completed. It is traditionally marked by fixing a small tree or branch to the highest point and often by holding a celebratory party for the construction workers and others concerned with the project.

top slice The profit rent from a leasehold investment where the leaseholder pays substantial rent, usually being more than 50% of the net rental value of the investment, with that liability continuing regardless of voids. The top slice is that part of the income at the greatest risk, being most vulnerable in adverse market conditions: the degree of risk is reflected in its value.

tort A wrongful act or omission, independent of contract, eg negligence, nuisance or trespass, for which damages can be obtained in a civil court. Some torts can also be breaches of contract and some can also be crimes, eg assault or criminal libel.

total extinguishment In compulsory purchase, a head of claim for disturbance based on the closure of a business, because either there is no suitable alternative accommodation available or the claimant is over the age of 60 and seeks compensation on the basis prescribed by section 46 of the Land Compensation Act 1973.

total yield *See* YIELD.

tower block A building, usually containing offices or flats of many storeys, (generally at least eight), especially if on a relatively small site. *Cf* HIGH-RISE BUILDING; MULTI-STOREY.

town and country planning The determination of policy for the development and use of land and the control of its implementation in urban and rural areas by district and county planning authorities under the supervision of the Secretary of State for the Environment in England, the Secretary of State for Wales or the Secretary of State for Scotland. The implementation of decisions relating to the development of property affected by planning policy involves the many specialisations concerned with the development and use of land, eg architects, surveyors, project managers and engineers, whether on behalf of public authorities or private owners, developers or occupiers of land and/or buildings.

town planner *See* PLANNER.

townscape A view of buildings, streets and other features of a town.

trade Under section 832(1) of the Taxes Act, defined as including "every trade, manufacture, adventure or concern in the nature of trade"; seemingly tautologous, but may be interpreted by reference to case law. *See* BADGES OF TRADE.

trade disturbance *See* DISTURBANCE.

trade fixtures *See* TENANT'S FIXTURES.

trading area 1. The demographic area which describes the major portion of a shopping centre's trade. It may be divided into primary (about 65% of trade), secondary (about 20%) and tertiary areas. 2. The area described in terms of the catchment population within isochrones.

trading company A company which, by virtue of its activities, is regarded by the Inland Revenue as one which trades (rather than invests) and is liable to corporation tax under Schedule D Case I accordingly. If necessary, the distinction between trading and investment companies may be determined by reference to case law on the badges of trade.

trading stock Under section 100 (2) of the Taxes Act, briefly, property whether real or personal being either "(i) property such as is sold in the ordinary course of the trade, or would be so sold if it were mature or if its manufacture, preparation or construction were complete; or (ii) materials such as are used in the manufacture, preparation or construction of any such property referred to in sub-paragraph (i) above . . . ".

traffic generation The build-up, or potential build-up, of vehicular traffic resulting from the use of land or buildings, eg a superstore or a sports stadium.

tranche A portion or instalment of a sum of money to be paid or advanced. For instance, during a building contract an arrangement may be made whereby at given intervals, usually related to the architect's certificates as work progresses, an instalment of the borrowing is drawn to cover the amount to which each certificate relates.

traverse A method of land surveying involving measuring the lengths of two adjoining lines and either measuring the internal or external angles between them or taking the bearing of each line.

traversing A method of land surveying by measuring angles with a theodolite, from each station to other stations, measuring the distance between stations and plotting the results.

treasure trove Ownership of bullion and gold and silver objects which have been buried or hidden in the past and found in recent times. A coroner will determine whether such objects are treasure trove, in which case they will belong to the Crown but the finder is usually rewarded. (If they are held not to be treasure trove, the finder is usually entitled to keep them.)

tree preservation order A means of special development control used by a local planning authority, under section 60 of the Town and Country Planning Act 1971, to preserve individual trees or groups of trees in the interests of amenity. The order may prohibit the cutting down, topping, lopping, uprooting, wilful damage or wilful destruction of the tree or trees except with the authority's consent.

trespass The tort of unlawful and direct interference with another person or his possession of goods or land. In relation to property, it signifies the entry upon another's land without licence from the owner or without statutory or other authority.

triangulation 1. (trigonometrical surveying) A method of land surveying involving the subdivision of an area of land into a network of triangles, the accurate measurement of one comparatively short base line (or possibly a few such base lines) and the measurement by theodolite of all the enclosed angles of the triangles. 2. The subdivision of a parcel of land (or the plan of such) into triangles in order to calculate its area.

trigger notice Colloquial term for a notice, the service of which is essential to initiate some legal process. Most commonly applied to a notice by a landlord or tenant setting in train a rent review procedure.

trigonometrical surveying *See* TRIANGULATION 1.

trotting The illegal practice of making or accepting a bogus bid at an auction sale in order to push up the price.

true net income Net income after allowing for any income taxation liability of the recipient.

true net yield The resulting yield after adjusting the remunerative rate which would otherwise have been appropriate to allow for any income taxation; it is therefore used to capitalise true net income.

trunking Types of conduit or trough (often rectangular in section) which are designed to carry out of sight, throughout a building, various services such as electrical or telephone wiring, water, drainage, ventilation or air-conditioning pipes.

trust An arrangement whereby an owner transfers property to one or more trustees to hold for the benefit of one or more beneficiaries who can enforce the trust by court action. Where land is held on trust, this is under either:

a a strict settlement, governed by the Settled Land Act 1925, or
b a trust for sale.

trust corporation The Public Trustee or a corporation, the latter having either been appointed by the court or entitled to act as trustee because it has issued capital of not less than a specified amount, of which a stated minimum must be in cash. A trust corporation has all the powers which would otherwise require two trustees, eg to sell land.

trustee A person, eg an individual or a company, holding nominal title to property for the benefit of one or more beneficiaries.

trustees of the settlement (Settled Land Act trustees) Two or more individual trustees or a trust corporation who are trustees of settled land.

trust for sale A trust where the trustees have a duty to sell the trust property and hold the proceeds of sale in trust for the beneficiaries, usually with a discretionary power to postpone the sale.

trust instrument A deed vesting property in trustees to hold on trust for the benefit of beneficiaries.

turbary A right, being a profit à prendre, to dig and remove peat or turf from another's land for use as a fuel.

turning The practice, sometimes carried on by property dealers, of buying a property and as soon as possible thereafter reselling it at an enhanced price in order to provide both the amount of the original purchase price and a profit on the deal. The term is applied particularly where the purchaser resells the property between the exchange of contracts and completion. *See* BADGES OF TRADE.

turnkey deal (turnkey package) An arrangement in which a vendor or lessor provides a building completely fitted out for immediate occupation (so that the occupier can simply turn the key and move in).

turnover The aggregate of receipts from the sales and takings of a business, ie before the deduction of any financial liability of the business for the cost of purchases, payroll, working expenses, rent, rates, or other outgoings necessarily incurred to enable the business to carry on. In turnover rent calculations the procedure for calculating turnover may be defined to exclude, for example, value added tax, other imposts such as tobacco tax, the apparent shortfall of income due to sales to staff at reduced prices, and discounts to certain customers.

turnover lease A lease, especially of retail property, in which the rent is an agreed percentage of the annual turnover. *See* PERCENTAGE LEASE.

turnover rent *See* PERCENTAGE RENT.

twilight zone An area of a town or city, generally situated between the centre and the suburbs, which is characterised by the deterioration of existing buildings and infrastructure. Such zones are associated with relative deprivation in economic, social, cultural and recreational matters.

U

ullage allowance In a valuation of licensed premises based upon the quantity of liquor sold, an allowance made to cover losses due to spillage, spoilage or evaporation, especially of draught beer.

ultra vires Literally "beyond the powers". It applies where a company, public authority or other body acts in a manner exceeding the powers granted to it by the relevant memorandum of association or other document. The term also applies where a court or tribunal exceeds its jurisdiction. *Cf* INTRA VIRES.

umpire In a dispute where each party has appointed an arbitrator and they subsequently disagree, a third person called in to adjudicate and resolve the dispute.

unadopted road A road for which the highway authority has not accepted responsibility as a public highway and which is not, therefore, maintained at public expense.

unconditional offer An offer made without conditions, such that its unqualified acceptance by the offeree will create a contract.

underlease *See* SUBLEASE.

underlessee *See* SUBLESSEE.

under offer Where an offer for a property has been made and accepted in principle but the transaction is still subject to contract.

underwood Immature trees and other low growth, cleared from time to time in the interests of good forestry. *Cf* COPPICE.

underwriter **1.** Any person who, for an agreed consideration, enters into a commitment which gives him a financial liability in the event of some specific happening, eg a member of an insurance company or syndicate who accepts the risks covered by a specific insurance policy. **2.** An individual or body, eg an issuing house, who accepts liability to purchase (at the issue price less an agreed discount) those stocks or shares not taken up by the public during flotation of a company or by the shareholders on a rights issue. *Cf* SUB-UNDERWRITER.

undisclosed principal A principal whose existence is not disclosed by an agent acting on his behalf in negotiations with a third party. In such circumstances both the principal and the agent may be liable on the contract but the third party may be able to disclaim liability to the principal, eg if he proves that he wished to contract with the agent personally, or that the (undisclosed) agency is not consistent with the terms of the contract.

undoubted covenant The characteristics of a covenantor, eg a tenant, whose financial standing and reputation are such that his ability and willingness to pay his dues and comply with his other obligations promptly are unquestioned. *See* COVENANT 2.

unencumbered Descriptive of a property the title of which is free of liens and other encumbrances, especially in relation to freehold titles.

unexpended balance of established development value (UBED) The total amount of any claims for loss of development value for a parcel of land originally made under Part VI of the Town and Country Planning Act 1947 but converted into rights to compensation now embodied in Part VII of the 1971 Act, including a one-seventh addition to represent interest. It is payable in certain circumstances on refusal of planning permission for new development or on compulsory purchase. *See* CLAIM HOLDING.

unfitness for human habitation The condition of a dwelling which renders it unfit for human habitation by failure to meet the criteria relating to repair, stability, freedom from damp, internal arrangement, natural lighting, ventilation, water supply, drainage and sanitary conveniences, facilities for the preparation and cooking of food, and arrangements for the disposal of waste water. *See* CLEARANCE AREA; CLOSING ORDER; DEMOLITION ORDER; SLUM CLEARANCE.

unfit property (unfit dwelling) A dwelling which has been formally declared by the local authority as failing to meet prescribed standards of fitness for human habitation under section 604 of the Housing Act 1985. *See* UNFITNESS FOR HUMAN HABITATION.

unilateral contract A contract in which one party, for the benefit of another party, undertakes to do or refrain from doing some act but without any corresponding promise by the other party at that stage of the agreement, eg the grant of an option (until it is exercised, when the contract will become bilateral).

unitary development plan A special form of development plan which, under the Local Government Act 1985, Schedule I paragraph 2, will replace structure and local plans within the areas of local planning authorities in Greater London and metropolitan counties, as from dates to be appointed by order of the Secretary of State.

unitisation A scheme of multiple but direct ownership of single properties in property units, eg in an authorised unit trust or by shares, similar to equities in a company, which can be traded by or on behalf of their owners.

unitisation yield A form of equated yield suitable for use in the valuation of unitised property. *See* DONALDSON'S INVESTMENT TABLES.

unit mix The different types of uses of buildings or parts of buildings in a development, eg in a shopping centre or on an industrial estate. *Cf* TENANT MIX.

unit of comparison A standard measure of value per unit, calculated by an analysis of the actual (or assumed) rent or sale price of a property used as a comparable in the direct comparison method. For instance, the rental value of offices expressed as £x per sq ft, or the capital value of a hotel expressed as £y per room.

unit trust An open-ended investment vehicle which enables subscribers to participate by acquiring units. The total subscriptions, as varied up or down subsequently (less administrative costs), become a fund for investment by named professional managers on behalf of trustees, who own the investments for the unit holders. Unit trusts are owned and managed in accordance with rules and regulations issued by the Department of Trade and Industry and the appropriate self-regulatory organisation. The units are not quoted on the Stock Exchange but are traded at bid and offer prices fixed by the managers at a level justified by the market values of the assets held. *Cf* INVESTMENT TRUST COMPANY. See PROPERTY UNIT TRUST.

unlimited company A company whose members have a liability for all the debts of the company regardless of the share structure or its total nominal value. *Cf* LIMITED COMPANY; COMPANY LIMITED BY GUARANTEE.

unliquidated damages Damages the amount of which has not been pre-determined but is settled by the court. *Cf* LIQUIDATED DAMAGES.

Unlisted Securities Market (USM) A second-tier market in stocks and shares, established by the London Stock Exchange in 1980, to permit dealings by those companies (usually smaller and/or newer) not wishing to go for a full Stock Exchange listing, ie quotation. *Cf* OFFICIAL LIST; THIRD MARKET.

unoccupied building For rating purposes, a building on which rates may become payable after being unoccupied for a prescribed minimum period under the General Rate Act 1967, as amended. *See* UNOCCUPIED RATE.

unoccupied rate The rate chargeable by a rating authority on empty commercial or residential property where that authority has adopted the provisions of section 17 of the General Rate Act 1967. For commercial properties, ie shops and offices, the amount is at present (1988) limited to a maximum of 50% of the occupied rate. However, empty residential property can be charged up to the full occupied rate. (The City of London has its own special provisions for rating of unoccupied property, which differ from the section 17 provisions; for over 100 years it has charged an empty rate and did not adopt the discretionary provisions of section 17.) *Cf* RATING SURCHARGE.

unsecured ground rent A rent for land upon which buildings have not yet been erected but where there is a lessee's right or commitment to build. *Cf* SECURED GROUND RENT.

up-front funding A commitment by a lender to provide long-term finance from the outset of a development. *Cf* FRONT MONEY. *See* FORWARD COMMITMENT; SPECULATIVE FUNDING.

uplift The additional amount of rent payable under a lease which has terms giving the tenant benefits not prevailing in the market. For example, where a lease has a longer than usual rent review pattern, the uplift is the extra rent which initially, or on review, can be secured to reflect those benefits.

uplifted rent A rent which reflects lease terms which are more beneficial to the tenant than prevailing commercial terms, eg a higher rent to reflect, say, 14-yearly reviews, rather than the more common five-yearly reviews. *See* RENT; PREMIUM RENT.

upset price The lowest acceptable or reserve price, eg at an auction. In Scotland, the term is usually applied in private treaty transactions to the price above which a vendor expects to receive bids.

upside and downside The optimistic and pessimistic views of the outcome of a risk venture. For instance, in development feasibility studies, a calculation is made assuming minimum estimates of cost, shortest building programme and maximum estimates of rent, indicating the maximum value that could be placed on a site. This is the "upside" view. A different calculation may be made assuming maximum cost, longest likely building programme and minimum rents. This produces a lower value for the site and is the "downside" view. Commercial decisions may then be made according to the degree of credibility attached to each assumption.

upward/downward rent review A rent review calculated under a clause in a lease which requires that such rent becomes payable, regardless of whether this is equal to, greater than or less than the rent payable immediately before the review. *Cf* UPWARD-ONLY RENT REVIEW. *See* UPWARD/DOWNWARD RENT REVIEW SUBJECT TO A BASE.

upward/downward rent review subject to a base A rent review which is the same as an upward/downward rent review, except that the rent payable cannot fall below a specified base rent. The base rent either remains constant throughout the term of the lease or may be adjusted at specified intervals. This type of arrangement usually arises in developments where the funding institution receives as a base rent an agreed minimum return on its funds committed to the property. *Cf* UPWARD-ONLY RENT REVIEW.

upward-only rent review A rent review where the rent payable following a review date is the greater of the rent payable immediately before the review or the amount calculated upon review under the terms of the lease. *Cf* UPWARD/DOWNWARD RENT REVIEW; UPWARD/DOWNWARD RENT REVIEW SUBJECT TO A BASE.

urban development area An area of land designated for regeneration by order of the appropriate Secretary of State under section 134 of the Local Government, Planning and Land Act 1980. In England such an area must be within a metropolitan district or an inner London borough (including land partly in an adjoining outer London borough). *See* URBAN DEVELOPMENT CORPORATION.

urban development corporation A corporation, established by order of the Secretary of State under section 135 of the Local Government, Planning and Land Act 1980, for the purpose of regenerating an urban development area and with formal powers to acquire land to promote development, eg the Merseyside and the London Docklands Development Corporations. Various local government functions for an area, including control of development, may be transferred from the local authorities to an urban development corporation by the Secretary of State. *See* REGENERATION.

urban development grant Under section 1 of the Local Government Specific Grants (Social Need) Act 1969, a central government cash subsidy for development on land in an urban area; it is intended to encourage the investment of private sector funds into projects which otherwise would be insufficiently attractive in commercial terms.

urban programme funds Under the Inner Urban Areas Act 1978, governmental financial assistance made to local authorities for approved environmental, economic or social projects in their designated areas submitted by them for consideration by the Department of the Environment.

urban regeneration grant Financial assistance under section 27 of the Housing and Planning Act 1986 for urban regeneration not being in an urban development area. The scheme enables grant aid to be given by central government direct to the private sector, without reference to local authorities, for the regeneration of medium-sized areas of urban and industrial dereliction of between 5 and 100 acres.

urban renewal The process of redevelopment or rehabilitation of worn-out or obsolescent parts of a town, perhaps with new infrastructure and improved amenities and facilities.

use and occupation action An action for the payment of damages from the use of property where there has been an owner and occupier relationship but no arrangement for payment of rent. *Cf* TRESPASS.

use class A class within the Town and Country Planning (Use Classes) Order 1987 (as amended or replaced). Any authorised use within a particular class can be changed to another use within the same class without planning permission, unless the original use was limited by an earlier planning permission.

use classes order A statutory instrument made under section 22(2)(*f*) of the Town and Country Planning Act 1971 defining the use classes. *See* USE CLASS.

use, reasonably beneficial *See* REASONABLY BENEFICIAL USE.

user **1.** The use or enjoyment of a property or of a right over property. **2.** A person who uses, enjoys or has a right over a property.

user clause (user covenant) A contractual provision, especially one in a lease, specifying the use or uses to which the property in question may be put and/or the use or uses which are prohibited.

use(s) In relation to property, generally the particular activity (or range of activities) carried on in a building or on an area of land. *See* USE CLASS.

usual covenants Those covenants which are included in a lease prepared in accordance with good conveyancing practice. They include, for example, covenants by the tenant to pay the rent, to pay tenant's rates and taxes and to keep the premises in repair, and a covenant by the landlord for quiet enjoyment. Sometimes an agreement for lease or the lease itself will refer to the parties being responsible for observing "the usual covenants". On the other hand such covenants are also implied by law to be incorporated in an agreement for lease where this does not specify all the relevant terms.

V

vacancy allowance *See* VOID ALLOWANCE.

vacant possession The attribute of an empty property which can legally be exclusively occupied and used by the owner or, on a sale or letting, by the new owner or tenant.

vacant possession search An inspection carried out immediately before completion of a property transaction to ensure that there has been compliance with a term in the contract requiring that the property will be transferred with vacant possession.

valuable consideration **1.** In property terms the money value, or something else which is tangible or real as distinct from something abstract. It is agreed as the payment due from one party to another in return for the benefit derived by the former. Where the parties have entered into a *bona fide* exchange, the consideration on each side must be equivalent but not necessarily adequate. **2.** Under section 205(1)(xxi) of the Law of Property Act 1925, valuable consideration includes marriage but not nominal money payments. *Cf* DISTRIBUTION IN KIND; GOOD CONSIDERATION.

valuation **1.** The process of making an estimate of worth of real property or other assets for a particular purpose, eg letting, purchase, sale, audit, rating, compulsory purchase or taxation. That purpose and the relevant circumstances will determine assumptions and facts that are appropriate and hence the process used. **2.** A statement, usually in writing, setting out the facts, assumptions, calculations and resultant value. **3.** Colloquially, the value arrived at as a result of the valuation process. *See* DATE OF VALUATION; SIGNING DATE; VALUATION CERTIFICATE; VALUATION REPORT.

valuation and community charge tribunal A court established under Schedule 2 to the Local Government Finance Act 1988 to hear:

a an appeal by a person aggrieved by any of the ten matters concerning the community charge set down in section 23(2) of the Act; or
b an appeal following a disagreement about the accuracy of a non-domestic

rating list between a valuation officer and a person making a proposal for its alteration.

valuation certificate A document in which a valuer certifies the amount of his valuation of a property or group of properties. There is no rigid form for such a certificate, although a suitable format is set out in the *RICS Guidance Notes on the Valuation of Assets*. It usually comprises a relatively short letter but may take the form of a detailed report and it will normally contain the valuation date, the purpose and basis of the valuation itself, its date, the factual information and any assumptions on which it is based, together with the name, address and qualifications of the valuer. *Cf* CERTIFICATE OF VALUE; VALUATION REPORT.

valuation date *See* DATE OF VALUATION.

valuation list Under the General Rate Act 1967, the statutory document listing all the rating assessments of hereditaments in a particular valuation area. It is prepared and kept up to date by the valuation officer of the Inland Revenue under the Valuation Lists Rules 1972 and is available for members of the public to inspect at the offices of the local rating authority. *Cf* CENTRAL NON-DOMESTIC RATING LIST; LOCAL NON-DOMESTIC RATING LIST.

Valuation Office A department of the Board of Inland Revenue appointed by central government having three main functions covering valuation matters, namely:

a taxation, eg capital gains tax, corporation tax and inheritance tax;
b rating, eg compiling and maintaining valuation lists; and
c compensation for compulsory purchase and allied matters on behalf of central government and some local authorities.

valuation officer For the purposes of the Local Government Finance Act 1988, a person appointed under section 61 by the Commissioners of Inland Revenue for each charging authority to compile, and then maintain, the local non-domestic rating list in accordance with section 41.

valuation report A report made for the purpose of advising on the capital and/or rental (or hiring) value of one or more properties (or other assets) and containing the valuation(s) and information relating thereto. It is usually longer and more detailed than a valuation certificate, although it may sometimes be so used.

valuation table A tabulated series of figures derived from a formula and used for valuation purposes, eg for discounting receipts and payments of a revenue or capital nature. The relevant facts and particular assumptions made by the valuer will lead to selection and use of the appropriate table. Typical sets of valuation tables include the following: amount of £1; amount of £1 per annum; annual sinking fund; annuity £1 will purchase; present value of £1; years' purchase (present value of £1 per annum). Among the principal published valuation tables are Bowcock's, Donaldson's, Parry's and Rose's.

value **1.** The price that an interest in property or some other asset might reasonably be expected to fetch if disposed of at a given time for a particular purpose or in particular circumstances. **2.** To make an estimate of the worth of a property or other asset. *See* VALUATION.

value added tax (VAT) Under the Value Added Tax Act 1983, as amended, a tax charged on the supply, actual or notional, of certain goods and services in the United Kingdom and on the importation of goods into the United Kingdom.

value in exchange The value, in terms of cash, of a property which is bartered for another asset or assets, cash being the yardstick by which the comparative value of each can be assessed.

value to the owner. *See* SUBJECTIVE VALUE.

variable rent Rent payable under a lease which provides that it will change at given times during the term by predetermined amounts, by formula or by other means.

variation Under a building contract, a change in the previously specified requirements for the building.

variety store A large retail shop selling many kinds of mainly small and relatively inexpensive items.

vassal (Scotland) The party in the subordinate position to the (feudal) superior, to whom he pays feu duty. *See* FEU.

vendee A purchaser, especially one who buys land.

vendor A seller, especially one who sells land.

vendor and purchaser summons A procedure for resolving disputes between parties to a contract for the sale of land where completion of the sale is being held up. It involves an application to a judge in chambers and is particularly useful in resolving questions of interpretation of the contract.

venture A risky undertaking or trade.

venture capital **1.** Funds made available for a risky undertaking of a commercial nature. **2.** Funds offered by financial organisations for relatively high-risk projects, such as start-ups, expansions, buy-outs and acquisitions, by unlisted companies: it usually involves equity participation and board representation by the funding body. *Cf* EQUITY FINANCE. *See* BRITISH VENTURE CAPITAL ASSOCIATION.

vertical income *See* VERTICAL SLICE.

vertical lease Another term for side-by-side lease.

vertical slice Where two or more persons wish to participate on comparable terms in an investment or property venture, usually a development, the amount received as a proportion of the total net income by each of the participants, all of whom own separate legal interests in the entire property by way of the freehold, head lease or a subordinate interest. The documentation usually provides that rental and other income as well as the cost of any revenue (or capital) liabilities in respect of the property are shared by the participants according to the value of contributions. Sometimes, one or more of the participants are entitled to a share of income, regardless of whether or not it is paid — this is not strictly a vertical slice. Also called a side-by-side share or income participation share. *Cf* HORIZONTAL SLICE; TOP SLICE. *See* SIDE-BY-SIDE LEASE.

vertical slice participation A method of multi-participation in a property venture, usually a development, whereby each of the participants owns a separate legal interest in the whole of the property concerned by way of the freehold, head lease or a subordinate interest. The documentation normally ensures that rental and other income and/or capital receipts as well as the cost of any revenue or capital liabilities are shared by the participants in predetermined percentages related to their respective contributions, whether financial or otherwise. *See* SIDE-BY-SIDE LEASE.

vest To bestow upon another a legal right, or the legal ownership of an estate or interest in land.

vested in interest Descriptive of a present right to a future interest in a property, eg that of the remainderman under a settlement. *Cf* VESTED IN POSSESSION. *See* VESTED INTEREST.

vested in possession Descriptive of a present right to enjoy an immediate interest in property, eg that of the life interest under a settlement. *Cf* VESTED IN INTEREST. *See* VESTED INTEREST.

vested interest A present right to an immediate or future interest in land (as opposed to one contingent on some future event). The interest vested may be either "in possession" or "in interest". *Cf* CONTINGENT INTEREST.

vesting assent A document transferring ownership of land from the personal representatives to the beneficiary under a will or under the rules of intestacy.

vesting declaration In a deed appointing new trustees, a statement that the trust property will vest in them and thus be in their possession.

vesting declaration, general *See* GENERAL VESTING DECLARATION.

vesting deed In a settlement made during the settlor's life, a deed transferring the legal estate in the settled land to the immediate beneficiary (or beneficiaries).

vicarious liability Legal liability for another's crime or tort resulting from the relationship between the persons concerned, eg any liability of an employer for a tort committed by his employee either in the normal course of his employment or where such act or omission has been authorised or ratified by the employer.

vi, clam or precario By force, secretly or by consent. In establishing a *prima facie* claim to a right by prescription these three factors must be absent. Thus the term is generally used negatively as *nec vi, nec clam, nec precario*.

virtual rent The true annual cost of a property to a lessee, representing the rent paid plus the annual equivalent of any capital sums expended from time to time, eg premiums. It is sometimes known as "sitting rent". *See* COSTS IN USE.

visibility line Another term for sight line. *See* VISION SPLAY.

vision splay A segment of land bounded by two diverging sight lines at the point of entry on to a road to ensure that visibility is unobstructed for a reasonable distance.

void **1.** Empty and unusable space, especially in a building or other structure. **2.** Unoccupied and unlet space, particularly in a multi-tenanted building. *See* VOID PERIOD; VOID RELIEF. **3.** Having no legal effect, eg of an alleged contract. *Cf* VOIDABLE. *See* VOID CONTRACT.

voidable In law, capable of being set aside as of no effect. *Cf* VOID. *See* VOIDABLE CONTRACT.

voidable contract A contract which, although *prima facie* valid when made, can subsequently be set aside on the grounds of misrepresentation, non-disclosure, undue influence or, in some instances, of mistake. *Cf* VOID CONTRACT.

void allowance (vacancy allowance) In valuations, a deduction made for the likely non-receipt of rent. *Cf* END ALLOWANCE.

void contract An alleged contract which has no legal effect *ab initio*, eg a contract to commit a crime, one contrary to public policy or one resulting from certain instances of mistake. *Cf* VOIDABLE CONTRACT. *See* VOID 3.

void period For Schedule A purposes, under section 25(1) of the Taxes Act, "a period during which the person chargeable was not in occupation of the premises or any part thereof but was entitled to possession thereof". *See* SCHEDULES.

void rate *See* UNOCCUPIED RATE.

void relief An allowance against rates for part or the whole of a period during which a property, or part of it, is not beneficially occupied. *Cf* UNOCCUPIED RATE. *See* RELIEF 1.

volenti non fit injuria That to which a person consents cannot be considered an injury, as applied to the legal defence that the plaintiff voluntarily consented to the injury or risk of injury.

voluntary body An association or society of persons, which is not a governmental or public body, with objects of a charitable, cultural, recreational or other non-profit-making nature.

voluntary disposition A conveyance (or other transfer of ownership) of real property made otherwise than for valuable consideration, eg a deed of gift.

voluntary improvement An improvement to a property carried out otherwise than under a legal obligation. *Cf* CONTRACTUAL IMPROVEMENT.

voluntary liquidation The termination of the operations of a company by the winding-up procedure initiated either by the shareholders or at the request of creditors (as distinct from a compulsory liquidation by the court, usually instituted on insolvency at the behest of creditors). *See* LIQUIDATION; WINDING-UP.

voluntary tax Descriptive of a tax which may be avoided relatively easily, ie a person who pays the tax has "voluntarily" done so, having taken no steps to avoid it. (Inheritance tax has been so called.)

voluntary waste Waste occurring by the positive act of a tenant's damaging the demised premises. *Cf* PERMISSIVE WASTE. *See* EQUITABLE WASTE.

W

waiver The actual or deemed abandonment of, or failure to assert, a legal right.

Waldram diagram Originally devised in the 1920s by the late Mr P J Waldram, a surveyor, a diagram which is used for testing the adequacy of daylight in a room. The effect of any obstruction to light in a room is plotted on a grid and that proportion of the unobstructed light from the sky available for illuminating individual points in the room can be calculated from the diagram. *See* RIGHT OF LIGHT; SUNLIGHT AND DAYLIGHT CODE.

walking possession In levying a distress, the act of the bailiff in listing the goods to be distrained but leaving them on the premises subject to an enforceable condition that they must not be removed therefrom.

walkway A footpath created in pursuance of an agreement under section 35 of the Highways Act 1980, enabling the public to go over, through, under or around (other than at ground level) buildings or structures. Such agreement may provide for the local authority to be liable for its maintenance.

walkway agreement *See* WALKWAY.

warehouse Premises designed and built or converted for the purpose of bulk storage of raw materials or finished or partly finished goods, pending either onward transit or division into smaller batches and subsequent distribution. *Cf* CASH AND CARRY (WAREHOUSE); DISCOUNT WAREHOUSE; RETAIL WAREHOUSE. *See* BONDED WAREHOUSE; GODOWN; QUEEN'S WAREHOUSE.

warehoused Descriptive of a loan or investment where interest or dividends respectively are rolled-up. *See* ROLLED-UP INTEREST.

warrandice (Scotland) A clause, usually in a disposition of heritable property (or heritage), ie property passing to heirs on the owner's death, by which the granter undertakes that the right conveyed will be effective.

warrant **1.** A document authorising an action or decision. **2.** A document of warranty. **3.** A document carrying the right to acquire equity shares at a predetermined price at some future date, the right being lost if not exercised by the due date.

warranty An express or implied undertaking of the truth of a statement, whereby the warrantor becomes legally responsible in the event of the facts being otherwise than as stated, eg a vendor may give a warranty that the property being sold is fit for a particular purpose or is in a given state of repair. *Cf* GUARANTEE. *See* SKILL AND CARE WARRANTY.

waste The doctrine of unlawful change, usually involving deterioration, in the physical condition of a property resulting from the positive act or neglect of the party responsible. It applies especially to a life tenant under a settlement, but also to a tenant under a lease. *Cf* FAIR WEAR AND TEAR. *See* AMELIORATING WASTE; EQUITABLE WASTE; PERMISSIVE WASTE; VOLUNTARY WASTE.

waste land **1.** In common parlance, uncultivated land not used for any purpose. **2.** For the purposes of section 65 of the Town and Country Planning Act 1971, this can include "any garden, vacant site or other open land" if its condition seriously injures the amenity of the area.

wasting asset **1.** An asset which in real terms will normally depreciate in value over time, eg a leasehold interest. **2.** Under the Capital Gains Tax Act 1979, section 37(1), an "asset with a predictable life not exceeding 50 years, but so that — (*a*) freehold land is not such an asset, whatever its nature and whatever the nature of the buildings or works thereon . . .". *See* DEPRECIATION; DEPRECIATING ASSET; SCRAP VALUE.

watercourse Either:

a a river, stream, canal or other channel for the flow of water, or

b the bed on which it flows.

See RIPARIAN RIGHTS.

water rate The amount charged to the occupier of a building for the supply of water and, perhaps, other related or incidental services. It may be calculated by reference to the rateable value of the property or to the quantity of water used, as measured by a meter installed on the premises.

water table The natural level to which underground water will rise relative to the surface of the land. It will usually vary with seasonal weather conditions and may be affected by, for example, the boring of deep wells, the construction of dams and deforestation.

waterway Under the Transport Act 1968, a canal or inland waterway within the jurisdiction of the British Waterways Board. *See* COMMERCIAL WATERWAY; CRUISING WATERWAY; REMAINDER WATERWAY.

wayleave Strictly, a determinable right of way to convey minerals extracted from land over another's land or to lay cables, pipes or conduits over, on or under another's land, especially one granted to a statutory undertaker. *See* OVERSAIL; RIGHT OF WAY.

way of necessity Where there would be no other means of access, a right of way implied in favour of an isolated parcel of land surrounded by other land, part or all of which was formerly in the same ownership. It results from severance of the ownership, either by the disposal of the parcel on its own or by its retention and the disposal of the remainder. The "necessity" must exist at the time of the disposal and not arise subsequently.

wear and tear *See* FAIR WEAR AND TEAR.

Wednesbury principle A principle by which the conduct of public authorities is judged and which is enshrined in the following sentence from the judgment of Lord Greene MR in *Associated Provincial Picture Houses Ltd* v *Wednesbury Corporation* (1947): "It is true to say that, if a decision on a competent matter is so unreasonable that no reasonable authority could ever have come to it, then the courts can interfere."

weekly tenancy *See* PERIODIC TENANCY.

weighbridge A machine used for weighing vehicles, loaded or unloaded; it is usually set into the roadway, with an ancillary office.

weighted rate (of return) An opportunity cost of money rate based on an organisation's historic average weighted cost of funding projects.

well **1.** A vertical hole or shaft in the ground, usually lined or piped and from which water or oil may be extracted. **2.** A vertical space in a building, sometimes containing stairs and/or lifts or providing light and air.

well maintained payment A colloquial term for a payment made under Schedule 23 to the Housing Act 1985 at the discretion of the local housing authority for an unfit house which has nevertheless been well maintained. The payment is made to the person(s) who incurred the cost of maintenance and is currently (1988) 14 times the rateable value but subject to its not exceeding the amount by which the full market value of the unfit house exceeds the site value compensation paid on its acquisition. (See Housing (Payments for Well Maintained Houses) Order 1982, section 1). *See* SLUM CLEARANCE; UNFIT PROPERTY.

Welsh Development Agency A government-sponsored organisation set up in 1976 under the Welsh Development Agency Act 1975 for the purposes of seeking, fostering, developing and implementing opportunities for the growth of business, employment and wealth in Wales. The agency concentrates its activities mainly in South Wales and North Wales. *Cf* SCOTTISH DEVELOPMENT AGENCY; DEVELOPMENT BOARD FOR RURAL WALES.

Western Corridor A colloquial term for a longitudinal area on both sides of the M4 motorway from London to Bristol, originally characterised by employment growth in the electronics industries.

white land A colloquial term for undeveloped, usually rural, land not the subject of any specific planning proposals or notation on a development plan; such land may have hope value for eventual (although unspecified) development.

White Paper A type of official publication, originally under a white cover, setting out government policy on a particular subject, especially that proposed for legislation. *Cf* GREEN PAPER; YELLOW PAPER. *See* COMMAND PAPERS.

Whitsunday May 15, a Scottish quarter day.

wholesale money market The financial market for funds derived from banks, pension funds and other institutions. *Cf* RETAIL MONEY MARKET.

wild animal For the purposes of Part I of the Wildlife and Countryside Act 1981, this means: ". . . any animal (other than a bird) which is or (before it was killed or taken) was living wild . . .".

wild bird For the purposes of Part I of the Wildlife and Countryside Act 1981 this means: ". . . any bird of a kind which is ordinarily resident in or is a visitor to Great Britain in a wild state . . ." excluding poultry or any game bird, except in section 5 (prohibition of certain methods of killing or taking wild birds) and section 16 (power to grant licences).

wild plant For the purposes of Part I of the Wildlife and Countryside Act 1981, this means: ". . . any plant which is or (before it was picked, uprooted or destroyed) was growing wild and is of a kind which ordinarily grows in Great Britain in a wild state."

will A written statement, duly witnessed, setting out an individual's intentions as to the distribution of his estate upon death: to be valid it must comply with the formal requirements of the Wills Act 1837 and subsequent statutes. *See* EXECUTOR(S); RULES OF INTESTACY.

"willing lessor, willing lessee" ("willing landlord, willing tenant") An assumption sometimes made for rental valuation purposes, eg when so required by a rent review clause, that the lessor is willing to let the property concerned and that there is at least one genuine prospective lessee, whether or not such is actually the case at the date of valuation.

"willing seller, willing buyer" ("willing vendor, willing purchaser") An assumption sometimes made for valuation purposes that the owner of the property concerned is willing to dispose of his interest therein and that there is at least one genuine purchaser in the market for that interest, whether or not such is actually the case at the date of valuation.

winding-up The procedure for terminating the affairs of a business, company or project. *See* LIQUIDATION; LIQUIDATOR.

"without prejudice" A phrase used to enable parties to negotiate an agreement or settle a dispute, either orally or in writing, without any statement or admission made being subsequently quoted or produced in evidence at any legal hearing bearing on the subject-matter of the proposed agreement or dispute. In claiming this privilege, care must be taken to avoid statements which are untrue or of a defamatory nature, which might entitle the court to allow their admission in evidence at the request of the other party. In any event, the privilege applies only to the proceedings in question, so that "without prejudice" statements (verbal or written) can, in certain circumstances, be produced in evidence in some other, unrelated, dispute.

without reserve Descriptive of a sale at auction or by tender made on the basis that no minimum price has been determined by the vendor.

working capital The capital required in the day-to-day running of a business, eg stock and/or cash.

working day For banking and financial purposes, any weekday other than a bank holiday.

workshop A building or part of a building in which some industrial activity or craft is carried on.

work station A place within an office or other work establishment where an employee works at some specialist equipment, eg a computer terminal or a word processor, as opposed to a desk.

worsenment (worsement) A colloquial term sometimes applied as an antonym to betterment and therefore meaning a decrease in the value of property, especially that arising as a result of some action by central or local government or some other body acting under statutory powers. *Cf* BETTERMENT 1 (UK).

wrap-around mortgage (USA) A second (junior) or subsequent mortgage with a face value of both the amount it secures and the balance due under the first or prior mortgage(s). In the event of default by the mortgagor, the wrap-around mortgagee has a legal responsibility for the balance of the first or prior mortgage(s) then outstanding.

writ An order issued by a court in the name of the sovereign directing the addressee to act or forbear from acting in some manner, eg a writ of summons (*writ simpliciter*) by which an action is begun in the High Court.

writing When used in a statute, this includes typing, printing, lithography, photography and other modes of representing or reproducing words in visual form: see the Interpretation Act 1978, Schedule 1.

writing down Reducing the book value of an asset; this may be done annually or on a special occasion, eg after an asset revaluation.

writing-down allowance Under the Capital Allowances Act 1968, as amended, an annual deduction from the allowable capital cost (or previous year's written-down value) of a qualifying asset. *See* CAPITAL ALLOWANCES.

written-down value At a given time, the result of making one or more annual or periodic deductions for depreciation against capital cost or worth.

X

xd *See* EX DIVIDEND.

xestobium rufovillosum An insect, commonly known as the death watch beetle, which attacks oak and other hardwoods by boring.

xi *See* EX INTEREST.

xylophagous Descriptive of those insects which eat or bore into wood, eg *xestobium rufovillosum*.

xystus **1.** A covered colonnade, as originally used for exercise by Greek athletes. **2.** A garden walk, usually bordered by trees.

Y

year *See* CALENDAR YEAR; FINANCIAL YEAR; FISCAL YEAR; LEAP YEAR; RATING YEAR; YEAR OF ASSESSMENT.

year of assessment For income and capital taxation purposes, a calendar year beginning April 6 and ending April 5 for which liability is calculated, eg "1988-89" describes the year of assessment beginning April 6 1988. *See* FISCAL YEAR.

yearly tenancy *See* TENANCY FROM YEAR TO YEAR.

yearly tenant *See* TENANCY FROM YEAR TO YEAR.

years' purchase (YP) In valuations by the investment method, the amount by which the net income is multiplied to arrive at capital value. It is synonymous with the present value of £1 per annum and is the reciprocal of the annuity £1 will purchase. For most purposes, tables of years' purchase are either single rate or dual rate.

year to year *See* TENANCY FROM YEAR TO YEAR.

Yellow Book The colloquial name for the loose-leaf publication issued by the Council of the International Stock Exchange and entitled "Admission of Securities to Listing", which has a bright yellow cover. It lays down minimum requirements for:

- a the admission of stocks and shares to listing, ie quotation,
- b the contents, scrutiny and publication of listing particulars, and
- c continuing obligations for those responsible.

Yellow Paper A limited circulation consultation paper embodying revised proposals by the government on a particular subject after consideration of submissions made in response to the relevant Green Paper. It is sent to official bodies, representative and professional organisations and others who have commented on or expressed interest in proposals put forward in the Green Paper. *See* WHITE PAPER.

yield *See* CROP YIELD; INVESTMENT YIELD. Refer to Appendix IV.

yield per head In agriculture, the average amount of milk, wool or other product per animal for a given period. *Cf* CROP YIELD.

yield up Give up possession, especially by the tenant at the end of a lease.

Z

zenith **1.** In land surveying, the point in the heavens vertically above the observer's head. **2.** The greatest height, the opposite, or lowest, point being the nadir.

zero grazing An intensive feeding system for cattle whereby the fodder is brought to the animals at one place, eg to a yard or byre; it may be employed, for instance, as protection from the climate, for animal security or because the farm's lands are dispersed or are devoted to growing crops.

zero-rated supply For value added tax, a supply of goods or services where tax is charged at nil rate but which is otherwise treated as a taxable supply, eg for the recovery of input tax. *Cf* EXEMPT SUPPLY; STANDARD-RATED SUPPLY.

zillmerising A procedure for modifying the net premium reserve method of valuing a long-term insurance policy by increasing the part of the future premiums for which credit is taken so as to allow for initial expenses: See Regulation 3 of the Insurance Companies Regulations 1981 (SI 1981 No 1654).

zone A defined area of land or part of a building which is allocated for a particular purpose, eg development plans may allocate areas of land for different uses or valuers of property may distinguish between areas of floorspace of a building and ascribe different values to them. *See* CENTRAL ACTIVITIES ZONE; CLEAN-AIR ZONE; ENTERPRISE ZONE; PLANNING ZONE; SIMPLIFIED PLANNING ZONE; TWILIGHT ZONE.

zone A *See* HALVING BACK; ZONING METHOD.

zone A value In the zoning method, the unit of comparison for rental purposes attributed to the frontal zone of retail premises, eg £x per sq ft. *See* HALVING BACK; ZONING METHOD.

zoning **1.** In planning terms, the dividing of an area by a local planning authority into zones for particular uses or activities. *See* PLANNING ZONE. **2.** *See* ZONING METHOD.

zoning method (zoning approach) A method of arriving at the rental value of retail space (usually on the ground floor) by dividing it into strips parallel with the main frontage. A different value per unit of space is attributed within each strip corresponding to its relative ability to achieve sales/profit, the most valuable space normally being towards the front. In standard shops the current (1988) practice in the central London shop market is to use a zone 30 ft deep as zone A, ie maximum value, and in outer London and the provinces a zone 20 ft deep. It is usual for zone A to have a value per sq ft (or m^2) twice that of zone B. *See* HALVING BACK; ZONE A VALUE.

zyzzy **1.** The authors' feelings on completion of an almost impossible task, ie euphoric self-deception. **2.** The sound of bubbling champagne.

APPENDIX I

TERMS GROUPED BY SUBJECT-MATTER

Lists enabling a reader to identify those terms (and definitions) which are relevant to a particular subject.

ACCOUNTS

accrued depreciation
accrued interest
amortisation
amortisation rate
amortisation term
asset valuation
balance sheet
balancing charge
book cost
book depreciation
book gain/loss
book value
capital appreciation
capital expenditure
cash flow
cash flow analysis/statement
current cost accounting
curved line depreciation
depreciated value
depreciation
deprival value
equalisation fund
financial year
fixed assets
gross trading profit
historical cost accounting
life-cycle cost(ing)
net trading profit (NTP)
non-recurring expense
outgoings
ratio analysis
reducing balance depreciation
Statement of Standard Accounting Practice (SSAP)
straight-line depreciation
turnover
writing down
written-down value

AGRICULTURE, FORESTRY AND FISHERIES

accommodation land
aeolian soil
agricultural building allowance
agricultural fixtures
agricultural holding
agricultural land
agricultural land tribunal
agricultural licence
Agricultural Mortgage Corporation (AMC)
agricultural tenancy
allotment
allotment garden
aquaculture
assart
autumn tenancy
away-going crop (way-going or off-going crop)
boosey pasture
bote
cattle
cattlegate
cattle trespass
coppice
cottage holding
crop yield
damage feasant
emblements
estovers
felling direction
felling licence
fish farming
game
game bird
ground game
holdover
kissing gate
land drainage
Land Improvement Company
ley
mariculture
model clauses (repair regulations)
occupier's drainage rate
owner's drainage rate
prairie value
smallholding
sod fertility

sod value
sporting rights
successions tenancy
tenant-right
tied cottage
underwood
wild animal
wild bird
wild plant
yield per head
zero grazing

BUILDING AND CONSTRUCTION

abutment
agrément certificate
air conditioning
alterations
approved inspector
architect
architect's certificate
atrium
balloon frame
bill of quantities
British Board of Agrément (BBA)
building
building byelaws
building contract
building contract certificates
building contractor
building control
building cost indices
Building Cost Information Service (BCIS)
building licence
Building Maintenance Cost Information Service (BMCIS)
building owner
Building Regulations
Building Research Establishment (BRE)
building survey
building surveyor
certificate of making good defects
certificate of practical completion
closed tender
construction period
contractor
cost-plus contract
dangerous structure notice
daywork contract
defects liability period (retention period)
demolition
Demolition and Dismantling Industry Register (DDIR)
Demolition Industry Group Training Association
design and build contract (design and construct contract)
double glazing/triple glazing
envelope
extras
façade
fascia board
final account
final certificate
finishes
fire-resisting construction
fire wall
fixed price contract
floor load
formal tender
gablet
gambrel roof
glazing
high point loading
improvements
incubator building (USA)
indirect construction costs
informal tender
interim certificate
JCT Contract
Joint Contracts Tribunal
layout
let
life-cycle cost(ing)
limited tender
load bearing
lump
lump sum (building) contract
maintenance period
mansard roof
non-loadbearing wall (partition wall)
one-hour door
package deal (building) contract
partial completion certificate (partial possession certificate)
party wall
party wall agreement
party wall award
performance bond
physical life
pitch
post-tensioned concrete
post-tensioning
practical completion certificate
pre-stressed concrete
pre-tensioning
prime cost contract

private tender (closed tender)
public tender (open tender)
rebuild
rebuilding clause
reconstruct
redevelopment
reinspection
remeasurement (building) contract
retained sum (retained amount)
retaining wall
sea wall
services
SfB
shell construction/finish
specification
sub-contractor
suspended ceiling
system(s) built
tender
tender document
tendering process
tender price indices
thermal insulation
topping out
trunking
variation
xystus

COMPANIES AND PARTNERSHIPS

advance corporation tax (ACT)
articles of association
asset valuation
bearer security
bonus issue
capitalisation
capitalisation of reserves (bonus, free or scrip issue)
close company
company
company limited by guarantee
company registration
compulsory liquidation (winding-up)
convertible bond
current cost accounting
debenture
director
disclosure
dissolution
distribution in kind
dividend
dividend yield
equity capital
equity finance
financial year
firm
fixed assets
franked investment income
free issue
gearing
historical cost accounting
investment trust company
joint development company
joint venture
limited company
limited liability
limited liability company
liquidation
liquidator
listed company
listing
market capitalisation
memorandum of association
ordinary share
par value
participators
partnership
preference share
private company
property investment trust
public limited company (plc)
quoted company (listed company)
receiver
rights issue
scrip issue
Statement of Standard Accounting Practice (SSAP)
unlimited company
venture capital
voluntary liquidation
winding-up

COMPULSORY PURCHASE AND COMPENSATION

abortive expenditure
accommodation works
acquiring authority
adjusted net trading profit
advance compensation
betterment
blight notice
ceiling value
certificate of appropriate alternative development
certificate of value
compensation
compulsory purchase
compulsory purchase order (CPO)

condemnation (USA)
"Crawley" costs ("Harvey" costs)
district valuer (DV)
disturbance
disturbance payment
enabling Act/enabling statute
equivalent reinstatement
ex gratia payment
general vesting declaration
grey property (grey land)
heads of claim
home loss payment
"Horn" principle
injurious affection
interest on unpaid compensation
inverse condemnation (USA)
key worker
limits of deviation
material detriment
maximum compensation
McCarthy rules
minor tenancy
mitigation of loss
modification order
no-scheme world
notice of entry
notice to treat
Part VI claim
permitted development value
physical factors
pink-hatched-yellow land
pink land
"Pointe Gourde" principle
principle of equivalence
purchase notice
Ryde's scale
scheme world
set-off
severance
short tenancy
site value
"six rules"
slum clearance
special Act
special parliamentary procedure
special suitability or adaptability
temporary loss of profits
total extinguishment
trade disturbance
unexpended balance of established development value (UBED)
Valuation Office
well maintained payment
worsenment (worsement)

CONVEYANCING AND TRANSFER OF LAND

abstract of title
agreement for lease or sale
alienation
amendment of documents
appurtenance
attornment
certificate of value
charges register
completion
completion statement
conditions of sale
consideration
constructive notice
contract deposit
contract for sale
conveyance
conveyancing
deed of gift
delivery
disposal (disposition)
engrossment
exception
exchange of contracts
execution
fittings
fixtures
land charges register
landlord's fixtures
land register
Land Registry
leaseback
letter of attornment
local land charges
local land charges register
missives of sale (Scotland)
notice to complete
parcel (of land)
patent (USA)
pre-contract deposit
premises
property register
proprietorship register
requisition
reservation
root of title
sale and leaseback
seal
search
stakeholder
tenant's fixtures
tendering process
trade fixtures

vacant possession
vacant possession search
vendee
vendor
vesting deed
voluntary disposition

COURTS, TRIBUNALS AND ARBITRATIONS

action
adjudication
agricultural land tribunal
appeal
appellate committee
arbitration
arbitration agreement
arbitration clause
arbitrator
award
case
case law
case stated
Chancery Division
citation
Commercial Court
county court
court
Court of Appeal
court of first instance
court of last resort
Court of Protection
court of record
Court of Session
damages
declaratory judgment
dictum
discovery of documents
Divisional Court
equitable remedies
European Court
ex parte
General Commissioners
High Court of Justice
House of Lords
independent expert
independent surveyor
independent valuer
inferior court
Inns of Court
Lands Tribunal
leasehold valuation tribunal
penalty
prerogative order
proof of evidence
puisne judge
Queen's Bench Division
reference
rent assessment committee
rent assessment panel
rent tribunal
sealed offer
Special Commissioners
sub judice
superior court
Supreme Court of England and Wales
third surveyor
umpire
valuation and community charge tribunal
writ

DEVELOPMENT

advance payments code
assembly of land
break-even (point)
break-even analysis
building agreement
building licence
building scheme (scheme of development)
buy-out rate
costs in use
critical path analysis
developer
developer's budget method
developer's profit (or loss)
developer's risk and profit
development appraisal
Development Board for Rural Wales
development brief
development expenditure
development management
development profit (or loss)
development return (developer's return)
development yield
discounted cash flow analysis (DCF)
draw down
envelope ratio
extrapolation forecasting
Family Expenditure Survey
feasibility study
forward commitment
forward finance
forward funding
forward letting/forward sale
front money
funding
green field site
infrastructure

interim finance rate
key property
land assembly
Land Authority for Wales
land availability study
land bank
letter of intent
market
mixed development
Monte Carlo simulation
network analysis
off-site improvements
on-costs
on-site improvements
opportunity cost
payback
precedence techniques
pre-funding
programme (project) evaluation (and) review techniques (PERT)
project management (development management)
redevelopment
Scottish Development Agency
sensitivity analysis
skill and care warranty
speculative development
speculative funding
turnkey deal (turnkey package)
up-front funding
upside and downside
Welsh Development Agency

ESTATE AGENCY AND AUCTIONS

accommodation agency
agency board
agency by estoppel
agent
agent of necessity
apparent authority
articles of roup (Scotland)
asking price
auction
auctioneer
bargain
bid
bidder
bidding agreement
board, estate agents'
break-up operation
brochure
broker
brokerage
buyer's market
buy in
candle auction
chain (of properties)
closed tender
commission
contract deposit
deposit
disclaimer
Dutch auction
earnest money
estate agency work
estate agent
exclusive agent
exposure
finder's fee
formal tender
gavel
gazumping
general agent
informal tender
in the market
joint agent
joint sole agent
limited tender
lot
lotting
market price
moiety
multiple agency
National Association of Estate Agents (NAEA)
negotiation
negotiator
particulars
pre-contract deposit
prelet
prime property
principal
private tender (closed tender)
private treaty
public tender (open tender)
puffing
realtor (USA)
reserve
retained agent
reverse gazumping
ring (bidding agreement; knock-out agreement)
roup
runner
seller's market
selling price
sole agent (exclusive agent)
sole selling/letting rights

special agent
stakeholder
sub-agent
tender
tender document
tendering process
trotting
under offer
undisclosed principal
upset price
without reserve

FINANCE

AAA (USA)
abortive expenditure
accumulative rate
add-on interest (USA)
adverse gearing
amortisation
amortisation rate
amortisation term
annual percentage rate (APR)
annual sinking fund (ASF)
annual sinking fund rate
arrears
back-to-back loan
balloon payment
bank rate
bankrupt
base rate
bearer security
bridging finance
bridging loan
British Venture Capital Association
building finance
bullet
buy-out
buy-out rate
call
call loan
capital improvement
capitalisation
capitalisation of reserves (bonus, free or scrip issue)
capital money
carrying charge
claw-back
collateral (security)
compound interest
construction loan (USA)
corporate treasury function
currency linked bond
daylight exposure limit
debenture
deficit financing
deposit
discount
draw-down
drop lock loan
effective rate of interest
equalisation fund
equity capital
equity finance
equivalent annual cost
Eurobond
facility letter
fixed charge
floating charge
forward commitment
forward finance
forward funding
forward letting/forward sale
fraudulent preference
front money
funding
geared leaseback
gearing
indexation
insolvency
interim finance rate
investment
Land Improvement Company
leaseback
letter of intent
leverage (USA)
LIBID (London interbank bid rate)
LIBOR (London interbank offer(ed) rate)
line of credit
liquidity
man of straw
minimum lending rate
non-recourse loan
payment on account
performance bond
pre-funding
priority yields
receiver
regional incentives
renewal fund
reserve fund
retail money market
reverse premium (negative premium)
risk capital
rolled-up interest
sale and leaseback
secured loan
security

shortfall
sinking fund
site finance
speculative funding
subscribing fund
surety
take-out
tender panel facility
tranche
up-front funding
venture capital
vertical slice
warehoused
warrant
working capital

GRANTS, ALLOWANCES AND OTHER INCENTIVES

agricultural building allowance
assisted area
capital allowances
derelict land grant
EEC grants and loans for industrial buildings
enterprise zone
enterprise zone allowance
Ferrous Foundry Industry Scheme
industrial improvement area
partnership area
programme area
regional incentives
section 4 grant
special area (partnership area)
urban development grant
urban programme funds
urban regeneration grant

HERITAGE

ancient monument
Ancient Monuments Boards
archaeological area
area of archaeological importance
area of outstanding natural beauty
building of special architectural or historic interest
building preservation notice (BPN)
building preservation order (BPO)
Civic Trust
conservation area
deemed listing
endowment trust
Friends of the Historic Houses Association
heritage body
heritage coast
heritage property
Historic Buildings and Monuments Commission for England
Historic Houses Association (HHA)
listed building
listed building consent
listing
monument
national park
protected monument
quinquennial
scheduled monument
site of special scientific interest
spot listing

HIGHWAYS

adoption
advance payments code
bridlepath (bridleway)
building line (set-back line)
carriageway
definitive maps
driftway
drove road
footpath
footway
highway
highway easement (USA)
improvement line
private street works code
rat run
return frontage
section 40 agreement
sight line
street
street works authority
street works code
traffic generation
unadopted road
visibility line
vision splay
walkway
walkway agreement

HOUSING

assured shorthold tenancy
assured tenancy
building society
clearance area
closing order
demolition order
disturbance payment
dwelling
dwelling-house

evict
ex gratia payment
flat
general improvement area (GIA)
grey property (grey land)
housing action area
housing association
housing authority
housing co-operative
Housing Corporation
housing society
housing trust
improvement notice
key money
long tenancy
maisonette
pink-hatched-yellow land
pink land
protected shorthold tenancy
protected tenancy
regulated tenancy
rent officer
repairs notice
restricted contract
secure tenancy
self-build society
service charge
service occupancy
service tenancy
shorthold tenancy
starter homes
starter housing
statutory tenancy
unfitness for human habitation
unfit property (unfit dwelling)
well maintained payment

INDUSTRY, MINING, OFFICES AND OTHER COMMERCIAL PREMISES

accident book
advance factory
aftercare
aftercare condition
Bürolandschaft business park
business premises
business space
common area
Council for Small Industries in Rural Areas (COSIRA)
dead rent
deposit
distribution
factory
flatted factory
godown
hi-tech building (high technology building)
incubator building (USA)
industrial building
mineral rights
mineral royalty
minerals
mining lease
mining operations
nursery units
prohibition notice
science park
sleeping rent
three-phase power
unit mix
warehouse
workshop
work station

INSURANCE

A & S fees
assurance
average
catastrophic perils (dry perils)
collective insurance
consequential loss of rent
contingency insurance
contribution clause
cover
endowment assurance policy
fire extinguishing appliances warranty
fire insurance
Fire Offices Committee
global cover
indemnity insurance
indemnity period
insurable interest
insurable value (USA)
insurance
insurance contract
insurance rent
insurance value
insured
insurer
long-term agreement
loss adjuster
loss assessor
non-catastrophic perils (wet perils)
non-tariff insurers
peril
premium
property owners' public liability insurance

proper valuation
reinstatement
reinstatement basis of insurance
reinstatement value
reinsurance
risk
shortfall
subrogation
sub-underwriter
sum insured
surrender value
title insurance
underwriter
zillmerising

INVESTMENT

accrued interest
annual sinking fund (ASF)
annuity
beta value
bond
capital
cash on cash (USA)
covenant
covenant value
current option
direct placement
discounted cash flow analysis (DCF)
diversification
dividend
froth income
good covenant
gross fund
hedge
institutional investors
investment
investment company
investment property
investment trust company
investment yield
investor in land
leaseback
managed fund
open-ended
opportunity cost
portfolio
prime property
property bond
property investment trust
property unit trust
retail money market
reversionary income
reversionary investment
risk capital
sale and leaseback
sinking fund
tenant's covenant
terminable income
terminal income
terminating income
top slice
true net income
undoubted covenant
unitisation
unit trust
venture capital
vertical income
vertical slice
vertical slice participation
warehoused
wholcsale money market
yield

LAND REGISTRATION

absolute title
cadastral
caution
charge certificate
charges register
estate contract
good leasehold title
inhibition
land certificate
land charge
land charges register
land register
land registration
Land Registry
minor interest
overriding interest
possessory title
property register
proprietorship register
qualified title
registered land
requisition
search

LANDLORD AND TENANT

(See also under RENT)

absolute covenant
acceleration
additional rent
Adler clause
agreement for lease or sale
agricultural fixtures
agricultural tenancy
alienation
alienation clause

animus revertendi
apportionment
assign
assignee
assignment
assignor
assured shorthold tenancy
assured tenancy
autumn tenancy
bote
break clause
break point (break date)
building agreement
building lease
building licence
business
business tenancy
case
cash back
certum est quod certum reddit potest
cesser of rent
clear lease
common area charges
common parts
competent landlord
concurrent lease
contractual improvement
contractual tenancy
controlled tenancy
converted tenancy
counterpart
covenant
created ground rent
cullery
current tenancy
deductions
demise
disregards
distress (distraint)
emblements
equitable lease (informal lease)
equity sharing lease
escalator clause
estovers
exception
excess charge
exempt lease
express covenant
extended lease
fag end
fair wear and tear (reasonable wear and tear)
fine
firebote (fuelbote)
forfeiture
full repairing (and insuring) lease (FRI lease)
future lease
geared leaseback
gold clause
gross lease
ground lease
guarantor
habendum
half a year
harassment
head lease
heads of terms
holding
holding over
holdover
horizontal slice
immediate landlord
implied covenant
interim rent
intermediate landlord
internal repairing lease
landlord
landlord's fixtures
landlord's improvements
lease
lease for life
leasehold
leasehold enfranchisement
leasehold improvements (USA)
leasehold reform
lessee
lessor
let
licence
life tenancy
long tenancy
maintain
merger of interests
mesne
mesne profits
mining lease
minor superior tenancy
minor tenancy
model rent review clause
normal wear and tear
notice to quit
notice to terminate
occupational lease
open rent review
ornamental fixtures
overriding lease
participating lease (participation lease)
percentage lease
percentage rent (turnover rent)

periodic tenancy
permissive waste
possession
prelet
premium
prime tenant
privity of contract
privity of estate
protected shorthold tenancy
protected tenancy
quiet enjoyment
rebuilding clause
reddendum
redevelopment clause
re-entry
regulated tenancy
renewal
rent cesser clause
rent-free period
rent review
repair
reservation
restricted contract
reverse premium
reversion
Scott schedule
secure tenancy
security of tenure
service charge
service occupancy
service tenancy
serviced accommodation
short lease
short tenancy
shorthold tenancy
side-by-side lease
sitting tenant
statutory tenancy
sublease (underlease)
sublessee (underlessee)
subtenancy
subtenant
succession tenancy
superior interest
superior landlord
superior lease (superior tenancy)
surrender (of lease or tenancy)
surrender clause
tacit acceptance
tenancy
tenancy agreement
tenancy at will
tenancy by estoppel
tenancy for life (or lives)
tenancy for years
tenancy from year to year
tenancy on sufferance
tenancy pur (or per) autre vie
tenant
tenant for life (life tenant)
tenant on sufferance
tenant-right
tenant's covenant
tenant's fixtures
tenant's improvements
tenant's repairing lease
term
term certain
term date
termination
term of years
term of years absolute
term of years absolute in possession
tied cottage
tied rent
trade fixtures
trigger notice
turnover lease
underlease
underlessee
undoubted covenant
uplift
upward/downward rent review
upward/downward rent review subject to a base
upward-only rent review
user clause (user covenant)
usual covenants
vertical income
vertical lease
voluntary improvement
voluntary waste
wear and tear
weekly tenancy
yearly tenancy
yearly tenant
year to year
yield up

LATIN TERMS

a coelo usque ad centrum
ab initio
ad hoc
ad idem
ad medium filium (viae or aquae)
ad valorem
a fortiori
animus possidendi
animus revertendi
audi alteram partem

bona fide
bona vacantia
caveat actor
caveat emptor
caveat subscriptor
caveat venditor
certum est quod certum reddit potest
consensus ad idem; consensus in idem (Scotland)
cujus est solum ejus est usque ad coelum et ad inferos
cum
de facto
de jure
de minimis
dominium directum (Scotland)
dominium utile (Scotland)
dubitante
ejusdem generis
ex gratia
ex officio
ex parte
in gremio (Scotland)
in personam
in rem
inter vivos
intra vires
jus quaesitum tertio (Scotland)
lex loci
lex loci actus
lex loci contractus
lex loci rei sitae (lex loci situs)
lex loci solutionis
locus poenitentiae
mala fide
mortis causa
nec vi, nec clam, nec precario
obiter dictum
opera citato (op cit)
pro indiviso (Scotland)
quantum meruit
quicquid plantatur solo, solo cedit
ratio decidendum
ratione soli
ratione solis
re
rebus sic stantibus
rei interventus (Scotland)
res nullius
solum (Scotland)
sub judice
ultra vires
vi, clam or precario
volenti non fit injuria

LAW — GENERAL

abandonment
abatement
absolute covenant
acceptance
accord and satisfaction
action
act of God
actual notice
ad idem
administration
administrative law
admissible evidence
adoption
affidavit
agency by estoppel
agent
agent of necessity
agreement
apparent authority
appeal
arm's length
attest
attorney
audi alteram partem
bailee
bailiff
bilateral contract (synallagmatic contract)
bill of sale
body of deed
bona vacantia
bond
breach of contract
breach of warranty
burden (of contract or covenant)
business name
byelaw (by-law)
case law
caveat emptor
caveat subscriptor
caveat venditor
certiorari
champerty (champertous maintenance)
chattel
chattel personal
chose
chose in action
chose in possession
circumstantial evidence (indirect evidence)
citation
collateral agreement
common law
competent

conclusive evidence
condition
conditional contract
condition precedent
condition subsequent
consensus ad idem; consensus in idem (Scotland)
consideration
constructive notice
contract
contract for sale
contractor
cost-of-living clause
counterpart
covenant
custom
cut-off date
cy-près doctrine
damages
declaration
declaratory judgment
deed
deed of gift
de facto
default
default notice
definitive maps
dehors
de jure
delivery
de minimis
derogate
devise
dictum
direct evidence
disclaimer
distress (distraint)
documentary evidence (written evidence)
dubitante
ejusdem generis
equitable
equitable estoppel (quasi-estoppel)
equitable lien
equitable remedies
equitable rights
equity
escheat
escrow
estoppel
evict
evidence
evidenced in writing
execution
exhibit
ex parte
expert
expert witness
express covenant
extinguishment
extrinsic evidence
fiduciary
fine
force majeure
frustrated contract
frustration of contract
full age
gale
general agent
good consideration (meritorious consideration)
guarantee, guaranty
guarantor
hearsay evidence (second-hand evidence)
holograph
implied notice
imputed notice
indenture
indirect evidence
in gross
injunction
in personam
in rem
interlocutory injunction
inter vivos
intra vires
joint and several obligation
joint obligation
jointure
judge
jurat
jurisdiction
laches
latent damage
latent defect
law report
legal memory
legal remedies
lex loci
lex loci actus
lex loci contractus
lex loci rei sitae (lex loci situs)
lex loci solutionis
licence
licensee
licensor
lien
limitation of actions
limited liability
liquidated damages
living memory

locus poenitentiae
mala fide
malfeasance
mandamus
misfeasance
misrepresentation
missives
mitigation of loss
mortis causa
mutual option
negligence
non-feasance
obiter dictum
offer
opinion evidence
option
oral evidence (parol evidence)
original evidence
override
part performance
patent defect
penalty
perpetual injunction
perpetuity
personalty (personal property)
positive covenant
power of appointment
pre-emption
prerogative order
prima facie evidence (presumptive evidence)
primary evidence
privity of contract
professional negligence
prohibition
prohibitory injunction
proof of evidence
property
property in action
put and take option (put and call option)
put option
qualified covenant
ratio decidendum
ratione soli
real evidence
real property (realty)
recital
recovery of land
rectification
relevant evidence
requisition
rescission
res nullius
restriction
restrictive covenant (negative covenant)
seal
sealed bid
secondary evidence
set-off
settlement
settlor
skill and care warranty
special agent
specific performance
statute law
subject to contract
surety
tacit acceptance
taxation of costs
tender
term
termination
time immemorial
time of the essence
tort
treasure trove
trespass
trigger notice
ultra vires
unconditional offer
undisclosed principal
unilateral contract
unliquidated damages
vest
vicarious liability
void
voidable
voidable contract
void contract
volenti non fit injuria
waiver
warrant
warranty
Wednesbury principle
will
"without prejudice"
writ
writing

LAW — PROPERTY

abandonment
abatement
abatement notice
absolute covenant
absolute title
abut
abuttals
acceleration
acceleration clause
accretion

acknowledgement and undertaking
a coelo usque ad centrum
ad hoc trust for sale
adjacent
adjoining
ad medium filium (viae or aquae)
adverse occupation
adverse possession
advowson
agreement for lease
agreement for lease or sale
airspace
alienation
alluvion
ameliorating waste (meliorating waste)
ancient demesne
ancient lights
animus possidendi
animus revertendi
apparent easement
appendant
approvement
appurtenance
appurtenant
assign
assignee
assignment
assignor
attornment
autre vie
avulsion
back-letter/back-bond
bare licensee
barren rent
base fee
beneficial interest
beneficial occupation
beneficial occupier
beneficial owner
bona fide purchaser
bote
boundary
breach of close
building owner
building scheme (scheme of development)
bundle of rights theory
butt
call option
cattle trespass
caution
cesser
charge
chattel personal
chattel real
chief rent
clear title
common
common land
common ownership
concurrent interests
conditional interest
consideration
contiguous
contingent interest
contract for sale
contractual improvement
conveyance
co-ownership
copyhold
corporeal hereditament
cross-easements
cross option
Crown land
cujus est solum ejus est usque ad coelum et ad inferos
curtilage
cy-près doctrine
damage feasant
dedication
defeasible
demise
demolition order
dereliction
determinable interest
devise
disentailing deed
disentailment
disposal (disposition)
domestic fixtures
dominant tenement
double option
easement
easement of light
emblements
encroachment
encumbrance (incumbrance)
enfranchisement
enlarge
entail
entailed interest
equitable charge
equitable easement
equitable estate
equitable interest
equitable lease (informal lease)
equitable mortgage
equitable waste
estate
estate contract

estate owner
estate pur (or per) autre vie
estovers
evidenced in writing
exception
fee
fee farm rent
fee simple
fee simple absolute in possession
fee tail
fief
firebote (fuelbote)
fittings
fixtures
flying freehold
free and clear
freehold
future estate
future interest
gavelkind
gift over
good marketable title
good title
hereditament
highway easement (USA)
holdover
housebote
implied covenant
improvements
incorporeal hereditament
inferior interest
inhibition
interest (in property)
joint ownership
joint tenancy
jointure
land charge
latent damage
leasehold
leasehold enfranchisement
legal charge
legal estate
legal interest
legal mortgage
licence
licensee
licensor
life interest
life tenancy
life tenancy under a settlement
light and air easements
local land charges
marketable title
merger of interests
mesne
mesne profits
messuage
minor interest
natural right
natural right of support
nec vi, nec clam, nec precario
notice to complete
nuisance
occupation
ornamental fixtures
overreach
overriding interest
owner
parcel (of land)
part performance
part possession
party wall
party wall agreement
party wall award
patent (USA)
permissive waste
perpetuity
perpetuity period
personalty (personal property)
positive covenant
possession
possessory title
power of appointment
pre-emption
premises
prescription
primogeniture
private nuisance
profit à prendre
property
public nuisance
put and take option (put and call option)
put option
qualified covenant
quasi-easement
quicquid plantatur solo, solo cedit
quitclaim deed (USA)
quit rent
real property (realty)
recovery of land
registered land
remainder
rentcharge
rent seck
requisition
reservation
restriction
restrictive covenant (negative covenant)
reversion
reversionary estate/reversionary interest

right of common
right of entry
right of light
right of support
right of way
riparian rights
root of title
search
seisin
servient tenement
settled land
settlement
settlor
squatter
squatter's title
statutory trust
strata title
strict settlement
superior interest
surrender (of lease or tenancy)
survivorship
tenancy
tenancy for life (or lives)
tenancy in common
tenancy in fee tail (tenancy in tail)
tenancy pur (or per) autre vie
tenant for life (life tenant)
tenant in fee simple
tenant in fee tail
tenant's fixtures
tenement
tenure
term of years
term of years absolute
term of years absolute in possession
title
title deeds
trade fixtures
trespass
trust
trustees of the settlement (Settled Land Act trustees)
trust for sale
turbary
unencumbered
use and occupation action
user
user clause (user covenant)
vacant possession
valuable consideration
vendee
vendor
vendor and purchaser summons
vest
vested in interest
vested in possession
vested interest
vesting assent
vesting deed
vi, clam or precario
voluntary disposition
voluntary improvement
voluntary waste
walking possession
waste
wayleave
way of necessity
yield up

LEASEHOLD REFORM

adverse differential
cleared site approach
"Delaforce effect"
entirety value
extended lease
good leasehold title
leasehold enfranchisement
leasehold reform
leasehold valuation tribunal
letting value
long tenancy
minor superior tenancy
modern ground rent
new-for-old approach
price payable
standing house approach

LEISURE AND RECREATION

access agreement
access order
amenity
amenity land
bank holiday
boarding house
common
Countryside Commission
cruising waterway
definitive maps
game
game bird
ground game
national park
park
section 4 grant
sporting rights
timeshare
Timeshare Developers' Group (TDG)

wild animal
wild bird
wild plant

LICENSED PREMISES

bonded warehouse (excise warehouse)
free house
off licence
on licence
tied house
tied rent
ullage allowance

MEASUREMENT, PLANS AND LAND SURVEYING

abut
adjacent
adjoining
aerial survey
bench-mark
block plan
block width
boundary
built depth
butt
cadastral map
cadastral survey
chain
circulation ratio
clear height
Code of Measuring Practice
contiguous
cross-hatching
cubic content
cubing
cubing code
decibel
dumpy level
eaves height
effective floor area
electromagnetic distance measurement (EDM)
floor area
floor load
floor plan
floorspace
foot super
frontage (line)
geodimeter
gross external area (GEA)
gross floorspace
gross internal area (GIA)
gross leasable area
Gunter's chain
hatching (hachures)
headroom
hide
linear interpolation
location plan
lux
map
National Grid
net internal area (NIA)
net lettable area
north point
Ordnance Survey
photogrammetry
photo interpretation
plan
planimeter
plot ratio
referencing
rentable area
retail price index (RPI)
RICS/ISVA Code of Measuring Practice
setting out
sight line
site plan
superficial area
survey
tellurometer
temporary bench-mark (TBM)
theodolite
traverse
traversing
triangulation
visibility line
Waldram diagram
zenith

MORTGAGES

acceleration clause
Agricultural Mortgage Corporation (AMC)
alienation clause
back-to-back loan
balloon payment
building society
bullet
charge by way of legal mortgage
charge certificate
clog on equity of redemption
collateral (security)
combination mortgage
consolidation of mortgages
deposit
drop lock loan
equitable charge
equitable mortgage

equity linked mortgage (equity participation mortgage)
equity of redemption
foreclose down
foreclosure
joint mortgage
judicial foreclosure (USA)
judicial sale (USA)
junior mortgage (USA)
law day (USA)
legal charge
legal mortgage
mortgage
mortgage broker
mortgagee
mortgagee's powers/remedies
mortgagor
non-recourse loan
principal
priority of mortgages
receiver
redeem up, foreclose down
redemption
redemption period
second mortgage
secured loan
wrap-around mortgage (USA)

NAMED ORGANISATIONS (other than courts and tribunals)

Agricultural Mortgage Corporation (AMC)
Ancient Monuments Boards
British Board of Agrément (BBA)
British Council of Shopping Centres (BCSC)
British Standards Institution (BSI)
British Venture Capital Association
Building Research Establishment (BRE)
CALUS
Church Commissioners
Civic Trust
College of Estate Management (CEM)
Commission for the New Towns
Council for Small Industries in Rural Areas (COSIRA)
Council of the International Stock Exchange
Countryside Commission
Crown Estate Commissioners
Demolition and Dismantling Industry Register (DDIR)
Demolition Industry Group Training Association
Development Board for Rural Wales
FIABCI
FIG
Forestry Commission
Friends of the Historic Houses Association
Historic Buildings and Monuments Commission for England
Historic Houses Association (HHA)
Housing Corporation
Incorporated Association of Architects and Surveyors (IAAS)
Incorporated Society of Valuers and Auctioneers (ISVA)
International Council of Shopping Centers
International Real Estate Federation
Joint Contracts Tribunal
Land Authority for Wales
Land Commission
Land Improvement Company
Land Registry
Local Enterprise Development Unit (Northern Ireland)
National Association of Estate Agents (NAEA)
National Water Authority
Panel on Takeovers and Mergers
Property Services Agency (PSA)
Rating and Valuation Association (RVA)
Rating Surveyors' Association
Royal Institute of British Architects, The (RIBA)
Royal Institution of Chartered Surveyors, The (RICS)
Royal Town Planning Institute, The
Scottish Development Agency
Takeover Panel
Timeshare Developers' Group (TDG)
Valuation Office
Welsh Development Agency

PARLIAMENT

Act of Parliament
appointed day
Bill (Parliamentary Bill)
chapter
clause
command papers
enabling Act/enabling statute
enactment
Green Paper

private Act
public Act
royal assent
special Act
special parliamentary procedure
statute law
statutory instrument (SI)
White Paper
Yellow Paper

PROPERTY MANAGEMENT

active management
energy management
equalisation fund
estate terrier
facilities management
fire certificate
full management
management
managing agent
outgoings
property asset management
property management
property management agreement
property portfolio management
rent roll
security
service charge
terotechnology

RATING

accounts method
assessment
assessor
beneficial occupation
beneficial occupier
central non-domestic rating list
central valuation officer
charging authority
community charge
completion notice
composite hereditament
compounding
contractor's basis/method
cumulo value
derating
differential rating
disability
domestic hereditament
effective capital value
empty rate
end allowance
enterprise zone
excepted rate
exemption
formula method
garden rate (square rate)
general rate
geometrical zoning (arbitrary or arithmetical zoning)
gross value
hereditament
hypothetical tenancy
hypothetical tenant
local non-domestic rating list
local taxation
local valuation court
mixed hereditament
mode or category of occupation
natural zoning
net annual value
notice of compliance
occupier's drainage rate
owner
owner's drainage rate
park
poundage
precept
precepting authority
profits basis (profits method)
proposal
quantity allowance (quantum allowance)
quinquennial
rateable hereditament
rateable occupation
rateable occupier
rateable plant and machinery
rateable property
rateable value (net annual value)
rate capping
rate demand
rate period
rate precept
rates
Rating and Valuation Association (RVA)
rating areas
rating authorities
rating officer
rating surcharge
Rating Surveyors' Association
rating year
rebus sic stantibus
rector's rate (church rate)
relief
remainder zone
revaluation
site value rating
statutory deductions ("stats")

statutory formula
tenets of rating
tone of the list
unoccupied building
unoccupied rate
valuation and community charge tribunal
valuation list
Valuation Office
valuation officer
void relief
water rate
zone A
zone A value
zoning method (zoning approach)

RENT

additional rent
arrears
barren rent
base rent
best rent
certificate of fair rent
cesser of rent
chief rent
concessionary rent
constant rent
controlled rent
cost rent (economic rent)
dead rent
distress (distraint)
English rose
equated rent
exclusive rent (exclusive rental)
fair rent
fee farm rent
fixed rent
full rent
full rental value (FRV)
gale
gales of rent
gavel
geared rent
gross rent
ground rent
hardcore rent
head rent
hypothetical tenancy
hypothetical use
improved ground rent
inclusive rent
mail or maill (Scotland)
marginal rent
minimum rent
model rent review clause
occupation(al) rent
open rent review
overage (income or rent)
passing rent
penal rent
peppercorn rent
percentage rent (turnover rent)
premium rent
profit rent
quit rent
rack-rent
reddendum
registered rent
rent
rentable area
rental value
rent assessment committee
rent assessment panel
rent cesser clause
rent-free period
rent officer
rent review
rent roll
rent seck
rent tribunal
rising rent
scarcity value
secured ground rent
secured rent
sitting rent
sleeping rent
tied rent
unsecured ground rent
uplift
uplifted rent
upward/downward rent review
upward/downward rent review subject to a base
upward-only rent review
variable rent
virtual rent

REPAIRS AND DILAPIDATIONS

adjoining owner
alterations
ameliorating waste (meliorating waste)
building survey
building surveyor
dilapidations
equitable waste
fair wear and tear (reasonable wear and tear)
heave

inherent defect
latent damage
latent defect
maintain
maintenance
maintenance trust fund
modernisation
normal wear and tear
patent defect
reconstruct
reinstatement
renewal
renewal fund
renovation
repair
repairs notice
reserve fund
schedule of condition
schedule of dilapidations
settlement
terotechnology
waste
wear and tear
xestobium rufovillosum
xylophagous

SCOTTISH LEGAL AND ALLIED TERMS

action for implement
adopted as holograph
alimentary liferent
arbiter
articles of roup
assignation (of lease)
attour
backhanded rent
blench (less commonly blanch)
Books of Council and Session
common interest
consensus in idem
common property
defender
delict
deposit receipt
dispone
disposition
dominium directum
dominium utile
eavesdrop
excambion
faculty
fee
feu
feuar
feu charter
feu contract
feu disposition
feu duty
feu farm
fiar
flit
fuel, feal and divot
fund in modic
furth
grassum
ground annual
hypothec
in gremio
interdict
interlocutor
irritancy
ish
iter
jus quaesitum tertio
law agent
liferent
locus poenitentiae
mail or maill
missives
missives of sale
multiple poinding
negative prescription (extinctive prescription)
personal bar (personal exception)
policy
pro indiviso
Register of Sasines
rei interventus
reporter
solum
subinfeudation
superior
vassal
warrandice

SHOPPING

anchor tenant(s)
arcade
British Council of Shopping Centres (BCSC)
business premises
cash and carry (warehouse)
catchment area
catchment population
chain store
checkout
clustering
common area
community shopping centre (USA)

comparison goods
comparison shop/store
concessionaire
consumer goods
convenience goods
convenience shopping
convenience shop/store
department store
discount store (discount warehouse)
district shopping centre
DIY (do-it-yourself) store
downtown (USA)
factory outlet
fascia board
fast-food shop
fooler (USA)
franchise
geometrical zoning (arbitrary or arithmetical zoning)
Goade plans
gravity model
halving back
hierarchy of shopping centres
hundred per cent location
hypermarket
independent retail outlet
International Council of Shopping Centers
isochrone
key money
key tenant
key trader
kiosk
lock-up shop
loss-leader
magnet store (magnet trader)
mall
managed shopping scheme
market
multiple position
multiple retail outlet
natural zoning
neighbourhood shopping centre
net retail floorspace (trading floorspace)
net sales area
off price centre (USA)
one-stop shopping
out-of-town shopping centre
percentage lease
percentage rent (turnover rent)
pitch
prime trading location
rabbit run
regional shopping centre
Reilly's law of retail gravitation
remainder zone
retail
retail gravity model
retail turnover (retail sales)
retail warehouse
return frontage
scrambled merchandising
shophouse
shopping arcade
shopping centre
shopping mall
shopping precinct
shop window display
speciality centre
standard shop unit
storage and preparation areas
sub-regional shopping centre
supermarket
superstore
tenant mix
trading area
turnover lease
turnover rent
unit mix
variety store
zone A
zone A value
zoning method (zoning approach)

STOCK EXCHANGE TERMS

account (Stock Exchange)
alpha, beta, gamma, delta
arbitrage
at best
bargain
bear
bearer security
bear market
beneficial owner
best efforts
Big Bang
blue chip
bond
bonus issue
break
broker
broker/dealer
bulge
bull
bull market
buy on opening
buy in
buy on close

call
call option
capital market
clearing house
Code on Takeovers and Mergers
contango
convertible bond
Council of the International Stock Exchange
coupon
cover
cross option
cum cap
cum dividend (*cum* div)
cum pref
cum rights
cumulative preference share
currency linked bond
debenture
discount broker
dividend yield
double option
earnings yield
equity capital
equity finance
ex dividend (ex div or xd)
ex interest (xi)
face value
float
flotation
free issue
gilts (gilt-edged securities)
insider dealing
listed company
listing
market capitalisation
nominal rate
nominal value
Official List
"open position"
Over the Counter Market
Panel on Takeovers and Mergers
par value
preference share
price/earnings ratio (P/E Ratio)
prospectus
put and take option (put and call option)
put option
quoted company (listed company)
real rate
redemption date
registered bonds
rights issue
scrip issue
security
sub-underwriter
Takeover Panel
Third Market
underwriter
Unlisted Securities Market (USM)
warrant
wholesale money market
Yellow Book, The

TAXATION (including CGT, Income and Corporation Tax, Inheritance Tax and VAT)

advance corporation tax (ACT)
agricultural building allowance
annual value
anti-avoidance
arm's length
assessment
asset
avoidance
badges of trade
balancing allowance
balancing charge
base value
betterment levy
business expansion scheme
cadastral
cadastral map
capital
capital allowances
capital gain
capital gains tax (CGT)
capital improvement
capital loss
capital transfer tax (CTT)
case
certificate of discharge
chargeable realised development value (CRDV)
claw-back
clearance
collector of taxes
Commissioners of Customs and Excise
Commissioners of Inland Revenue
concession
corporation tax
current use value (CUV)
dealer in land
death duty
deemed disposal
deemed premium
depreciating asset
depreciation
development charge

development gains tax (DGT)
development land tax (DLT)
disposal (disposition)
domicile
eligible objects
enhancement expenditure
enterprise zone
enterprise zone allowance
estate
estate duty
evasion
excluded property
excluded services
exemption
exempt supply
extra-statutory concession
first year allowance
fiscal year (tax year)
flooded market clause
forestry land
franked investment income
full rent
General Commissioners
heritage body
heritage property
holding period (USA)
income (revenue)
income tax
income tax year
indexation allowance
industrial building
industrial building allowance (IBA)
inheritance tax
input tax
inspector of taxes
interaction of taxes
investment company
investment property
investor in land
know-how
maintenance
major interest
material development
national taxation
net income
output tax
part disposal
payment in kind
prairie value
protected building
realised development value (RDV)
registered supplier
reiteration
retirement relief
rollover relief
Schedule A
Schedules
scientific research
scrap value
sea wall
section 776
short lease
Special Commissioners
stamp duty
standard rate
standard-rated supply
supply
taxable person
taxable supply
Tax Acts
tax avoidance
Taxes Act
Taxes Acts
tax evasion
tax relief
tax year
tenant's repairing lease
time apportionment
trade
trading company
trading stock
Valuation Office
value added tax (VAT)
void period
voluntary tax
wasting asset
writing-down allowance
year of assessment
zero-rated supply

TOWN AND COUNTRY PLANNING

access agreement
access order
action area
advertisement
advertisement control
agency board
amenity
amenity land
ancillary use
area of outstanding natural beauty
area of special control
article 4 direction
assessor
authorised
authorised development
authorised use
buffer zone

building of special architectural or historic interest
building preservation notice (BPN)
building preservation order (BPO)
burial ground
call-in
central activities zone (CAZ)
central business district (CBD)
certificate of appropriate alternative development
certificate of non-listing (certificate of immunity)
Civic Trust
claim holding
clean air zone
Commission for the New Towns
community land scheme
completion notice
comprehensive development area (CDA)
condition
conditional planning permission
consent
conservation area
conurbation
deemed listing
deemed planning permission
density
design guide
designation order
development
development control
development corporation
development notice
development plan
discontinuance order
district plan
eighth schedule development
enforcement notice
enterprise zone
envelope
envelope ratio
established claim
established use
established use certificate
existing use rights
existing use value
garden city
general development order (GDO)
green belt
green wedges
growth area
industrial building
industrial development certificate (IDC)
industrial process
intensification of use
joint board
joint planning board
lawful use
listed building
listed building consent
listing
local plan
local planning authority
local user restriction
material change of use
minimum compensation
mining operations
modification order
national park
new town
new town development corporation
non-conforming use
"old-style" development plan
outline planning application
outline planning permission
owner
parking ratio
Part VI claim
partnership area
permitted development
permitted development value
permitted use
planner (town planner)
planning appeal
planning application
planning blight
planning brief
planning consent
planning gain
planning permission
planning unit
planning zone
plot ratio
primary use
purchase notice
reasonably beneficial use
regeneration
repairs notice
reporter
reserved matters
revocation order
Royal Town Planning Institute, The
section 52 agreement
service trade
sight line
simplified planning zone (SPZ)
site coverage
site of special scientific interest (SSSI)
special development order (SDO)
spot listing

statutory undertakers
stop notice
structure plan
subject plan
sunlight and daylight code
town and country planning
town planner
tree preservation order
unexpended balance of established development value (UBED)
unitary development plan
urban development area
urban development corporation
urban renewal
use class
use classes order
visibility line
vision splay
waste land
white land
zone
zoning

TRUSTS

active trust (special trust)
ad hoc trust for sale
administration
alimentary trust (protective trust)
bare trust (naked or simple trust)
beneficial interest
beneficial owner
beneficiary
breach of trust
capital money
cestui que trust
charitable trust
constructive trust
custodian trustee
declaration of trust
discretionary trust
endowment
endowment trust
executed trust (completely constituted or perfect trust)
executory trust (incompletely constituted or imperfect trust)
express trust
fiduciary
implied trust (resulting trust)
investment trust company
judicial trustee
life beneficiary
life tenancy under a settlement
maintenance trust fund
managing trustee
overreach
property unit trust
public trust
Public Trustee
real estate investment trust (REIT) (USA)
secret trust
settled land
settlement
settlor
statutory trust
strict settlement
trust
trust corporation
trustee
trustees of the settlement (Settled Land Act trustees)
trust for sale
trust instrument
unit trust
vesting declaration
vesting deed

VALUATION AND APPRAISAL

accounts method
adjusted net trading profit
adverse differential
all risks yield (ARY) (market yield)
alternative use value
amount of £1
amount of £1 per annum
annual equivalent
annual sinking fund (ASF)
annual value
annuity £1 will purchase
appraisal (appraisement)
appraiser
asset valuation
before-and-after valuations
benefit/cost ratio
betterment
Bowcock's Tables
break-even (point)
break-even analysis
break-up value
capital improvement
capitalisation
capitalisation rate
capital value
cash flow analysis/statement
ceiling value
cleared site approach
comparable
constant rent tables

contractor's basis/method
cost-benefit analysis
covenant value
criterion rate
critical path analysis
current use value (CUV)
current yield
curved line depreciation
date of valuation (valuation date)
decapitalisation
depreciable amount
depreciated replacement cost basis (DRC)
depreciated value
depreciation
deprival value
depth factor (USA)
desk valuation
devaluation
developer's budget method
developer's risk and profit
development appraisal
development return (developer's return)
development value
direct comparison method (comparative method or market value approach)
discounted cash flow analysis (DCF)
discounted cash flow yield
discounting
discount rate
disregards
district valuer (DV)
divisible balance
divorce value
Donaldson's Investment Tables
double sinking fund method
dual rate method
dual rate table
dual rate years' purchase
economc life
entirety value
equated yield
equivalent annual cost
equivalent yield
existing use value
expected value
external valuer
face value
fair value
fall-back figure
forced sale value
frontage method
full rental value (FRV)
geometrical zoning (arbitrary or arithmetical zoning)
going concern value
goodwill
gross development value (gross realisation)
gross income
gross realisation
gross redemption yield
gross replacement cost
gross value
growth rate
halving back
hardcore method (layer method)
hardcore rent
hope value
Hoskold factor (USA)
hundred per cent location
hypothetical tenancy
hypothetical tenant
hypothetical use
implied growth rate
improved value (USA)
incremental yield
incremental yield analysis
initial return (initial yield)
inspection
internal rate of return (IRR) (money weighted rate of return)
internal valuer
investment method
investment yield
isoval
joint valuers
latent value
letting value
linear interpolation
marginal yield
market price
market value
marriage value
modern ground rent
multiple regression analysis
natural zoning
negative development value
negative value
net income
net present value (NPV)
net present value method
net rent
net replacement cost
net trading profit (NTP)
network analysis
net yield
new-for-old approach
nil value
nominal consideration

nominal value
open market value
opportunity cost
opportunity cost of money rate
outgoings
overall yield
Parry's Valuation Tables
permitted development value
precedence techniques
present value
present value of £1
present value of £1 per annum
prime yield
procedure diagram
profit rent
profits basis (profits method)
programme (project) evaluation (and) review techniques (PERT)
proper valuation
prudent lotting
qualified valuer
quantity allowance (quantum allowance)
rate (of interest)
rate of return
ratio analysis
reasonable period
regression analysis
reinspection
remainder zone
remunerative rate
rental value
replacement value
residual amount
residual method (residual valuation)
residual value
return for risk and profit
return (on capital)
revaluation
reversionary return (reversionary yield)
reversion yield
Rose's Constant Rent Tables
royalty method
scarcity value
scrap value
selling price
sensitivity analysis
signing date
single rate method
single rate table
single rate years' purchase
sinking fund
site value
sitting rent
sitting tenant value
slice method
special purchaser
special purchaser value
standing house approach
subjective value (value to the owner)
surrender value
tax-adjusted table
tenant's share
term and reversion method
term yield
throughput method
time-value of money
true net yield
unitisation yield
unit of comparison
valuation
valuation certificate
valuation date
Valuation Office
valuation officer
valuation report
valuation table
value
value in exchange
virtual rent
void
void allowance (vacancy allowance)
weighted rate (of return)
"willing lessor, willing lessee" ("willing landlord, willing tenant")
"willing seller, willing buyer" ("willing vendor, willing purchaser")
written-down value
years' purchase (YP)
yield
zone A
zone A value
zoning
zoning method (zoning approach)

WILLS AND ADMINISTRATION OF ESTATES

administration
assent
beneficiary
bona vacantia
cy-près doctrine
devise
escheat
executor(s)
gavelkind
intestate
personal representative
primogeniture

rules of intestacy
rules of succession
vesting assent
will

YIELDS, RATES AND RETURNS

accumulative rate
all risks yield (ARY) (market yield)
amortisation rate
annual percentage rate (APR)
annual sinking fund (ASF)
annual sinking fund rate
capitalisation rate
cash on cash (USA)
current yield
development return (developer's return)
development yield
discounted cash flow yield
discount rate
discount yield
earnings yield
equated yield
equivalent yield
gross redemption yield
implied growth rate
incremental yield
incremental yield analysis
inflation-prone yield
inflation-risk-free yield
initial return (initial yield)
interim finance rate
internal rate of return (IRR) (money weighted rate of return)
investment yield
marginal rate
marginal yield
net redemption yield
net yield
nominal rate
opportunity cost of money rate
overall yield
prime yield
priority yields
rate (of interest)
rate of return
real rate
redemption yield
remunerative rate
return (on capital)
reverse yield gap
reversion yield
reversionary return (reversionary yield)
running yield (straight yield)
sinking fund
target rate
target redemption yield
term yield
total yield
true net yield
unitisation yield
weighted rate (of return)
yield

APPENDIX II

ABBREVIATIONS

AAA (USA) triple A (top credit rating)
AAD cert appropriate alternative development certificate
AAIV Associate of the Australian Institute of Valuers
A & S fees architects' and surveyors' fees
AAR average annual return
ABI Association of British Insurers
a/c air conditioning
AC Appeal Cases (law reports)
ACA Association of Consultant Architects; Associate of the Institute of Chartered Accountants
ACC Association of County Councils
ACIArb Associate of the Chartered Institute of Arbitrators
ACT Advanced Corporation Tax; Association of Corporate Treasurers
ad val *ad valorem* (according to the value)
ADAS Agricultural Development Advisory Service
ADC Association of District Councils
AEA Atomic Energy Authority
AFAS Associate Architect Member of the Faculty of Architects and Surveyors
AFBD Association of Futures Brokers and Dealers
AFS Associate Surveyor Member of the Faculty of Architects and Surveyors
AGI Association for Geographic Information Ltd
AHA Accepting Houses Association
AIA American Institution of Architects; Associate of the Institute of Actuaries
AIBA Associate of the Institution of Business Agents
AIBD Association of International Bond Dealers
AILAM Associate of the Institute of Leisure and Amenity Management
AIP American Institute of Planners
AIREA American Institute of Real Estate Appraisers
AITC Association of Investment Trust Companies
AJ Architects Journal
ALA Association of London Authorities
All ER The All England Law Reports
All ER Rep The All England Law Reports Reprint
ALT agricultural land tribunal
AMA Association of Metropolitan Authorities
AMC Agricultural Mortgage Corporation
AMIAS Associate Member of the Incorporated Association of Architects and Surveyors
ANAEA Associate of the National Association of Estate Agents
AONB area of outstanding natural beauty
APR annual percentage rate
ARC Agricultural Research Council
ARCUK Architects' Registration Council of the United Kingdom
AREI Associate of the Real Estate Institute of Australia
AREINZ Associate of the Real Estate Institute of New Zealand
ARICS Professional Associate of the Royal Institution of Chartered Surveyors
ARR average rate of return
art article (of an order)
ARVA Associate of the Rating and Valuation Association
ARY all risks yield
ASA American Society of Appraisers
asf/ASF annual sinking fund
ASLE Associate of the Society of Land Economists (Australia)
ASREC American Society of Real Estate Counselors

ASVA	Associate of the Incorporated Society of Valuers and Auctioneers
AV	annual value
BACMI	British Aggregates Construction Materials Industries
BBA	British Board of Agrément; British Bankers' Association
BCB	British Consultants Bureau
BCIS	Building Cost Information Service
BCSC	British Council of Shopping Centres
BDFA	British Deer Farmers' Association
BER	Bureau Européen de Recherches
BES	business expansion scheme
BHD	breast height diameter
BIDS	British Institute of Dealers in Securities
BIM	British Institute of Management
BLAISE	British Library Automated Information Service
BM	bench-mark
BMBA	British Merchant Bankers and Securities Association
BMCIS	Building Maintenance Cost Information Service
BOMA	Building Owners' and Managers' Association
BOTB	British Overseas Trade Board
BPF	British Property Federation
BPN	building preservation notice
BPT	building preservation trust
BRB	British Railways Board
BRE (BRS)	Building Research Establishment (formerly Building Research Station)
BRPB	British Rail Property Board
BRR	book rate of return
BSA	Building Societies Association
BSI	British Standards Institution
BST	British Summer Time
BV	Besloten vennootschap (Dutch private limited liability company)
BVCA	British Venture Capital Association
BWB	British Waterways Board
c	chapter (as in statutes); *circa* (about)
C Eng	Chartered Engineer
CA	Court of Appeal; chartered accountant (Scotland)
CAA	Civil Aviation Authority
CAAV	Central Association of Agricultural Valuers
CAD	computer assisted design
CALUS	Centre for Advanced Land Use Studies
CAMIFA	Campaign for Independent Financial Advice
CAP	Common Agricultural Policy
CAP rate	capitalisation rate
CASLE	Commonwealth Association of Surveying and Land Economy
CAZ	central activities zone
CBD	central business district
CBI	Confederation of British Industry
CC	county council
CCA	current cost accounting
CCAB	Consultative Committee of Accounting Bodies
Cd	Command Paper (for White Papers 1900 to 1918)
CD	certificate of deposit
CDA	comprehensive development area
CEEC	European Committee of Construction Economics
CEED	Centre for Economic and Environmental Development
CEGB	Central Electricity Generating Board
CEM	College of Estate Management
C Eng	chartered engineer
CET	Central European Time
Cf	compare with
CGT	capital gains tax
Ch	Chancery (law reports)
CH	central heating
ChD	Chancery Division
cif/CIF	cost insurance and freight
CIPFA	Chartered Institute of Public Finance and Accountancy
CIR	Commissioners of Inland Revenue
CIRIA	Construction Industry Research and Information Association
Circ	Circular
CJ	Lord Chief Justice or Chief Justice
CL	Current Law (legal journal)
CLOR	Central London Office Research

CLY	Current Law Yearbook
cm	centimetre
Cm	Command Paper (for White Papers from 1987)
Cmd	Command Paper (for White Papers 1919 to 1956)
Cmnd	Command Paper (for White Papers 1956 to 1987)
CNT	Commission for the New Towns; confectioners, newsagents, tobacconists
CO	certificate of occupancy
COLAS	City of London Archaeological Society
COSIRA	Council for Small Industries in Rural Areas
CPA/M	critical path analysis/method
CPD	Continuing Professional Development
CPI	co-ordinated project information; consumer price index
CPO	compulsory purchase order
CPRE	Council for the Protection of Rural England
CRDV	chargeable realised development value
CRT	composite rate tax
CSO	Central Statistical Office
CSW	Chartered Surveyor Weekly
CT	corporation tax
CTT	capital transfer tax
CUV	current use value
DBH (USA)	diameter breast high
DBMS	database management system
DC	district council; Divisional Court
DCF	discounted cash flow
DDD	*dat dicat dedicat* (gives, devotes and dedicates)
def	deferred
del	*deliniavit* (he/she drew it)
DF	depreciation factor
DGT	Development Gains Tax
div	dividend
DLT	Development Land Tax
DO	demolition order
DoE	Department of the Environment
DDIR	Demolition and Dismantling Industry Register
DRA	Derating and Rating Appeals (law reports)
DRC	depreciated replacement cost
DTI	Department of Trade and Industry
DV	district valuer (of the Inland Revenue)
EA	environmental assessment
E and OE	errors and omissions excepted
EC	Electricity Council; European Community
ECU	european currency unit
ECV	effective capital value
EDM	electro-magnetic distance measurement
EEC	European Economic Community
EEO	Energy Efficiency Office
EFA	effective floor area
EG	Estates Gazette
EGCS	Estates Gazette Case Summaries
EGD	Estates Gazette Digest of Cases
EGI	effective gross income
EGLR	Estates Gazette Law Reports (bound volumes)
EIA	environmental impact assessment
EIB	European Investment Bank
EIS	environmental impact statement
EIU	Economist Intelligence Unit
EMS	European Monetary System
ENEA	European Nuclear Energy Agency
EPA	Environmental Protection Agency
ERV	estimated rental value
ESA	environmentally sensitive area
ESRC	Economic and Social Research Council
Est Man	estate management
ET	Estates Times
et al	*et alii* (and others); *et alibi* (and elsewhere)
ETB	English Tourist Board
EUV	existing use value
Exch	Exchequer Reports (law reports)
ex div	(see xd)
EZ	enterprise zone
FAI	fresh air inlet
FAIV	Fellow of the Australian Institute of Valuers
FAO	Food and Agricultural Organisation
FAS	Faculty of Architects and Surveyors

FCA	Fellow of the Institute of Chartered Accountants
FCIArb	Fellow of the Chartered Institute of Arbitrators
Fec	*fecit* (he did it)
FEOGA	Fonds Européan d'Orientation et de Garanties Agricoles (European Agriculture Guidance and Guarantee Funds)
FFAS	Fellow Architect Member of the Faculty of Architects and Surveyors
FFS	Fellow Surveyor Member of the Faculty of Architects and Surveyors
FHA	Finance Houses Association
FIA	Fellow of the Institute of Actuaries
FIAA	Fellow Architect Member of the Incorporated Association of Architects and Surveyors
FIABCI	Fédération Internationale des Administrateurs de Biens Conseils et Immobiliers (International Real Estate Federation)
FIAS	Fellow Surveyor Member of the Incorporated Association of Architects and Surveyors
FIBA	Fellow of the Institution of Business Agents
FIG	Fédération Internationale de Geomètres (International Federation of Surveyors)
FIMBRA	Financial Intermediaries, Managers and Brokers Regulatory Association
F Land Inst	Fellow of the Land Institute
FMV	fair market value
FNAEA	Fellow of the National Association of Estate Agents
FNZIV	Fellow of the New Zealand Institute of Valuers
Fob	free on board
FREI	Fellow of the Real Estate Institute of Australia
FREINZ	Fellow of the Real Estate Institute of New Zealand
FRI lease	full repairing and insuring lease
FRICS	Fellow of the Royal Institution of Chartered Surveyors
FRV	full rental value
FRVA	Fellow of the Rating and Valuation Association
fs	foot super
FSI	floor space index
FSLE	Fellow of the Society of Land Economists (Australia)
FSVA	Fellow of the Incorporated Society of Valuers and Auctioneers
FT	Financial Times
FT 30	Financial Times 30 Share Index
FT-SE 100	Financial Times Stock Exchange 100 Index
GATT	General Agreement on Tariffs and Trade
GBA	gross built area
GDI	gross domestic income
GDO	general development order
GDP	gross domestic product
GDV	gross development value
GEA	gross external area
GIA	general improvement area; gross internal area
GLA	gross lettable area
GLC	Greater London Council (now defunct)
GLDP	Greater London Development Plan
Gmbh	Gesellschaft mit beschrankter Haftung (German limited liability company)
GMC	Greater Manchester Council (now defunct)
GMT	Greenwich Mean Time
GNP	gross national product
GP	general practice
GRA	General Rate Act
GRC	gross replacement cost
GRY	gross redemption yield
GTP	gross trading profit
GV	gross value
GVD	general vesting declaration
ha	hectare
HAT	housing action trust
H & C	hot and cold (water)
HBC	Historic Building Council (now defunct)
HBRV	House Buyers Report and Valuation
HCPT	Historic Churches Preservation Trust
HHA	Historic Houses Association
HIDB	Highlands and Islands Development Board (Scotland)
HIP	Housing Improvement Programme
HL	House of Lords

HL Cas	House of Lords Cases (Clark Law Reports)
HMO	house in multiple occupation
HMSO	Her Majesty's Stationery Office
HWM	high-water mark
IAAS	Incorporated Association of Architects and Surveyors
IAP	inner area policy/programme
IBA	industrial building allowance
ibid	*ibidem* (in the same publication)
IBRD	International Bank for Reconstruction and Development
ICA	Institute of Chartered Accountants
ICC	International Chamber of Commerce; Institution and College Conferences (RICS/CEM)
ICFC	Industrial and Commercial Finance Corporation Ltd
ICSC	International Council of Shopping Centers
ICE	Inner City Enterprise
id	*idem* (the same)
IDC	industrial development certificate (now defunct)
IDHE	Institute of Domestic Heating and Environmental Engineers
IHT	inheritance tax
IIA	industrial improvement area
ILA	Institute of Landscape Architects
ILAM	Institute of Leisure and Amenity Management
IMF	International Monetary Fund
IMRO	Investment Management Regulatory Organisation
inst	instant (of the current month)
IOU	I owe you
IPC	Investor Protection Committee
IPD	Investment Property Databank
IR	Inland Revenue
IRC	Inland Revenue Commissioners; Internal Revenue Code (USA)
IRR	internal rate of return
IREF	International Real Estate Federation
IREM	Institute of Real Estate Management (USA)
ISBA	Incorporated Society of British Advertisers
ISE	International Stock Exchange
ISVA	Incorporated Society of Valuers and Auctioneers
IT	income tax; information technology
ITZA	in terms of zone "A"
J	Judge (of the High Court)
JCT	Joint Contracts Tribunal
JMO	Junior Members Organisation (of the ISVA)
JO	Junior Organisation (of the RICS)
JP	Justice of the Peace; Justice of the Peace Journal
JPL	Journal of Planning and Environment Law
JTC	joint (RICS/SST) test of competence
KB	King's Bench (law reports)
kg	kilogram
kilo	one thousand times
km	kilometre
kV	kilovolt
kW	kilowatt
L(£)	pounds (money)
lb	pound(s) (weight)
LA	local authority
LACSAB	Local Authority Conditions of Service Advisory Board
LAMIS	Local Authority Management Information System
LAUTRO	Life Assurance and Unit Trust Regulatory Organisation
LAW	Land Authority for Wales
LBA	London Boroughs Association
LBC	London borough council
LCIA	London Court of International Arbitration
LCJ	Lord Chief Justice
LDDC	London Docklands Development Corporation
LGR	Local Government Reports
LIBOR	London interbank offered rate
LICOM	London interbank currency option market
LIFFE	London International Financial Futures Exchange
LJ Ch	Law Journal Reports Chancery (law reports)
LJ(J)	Lord(s) Justice(s) of Appeal
Lloyd's Rep	Lloyd's Law Reports
LPA	local planning authority; Law of Property Act
LR Eq	Law Reports Equity

LRB	London Residuary Body
LT	Lands Tribunal
LVC	local valuation court
LVT	leasehold valuation tribunal
LWM	low-water mark
m	metre; million
M	motorway
M Land Inst	Member of the Land Institute
m^2	square metre(s)
MAFF	Ministry of Agriculture, Fisheries and Food
mega	one million times
MEP	Member of European Parliament
MHLG	Ministry of Housing and Local Government
MIAA	Architect Member of the Incorporated Association of Architects and Surveyors
MIAS	Surveyor Member of the Incorporated Association of Architects and Surveyors
MIAVI	Member of the Irish Auctioneers and Valuers Institute
MIB	Motor Insurers Bureau
micro-	one millionth part
milli-	one thousandth part
MIRAS	mortgage interest relief at source
MLC	Meat and Livestock Commission
MLR	minimum lending rate
mm	millimetre(s)
mm	*mutatis mutandis* (the necessary changes having been made)
MMC	Monopolies and Mergers Commission
MP	Member of Parliament
MR	Master of the Rolls
MRA	multiple regression analysis
MRC	major retail centre
MREINZ	Member of the Real Estate Institute of New Zealand
MSST	Full Member of the Society of Surveying Technicians
MV	market value
NABM	National Association of British Manufacturers
NAEA	National Association of Estate Agents
NAO	National Audit Office
NAPF	National Association of Pension Funds
NAR	National Association of Realtors (USA)
NAV	net annual value; net asset value
NCC	Nature Conservancy Council
NCVQ	National Council for Vocational Qualifications
NEDC	National Economic Development Council
NEDO	National Economic Development Office
nem con	*nemine contra dicente* (no one contradicting)
NERC	Natural Environment Research Council
NHBC	National House-Building Council
NIA	net internal area
NLA	net lettable area
NLJ	New Law Journal
NLUC	National Land Use Classification
NNDR	national non-domestic rate
NNR	National Nature Reserve
No	number
NPFA	National Playing Fields Association
NPV	net present value
NRA	National River Association
NRV	net realisable value
NT	National Trust
NTP	net trading profit
NV	Naamloze vennootschap (Dutch public limited liability company)
O & M	organisation and method
OAS	Organisation of American States
ob	*obiit* (died); *obiter* (in passing)
ODP	office development permit (now defunct)
OECD	Organisation for Economic Co-operation and Development
OFT	Office of Fair Trading
OMV	open market value
OPAS	Occupational Pensions Advisory Service
OPCS	Office of Population Censuses and Surveys
OS	Ordnance Survey
OSA	Open Spaces Association
OXIRM	Oxford Institute of Retail Management
oz	ounce
p	page; penny or pence

P	President (of the Family Division)
pa	per annum
PABX	private automatic branch (telephone) exchange
PAG	Property Advisory Group
P & CR	Planning and Compensation Reports
P & I	principal and interest
para	paragraph
PAYE	pay as you earn
pc	per cent
PC	Privy Council; personal computer
PDQ	process data quickly
PDV	permitted development value
P/E ratio	price/earnings ratio
PEP	personal equity plan
perp	perpetuity
PERT	project evaluation review technique
PET	potentially exempt transfer; property enterprise trust
pH	measure of acidity/alkalinity
PIC	property investment certificate
PINC	property income certificate
plc/PLC	public limited company
PLR	Planning Law Reports
PMBX	private manual branch (telephone) exchange
pp	pages; *per procurationem* (by proxy)
PR	plot ratio; public relations
pro tem	*pro tempore* (for the time being)
prox	*proximo* (of the next month)
PSA	Property Services Agency
psf	per square foot
PSBR	public sector borrowing requirement
Pt	Part (of an Act or statutory instrument)
PUT	property unit trust
PV	present value
QB	Queen's Bench (law reports)
QBD	Queen's Bench Division
QC	Queen's Counsel
QS	quantity surveyor
qv	*quod vide* (which see)
R	Regina (Queen); Rex (King)
R & D	research and development
RA	Rating Appeals (law reports)
RCA	reduced covered area
RCI	Resort Condominium International
RDC	rural district council (now defunct)
RDV	realised development value
REIA	Real Estate Institute of Australia
REIT (USA)	real estate investment trust
RIBA	Royal Institute of British Architects
RICS	Royal Institution of Chartered Surveyors
ROA	return on assets
ROI	return on investment
RPB	recognised professional body
RPI	Retail Prices Index
RRC	Ryde's Rating Cases
RSC	Rules of the Supreme Court
RTPI	Royal Town Planning Institute
RV	rateable value
RVA	Rating and Valuation Association
RVR	Rating and Valuation Reporter (journal)
s	section (of an Act of Parliament)
S & L	sale and leaseback
S of S	Secretary of State
SA	*société anonyme* (French limited liability company); *sociedad anónima* (Spanish limited liability company); *società anonima* (Italian limited liability company); Securities Association
SAPCO	Single Asset Property Company
SC	Session Cases (Scotland) (law reports)
Sched/Sch	Schedule
SDD	Scottish Development Department
SDO	special development order
SEAQ	Stock Exchange Automated Quotations
SEC	Securities Exchange Commission
SEME	Society of Estate Managers in Education
SERC	Science and Engineering Research Council
SERPLAN	South East Regional Planning Conference

SERPS	State Earnings Related Pension Scheme.
sf/SF	sinking fund
SfB	(From the Swedish *Samarbets-kommittén för Byggnadsfrågor*) building materials classification. Colloquially, "safe for building"
SI	Statutory Instrument; *Système International d'Unités* (International System of Units)
SIB	Securities and Investments Board
SIC	Standard Industrial Classification
sic	so written
SIS	Satellite Information System
SJ	Solicitors' Journal
SLT	Scots Law Times
sp	*sine prole* (without issue)
SPA	special protection area (for wild birds)
SpA	*società per azioni* (joint stock company)
SPAB	Society for the Protection of Ancient Buildings
SPOT	single property ownership trust
SPZ	simplified planning zone
SRL	*società a responsabilità limitata* (Italian limited liability company)
SRO	Staff Regulatory Organisation; Self Regulatory Organisation
SSAP	Statement of Standard Accounting Practice
SSC	Solicitor before Supreme Court (Scotland)
SSSI	site of special scientific interest
SST	Society of Surveying Technicians
stats	statutory deductions
STC	Simon's Tax Cases
stet	let it stand, ie cancel correction
TBM	temporary bench-mark
TC	Tax Cases (law reports)
TCPA	Town and Country Planning Association
TDA	Time-share Developers' Association
TLR	Times Law Reports
TOP	Takeover Panel
TPC	test of professional competence
TPO	tree preservation order
TSA	The Securities Association
TVA	*taxe sur la valeur ajoutée* (French VAT)
TWR	time-weighted rate of return
UBED	unexpended balance of established development value
UBR	uniform business rate
UDA	urban development area
UDC	urban development corporation
UDG	urban development grant
ULI	Urban Land Institute
ult	*ultimo* (of the previous month)
UNCTAD	UN Conference on Trade and Development
UPRN	unique property reference number
URA	Urban Renewal Administration
URG	urban regeneration grant
URPI	Unit of Retail Planning Information
USM	Unlisted Securities Market
UTA	Unit Trust Association
UXB	See UBED
v	versus
V	volt
VAT	value added tax
V-C	Vice-Chancellor
VCCT	valuation and community charge tribunal
VDU	visual display unit
VMIS	video maps imaging system
VO	valuation officer (of the Inland Revenue)
vol	volume
VP	vacant possession
VRM	variable rate mortgage
WCH	wet central heating
WDA	Welsh Development Agency
WLR	Weekly Law Reports
WN	Weekly Notes (1866-1952) (law reports)
WO	Welsh Office
WOW	waiting on weather
WP	White Paper
xd	without dividend
xi	without interest
YP	years' purchase

APPENDIX III

REFERENCES FOR LAW REPORTS

Law cases (and administrative tribunal decisions) are reported in a large variety of publications in the United Kingdom, but those concerning real property matters in the period since 1945 have usually been reported in one or more of the following series. The abbreviations are the conventional ones used in case references.

AC	Appeal Cases (House of Lords and Privy Council decisions in The Law Reports)
All ER	All England Law Reports
BLR	Building Law Reports
Ch	Chancery Division (The Law Reports)
CLY	Current Law Yearbook
CMLR	Common Market Law Reports
Con LR	Construction Law Reports
EG	Estates Gazette (journal)
EGCS	Estates Gazette Case Summaries
EGD	Estates Gazette Digest of Cases (1902–1984)
EGLR	Estates Gazette Law Reports (bound volumes from 1985)
HLR	Housing Law Reports
JP	Justice of the Peace Reports
JPL	Journal of Planning and Environment Law
KB	King's Bench Division (The Law Reports)
LGR	Local Government Reports
Lloyd's Rep	Lloyd's Law Reports
P&CR	Planning and Compensation Reports
PLB	Property Law Bulletin
PLR	Estates Gazette Planning Law Reports
QB	Queen's Bench Division (The Law Reports)
RA	Rating Appeals
R&IT	Rating and Income Tax (1924–60)
RRC	Ryde's Rating Cases
RVR	Rating and Valuation Reporter
SC	Session Cases (Scotland)
SJ	Solicitors' Journal
SLCR	Scottish Land Court Reports
SLT	Scots Law Times
STC	Simon's Tax Cases
TC	Tax Cases
TLR	Times Law Reports (1884–1952) (a separate series from the reports published in *The Times* newspaper)
VATTR	Value Added Tax Tribunal Reports
WLR	The Weekly Law Reports
WN	Weekly Notes (1866–1952)

References to law reports usually consist of a year, a volume number (if any), the report series abbreviation and the number of the page on which the case report begins. There are two conventional forms of reference, eg [1987] 1 EGLR 75 and (1986) 281 EG 531, and each report will be referenced in one or other of these forms according to the following rules:

(i) Where volume or issue numbers do not extend beyond a year or there is no volume or issue number, the year of publication of the report is shown in square brackets and is an integral part of the reference. Thus [1987] 1 EGLR 75 refers to a case reported in volume 1 of Estates Gazette Law Reports published in 1987 and beginning at page 75.

(ii) Where there is a continuous series of volume numbers over years, the year in which the case was decided is shown in round brackets and is not an integral part of the reference, since the report can be identified by the volume number alone. Thus (1986) 281 EG 531 refers to the same case instanced in (i), which was decided in 1986 and reported in volume 281 of the "Estates Gazette" journal (published in 1987) beginning at page 531.

(iii) Commencing in 1988 the references for the "Estates Gazette" journal have, however, changed to the square bracket form, as the continuous volume numbers (No 1 in 1858 to No 284 in the last quarter of 1987) have been replaced by issue numbers relating to only a single year, eg [1988] 37 EG 110 refers to a case published in the 37th weekly issue of 1988 beginning at page 110.

(iv) For Scottish reports, the convention is for the relevant year to be shown without brackets, eg 1988 SLT 84.

Some authors and reports use the following abbreviations in references and indexes to indicate the court in which a case has been decided.

CA	Court of Appeal
CC	county court
Ch	Chancery Division
DC	Divisional Court of the Queen's Bench Division
HL	House of Lords
LT	Lands Tribunal
PC	Privy Council
QB	Queen's Bench Division

APPENDIX IV

YIELD, RATE (OF INTEREST) AND RETURN (ON CAPITAL)

The words "yield", "rate" and "return", although not synonymous, are similar and tend to be used indiscriminately when related to the ratio of net income to capital worth (or cost) expressed as a percentage.

While it is desirable to achieve consistency, and thereby greater precision and accuracy in understanding, it must be accepted that definitions cannot be imposed just for convenience, or even avoidance of doubt, especially when different shades of meaning have been used for so long by so many.

We have formed the view that it would be helpful to suggest a preferred use for each of the three words in certain definitions of terms incorporating them, hoping that such a choice meets with approval and acceptance.

Our endeavours may be prejudiced by falling ourselves into the trap of imprecision when defining some of those terms in the glossary relating directly or indirectly to the subject. We do, nevertheless, suggest:

1. "Yield" should represent the annual percentage amount which is expected to be produced by a specific investment having regard to relevant facts, ie what it should be in market terms. Thus an investment valuation will need the selection of the appropriate percentage by way of yield, and such yield is used when capitalising (actual or estimated) income.
2. "Return" (on capital) should be confined to the measure of the annual percentage amount produced by an investment, whether by reference to cost or to a value not reflecting current market conditions, eg low book value. Thus an investment showing a return in excess of the yield appropriate to it will be a good bargain and one with a return which is less than yield will be a poor bargain. NB: The yield will be the same as return when the capital value is the same as the relevant cost or book value.
3. "Rate" should more properly be concentrated upon its significance as the annual percentage amount charged on borrowed money by way of interest, or as the figure of interest applied when discounting a future receipt or payment.

Terms such as "initial yield", "reversionary yield", "initial return" and "reversionary return" typically lack consistency in use. It would be helpful if the word "yield" were adopted where the capital figure from which it is calculated is one which is estimated at a market level, and "return" when such capital is a different actual figure. The same arguments can be applied to "term yield" and "reversion yield".

Again, it seems that the expressions "flat yield", "running yield" and "straight yield" can mean the same thing. The panel are of the view that "running yield" is the most appropriate term, since it gives the impression of averaging over a period of time.

There has been confusion between the meanings attributed to "equated yield" and "equivalent yield", but the editorial panel have adopted the definitions which they believe to be generally acceptable in the property industry. The same arguments as in the text of our definitions could justify two definitions not yet included in the Glossary, ie "equated return" and "equivalent return".